THE MEDIA GAZE
Representations of Diversities in Canada

Augie Fleras

UBCPress · Vancouver · Toronto

21 20 19 18 17 16 15 14 13 12 11   5 4 3 2 1

Printed in Canada on paper that is processed chlorine- and acid-free.

_____

Library and Archives Canada Cataloguing in Publication

Fleras, Augie, 1947-
    Media gaze : representations of diversities in Canada / Augie Fleras.

Includes bibliographical references and index.
Also issued in electronic format.
ISBN 978-0-7748-2136-0 (bound); ISBN 978-0-7748-2137-7 (pbk.)

    1. Mass media – Social aspects – Canada. 2. Minorities in mass media – Canada.
3. Multiculturalism in mass media – Canada. I. Title.

P94.5.M552C334 2011   302.23080971   C2011-903652-5

_____

Canadä

UBC Press gratefully acknowledges the financial support for our publishing program of the Government of Canada (through the Canada Book Fund), the Canada Council for the Arts, and the British Columbia Arts Council.

This book has been published with the help of a grant from the Canadian Federation for the Humanities and Social Sciences, through the Aid to Scholarly Publications Program, using funds provided by the Social Sciences and Humanities Research Council of Canada.

UBC Press
The University of British Columbia
2029 West Mall
Vancouver, BC V6T 1Z2
www.ubcpress.ca

Contents

Preface

To say that Canada is a society of diversities and difference is surely an understatement. Canada represents an extremely diverse society in terms of new Canadians and racialized minorities, including over two hundred different ethnic groups, as well as some eighty distinct Aboriginal nations. In addition to its racial, ethnic, and Aboriginal differences, Canada is home to class diversities, ranging from ruling to working to underclass; diversities in gender, including the transgendered and intersexed; and diversities associated with religion, sexual orientation, and age. Difference is no less prevalent a reality. In contrast to the descriptive terms "diversities" and "differences," both of which denote human variation along physical, cultural, social, and psychological lines, references to "difference" connote a more politicized concept that contextualizes diversities within a contested framework of inequality and power. To the extent that mainstream media have proven diversity-friendly by embracing superficial differences yet difference-aversive in rejecting deep differences and politicized diversities, the distinction is critical.

The profusion of diversities and difference in Canada cannot be denied. Expressions of politicized diversities (i.e., difference) include, among others, the politics of aboriginality, the proliferation of identity politics around race or gender, and the politicization of sexuality in claiming public space. Nor should we refute the reality of both government and institutional initiatives for accommodating diversities and difference. On one side are equity-based initiatives for levelling the playing field, including those under the Employment

Equity Act or a gender-based analysis as policy-making framework. On the other side are diversity-inspired models for accommodating different ways of accommodating difference(s) related to the status and rights of Aboriginal peoples, the place of Quebec within an English-speaking Canada, and the increasingly politicized demands of immigrants and racialized minorities (Fleras 2010). On yet another side are the human rights statutes and Charter provisions that purport to protect and empower those whose differences are disadvantaging.

Principles are one thing; practices are proving to be something else. However valorized as a relatively open and tolerant society that abides by the multicultural principle of inclusiveness (Ibbitson 2005; Adams 2007), Canada's commitment to institutional inclusion has left much to be desired. Good intentions notwithstanding, institutions have generally fumbled the challenge of inclusiveness, largely because prevailing notions of "how things should be done around here" remain deeply etched within (1) institutional design and organization, (2) working assumptions, (3) operational protocols and procedures, and (4) organizational outcomes. In that the foundational principles of mainstream institutions are likely to remain structured in dominance, the prospect of transformative change is iffy at best.

Mainstream media are no inclusionary exception to this exclusionary rule. Yes, compared to the past, mainstream media are generally more inclusive in representing diversities and difference (Gauntlett 2008). Both the quantity and quality of media representations have improved to the point where critics (McGowan 2001) now vilify these improvements as a political correctness gone wild. Yet there is also a less flattering spin. Lip service to the contrary, too many media messages remain stuck in the past. When not ignored as irrelevant or inferior, those demographics considered diverse and different are routinely framed as "troublesome constituents" who constitute problems in their own right or who create problems involving cost or inconvenience. Even initiatives for accommodating diversities and difference continue to be mired in controversy or marred by inconsistencies – thanks to an array of conflicting priorities and stubborn agendas. Not surprisingly, the interplay of institutional biases with organizational priorities continues to advance dominant interests and agendas, often at odds with those of diversities in Canada, with the result that audiences rarely get what they want but end up wanting what the media want them to have.

In acknowledging a need for challenge and change, this book addresses (describes, analyzes, and explains) the logic behind media (mis)representations of diversities and difference against a backdrop of Canada's evolving mediascape. The book is anchored in a simple yet powerful theme: that mainstream media exist primarily as channels of persuasion whose primary objective is implicitly consistent yet expertly concealed — namely, to convert and co-opt audiences into *"seeing like the media," as if this media gaze was untouched by bias or perspective.* The implications of this media-centred (mediacentric) gaze are inescapable. In decoding how mainstream media encode (frame) images of diversities and difference, institutional designs and media processes are exposed as raced, gendered, and classed, as well as sexualized, secularized, and ageist. This book also addresses how the fundamental principles of the media's foundational order remain structured in dominance because of media gazes that extol the normalcy and normativeness of whiteness, Eurocentrism, secularism, heterosexism, and androcentrism. Even the popularity and power of social networking media, with all its democratic and liberating potential, may not have as much transformative clout in challenging a mainstream media gaze as many have anticipated (Hackett and Anderson 2010).

The goal of this book is both constructive and deconstructive: to analyze media constructions of diversities and difference by deconstructing the logic and dynamics of a blinkered media gaze. This critically (de)constructive tone is predicated on the premise that there is nothing normal or inevitable about what we see, hear, or experience, despite media efforts to naturalize their representational gazes. To the contrary, mainstream media messages continue to reflect, reinforce, and advance discourses in defence of dominant ideology. The agendas, interests, and priorities of those who own or control media are embraced as desirable or inevitable, yet are expertly concealed so that the resultant media gaze comes across as natural and normal rather than constructed and contested. The explanatory value of a media gaze for understanding the what, why, and how is crucial not only in securing an analytical framework for seeing through a seeing like the media, but also in pinpointing the politics and dynamics of a media-centred gaze as demonstrated below:

- We live in an information society. In the absence of personal experiences for understanding social reality, media secure a preliminary and/or primary point of contact with the world out there, often without individual awareness or resistance. In that sense, media are primarily a socializing institution of social control (Critcher 2006; Kimmel 2008).
- How do mainstream media construct images of race, ethnicity, and aboriginality; women and gender relations; the poor and the working classes; and

the historically disadvantaged, including gays and lesbians, youth and elderly, and religious minorities? Are constructions based on a relatively accurate appraisal of reality or, alternatively, are images refracted through the prism of preconceived notions that privilege whiteness, masculinity, and heteronormativity. But what kind of information is yielded when media messages about diversities and difference are raced, classed, and gendered as normal and acceptable?

- On the assumption that media representations of diversities and difference constitute mainstream projections rather than minority realities (M.J. Miller 2008), do media images of race, gender, and class say more about the fantasies or fears of those doing the projecting than about the experiences and aspirations of those projected?

- Are mainstream media too accommodative of differences or not accommodative enough? Is there any truth to the accusation that news media embrace a corrosive political correctness that recoils from criticizing either minority actions or diversity initiatives for fear of courting accusations of racism (McGowan 2001)?

- The verdict on media inclusiveness is inconclusive, with signs of progress alongside patterns of resistance. Why, then, are some media processes such as advertising inclusive of diversities and difference, whereas other media processes – for example, newscasting – seemingly stagnate?

- Why is it that mainstream media are diversity-friendly (i.e., they accommodate superficial differences – an empty pluralism) yet difference-aversive (i.e., they reject deep difference unless it is depoliticized or whitewashed)? Is it because of attitudes or structure? Can fundamental change be advanced by tinkering with the conventions that refer to the rules? Or is the onus on challenging those foundational rules that inform media conventions?

- What responsibility do mainstream media have in facilitating the integration of diversities and difference? If responsibility prevails, what is the appropriate role? Should differences be ignored by emphasizing commonalities, even at the risk of glossing over identities? Should differences be foregrounded despite risks in reinforcing stereotypes?

- Many concur that mainstream media are raced, gendered, classed, ageist, and Eurocentric. Is it logically or existentially possible for mainstream media to become de-raced, de-classed, and de-gendered? What would such a media look like in a world where, ideologically speaking, there is no position from nowhere?

- What are the implications of seeing like the media in a wireless world where the new media are competing with mainstream media for placement and primacy in Canada's mediascape (Lee 2010)? Does a "power to the ordinary people" implicit within populist and social media portend the possibility of a more democratic gaze (G. Turner 2010)?

There is much of value in the belief that true insight arises from asking the right questions. But as this book amply demonstrates, responses to these questions are neither readily forthcoming nor wholly accepted. Each of the themes yields an astonishing range of often conflicting responses that elude any consensus or certainty. And yet, exploring these issues in a mediated world both rapidly changing and increasingly diverse is necessary and relevant – *necessary* because everybody must become more critically reflective of what it means to live in our richly saturated media world; *relevant* because the blueprint for living together with our diversities and difference relies on the media to do their part in empowering Canadians accordingly. Perhaps *The Media Gaze* will equip Canadians with the insight and initiative for advancing the prospects of living together with our differences, equitably, and in dignity.

THE MEDIA GAZE

part 1

Seeing Like the Mainstream Media

* * * * * * * * * *

anadians live in a mediated world. Few would dispute the centrality of mainstream media as an information source with persuasive powers to motivate or manipulate. But many believe that while others are susceptible to media's intoxicating brew of persuasion and fantasy, they themselves are largely immune to media messages – a mistaken belief that, paradoxically, bolsters the industry's powers of persuasion. Rather than a frivolous diversion for amusement or distraction, mainstream media are influential in framing who we think we are, what we think about, the nature of our experiences, how we relate to others, and how they relate to us. Media coverage draws attention to some aspects of reality as normal and necessary – primarily by focusing on what issues to think about, how to think about these issues, and whose voices will prevail in public discourses. Other aspects of reality are framed as inferior or inconsequential and dismissed accordingly. In short, far from passively reflecting a so-called objective world "out there," the media actively contribute to constructing public discourses about this mediated reality. When mainstream media provide a relatively accurate rendition of social reality, they are doing their job. But when conflict-driven and celebrity-obsessed coverage prevails over wisdom and insight, mainstream media may be doing a disservice to Canadians.

Nowhere are the politics and provocations more evident than in the framing of diversities and difference. Evidence overwhelming demonstrates how mainstream media have faltered in depicting women, racialized minorities, youth and the elderly, working classes, and homosexuality (Wilson, Gutiérrez, and Chao 2003). Those outside the framework of a preferred demographic have been either ignored as irrelevant or stigmatized as inferior. Alternatively, they have been portrayed as troublesome constituents who posed a threat to society because of their problematic status. Media coverage of marginalized demographics has embraced a set of binary oppositions ("us" versus "them") that has compromised their status in society (van Dijk 1995; Cushion 2004). To the extent that media have been reflective of reality, the prevailing media gaze has reflected the realities of those who owned or controlled what people consumed and communicated.

But yesterday's agendas are today's challenges (Gauntlett 2008). An exclusive reliance on monocultural frames as prevailing media gazes are relinquishing ground to depictions more reflective of and responsive to diversities and difference. Both the quantity and quality of representations in new and conventional media have improved to the point of guarded optimism (Hier 2008, 2010). However commendable these moves toward inclusivity are, contradictions prevail, as demonstrated by the following inconsistencies:

1   In theory, media institutions are under pressure to incorporate minority in-
    clusiveness in line with Canada's multicultural principles, provisions of the
    Broadcasting Act, and human rights protocols. In reality, however, patterns
    of inclusiveness have proven erratic, shallow, and tokenistic in challenging
    traditional representations of minorities.
2   The gendered nature of mass media communication persists as well. Women
    and men continue to stand in a different relationship to media because of
    a privileged male gaze as the unquestioned media norm that defines ac-
    ceptability and legitimizes normalcy.
3   In that media institutions remain in the hands of big business and corporate
    interests, depictions of the working classes, labour unions, and the un-
    deserving poor tend to be slanted accordingly.
4   Other minority sectors of society are marginalized as well. Young men are
    routinely discredited as a problem demographic in need of monitoring and
    control. Their interests, realities, and accomplishments are routinely dis-
    carded in favour of delinquency frames. References to the elderly are no less
    unflattering because of their diminished status as nonproductive members
    of society.
5   Both gays and lesbians are finally receiving the kind of exposure that histor-
    ically eluded their grasp. Nevertheless, depictions of homosexuality remain
    problematic, with seemingly progressive coverage undercut by the super-
    ficial and stereotypical – in part to placate the squeamishness of audiences
    and advertisers in seeing what was once unsightly.
6   The politics of religion at both national and international levels has leapt to
    the forefront in challenging the prospect of living together with differen-
    ces. But this emergent reality is poorly reflected in media depictions of re-
    ligiosity, religion, and religious differences for reasons that are not yet fully
    understood.

Does it matter? Should we care? Can anything be done? Regardless of the
response or assessments, the cumulative effect of mixed media messages ex-
acts a cost. Because media gazes are known to conceal as much as they reveal,
media representations are pivotal in defining what is normal, acceptable, or
desirable. For audiences who lack meaningful first-hand contact with diversities and difference, these representations are taken at face value, despite
their potential to distort or inflame. They are no less powerful in circumscribing the lives and life chances of those framed as dangerous or diminished. The images conveyed by media gazes may be constructed; nevertheless,
the construction of these images constitutes the lived realities for minorities

and diversities whether they like it or not. The conclusion seems inescapable: media representations of diversities and difference persist with respect to women, racialized minorities, Aboriginal peoples, and the poor and working classes, in addition to youth, homosexuals, and faith-based communities. These so-called demographics continue to be under-represented in areas that count, overrepresented in areas that don't count, and misrepresented on both accounts. That alone should be cause for concern, a commitment to action, and a catalyst for change.

Chapter 1 addresses these core questions: (1) What are media? (2) What do the media say they are doing? (3) What do the media really do? and (4) How do media matter in (mis)representing diversities and difference? Canada's mediascape comprises four sectors, each of which is animated by a different logic that informs content, relationship to audience, and corresponding patterns of media gaze. Particular attention is devoted to the idea that media gazes in general, and news media coverage in particular, may be interpreted as though they are systemically biasing because of consequences rather than intent. Chapter 2 theorizes the concept of a media gaze. By decoding those media gazes that frame (or encode) representations of diversities, the chapter focuses on deconstructing (decoding) the conventions behind a seeing like the media. Accounting for representations of diversities in this book taps into a recurrent theme. Biases that inform the media gaze are shown to be structural rather than attitudinal, institutional rather than individual, patterned rather than random, and consequential (systemic) rather than deliberate (systematic). That insight provides a sobering reminder of the obstacles that await in deconstructing media gazes for seeing through a seeing like the media.

1

Disassembling Media Representations 101

Mainstream media are thought to communicate by providing information and entertainment. However trite but true that may be, mainstream media do more than tabulate and transmit. More accurately, they communicate by manipulating patterns of persuasion while suspending belief to achieve the desired effect of drawing audiences into seeing like the media. Nor is there any validity to claims that mainstream media are neutral and dispassionate conveyors of information. To the contrary, they are laced with commercial values, systemic biases, and hidden agendas that draw attention to mainstream aspects of reality as normal and necessary. Other aspects are discredited as irrelevant or inferior or problematic because they fall outside normative standards. Inasmuch as media cannot not communicate (in part because communication is receiver dependent), media representations of diversities are filtered through a prevailing media gaze.

The end result of such one-sidedness is entirely predictable, if unnerving: mainstream media not only constitute tools of persuasion in articulating right from wrong, acceptable from non-acceptable, normalcy from the deviant, and what counts from who doesn't. They also reinforce vested interests and priorities by consolidating patterns of power and privilege contrary to democratic principles (Hackett and Anderson 2010). The representational content of media persuasion is not necessarily deliberate (systematic); rather, the largely slanted coverage of media content tends to be systemically biasing owing to its predominantly negative messages. In that mainstream media portrayals can be interpreted as discourses in defence of dominant ideology, a mediacentric gaze is critical in framing audience understanding of diversities and difference.

Reference to the concept of media in the singular is misleading. Media themselves differ in terms of what they look like, what they set out to do, and what they really do. Failure to acknowledge these distinctions does a disservice. Nevertheless, patterns and commonalities can be discerned, thanks to shared similarities in terms of rationale, structure, and dynamics. This chapter is focused on deconstructing mainstream media by disassembling their inner logic with respect to tacit assumptions, unanticipated outcomes, operational dynamics, and latent functions. The chapter compares the different media sectors (private, public, populist, and participatory/social); conceptualizes mainstream media as discourses in advancing dominant ideologies; frames news media as "soft" propaganda; and explores the concept of media impact and effects by reference to media hype and moral panic. In promoting a critically informed understanding of what, why, and how, the chapter goes beyond what the media say they do. Emphasis instead is focused on what the media are really doing in advancing hidden agendas while securing vested interests.

Defining Media Sectors

It's commonly known that definitions differ in focus and scope, with points of emphasis ranging from what something looks like to what it says it does and to what it really does. Media too can be differently defined along these lines, that is, what media look like, what they say they are doing, and what they really do. As well, media themselves are internally varied because of underlying assumptions (elitist or populist), content (information or entertainment), structures (content or delivery focus), intended audiences (mass or niche), revenue source (direct or indirect), and anticipated outcomes (enlighten or entertain). The logic behind each definition also reflects differences in what is being communicated, why, and how, and with what purpose. Four major media sectors can be discerned for purposes of analysis: private, public, populist, and participatory/ social. In reality, simple typologies cannot accurately describe the current media environment given its complex interdependencies and blurring of distinctions between "new" and "conventional" media (Miel and Faris 2008).

Private (commercial) media are privately owned enterprises, concerned primarily with profit making on behalf of shareholders (usually through advertising or subscriptions/ticket sales). As money-making machineries through advertising or subscriptions/ticket sales, they are focused on providing consumers with safe and formulaic content that appeals to the lowest common denominator that advertisers can tap into. According to their underlying logic, private commercial media per se do not exist to inform, entertain, or enlighten. Nor do they see their role as one of progressive social change unless the bottom line is involved. Their primary goal is to generate revenue by providing a commodity (or programming) that connects the preferred demographic with profit-driven advertisers. The preferred media gaze is aligned accordingly, so that commercial media rarely give people what they want but persuade people to want what the media have to give (see Ash 2007).

Public media are viewed as public service institutions. Their mandate is to provide audiences with a broad range of programs for advancing the goals of citizenship, belonging, and participation. Public media are government- or taxpayer-owned, focused largely on the enlightenment of individuals as citizens across a broad range of programming, and geared to maximizing the public good or advancing national interests. Like the commercial media, public media too are concerned with making audiences want what the media want them to have. To be sure, references to public media embrace a wide range of arrangements, from the publicly funded BBC to the mixed-funding model of the CBC in Canada and PBS in the United States to the state-owned and government-controlled system in China (Lincoln, Tasse, and Cianciotta 2005). Nevertheless, public media operate on the somewhat elitist premise that they know what is best for you.

The concept of *populist media* encompasses a broad range of printing and broadcasting enterprises, including *alternative, community, ethnic (multicultural), and Aboriginal media.* The term "populist" itself is generally employed to incorporate everything from right-wing conservative ideologies to radical polemics, with references in between that pit common folk against ruling elites. Here, however, the concept is used primarily in the latter sense of people-oriented media – media by, for, and about those demographics that public and private media tend to ignore or distort.

The customizing of content for specific audiences ensures that populist media differ from mainstream (public and private) media in terms of underlying logic, operational procedures, content, structure, and distribution (Skinner 2010). In occupying space abandoned by mainstream media, populist media provide a much-needed service for those poorly serviced because they lack financial clout and political power. Despite significant differences in form and function, populist media appear to share common attributes. They tend to be independently owned and operated, reflect localized interests by providing information of direct relevance to the communities they serve ("news they can use"), embrace news values that supplement or challenge mainstream news media (Howley 2010), operate largely along horizontal lines rather than through top-down hierarchies, and encourage community-wide participation consistent with their grassroots orientation (Rennie 2006). Populist media also are highly partisan in defending the interests of those communities either ignored or marginalized by unflattering mainstream representations (M.J. Miller 2008; Roth 2010b). As Skinner (2006, 217) writes:

> Rather than tailor content, organizational structure, and production practices to maximize return on investment, alternative media foreground special social issues and values. In terms of organizational structure, they often purposefully shun traditional hierarchical models of organization to facilitate as much input as possible into the production. And in terms of production, in order to countermand the tendency to have professional values dictate the subjects, structures, and sources of content, they often seek participation and contributions from the communities they serve rather than rely on professional journalists.

Clearly, then, populist media fill a gap. They offer an alternative to mainstream media's indifference to country-of-origin issues, provide useful information for settling down and fitting in, promote public dialogue and exchange of ideas for the mobilization of audiences into social action, and challenge a highly corporatized media status quo (Rennie 2006; Downing 2009). Populist media may also prove pro-transformative. In acknowledging that social justice rarely originates within government circles or existing power structures, but rather from networks of resisters and agitators, populist media provide a mobilizing wedge for activists to foster dissent, challenge and resist power structures, and generate social movements on both the right and the left (Cultural Survival Voices 2008; J.D. Atkinson 2010; see also Chapters 13 and 14).

The expansion and popularity of digital, interactive, and mobile communication have ushered in a *social/participatory* media sector. Emergence of user-generated online content suggests the possibility of a new participatory media model, one based on ordinary citizens creating, distributing, and consuming media products outside of conventional channels (Ojo 2006; Rennie 2006; G. Turner 2010). "Participatory media" describes those online tools, spaces, and practices through which people interact, connect, and share information online. They include social network sites such as Facebook, YouTube, and Twitter, in addition to information-sharing platforms such as blogs and wikis. The participatory nature of online media reflects what Mark Deuze (2006) refers to

as "people becoming the media," that is, a worldwide trend in which actors –
formerly known as the audience – become increasingly engaged in active media
making of their own.

The implications of this communication shift cannot be underestimated.
Unlike conventional media, which tend to treat content as a thing (a product
to be consumed), social media reflect a process or activity that significantly
shifts the balance of power from producer to consumer (or "produser," to bor-
row Graeme Turner's terminology). They not only create personal online space
but also construct virtual communities by exchanging stories, experiences,
and shared meanings (K. Anderson 2009). Macro-level changes are no less
significant (Kumar 2010). Or to rephrase Manuel Castells (2009, 8), in a networked society where digital technologies figure prominently in contemporary organizational forms, social reality is fundamentally a mediated social
reality.

Shifts toward the participatory and social reflect – and are reflected in –
changes to Canada's mediascape (Shade 2010). Of particular note in this shape-
shifting dynamic are the following emerging themes: the fragmentation,
globalization, and deregulation of markets for media products; increased competition for smaller or niche markets; and the decline of mass audiences (the
largest possible audience all of the time) (G. Turner 2010). Media audiences are
migrating from conventional broadcasting models toward the more interactive
models of participation. Digital platforms have also altered the logic of media
production, distribution, and marketing through social networking of user-
generated content. In short, the explosion of digital and mobile media has
proven transformative, not only in taking the "mass" out of the mass media but
also in challenging mainstream media gazes (see Chapter 12). Table 1 compares
the different media sectors. The far left-hand column provides the criteria for
comparison. The other four columns secure the content, albeit in ideal-typical
terms that reflect categorical rather than contextual differences.

As the table demonstrates, each media sector differs in underlying assumptions, operational logic, articulated and assumed goals, preferred channels of
communication, institutional processes, and anticipated outcomes. To be sure,
some degree of caution must be exercised because of inconsistencies in boundaries and content. After all, ideal-typical descriptions are abstract constructs
that do not necessarily exist in reality, rarely claim to be exhaustive in their
descriptions of reality, and can hardly claim internal consistency in a world that
is contextual rather categorical. Nevertheless, there is much to commend in a
typology that provides a heuristic tool for organizing a wide range of media
institutions and their corresponding gazes.

TABLE 1

Typology of media sectors

	Private (commercial)	Public (public service)	Populist[a]	Participatory/social[b]
Logic	Escapist (Give consumers what they want.)	Elitist (Give citizens what they need.)	Empower (we-media) (Give the community the power/voices they lack.)	Egalitarian (me-media) (People creating, circulating, and consuming what they want, when, and how.)
Goal	Profit (market-driven)	Common good and national interests	Partisan – for the people, by the people, about the people	Social networking: create online communities + identity construction
Means	Entertain	Enlighten	Embolden – inform, adapt, challenge	Engage (interact) by bonding (internal) + bridging (external)
Scope	Mass commercial-casting + niche markets[c]	Universality (broadcasting)	Narrowcasting – untapped "minority" group	Egocasting/me-media (customized)
Perception of audience	Consumer: Passive consumption + interactive users[c]	Citizen	Community/minority	Netizens (Internet citizens) (People/citizens becoming the media.)

	Corporate-owned	General public, taxpayer-funded	Locally owned/controlled/produced	No one and everyone because everybody is connected but no one is in charge + corporate-owned
Ownership	Corporate-owned	General public, taxpayer-funded	Locally owned/controlled/produced	No one and everyone because everybody is connected but no one is in charge + corporate-owned
Information flow	• top-down • hierarchical/authority • one to many + interactivity[c]	• top-down • hierarchical/authority • one to many	• top-down – bottom-up • hierarchical/interactive • one to many/many to one	• anarchic – people becoming the media + power to the interactive person • bottom-up • fluid/decentred • user-generated • many to many/P2P
Contents	Safe/routine/familiar	Broad range, with emphasis on high-brow/high culture	Based on alternative media values and norms (Give the people what the mainstream media ignore.)	Whatever you want – anytime, anywhere, anybody (communicating without filters/publishing without editors)
Metaphorical description	"thing" (commodity)	"thing" (citizenship)	"thing-process" (inclusion)	"process" (conversing, connecting, mobilizing)

a The populist sector can be alternative, ethnic, Aboriginal, and/or community media.

b The participatory/social sector includes citizen media and social media (Web 2.0/wikis/blogs/Twitter, Facebook/YouTube).

c To create a more participatory and interactive format, mainstream media have adjusted their business style by capitalizing on digital media.

Mainstream Media: Discourses in Defence of Dominant Ideology

Mainstream media have long been equated with the Althusserian notion of ideological state apparatus. They are thought to be complicit in colluding with the powerful and the rich to maintain the ideological hegemony of contemporary capitalism (Winseck 2008; Winseck and Pike 2008; Hackett and Anderson 2011). Ideas and ideals are promulgated whose intent is to channel people's thoughts and behaviour into a dominant ideology. This indoctrination process is not necessarily deliberate or malevolent. Mainstream media may invoke claims of neutrality and objectivity yet conceal vested interests behind a smokescreen of platitudes and polemics, while embracing a tacitly accepted agenda of power and privilege without seeming to do so. This passage from John Fiske (1998, 307) astutely captures how ideological neutrality can skew media discourses:

> Social norms are realized in the day-to-day workings of the ideological state apparatuses. Each of these institutions is "relatively autonomous" ... yet they all perform similar ideological work. They are all patriarchal; they are concerned with the getting and keeping of wealth and possessions; and they all endorse individualism and competition between individuals. But the most significant feature is that they all present themselves as socially neutral, as not favoring one particular class over any other. Each presents itself as a principled institutionalization of equality: the law, the media, and education all claim, loudly and often, to treat all individuals equally and fairly.

How do media reinforce their sociological status as discourses in defence of dominant ideology? First and foremost, mainstream media are ideological because of a tendency to embody (reflect, reinforce, and advance) the agendas (the interests, perspectives, and priorities) of the dominant sector. Their ideological assumptions draw attention to preferred aspects of reality by normalizing dominant ideas and ideals as natural or superior while problematizing as irrelevant and inferior those who challenge or resist (Abel 1997; Henry and Tator 2002; Lambertus 2004). Consider the news media: as discourses of domination that conceal as they reveal, news media legitimize and naturalize social and ethnic inequality by focusing on the spectacular (from coups and quakes to drug cartels and ethnic conflict) at the expense of stories that make society look bad, including (a) poverty and its causes in rich countries, (b) everyday racism and cultural ethnocentrism, (c) imbalances because of globalization and world trade, and (d) legacies of colonialism within the context of neo-colonialism (van Dijk 1995). In reflecting and advancing the interests of the

FYI: Framing Matters

The concept of framing is critical in constructing media gazes. That should come as no surprise; after all, few would dispute the centrality of media frames in influencing how people interpret the world and act upon that interpretation. Framing represents a process for organizing information by drawing attention to some aspects of reality as normal and desirable, but away from others as irrelevant or inferior — in the hopes of encouraging a preferred reading consistent with seeing like the media. The framing experience is anything but neutral. The interplay of deeply embedded news values and norms with institutional routines and organizational imperatives imposes limits on the boundaries of discourse (Lakoff and Ferguson 2006). Furthermore, according to Robert Entman (1993), the framing process itself is inherently communicative. Implied within each frame is a particular problem definition, a causal interpretation or diagnosis (what), a moral evaluation or judgment (why and who), and a proposed solution or remedy. For example, as widely noted, news media coverage of 9/11 was framed along these lines: (1) defining the problem (thousands killed by terrorists), (2) diagnosis (terrorists caused it),

elite through the power of distraction or divisiveness ("us" versus "them," hegemonic news media circumscribe the limits of legitimate debate by normalizing conformity while problematizing dissent [Bales 2003; for discussion, see Henry and Tator 2006]). Those who conform and comply receive favourable coverage; those who provoke or protest are framed as troublesome constituents in need of control or correction. Noncompliance is "otherized" as deviant or dangerous — not necessarily through overt expressions of racist discourse but through narratives, images, and rhetorical devices that demean or deny behind a facade of neutrality or objectivity (Mahtani, Henry, and Tator 2008). Clearly, then, how issues and persons are framed is crucial in advancing a preferred reading, as is explained in the accompanying sidebar.

Media are ideological in a second way. In addition to securing dominant ideologies in defence of mainstream interests, they themselves are loaded with ideological assumptions that influence the framing of which stories and whose voices. For example, consider how the concept of newsworthiness reflects a patterned yet unintentional institutional bias. News is essentially biased as a "medium of the negative" in embracing abnormality, negativity, crime, or conflict (as exemplified by a raft of clichés, such as "the only good news is bad news," "if it bleeds, it leads," and "if it scares, it airs"). Incidents and issues are routinely chosen for their conflict value or, alternatively, framed in ways that hype the "hot" by playing the angle (e.g., "race card") or spinning a conflict (e.g., "gender wars"). The former editor of the *Globe and Mail*, Edward Greenspon spoke frankly of a profession obsessed with the abnormal: "Let's not be coy here. Journalists thrive on the misery of others. It's not, as some have supposed, that the media dwell on the negative. It is that we dwell on the unusual and extraordinary ... If it happens everyday, it ain't news. Which creates a natural bias toward the negative since most of life actually unfolds as expected" (Greenspon 2003).

The centrality of conflict and negativity as newsworthy encourages an adversarial format as a preferred media gaze. Disproportionate coverage is accorded to extremists with loud voices, contrary perspectives, strange appearances, and bizarre behaviour (Weston 2003). Incidents involving mass protest and civil disobedience are pigeonholed into a confrontational framework, with clearly marked positions and protagonists, from heroes to villains to victims (van Dijk 2000). Isolated and intermittent events are spliced together into a spiced-up story that inflames as it frames, thereby implying a looming crisis where none actually existed (Henry and Tator 2002; Hier and Greenberg 2002). Compounding this negativizing process is the growing tabloidization of news. Not only is reality morselized into biteable bits for easy consumption, but a "gotcha" journalism mentality is also promulgated that sacrifices substance for the scoop or the scandal.

Clearly, then, a paradox is at play. News discourses uphold a commitment to notions of public good, common values, and social order, yet they overwhelmingly emphasize negativity and conflict as newsworthy. Instead of tapping into the "silent majority" as news source, those on the margins capture the bulk of coverage precisely because of their inherent newsworthiness. News items consistent with prevailing media norms receive ample placements, regardless of their triviality. By contrast, stories outside conventional frames are peripheralized, despite their significance. As a result, important events in society may be under-reported because they lack striking visuals or catchy hooks, whereas relatively unimportant but visually arresting incidents monopolize news media attention. As Sauvageau, Schneiderman, and Taras (2006, 29) concede: "Stories that feature sharp conflict, can be easily explained and condensed, involve

(3) evaluation (terrorists are evil), and (4) solution (eliminate terrorism by fighting against terror). Finally, in framing both problem and solution, what is excluded from the "frame game" may prove just as informative as what is included. As Entman (1993, 54) writes, "Most frames are defined by what they omit ... Receivers' responses are clearly affected if they perceive and process information about one interpretation and possess little or incommensurable data about alternatives."

Clearly, then, frames are critical in constructing people's understanding of social reality. With frames, attention is drawn to some aspects of reality (but not others) as meaningful or memorable — thus reflecting political power and reinforcing boundaries of acceptable political discourse (what is and can be discussed and how). Without frames, effective communication is impossible, since there is no clue as to how to define the situation and respond or interact accordingly. Finally, reference to framing is closely aligned with the concept of hegemony. Media and political elites control the framing of issues for influencing public opinion and societal discourses by (1) creating consensus and cooperation without coercion, (2) changing people's attitudes without their awareness that attitudes are changing, (3) bolstering the status quo as natural and normal, and (4) securing power over others without provoking resistance (Rosas-Moreno 2010).

In short, the power of frames arises from their perceived status as natural and normal rather than constructed and conventional. Their potency is secured by a gloss of invisibility, an absence of visible intent, and an uncanny knack to work in hidden ways — not only in shaping the media gaze as if it were no gaze at all but also in ensuring people's complicity in seeing like the media without their explicit consent (N.J.G. Winter 2008).

people in positions of authority, or who are compelling in some other way, either as villains or victims, and have eye-catching visuals are the stories that contain the ingredients most sought after by journalists."

The paradox is unmistakable: what should be newsworthy (however that may be defined) does not necessarily become the news; conversely, what becomes news would not be newsworthy if judged by standards of importance or relevance. This paradox is especially evident when privileging deviance as significant, while routinely attaching significance to the deviant (Shoemaker and Cohen 2006, 337). Maude Barlow (2004, 35) captures this anomaly by recounting her experience with a reporter who had internalized only too well the prevailing news norms: "I was congratulated by a reporter from a national newspaper who said, 'You know, it was really good that there wasn't violence from your side. But you know, one or two more peaceful demonstrations like that and we won't cover you anymore.'"

A conflict of interests is apparent. However illogical by conventional norms of morality and justice, a news media commitment to conflict and abnormality dovetails with the principle of newsworthiness. Inasmuch as what passes for newsworthiness is driven by the news norms of a prevailing news paradigm than by the needs of a democratically informed citizenship, the news media are fundamentally mediacentric. Reality is shoehorned into a media-centred point of view as natural and normal; other perspectives are dismissed as inappropriate or dangerous. The logic behind this mediacentricity is driven by the institutional, not the personal; by the consequential, not the intentional; by the routine, not the random; by the cultural, not the conspiratorial; and by the structural, not the attitudinal (see Weston 2003). Not surprisingly, there is a cost in framing news around a mediacentric perception of reality. A capacity to convey accurate and impartial information is sharply compromised, to the detriment of fostering a democratically informed citizenship. The next Case Study demonstrates how news media coverage of Aboriginal peoples' protest actions reinforces their discursive status as problem people who protest.

As discourses in defence of dominant ideology, news media constitute systems of soft or systemic propaganda (Fleras and Kunz 2001). This is not propaganda in the conventional sense of deliberate and organized brainwashing; after all, negative depictions of aboriginality are not necessarily reflective of a racist news media that deliberately amplifies negativity through exaggerated and sensationalized coverage. Rather, repeated coverage of First Nations peoples as troublesome constituents exerts a softer propaganda effect. This negativity is conveyed not through biased coverage but by coverage that is systemically biasing. A one-size-fits-all formula of newsworthiness (conflict, negativity) is applied to all situations and groups, although some are more vulnerable than others to this one-sided coverage. Instead of something deliberate and malevolent, the typecasting of Aboriginal peoples as a troublesome constituent reflects the nature of news media to negatively frame (or problematize) those who challenge or fail to conform.

In short, media do not set out to deliberately create propaganda or wilfully control people's thoughts. But coverage can be interpreted as soft propaganda when it reflects the inevitable consequence of creating one-sided messages that privilege one point of view to the exclusion of others. The politics of propaganda is further explored in Chapter 15.

―― case study

Framing Aboriginal Protest

Mainstream news coverage of Aboriginal issues is subject to intense scrutiny and criticism (Fleras and Kunz 2001; Weston 2003; J. Miller 2005; Wilkes, Corrigall-Brown, and Myers 2010). Newscasting media are accused of perpetuating errors of omission or sins of commission by refracting Aboriginal realities through the prism of mainstream whiteness (Fleras 2003). Images of aboriginality continue to be refracted through the prism/prison of a white cultural paradigm that asserts the normalcy of white dominance while precluding alternative narratives. Few Aboriginal news stories are situated within a historical context; fewer still incorporate Aboriginal concerns from Aboriginal perspectives (Abel 1997; Sheffield 2002; Glynn and Tyson 2007; M.J. Miller 2008). Coverage is conveyed from an outsider's point of view without much Aboriginal input. This oversight is due in part to fear, laziness, inexperience, or just plain ineptitude. The end result is profoundly regressive: media representations of Aboriginal politics and protest are unbalanced, decontextualized, focused on the extreme, deviant, or threatening, and likely to foster tensions or promote divisive politics (RCAP 1996; Weston 2003; David 2004; see also Kupu Taea 2007).

Such pejorative coverage paints a villainous picture of Canada's First Peoples as a population with a plight who have lost control of the plot (Weston 2003; Harding 2010). Paradoxically, Aboriginal efforts to bring about social change through blockades and occupations are no less problematized, as demonstrated in this Case Study on the news media's framing of Aboriginal protest. An assessment of this nature should come as no surprise. Aboriginal issues are much too complex, contradictory, and contextual for capture by the quick-fix mandate of junk food journalism (see Lasica 1996; Meadows and Molnar 2001).

Packaging Protest

Protests and demonstrations are thought to play a critical role in advancing a healthy democracy (Cottle 2008). They constitute a bridge for overcoming disconnects between publics and policy makers, while helping to revitalize moribund parliamentary democracies. The issues that animate protests and demonstrations are conveyed by the media, which can make or break them, depending on the quality of coverage. However, to take advantage of the media's agenda-setting reach for getting across their message, mobilizing wider support, and gaining legitimacy for these actions, a price must be paid. Increasingly driven by their pursuit of media attention, dissidents and protesters must sensationalize their tactics by spiking the drama (from flamboyant theatre to open violence to fiery rhetoric) to attract news media attention to their cause. Yet the packaging of protest as spectacle rather than substance reinforces news routines that dwell on the superficial instead of the substantial (Wilkes, Corrigall-Brown, and Myers 2010). In the end, the underlying message is lost in the shuffle (Boykoff 2006) by a media tendency to trivialize protests or to criminalize protesters. Emphasizing violence or law breaking defines (frames) a situation in a way that delegitimizes challenges while reinforcing dominant interests (see Cottle 2008).

Mediating First Nations Peoples: Images That Injure

Media coverage of Aboriginal peoples may be charitably described as uneven at best, criminal at worst (Harding 2010). Such an ambivalence reflects media pigeonholing of Aboriginal peoples as pathetic victims, noble environmentalists, or angry warriors (RCAP 1996). On one side, Aboriginal peoples are defined as pure, innocent, vulnerable, and deserving of government protection. On another side, they are depicted as ruthless thugs who must be firmly controlled. On still another side is their portrayal as hapless victims in dire need of government assistance or protection from internal lawlessness. By tapping into a cultural and historical reservoir of stereotypical negativity, namely, the motif of cowboys and Indians, news media coverage fixates on the confrontational rather than the normative, typical, or cooperative (Weston 2003; Lambertus 2004). The stereotyping of Aboriginal peoples as problem people is further compounded by funnelling Aboriginal protest and resistance into the framework of conflict, crisis, or crime. Finally, the linking of Aboriginal disputes across Canada tends to generate a moral panic over fears of Aboriginal peoples on a twenty-first-century warpath (J. Miller 2005).

Aboriginal protests are highly varied in terms of purpose, duration, and tactics, with corresponding difference in media coverage of these collective actions. Five major frames prevail, each with several themes: (1) political (from unrest to militancy), (2) social justice (defence of rights), (3) racial (discrimination to stereotypes), (4) legal, and (5) economic (costs or benefits). For the most part, however, Aboriginal protest or civil disobedience is routinely framed by a confrontational theme: one side is deified as good while the other is demonized as bad in the ensuing struggle between competing forces. Protesters are branded as dangerous or irrational because their prevarications fall outside the Eurocentric norms of engagement; by contrast, lawful authorities are framed as above the fray (Abel 1997). As Professor John Miller (2006) of Ryerson's School of Journalism in Toronto writes in lampooning journalists for framing the Ipperwash Ontario protest around negative stereotypes: "They framed the story as a bunch of First Nations people who were causing trouble instead of a land dispute that has not been resolved for 52 years." The intensity and repetitiveness of Aboriginal resistance (from Oka to Caledonia) has proven both puzzling and infuriating to many Canadians who "just don't get it" (D. Miller 2004), prompting this blistering indictment by Dan David (2004) over media coverage of a crisis at Kanehsatake, near Montreal:

> In mid-January [2004], Kanehsatake exploded in the national consciousness once more. Looking back at the media coverage of the events, familiar patterns

emerge. Major Canadian news organizations immediately pumped up the volume by resurrecting images of the 1990 Oka crisis, masked Mohawk warriors and all. They soon transformed the story into one of criminals versus a crime-fighting chief. Then journalists painted Kanehsatake as a community with never-ending problems, doomed by petty family squabbles ... Few journalists looked much deeper into the story or deviated from these easy stereotypes.

In short, news media contextualize protests as acts of criminality and threats to Canada's social order while simultaneously promoting a lawful and ordered Canadian establishment. They also tend to isolate Aboriginal discontent by framing protests as relatively independent of one another, ignoring a diversity of multi-faceted Aboriginal voices in the process (Ricard and Wilkes 2007). But framing protest outside any socio-political context not only trivializes Aboriginal struggles for righting historical wrongs but also criminalizes the very problem under protest (Lambertus 2004; Harding 2006). With its ominous overtones of a people on the brink of violent revolt (J. Miller 2005), coverage of Aboriginal peoples as trouble-makers masks their realities as complex individuals with legitimate grievances. It also overrides more fundamental issues related to Aboriginal constitutional rights unless themselves framed as conflict, a problem, or a threat to Canada (ibid.). And although space for dissenting views is not altogether absent when drawing attention to Aboriginal protest, news discourses continue to endorse dominant interests and unequal power relations (Harding 2006).

Coverage: Informing or Inflaming?

Stuart Hall in his landmark 1978 work *Policing the Crisis* argues that times of crisis yield insights into how an ideological frame works. Conventional frameworks are rendered problematic because of counter-discourses that challenge a business-as-usual mindset (Henry and Tator 2005). For example, news coverage of the Atlantic lobster-fishing crisis exposed deep fissures between Canada's Aboriginal peoples and the mainstream news media. In late 1999, Canada's Supreme Court ruled that some Aboriginal groups in Atlantic Canada (including the Mi'kmaq and Maliseet) were entitled by virtue of unextinguished Aboriginal and treaty rights to hunt and fish without a licence and out of season for subsistence purposes or in pursuit of a modest livelihood (Coates 2000). The exercise of Aboriginal customary rights over the harvesting of lobster proved to be a flashpoint. In an industry in which a licence to fish for lobster was tantamount to printing money, lobster-fishing licences

case study

have proven tricky to come by, in the process excluding Aboriginal fishers from access to this lucrative industry.

Not surprisingly, tensions between Aboriginal peoples and lobster fishers escalated, especially when non-Aboriginal fishers smashed hundreds of Aboriginal lobster traps in the aftermath of the Supreme Court ruling. A subsequent Supreme Court ruling bowed to public pressure by conceding federal authority over managing fisheries on behalf of national and environmental interests, but not before Aboriginal fishing fleets were pillaged and burned, four thousand Aboriginal lobster traps were destroyed, and graphic video footage of open violence undid Canada's much-touted reputation as a kinder, gentler society (Toughill 2000). Eventually, calm was restored through negotiated compromises with most but not all the Aboriginal groups involved, only to be shattered again by violent episodes, including the pelting of federal fishing officers with fish entrails, federal boats ramming Mi'kmaq fishing vessels, and reported exchanges of shotgun fire.

How, then, did the news media respond to these crises in cutting up the catch? Mainstream news coverage of the Burnt Church lobster crisis proved no less myopic than that during the Oka crisis in 1990, which also attracted both national and international media attention (Kalant 2004; Conradi 2009; Swain 2010). The overall thrust of the news media's Oka coverage was framed around the theme of criminality ("law and order") and conflict instead of a struggle over land or Aboriginal rights. With confrontation as the preferred slant, the saga was recast into a morality play invoking a titanic struggle between the forces of order and those of disorder, with the police and government squaring off against Mohawk factions (York 1991). Media preoccupation with criminality might have prolonged the dispute. Focusing on the spectacle most certainly distracted public attention from the more substantial issues pertaining to Aboriginal rights. Admittedly, insightful articles were published that put the controversy into a historical context from an Aboriginal perspective. But most coverage hid behind catchy headlines or photogenic visuals that titillated rather than taught.

Similarly, news media coverage of the crisis at the "Maritime Oka" proved to be equally lopsided. In its fixation with conflict and confrontation, the news media's references to Burnt Church conjured up images of armed conflict involving a rump of white fishers against a rabble of lawless Aboriginal peoples. On one side were Aboriginal peoples who endured criticism for recklessly defending an indefensible position foolishly espoused by the Supreme Court. On the other side were non-Aboriginal fishers who too defended their interests, violently at times and by taking the law into their hands, against a backdrop of protecting their livelihood from environmental ruin. A double standard prevailed: Mi'kmaq were demonized as hot-blooded thugs who offended Canadian law and clashed with authorities. Their criminality was also framed as contrary to core Canadian values and national interests. By contrast, overfishing and illegal poaching by non-Aboriginal fishers tended to be underplayed, while police violence to crush Aboriginal resistance was condoned by the simple expedient of criminalizing Aboriginal behaviour (see Lambertus 2004).

Admittedly, news coverage did not recoil from emphasizing non-Aboriginal aggressiveness. Nevertheless, emphasis was tilted toward the righteous anger of non-Aboriginal fishers, many of whom were portrayed as law-abiding conservationists in defending their interests against special Aboriginal privilege. Through language and presuppositions implicit from reading between the lines (van Dijk 2000), a coded subtext was clearly implied: for openly breaking the law by fishing without a licence and out of season, Aboriginal fishers deserved what they got from white vigilantes. The framing of Aboriginal fishers as environmental predators could not be more ironic, given long-standing stereotypes of Aboriginal peoples as environmental custodians, but it is precisely this contradiction that constituted newsworthiness.

Criminalizing Aboriginality, Aboriginalizing Crime

Equally disconcerting in packaging protests were the preferred sources of information. Whether by intent or inadvertently, media coverage of Aboriginal protest was largely aligned with the position of the Department of Fisheries and Oceans, whose news releases could hardly be defined as either neutral or even-handed. Mainstream media uncritically accepted a federal communications strategy that pounced on Mi'kmaq as law-breaking renegades, both greedy and irrational and hell-bent on illegally plundering depleted resources without much thought for the rule of law or rights of conservation. By contrast, the government position was praised as balanced, just, and reflective of national interests in restoring peace, order, and good government. But the framing of Aboriginal resistance as a law-and-order issue tended to downplay the broader context that sparked the struggle. References to the legitimacy of Aboriginal and treaty rights were dismissed as a smokescreen to rationalize a host of criminal activities at odds with the so-called Canadian way. An Aboriginal perspective rarely appeared as a counterbalance, in effect glossing over the competing perspectives that informed the crisis.

case study

To sum up: one of the core functions of the news media is providing news that people can use, that is, it is to construct a common sense view of the world for interpreting what is going on (Harding 2005). Once the news media establish a commonsensical agenda, a closed form of thought is entrenched that resists challenge or change (Nesbitt-Larking 2001). But the commonsensical coverage of Aboriginal peoples' protest misses the point of the struggle.

First, the demonizing of Aboriginal activism and Aboriginal protesters as dangerous militants or irrational ideologues is critical. Such a slant not only marginalizes the legitimacy of dissent, it also trivializes Aboriginal concerns by distracting from the issues at hand. Aboriginal peoples are framed as ill-prepared to exercise control over their lives by portraying them as childlike and in need of state benevolence and care (Harding 2010). In cases where agency is displayed, Aboriginal actions are framed as militant (overdemanding and unreasonable), as might be expected of the petulant and emotional. Members of the dominant society are framed as reasonable and law-abiding.

Second, the struggle was not about breaking the law, nor was it about violence between the lawbreakers or law enforcers. Rather, the fundamental issue revolved around the politics of jurisdiction in determining who owned what, and why. Whose rights – those of Aboriginal nations or the Canadian state – would prevail when contesting competing claims to the same territory? Was it possible to balance constitutionally guaranteed Aboriginal and treaty rights to forage and fish with that of the government's responsibility to regulate on behalf of all Canadians and for conservation purposes? Who would decide, and on what grounds? Do rights in Canada entail a one-size-fits-all formula, or can entitlements be customized to fit the distinctive status of Aboriginal peoples? Was the conflict about re-dividing the existing resource pie (cutting up the catch), or was it about challenging the colonial foundational principles that govern the constitutional order of settler society (Maaka and Fleras 2005)? In that the news media did not address these concerns – after all, the confrontational aspects monopolized media attention while more fundamental issues drew a blank – the struggles at Burnt Church were depoliticized by reducing the resistance to the level of a classic cowboys and Indians dust-up.

Third, the news media do not appear to have learned their lesson. In yet another all-too-familiar storyline, Aboriginal peoples are confronting non-Aboriginal Canadians over competing agendas and contested land claims in a case involving a housing development site in Caledonia, Ontario. With the site now into its fifth year of occupation, images of provocation are equally familiar, including Aboriginal flags, irate citizens, masked warriors, police in riot gear, the obligatory plumes of black smoke, barricades that inconvenience, government waffling, and a cacophony of apoplectic voices. No less predictable is news media coverage of the issues at hand in Caledonia. A focus on conflict and enforcement and spectacle and superficiality superseded the political and prosaic, resulting in coverage that is systemically biasing because of its one-sided negativity. Not surprisingly, constitutional issues behind the dispute rarely make the six o'clock news since they lack exciting visuals and cannot be morselized into biteable bits.

But there is a cost in emphasizing the episodic and dramatic at the expense of the contextual and thematic. Instead of information and enlightenment, entertainment values prevail so that the crisis is dumb-downed to the level of a video game in real time (Fleras 2006; see also Austerberry 2008). Inasmuch as a few hotheads on both sides of the confrontational divide drive the frenzy that feeds the news media beast, little is done to probe the what and the why, with the result that many Canadians – both Aboriginal and non-Aboriginal – remain frustrated and angry (M. Campbell 2006; *Christchurch Press* 2006).

Critical-Thinking Questions
How and why do mainstream news media frame Aboriginal protest the way they do?

* * * * * * * * * * *

Do Media Matter? Media Impacts, Media Effects
People's fascination with media communication is piqued by the topic of effects (on individuals) and impacts (on society). What influence do media have on people's attitudes and behaviour (J.P. Murray 2008)? Are media impacts and effects powerful, direct, and long-lasting? Or are they indirect, diffused, short-term, highly variable, and conditional on context, criteria, and consequences? Why are some seemingly susceptible to media messages, whereas others appear to be relatively immune to the lure of media messages? Which dumbing down came first – of audiences or of media? Do the media give an already dumbed-down people what they want? Or have audiences become conditioned to accept less than they deserve by commercial media that cater to the lowest common denominator? Answers to these questions are sharply contested and rarely yield consensus. Even notions of audience are problematic: with the introduction of social-networking sites like Facebook or Twitter, problems arise with any proposed distinction between active producer and distributor as well as between consumer or critic (Gauntlett 2008).

Reference to media effects on individuals are highly varied, even contradictory, ranging from maximal to minimal (Gunter 2008). For some, excessive exposure to media breeds passivity; for others, aggression is the result. For some, such exposure contributes to crime by glamorizing criminal role models; for others, it contributes to collective consensus by fostering shared values for doing the right thing. For some, media trivializes reality; for others, public debate and social action are fostered. For some, the media do little more than pander to the lowest common denominator; for others, the effect is cognitively empowering (as Rob Salem, TV critic for the *Toronto Star,* once pointed out, a forty-four-minute episode of the TV series *24* involves the lives of twenty-one distinct characters and nine primary narrative threads). Or consider a *New York Times* article's claim that by featuring strong black male leads in positions of authority (from James Earl Jones to Morgan Freeman to Denzel Washington), Hollywood prepared America for the election of a black president – a case of life imitating art (Rosas-Moreno 2010).

Explanatory frameworks remain polarized. On one side, the magic bullet theory points to media as powerful and persuasive because audiences are thought to uncritically absorb media messages and blindly act upon them. On the other side are skeptics and media scholars who reject this claim. According to the latter, audiences do not resemble empty wheelbarrows that can be loaded up with media content and pushed around with impunity (Fleras 2003). To the contrary, audiences are generally perceived as active and interactive agents taking the initiative to negotiate and interpret media messages. Moreover, media effects cannot be seen in isolation but within the broader context of other influences (Potter 2005). Canada is a complex society involving a variety of forces at work, often at cross-purposes to one another, with the result that media are but one of many important players in accelerating the pace of social change. Not surprisingly, mainstream media are increasingly seen as contested sites of struggle between prevailing media gazes and the oppositional messages of critics or audiences.

Media effects are not just restricted to individuals. Institutions are also affected in ways both direct or indirect and immediate or delayed, as well as in the short run or long term. Political institutions have changed dramatically because of new media dynamics. Instead of old-fashioned speech making and good ol' backroom deals, politics is increasingly driven by opinion polling, slick and expensive negative ads, and media-savvy spin doctors to massage the narrative (McChesney 1999). The impact of media on society can be analyzed in another way. Media outputs do not directly impact on society as much as they generate public discourses about what is normal and necessary. Attention is drawn to some dimensions of reality as acceptable or superior, whereas other aspects are glossed over as inferior, irrelevant, or a threat. This agenda setting activity is interpreted differently within various sociological perspectives. For functionalists, media messages contribute to the smooth functioning of society; for conflict theorists, media are complicit in reinforcing domination and control; and for symbolic interactionists, the agenda itself is under negotiated construction. These discourses and debates become the basis by which individuals become informed – or misinformed – about the society they live in.

Interrogating a Media Gaze: Encoding Media Hype/Decoding Moral Panic

> *Societies appear to be subject, every now and then, to periods*
> *of moral panic: a condition, episode, person or group emerges to*
> *become defined as a threat to societal values and interests; its*
> *nature is presented in a stylised and stereotypical fashion by the*
> *mass media. (S. Cohen 1972, 1)*

With so much power at their disposal, media possess the potential to expose, conceal, or transform. Media power stems in part from patterns of private ownership or corporate linkages. This power also reflects an ability to shape agendas by emphasizing some aspects of reality while disregarding others. Media preferences for news items that encompass the bizarre or diabolical are well established. Audiences are no less captivated by this menu of danger and disgust, if for no other reason than a yearning for novelty and distraction. In that media possess the power to generate as well as control public reactions to deviant acts, such selective exposure may prove galvanizing (Critcher 2003). But when media coverage appears disproportional to the significance of the event or the risk involved, according to David Altheide (2002, 2009), a dynamic of fear is activated that incites panic or paralysis.

It is commonly known that, when the unthinkable happens, news media are prone to exaggeration (Killingbeck 2001). Often unrelated incidents involving unnerving challenges to society are packaged into a crisis frame that imparts the worst possible spin. Unrelated stories may be pastiched together to manufacture scare stories related to personal safety or national security. Since an isolated event is rarely problematic until *constructed* as such by news media reworking it as a profound societal crisis that imperils the nation (Hier and Greenberg 2002), the accumulation of negative and often unsubstantiated claims may spiral out of control. A media-hyped moral panic materializes when people experience a loss of control over conventional rules, cherished values, or threats to the social and moral order. A generalized fear is activated by the perceived decay and collapse of civilized society, especially when the apparently random danger shows no respect for the age, social standing, or gender of victims (Critcher 2003). The fear mobilizes around a seemingly exaggerated overreaction toward perceived threats to societal values or interests by persons who can be easily demonized (folk devils). Actions thought to be repugnant, unpredictable, and uncontrollable generate a generalized sense of dread or outrage, thus prompting calls for action and intervention. Paradoxically, an official (over)reaction to the moral panic often reinforces perceptions about the severity of the threat, thus justifying media hype (coverage) in the first place (S. Cohen 1972).

But the hyping (exaggerating) of news events comes with a cost. A crisis of confidence is triggered that escalates into a moral panic, namely, a belief in a dissolving moral order. Hyping the panic not only elicits an irrational public reaction but also distorts official responses to the incident. Mainstream media are inextricably involved in generating moral panics by labelling and publicizing certain actions as a threat, amplifying their danger, and uncovering scapegoats (folk devils) to blame. Political response to this media-hyped and publicly driven moral panic is no less problematic. Laws, policies, and programs may be introduced to appease a panicky public rather than to carefully analyze the problem. Frenzied public and political reaction may justify yet additional media exposure, which, in turn, further incites public anxieties – and so on and so forth in a circular process. In that both media coverage and public/political responses constitute a symbolic projection of people's worst fears of the "other," media hyping and moral panicking often say more about society at large than about those under scrutiny (Fleras 2003).

In short, neither the incident nor the threat per se is the issue. Attention must focus instead on how media frame the defined threat into an easily recognizable trope with a highly connotative label, together with appropriate remedies aimed at isolating or removing those demonized as scapegoats. A rapid escalation of public unease or outrage (moral panic) is further reinforced by an elite exaggeration of the scope and seriousness of the situation. This focus on societal reaction to such media dramatization and sensationalism (hype) demonstrates the demonizing (labelling and stereotyping) of those events or persons responsible for the panic (hysteria). Often, these panicky insecurities far exceed the actual threat or danger; nevertheless, they are real in their conse-quences, especially for those most vulnerable, thus confirming the sociological axiom that things do not have to be real to have real effects.

Admittedly, there are problems in operationalizing concepts related to hype or panic. For example, if moral panics are by definition disproportionate responses to perceived threats (Critcher 2006), what constitutes a proportion-al response? When does a legitimate concern qualify as a moral panic, and who says so and why? When is the irrational rational, and vice versa? What is the relationship between those who do the hyping and those targeted by this hype? Moreover, accusing both the media and the public of excessive and dispropor-tionate reaction to the threat is a luxury afforded in hindsight. In that these panics tend to say more about the public in terms of its anxieties than anything about the world out there, their socially constructed nature cannot be under-played. Despite these conceptual conundrums, there is sociological value in studying how intense media coverage (hype) can contribute to a public dis-course of panic. The next Case Study offers an illustration of how exaggerated media discourses can distort people's understanding of social reality to the point of unsettling a society.

case study

Toronto Terror Scare: Moral Panic as Media Hype? Media Hype as Moral Panic?

> *The media commands immense influence on the development of public discourse on most subjects and its influence on the subject of ethnic diversity is profound. The public relies on the media to provide them with information in particular about events taking place outside of their direct experience. This places journalists and editors in a powerful position and it is vital, therefore, that the practices and beliefs of news organizations are held to account and subject to contestation and debate. (Samir Shah, chair, Runneymede Trust, Foreword to Sveinsson 2008, 2)*

Occasionally, incidents occur that are so disturbing that they mobilize political and public debate over a complex web of contentious issues. The Toronto Terror Scare is one example of how a sensationalistic news media hyped issues and created a moral panic – or capitalized on an existing moral panic – with wide-ranging repercussions that say a lot about the politics of seeing like the media.

Reference to media hype and its relationship to moral panic received a thorough workout when Canadian authorities in June 2006 apprehended an Islamist terrorist cell in the Greater Toronto Area. If the British air terror scare and the suitcase bomb fright at a Dortmund train station are included, the Toronto sweep expanded the number of terror plots exposed that summer by those born on native soil, speaking the vernacular, protected by rights of legal citizenship, and claiming Islam as a justifying ideology (Frum 2006). News coverage tended to border on the hysterical: news media hype capitalized on an existing moral panic to accentuate the conflicting and confrontational without much in the way of context or evidence. The conflict theme prevailed, as might have been expected, in the process demonizing the entire Muslim community by conflating the criminality of a few with the commonality of the many. In other words, media coverage of this embryonic plot proved both sensationalistic and misleading: sensationalistic because episodic coverage superseded the thematic or contextual; misleading because of a systemic bias against religiosity unless framed as negative, confrontational, or problematic. To the extent that the quantity of coverage superseded the quality of coverage, both Canadian Muslims and non-Muslim Canadians were done a disservice.

In early June 2006, Canada joined the global big leagues when seventeen (later increased to eighteen) relatively young men in the Greater Toronto Area were apprehended by police and security agencies for an alleged plot to stage a terror strike on home soil – forever changing the theory that terrorism could not happen here. True, nothing did happen; nevertheless, the suspects were charged under anti-terrorism legislation passed by the Canadian government in December 2001 in the aftermath of 9/11. The arrests sparked a blaze of media attention and national debates over a range of issues, from stereotyping to national security to Canadian-American relations. Two news media narratives emerged (Kay 2006). One reading took the terror scare as a deadly threat – Canada's equivalent to the 7/7 London bombings and a sign that Canada too was under siege from a militant subculture within the Islamic community. The other reading preferred to frame the scare as little more than a youthful hoax concocted by a bunch of mixed-up adolescents with too much testosterone on their hands – less hard-core terrorists than amateur poseurs enthralled with the quixotism of youthful rebellion. This brash plot, with its bracing mix of bombings and beheadings, was exposed as amateurish and bungled from the start. Authorities had long monitored the suspicious activity; heck, they even supplied the suspects with the potentially explosive ammonium nitrate (the same material used in the 1995 Oklahoma blast) as part of the sting operation – prompting some critics to suggest that authorities deliberately misled ("entrapped"?) the suspects for political reasons (Friscolanti, Gatehouse, and Gillis 2006).

Whether the crisis was orchestrated or coincidental, the news media took the terrorism bait – hook, line, and sinker. Any sense of balance quickly dissipated as newsroom decorum gave way to speculation and sensationalism. Admittedly, many acknowledged the difficulty of balancing objectivity with fairness without stigmatizing the overwhelming number of law-abiding Muslims or denying the accused the right to a fair trial (Burnside 2006). Still, Canadians were gripped with coverage so saturated in conjecture and hyperbole that it nearly bordered on overkill. Countless pages were devoted to deconstructing the chain of events, dissecting the possible causes, speculating on the connections to overseas terrorism, and debating what, if anything, could prevent a repeat occurrence. Fingers were pointed in all directions, including the clash of civilizations, the belligerence of Western foreign policies, the impact of global politics, the failure of Canada's immigration and multiculturalism policies (Ryan 2010), youthful indiscretion or radicalization, and the Islamification of terrorism (see Elmasry 2006). But although the news media cast about for a single cause or explanatory framework, reality is rarely so accommodating. According to Jessica Stern (2003), understanding the causes of terrorism and terrorist motivations involves a thoughtful and multilayered approach at different levels: global, national, intergroup, and personal.

The crisis also exposed the perils of assuming a linear mono-causality between media hype and moral panic. Could the crisis be attributed to a media-driven scare that terrorized Torontonians? Or was an already panicked public primed to be frightened by an opportunistic media? Moral panic can be defined as a public reaction (from a spontaneous outburst to an organized social movement) to a perceived and often exaggerated threat that, by challenging its values and norms, imperils the very moral fabric of society (S. Cohen 1972). For the most part, these mass panics (or hysterias) are fuelled by intense news media coverage, resulting in what Stanley Cohen calls a "deviancy amplification spiral" (118). That is, the very process of labelling those who pose a threat to public morality tends to amplify their status as problem people. Once labelled as problematic, the stigmatized may act in ways that amplify the crisis. The resultant media-hyped moral panic also yields another effect: a misperception of the magnitude of the threat. Unrelated stories involving religious-inspired extremism may be pastiched together to launch scare stories about possible national threats. In that terrorism is about intimidating the hearts and minds of the general public (Stern 2003), the actions of a few are amplified out of proportion, thus intensifying public panic over the possibility of an apocalyptic insurrection (Walkom 2006).

It is widely accepted that news media hype generates moral panic. Can this causal relationship be inverted by suggesting the opposite, namely, that an existing public or moral panic – based on previous news media hype – may trigger excessive coverage as consumers clamour for more information about the dangers at hand? To what extent does the threat of terrorism drive the dynamic rather than public fears based on media misperceptions (Huysmans 2006)? For example, with the acquittal of the suspects in the 1985 Air India bombing still in the public mind, Canadians remained uneasy over the capacity of faith-based groups to wreak havoc (McLeod 2006). The act of violence of 9/11 and the events of 7/7 in London also bolstered the dread factor by catapulting terrorism to the top of the security agenda. In other words, there was so much anxiety and fear in the air that reality was already spinning out of control (see Altheide 2009). The media simply took advantage of a public in moral panic mode.

To be sure, the risks of victimization by terrorism are low when measured against facts, probabilities, or statistics. But perception *is* reality when coping with risk. In that public perceptions of threat rather than statistical evidence drive public opinion (Leroy 2005), the combination of unpredictability and uncontrollability triggers a generalized sense of dread, especially when inflamed by relentless media coverage over security breaches (both real and imagined). An obsession with security is not surprising; after all, the external world has become more frightening in a vaguely dangerous manner because of strange viruses (like SARS) or geopolitical instabilities (Graves 2005; Altheide 2009). Governments may be equally complicit in transforming a culture of privatized fear into a public panic (Giroux 2006). By projecting the worst fears into a terrifying nightmare, hidden agendas masquerading as national interests can sway a suspecting public. In short, terrorism will succeed even when it fails, as noted by terrorism expert Roland Jacquard (quoted in Crumley 2006). Terrorist-inspired fear mongering may generate such a societal paranoia about future attacks that a heightened vigilantism begins to erode the very freedoms and rights under attack by terrorists.

In a frightened society, then, the real war against terrorism should be the war against fear. Vigilance, yes, but a vigilantism that purges any freedom that remotely

threatens security can make a bad situation even worse (Trudeau 2006). Both terrorists and the news media know exactly which mass panic buttons to push for max-
imum impact. In the final analysis, the real problem is not a failure of imagination
by the news media. More to the point, it's about an imagination of failure by the
consuming public (see Harvey 2006).

Critical-Thinking Question
How do the concepts of media hype and moral panic apply to media coverage of
the 2006 Toronto Terror Scare?

* * * * * * * * * *

Terrorists have long acknowledged the importance of media (especially
CNN and the Internet) as an effective vehicle for disseminating their message.
Without the global reach of media communication, terrorism would be a shad-
ow of itself. The terror in terrorism reflects its symbolism as political theatre;
after all, terrorist acts are designed as a media spectacle to maximize fear and
panic. Mainstream media, in turn, like to report on terrorism because of its
intrinsic newsworthiness in providing graphic visuals, easy-to-identify protagonists, and the corresponding suspense. In that terrorism is about theatre for
intimidating the hearts and minds of the general public (Stern 2003), the actions of a few are amplified out of proportion, thus intensifying public panic
over the possibility of a catastrophic scenario (Walkom 2006). Not surprisingly,
coverage takes on a life of its own, pushed forward by a self-reinforcing process
or self-referential feedback loop: more coverage = more panic = more coverage
= more reaction = more coverage. Several insights into seeing like the media
can be gleaned by examining the politics of media hyping and panicky publics:

- Moral panics are increasingly intrinsic to a media that thrives on negativity
  and conflict. As J.M. Gray (2006) wrote in his *Globe and Mail* column,
  "[Given] North American media's structural inclination to ratchet up the ten-
  sion and fear in any story ... Inflated drama is in the genetic code of TV news."
  The media may have an uncanny knack for creating stories that culminate in
  public hysteria. Yet they also possess the ability to criticize or even mock
  those who take the paranoia seriously – in the same way media put celebrities
  on a pedestal, only to topple them, while criticizing the public for its obsession with a media-driven cult of celebrity worship. Finally, the relatively
  muted coverage of local media stands in sharp contrast to the international

media's commitment to sound bites, sensationalism, and exaggerated angles (Appelbe 2003).

- Rather than an unintended and isolated consequence of a well-meaning if pressured media, such hype may not be entirely random. Media-driven moral panics are not simply discrete episodes that randomly flare up but are part of a broader media dynamic (Thompson 2005). Vested interests may deliberately generate panics about relatively harmless issues as a way of diverting attention from more serious problems (Hall 1980). Media-hyped moral panics are increasingly attractive to (1) politicians, to orchestrate consent, (2) authorities, to rationalize excessive control or intrusion, (3) businesses, to promote sales, and (4) media, to bolster profit levels and market shares (McRobbie and Thornton 1995). Not surprisingly, governments will inflate marginal nuisances into a colossal bogeyman to distract the masses while capitalizing on these threats to pass unpopular legislation or impose social controls in the name of national security (Dyer 2003).

- The politics of media hyping reveals a lot about the exercise of power in society. In defining who is a social problem and what is the appropriate solution (Critcher 2006), the media are especially adept at hyping the panic. Conventional wisdom contends that a lack of information feeds public fears. A dearth of information may create a vacuum whose void is rapidly filled with rumour and innuendo, in turn leading to fear, anxiety, and paranoia. The public respond to this void by acting (ir)rationally as a coping mechanism to assert control (or at least the illusion of control) – however simplistic – over a bewildering and complex scenario. Yet there is no evidence that better information would dampen the jitters. The very act of expanding space for crisis stories is as likely as withholding information to amplify public anxieties. Proposing solutions is just as likely to inflate people's worries as are stories about government indifference or complacency. In short, there are no grounds for assuming that panic is created by keeping people in the dark. To the contrary, both informed and misinformed doomsday talk is likely to have a panicking effect on the audience. And there is little the media can do because of the public's seemingly insatiable capacity to be simultaneously alarmed and assured.

Are media and terrorism partners in crime? Yes and no. No because the media are neither complicit nor accomplices. There is no evidence to suggest the media act in collusion with terrorists as a pipeline to the spectacular and the menacing. Yes because media coverage unwittingly supplies terrorists with the oxygen of publicity. The paradox is inescapable and cruel: just as the Israelis learned long ago, the greater the force of retaliation to terrorist attacks, the greater the lure of the terrorist cause. Such as Faustian bargain can be applied to news media. In publishing articles that panic the public to the point of paralysis, the media may inadvertently advance the terrorist agenda.

2 Conceptualizing Media Gazes

Quickly, now, define television. Easier said than done. Your definition might focus on what television looks like (e.g., a forty-six-inch HD flat-screen model). Or perhaps it's based on what television does in conveying programs for entertainment or information. Another way of defining television is by analyzing what it really does rather than what it says it does. Is television a medium of persuasion whose primary function is to foster consumerism as ideology and lifestyle? A reliance on playful inversions is helpful in thinking outside the box – namely, the inverting of conventional wisdom on its head in hopes of coaxing fresh insights from a tired topic. Consider television programming as a prime-time example of inversion in practice:

Convention Television is a medium for providing programming, with commercials as the filler.

Inversion More accurately, television as the consummate marketing device is primarily about selling advertising, with programming as the filler in between the commercial breaks.

Convention Audiences are perceived as the main customers, who must be catered to through consumer-pleasing programming.

Inversion In reality, it is advertisers that are television's main customer, with audiences as a commodity for sale to advertisers. The larger the (right kind of) audience, the higher the price that can be charged.

Convention	People watch television.
Inversion	Television also watches us to monitor those preferences, relationships, and anxieties that can be alleviated only through product purchase. Insofar as most commercial media are conduits for advertising or brand awareness, the idea that television is watching us puts an entirely new spin on the relationship.

Two conclusions follow. First, media see and interpret the world in a self-serving way. Given their dependence on readers/viewers, ratings, and revenue, how could it be otherwise? Second, the media are instrumental in getting audiences to see reality from their perspective while pretending this perspective is perspective-less. This media sleight of hand is accomplished in large part by co-opting the viewer into a media-centred view of social reality as if it were natural, normative, and normal, rather than conventional, constructed, and contested.

This chapter explores the politics of the media gaze in explaining the dynamics of a seeing like the media. A prevailing media gaze is shown to encode media messages that are ideologically loaded because they are socially constructed. That alone makes it doubly important to decode (or deconstruct) those hidden values, beliefs, and norms that make up the encoding process. The chapter addresses the media gaze as a pattern of persuasion that co-opts audiences into uncritically seeing like the media. Two major case studies delve into the dynamics of persuasion by stealth: how a Hollywood gaze framed depictions of Canada and its Aboriginal peoples, and how a "whitestream" media gaze depoliticizes controversial issues in the television series *Little Mosque on the Prairie*. The chapter concludes by demonstrating how a mediacentric gaze constitutes coverage that is systemically biasing in its consequences.

Media Gaze as Mediacentrism

Let's be upfront about this: first, there is no such thing as a pure and unmediated gaze. Whether aware or not, people are always interpreting social reality through the prism of situated lenses – one that reflects the commonly held assumptions of the day, another that involves ingrained but often unconscious mindsets for interpreting social reality, and yet another that refracts reality through stereotypes instead of a rational assessment based on particular facts

(Bahdi 2003). Second, by suspending belief, a gaze is more than the simple act of looking at something. As bell hooks (1992) and others, including Foucault (1977), point out, a gaze entails looking with intent, in the process conferring meaning on the object of attention while establishing an asymmetrical power relationship between gazer and the gazed upon. For example, Cornel West (2001) invokes the concept of a Eurocentrically normative gaze to demonstrate how whiteness – by projecting white fears and fantasies upon the "other" – frames the inferiority of others as natural and normal.

The conclusion seems inescapable: people's experiences with reality are influenced by largely unconscious preconceptions and often irrational biases that frame what is seen or thought (Ariely 2009). As Foucault recognized long ago, what we know about the world is not based on what the world is but a reflection of who we are. Or alternatively phrased, where we are socially located in society with respect to the intersections of class, gender, race, ethnicity, sexuality, and age will profoundly influence the shaping of our identities, experiences, relationships (how we relate to others, and they to us), and opportunities/ outcomes.

The same goes for the concept of media gaze. Just as there is no neutral gaze among individuals, so too is the notion of media neutrality a myth. As noted in Chapter 1, mainstream media are neither neutral nor value-free. Rather, they are so loaded with deeply embedded ideas and ideals about what is normal and acceptable with respect to race, gender, and class that media representations of diversities and difference are invariably raced, gendered, Eurocentric, and classed. These foundational ideas and fundamental ideals draw attention to some aspects of reality as normal and necessary while drawing the gaze away from others as irrelevant or inferior. These ideas and ideals also reflect, reinforce, and advance the interests, experiences, and agendas of those who create or control what audiences see or hear. In that some interests are advanced as normal, acceptable, or desirable while others are excluded or caricaturized, a media gaze involves a mediated process of formulating representations according to media priorities.

But the concept of the media gaze goes beyond a mediacentric way of framing social reality. Rather, a media gaze refers to the process by which readers and viewers are painted into the media picture so that they begin to see like the media without realizing they are doing so. More specifically, a media gaze reflects a tendency by a mainstream media to frame the social reality from an institutional point of view (i.e., predominantly straight, white, middle-aged, middle-class, male) as natural and normal, while dismissing other aspects as inferior and irrelevant, *in the process drawing audiences into seeing like the media as if this seeing did not involve any perspective or bias.* The media are hegemonic in coaxing the public to absorb a media interpretation of reality as if it were true, normal, and desirable (Kuypers 2002). Audiences are co-opted into seeing reality from a media-centred perspective yet are rarely aware that their attitudes are undergoing change along mediacentric lines.

In general, a media gaze represents a media tendency to impose a specific view of the world without announcing its intention or underlying biases. These gazes entail a process in which the media (and media actors) construct media-centric images of the world by framing social reality in a manner consistent with media values, norms, priorities, and interests.[1] Information is organized (framed) in a way that draws attention to some aspects of reality and away from other aspects by encouraging a preferred reading consistent with a prevailing media gaze. Take, for example, media portrayals of diversities and difference. By whitewashing minorities into something familiar, acceptable, non-threatening, and under control, they are rendered more palatable for mainstream audiences. But the whitewashing of minorities along dominant frames is consequential. Their agency, agendas, and subjectivity are compromised by transforming them into *objects of representation commensurate with a mainstream media gaze,* especially when they unknowingly *objectify themselves by imagining how the media are seeing them* (Sheffield 2002). The resulting mediacentric bias erodes any pretence of media neutrality; it also confirms the status of media representations as socially constructed conventions that conceal as they reveal.

To sum up: a media gaze is mediacentric in framing diversities and difference. With mediacentrism, the media tend to gaze at (i.e., see, interpret, and frame) reality from their vantage point as natural and normal. Other interpretations of reality are dismissed as inappropriate and inconsistent, primarily because media want audiences *to see like the media* by pretending that this seeing is bias-free. In the final analysis, media do not reflect reality per se but rather a version of reality by those who construct media content through techniques that make this reality construction seem natural and normal – in effect saying more about those doing the constructing than about the constructed. Over time, viewers and readers come to believe that news media frames of

---

1 Reference to "mediacentric" borrows from the more widely used term "ethnocentric." Ethnocentrism reflects a tendency for people to frame (see, interpret, evaluate) social reality from their point of view as natural and normal, and to assume others are doing so (or should be doing so) as well, while dismissing other interpretations as inferior or irrelevant. This ethnocentric tendency to frame or judge others by one's own standards of normalcy or acceptability clearly leads to assumptions of superiority over the "other."

reality are neutral in accurately depicting an objective and external reality. In reality, newsworthiness under a mediacentric gaze is biased and filtered through frames that prioritize the negative over the positive, deviance over normative, conflict over cooperation, the sensational over the mundane, the episodic over the thematic, and vested interests over marginal interests.

The impact and implications of a media gaze cannot be underestimated. In that media constitute a socially constructed convention rather than something natural or normal, a media gaze is socially constructing. For example, a newscasting focus on negativity and conflict constructs an image of a world both dangerous and to be feared, especially when diversities and difference are involved. In encouraging audiences to see like the media, a media gaze influences not only how people look at the "other" but also how the "other" looks at itself. For example, depictions of racialized minorities as problem people dwell on their personal shortcomings while drawing attention away from racialized violence, systemic bias, and structural barriers. Coverage of the "other" under a media gaze is so systemically biasing in its consequences that it virtually amounts to an exercise in soft propaganda. Control by hegemony – that is, how the powerful create consensus and control through consent rather than coercion, largely by changing people's attitudes without a corresponding awareness – could not be more skillfully conveyed. The following Case Study demonstrates the power of the media gaze in terms of seeing Canada and First Nations peoples through the prism of a Hollywood lens.

---

case study

Seeing Canada Like Hollywood Did: Putting Tinseltown's Media Gaze to the "Reel" "Indian" Movie Test

In 1975, McClelland and Stewart published a book titled *Hollywood's Canada*. The author, Pierre Berton, castigated the film industry for its misrepresentation of Canada and Canadians. From 1907 onward, according to Berton, a total of 575 films were made about or specifically set in Canada and distributed worldwide. But the Canada that appeared on Tinseltown celluloid differed sharply from the realities of Canada or that of Canadians. For Hollywood, Canada consisted almost exclusively of boundless forests and snow-swept mountains (no prairies), was devoid of large cities (except Montreal), and was peopled by happy-go-lucky French Canadians, savage Indians, wicked half-breeds, and grim-jawed Mounties in charge of policing an American-style wild West frontier. Not only did these fabrications and caricatures influence generations of moviegoers both in Canada and abroad – keeping in mind that what the world knew of Canada or Canadians was largely gleaned from movies – but the refraction of these demeaning images through the prism of Hollywood's fantasy machine aborted the search for a Canadian national identity.

This Case Study on Hollywood's depiction of Aboriginal peoples (normally referred to as "Indians" in "La-La Land"), including Metis (called "half-breeds" by Hollywood), is instructive in demonstrating how a constructed media gaze reflected a distinction between a reel reality and real realities. Native Americans (indigenous peoples) proved reliable film fodder for reeling in the audiences, all the time perpetuating myth-conceptions of the wild West as the quintessential proving ground for American expansionism. Movie directors were drawn to the winning combination of non-stop action, arrows zipping through the air, blood-curdling shrieks, acrobatic pony manoeuvres, and high body counts. Equally mesmerizing were eye-popping images that embraced rapid physical movement, exotic appearance, violent confrontations, and barbaric personalities. Dramatic cinematic narratives pertaining to the saga of greed, broken treaties, and mutual betrayals were no less appealing (Herzberg 2008). This focus on action and treachery reinforced the "othering" of Aboriginal peoples as life forms from a different time and place. Their histories began with the arrival of whites; subsequent realities made sense only within the context of settler interaction (see Razack 2002); and their future could be crudely encrypted in the title of the acclaimed book by Ralph and Natasha Friar, *The Only Good Indian Is a Dead Indian*.

Although Canada's Aboriginal peoples comprised a culturally and socially different groups whose distinctiveness reflected variations in history, geography, and culture, a one-size-fits-all mindset prevailed for Hollywood's "injuns" (Buscombe 2006). Regardless of where they lived or how they lived, Canadian "Indians" – Blackfoot, Iroquois, Cree, Salish, or Ojibwa – were bunched together as uniformly the same and largely indistinguishable from their American counterparts – in effect reinforcing a "seen one Indian, seen them all" mentality. Film portrayals embraced a mythical image of an imaginary warrior who occupied the Plains during the nineteenth century (Francis 1992). A generic appearance standard was culled from a so-called Indian (male) Identity Kit (Friar and Friar 1972) consisting of a wig with hair parted in the middle into hanging plaits, a feathered war bonnet or headband (not an indigenous artifact but introduced by white actors for securing their wigs), buckskin leggings, moccasins, painted skin teepee, and a spear, bow and arrow, or

case study

tomahawk. Aggressive actions by unfriendly Natives conformed to a standard Primitive Savagery Kit, including attacking wagon trains, swooping down on horseback to torch settler cabins, torturing prisoners, pounding on tom-toms or whooping it up or fanning menacing smoke signals as a prelude before attack, and being prone to uncontrollable drunkenness and cruelty ("It was in their blood"). Collective resistance to their colonization was rarely depicted, although individual acts of protest were acknowledged and justified (but not excused) in halting the march of civilization across their hunting grounds – in effect depoliticizing the politics of aboriginality.

Of those most maligned by Hollywood's propaganda machine, the Blackfoot Confederacy in Canada's western foothills suffered the severest slings. According to Berton, Hollywood's movie moguls were enamoured by the Blackfoot as the quintessential expression of Canadian "Indianness," despite their limited geographical locale. Worse still, they were usually framed as barbaric and bloodthirsty savages, whereas, in reality, the Plains Indians in general and the Blackfoot in particular were for the most part peaceful. It was not part of their culture to torture or burn or attack either the RCMP or settlers in their homes or wagon trains. As proof, Berton points out, they not only signed one of the earliest western treaties but refused to join the Metis and Cree in the Northwest Rebellion of 1885. Paradoxically, it was the whites who committed some of the worst atrocities that kept the Mounties busy.

Indian women received more humane treatment by Hollywood's mythmaking gaze. Nevertheless, their appearance and behaviour conformed to a Hollywood Female Indian Kit. With their beaded headbands, single eagle feather, necklaces of beads or animal teeth, buckskin or leather skirts, and long black hair in braids, they were portrayed as small, gentle creatures whose compassion for captured white males often proved a fatal attraction. In sharp contrast were depictions of bad Indian women ("squaws") and their hot-blooded half-sisters ("half-breeds"), who would go to any length to seduce hapless white males. Ultimately, however, they too paid for these indiscretions with their lives. Half-breed males suffered worse indignities. Unlike the generally affable rogues that the French Canadian represented, the Metis were vilified as proof of the evils of miscegenation (Friar and Friar 1972). These half-breeds were depicted as the worst sort of dirty, no-good scoundrels and untrustworthy degenerates who coveted defenceless white women or sold bad whisky to Indians. Yet what was filtered through the Hollywood gaze proved fanciful. The Metis were not a lawless folk constantly pursued by Mounties; more accurately, Berton writes, the real Metis were a people whose code of honour and protocols established a precedent for law and order in the West. Nor did they engage in the selling of boot-legged booze to other Indians – it was the white men who did so, initially those in the large fur-trading companies, then opportunistic American entrepreneurs.

Berton's book yields a bundle of insights into Hollywood's misinformation industry. A seeing like Hollywood saw included distorted geography, inaccurate costuming, insulting stereotypes, and incorrect interpretations of Canadian history, its peoples, and its character, all contributing to perceptions of Canada and Canadians. This way of seeing had two implications (J. Nelson 1976). First, Hollywood's portrayal of Canada could be deployed as a justification for American cultural imperialism. American exploitation of its northern neighbour was justified on the grounds that Canada was a *terra nullius* – an empty and largely under-utilized country, save for a few primitives and prospectors – ripe for the picking. Second, Hollywood's gaze helped to mystify, obscure, engulf, and unsettle Canada's march toward identity and real autonomy, writes Joyce Nelson (1976) in reviewing Berton's book. That alone should compel any dominated peoples to take back their own fictions, to tell their stories and myths, to excavate their histories, and to repossess their imaginations. Such a reclamation is particularly valid for Canada's First Nations peoples, who have historically endured images and representations crafted for non-Aboriginal audiences (M.J. Miller 2008). After all, to continue seeing like Hollywood, with its stereotypes of "reel" Indians as drunken, savage, treacherous, unreliable, and childlike (Friar and Friar 1972), without challenging this prevailing movie-media gaze is tantamount to the symbolic annihilation of society and culture.

Critical-Thinking Questions
How has a Hollywood gaze depicted Canada's Aboriginal peoples? How might an Aboriginal gaze portray Hollywood as a medium? (To assist in this debate, the NFB film *Reel Injuns* by Neil Diamond may prove useful.)

* * * * * * * * * *

The Multi-Dimensionality of Media Gazes
Despite its singular-sounding connotation, a media gaze represents a multi-faceted phenomena. A media gaze incorporates a multi-dimensional interplay of gazes (perspectives) for framing diversities and difference, including a corporate (classist) gaze, an androcentric (male)/gendered gaze, a heterosexist gaze, a Eurocentric (liberal universal) gaze, and a racialized gaze. Although each of these media gazes will be separately analyzed, in reality they tend to

concurrently intersect with one another to normalize invisibility yet problematize visibility.

Corporate (Classist) Media Gaze

The concept of a corporate media gaze is rooted in A.J. Leibling's prescient notion that the freedom of the press belongs to the owners. Phrased alternatively, corporate interests are favourably positioned to influence how media look and frame realities. Reality is subsequently refracted through the prism of those who own or control media outputs. For example, the ownership and control of profit-oriented commercial media by the rich and powerful may indirectly influence how social class is portrayed. Mainstream news media tend to highlight pro-white issues of relevance to middle-class readers, and its organizational culture and news routines favour coverage of those with privileged access to the news industry. The conflation of media interests with national elites fosters a sharing of common viewpoints with other corporate rulers about important political and economic issues (Kollmeyer 2004). This convergence of interests ultimately influences how news media cover the economy or society, with preference given to corporate events and investment issues over those affecting labour unions or the working classes. Media representations of class will be discussed in Chapters 5 and 10.

Androcentric (Male)/Gendered Media Gaze

References to a media gaze are often associated with a male gaze. Historically, of course, media content reflected, reinforced, and advanced male interests and experiences as acceptable and superior; women's voices were dismissed accordingly. In advancing the notion of media as a blank screen (or page) for projecting male fears and fantasies, preferred images of women were formulated along androcentric lines. This gendered media gaze materializes when audiences assume the perspective of seeing and interpreting the world from a male's vantage point as being natural and normal (i.e., as if it were no perspective at all). Then and now, as Laura Mulvey (1975) writes of film, the camera's eye prompts women to look and act in a way that pleases men – for example, in that subservient and helpless way that many men apparently find appealing. Or, as conveyed by the Boston-based Our Bodies, Ourselves health resource centre (http://www.ourbodiesourselves.org),

> In trying to understand the media's objectification of women and how it makes us feel, it can help to think of the camera lens as a white male eye. Have you noticed that the covers of women's and men's magazines are almost always

female? The female stars of mainstream movies and TV shows not only look sexy, but often behave in the kind of subservient, helpless way that many men find appealing. The camera eye is usually focused on women who look and act in a way that pleases men; men look (active), and women receive their gaze (passive). We are so accustomed to seeing things through the dominant male perspective that we might not even notice the dynamics at play.

In short, how women are portrayed – from sex objects and objects of physical attractiveness to sterner stuff related to maternal-domestic activities – is less natural than many think but reflects hidden ideological biases that display women's bodies and actions for male edification. Sut Jhally confirms this in the video "Dreamworlds 3" (Jhally 2007) when referring to the unwritten rules and unspoken codes of a prevailing male gaze that are deeply sexist in reinforcing how the most important thing about a woman is her sexuality and sexual prowess.

Put bluntly, when seeing like the media, men gaze; women are gazed at (Berger 1972). Men voyeuristically look (gaze) at women, while women watch themselves being looked at (gazed). Media representations of women's bodies are seen through the lens of the dominant gender, thereby reinforcing the primacy of a male perspective, even if the intended viewer is female. In treating the lens as a substitute for the eyes of an imaginary onlooker, the ideal spectator is always assumed to be a male (point of view), and the image of the woman is designed to flatter him (ibid; see also Chandler 2000). Tricia Sheffield (2002, 3) puts it nicely in positing the politics of gazing as a power relationship that positions the male gazer as superior to the feminized object of the gaze (see Karan and Khoo 2007). She writes: "Knowing that the male gaze functions as the dominant form of approval and power in society, and that the gaze is ever roaming ... She is always aware that she may be observed from the 'tower' at any given time, so she takes over the job of surveying herself and modifying her behaviour. She internalizes the gaze of the surveyor and the structure, which is patriarchy." Admittedly, women are increasingly subverting the intended male gaze of the dominant paradigm (see Chapter 9), with the result that men are now learning what it means to watch oneself being watched by a gendered media gaze.

A Heterosexist Media Gaze
Straight white males continue to represent the dominant group in society with the political clout to reflect, reinforce, and advance their social and cultural agendas at institutional levels. With respect to the media, a heterocentric

gaze tends to dominate social norms and cultural values about sexuality and sexualization, for example, by sanitizing and repackaging homosexuality for straightstream consumption. The paradox is nicely captured in the following way: "When previously ignored groups or perspectives do gain visibility, the manner of their representation will reflect the biases and interests of those powerful people who define the public agenda. And they are mostly white, mostly middle aged, mostly male, mostly middle and upper middle class, and overwhelmingly heterosexual" (quoted in Shugart 2003, 68). To be sure, with modern masculinities under siege and changing (Kimmel 2010; Vitales 2010), positive images of homosexuality are flourishing on television and film (GLAAD 2010). Nevertheless, heterocentric gazes of homosexuality remain in force, resulting in mixed signals that simultaneously empower and marginalize.

Racialized Media Gaze
A media gaze also incorporates a racialized agenda. Cornel West's reference to a normative gaze describes how a racialized (white or Eurocentric) perspective provides a conceptual lens ("the norm" or frames) for framing racialized minorities. Take newscasting: in fostering a colour-coded news discourse whose "palemale" gaze is deemed to be pro-white rather than anti-minority (Jiwani 2006), images of "them" as "those people" are filtered through the norms of "whiteness" as the unmarked yet universal standard that defines and discredits others. With a racialized gaze, minorities are looked at from a white-o-centric point of view, thus reinforcing pre-existing beliefs (Sommers et al. 2006), while minority women and men internalize a white way of being looked at. Jennifer Kelly (1998, 19) writes of the controlling effect associated with a racialized gaze: "The importance of the gaze is that it allows a dominant group to control the social spaces and social interactions of all groups. Blacks are made visible and invisible at the same time under the gaze. For example, when black youth are seen it is often with a specific gaze that sees the 'troublemaker', 'the school skipper' or the 'criminal.'"

A Eurocentric media gaze represents an extension of a racialized gaze. Like ethnocentrism, Eurocentrism reflects an inclination to frame (see, interpret, assess) social reality in ways consistent with European ideals of desirability, normality, and acceptability, while dismissing alternative frames or perspectives as inferior, irrelevant, or threatening. For example, a Eurocentric news media embraces a commitment to liberal universalism, with its attendant notion that what we share in common as morally autonomous individuals – at least for purposes of reward and recognition – supersedes what divides us as members of groups. Such a liberal view works well when excluded groups demand to be treated similarly because of previous exclusions. But problems arise when certain groups want their differences to be taken seriously or, alternatively, when they want differences to be publicly recognized and accommodated. Media reactions to those who challenge or contravene the principles of liberal universalism should come as no surprise. Those with left-leaning views are ignored or framed as troublesome constituents, whereas those to the right of centre are dismissed as biased or ideologues. By contrast, positive coverage is accorded to those whose views reflect a range of acceptable media discourses. And yet, paradoxically, the extremes monopolize coverage.

Racialized minorities are framed under a Eurocentric gaze by repositioning (whitewashing) them as objects for mainstream acceptance (MacNeill 2009). Whitewashing minorities reflects a media gaze that can assume several forms, including the idea of miniaturizing their presence on the screen or in print. Whitewashing can also incorporate a sanitizing of minority appearances by ensuring that any differences comply with a white-o-centric standard of acceptability. The representation of minorities is depoliticized (or neutered) so as not to discomfort mainstream viewers (see Rockler-Gladen 2008). Mainstream media employ several depoliticizing strategies to allay audience concerns over potentially awkward viewing experiences, including the following:

- Representations of minorities focus on universal experiences with widespread mainstream appeal rather than on experiences unique to a specific group, thus a defusing by diffusing. This normalization process is consistent with the universalizing principles of liberal universalism (we are all basically the same). It also contributes to the whitewashing or depoliticizing of those differences deemed to be incompatible with Canada's multicultural kaleidoscope.
- Representations ignore prickly issues related to poverty, discrimination, or powerlessness. If introduced, such representations gloss over systemic structures of inequality while blaming minorities for their predicaments, thus avoiding narratives that challenge the prevailing distribution of power and privilege.
- Representations focus on minorities as laughably quirky or treacly sweet rather than as complex individuals with personalities. Storylines focus on "playing minorities for laughs" by capitalizing on their status as fish out of water.
- Representations about minorities are less about them and more about how others are baffled by them and (re)act accordingly.

In short, a whitewashing is prevalent because commercial media are not in the business of offering representations contrary to consensus ideologies. The centrality of ratings and advertising revenue ensures the whitewashing of controversial representations to placate audiences and sponsors. By taking what is potentially controversial and sanitizing it into something more palatable for the mainstream, a depoliticized media gaze says more about the doer than the done-to. The next Case Study demonstrates how differences may be whitewashed to make them more palatable for viewing audiences.

_____ **case study**

Whitewashing Difference as Racialized Media Gaze: *Little Mosque on the Prairie*

The centrality of a racialized media gaze can be applied to the CBC sitcom hit *Little Mosque on the Prairie*, which premiered in January 2007. Taking its cue from the popular books by Laura Ingalls Wilder and the television series *Little House on the Prairie*, *Little Mosque* unfolds as a typical sitcom series, except that it revolves around Muslim individuals in the small rural prairie community of Mercy, Saskatchewan (see Wikipedia for more details regarding the series). The show consists of stock characters with overly exaggerated and stereotyped qualities; plot lines and gags revolve around misunderstandings between Muslims and their dealings with a host of friendly yet eccentric and bumbling townsfolk (Mohammed 2007). With its tagline "Small-town Canada with a little Muslim twist," the show derives its humour from exploring the fish-out-of-water interactions of Muslims (from conservatives to liberals) with non-Muslims.

The series has garnered considerable praise both nationally and internationally, and a number of countries have purchased syndication rights (B. Anderson 2007). Critical reaction to the show is varied. For some, it's groundbreaking programming in a multicultural society in which making fun of religion is not socially acceptable. Admittedly, the series is not the first media initiative to dispel negative stereotypes through comedy, although the show does normalize Muslims by situating them within Canada's multicultural experiences, rather than framing them as stoic sojourners with alien allegiances (Nicolo 2007; Sheikh and Farooq 2007). In contrast to conventional negative stereotyping as typically found in newscasts, the series seeks to humanize Muslims by poking fun at the stereotypes that distort or demean (ibid.). The attraction of the series reflects a portrayal of

Muslims as never before seen on TV – as regular people with everyday problems who do not take themselves too seriously (B. Anderson 2007). Moreover, in contrast to American TV dramas that routinely frame Muslims as dangerous immigrants and Islam as an evil and violence-prone religion (Aydin and Hammer 2010), the series represents one of the first attempts by Muslims to televisually reflect upon Islamic communities and the type of image they as citizens of a country are projecting (Mohammed 2007).

Others are more critical of the show's popularity and success. Although sitcoms understandably distort reality and exaggerate differences for comic relief (Sheikh and Farooq 2007), poking fun of Muslims in Canada runs the risk of perpetuating new stereotypes while sweeping aside real issues. Even if the series has broken a media taboo by framing Muslims as personalities or characters within a broader Canadian context, there is no escaping the centrality of a racialized mediacentric gaze in whitewashing (depoliticizing) the series, the storylines, and its characters:

1 By focusing on universal experiences rather than Muslim realities, the series tells universal stories about the foibles and follies of individuals with diverse backgrounds in sustained contact of mutual incomprehensiveness (B. Anderson 2007). As one of the executive producers, Mary Darling, said, "One thing that attracted us was the universal nature of the idea. I mean anyone in any religious congregation would recognize the kinds of people who are our characters. I mean, people are people. We are one human family, really" (quoted in Mohammed 2007).

2 The series depoliticizes the tensions and potential conflicts associated with Islam in a nominally secular Canada. According to its creator, Zarqa Nawaz, in subscribing to the view that humour fosters intergroup conviviality, the series provides "an unabashedly comedic look at a small Muslim community living side by side with the residents of a little prairie town" (Meer 2007). By playing off Muslims with non-Muslim for laughs, potentially politicized situations in the post-9/11 era are channelled into harmless venues.

3 The politics of religion are largely sanitized and stripped of their potential disruptiveness. For example, critics like Tarek Fatah (2008) suggest the show glosses over what really happens in those mosques whose preachers convey political messages. To the extent that the series explores religious-based storylines, politically tinged issues like the use of headscarves or prayer rugs are included as much for their laughs as for their politics.

case study

4   Although the series does provide some insight into Muslim experiences and the Islamic faith, including their difficulties in adapting to a mainstream Canada, the primary focus is unmistakable: eliciting townsfolk reactions to the presence of the strangers within. Muslims are framed primarily as comedic fodder for driving plot lines that reinforce the universality of the immigrant experience at the expense of being Muslim in Canada.

Clearly, then, a media gaze has managed to depoliticize what in reality may be an awkward 9/11 situation. The whitewashing of Muslim experiences into something that is palatable for audiences, advertisers, and overseas sales alike is cleverly concealed behind the smiles of a happy-face multiculturalism. To be sure, mainstream media often find themselves in a no-win situation. Depictions of diversities and difference that emphasize normalcy may be accused of whitewashing, whereas those that emphasize difference(s) are charged with "othering" minorities who don't quite fit into how things are done around here. Still, a commitment to normalization is surely an improvement over the framing of Muslims and Islam as evil personified. But such a shift comes with unintended costs because of prevailing media gazes that universalize as they homogenize.

Critical-Thinking Questions

How and why does a racialized media gaze tend to whitewash (depoliticize) diversities and differences? Watch an episode of *Little Mosque on the Prairie* to see these depoliticizing (whitewashing) strategies in action.

* * * * * * * * * * *

Media Gaze and the Politics of "Diversities and Difference"

As the Case Study on *Little Mosque on the Prairie* demonstrates, more can be less. In refusing to take differences seriously because of an Eurocentric media gaze, mainstream media have proven diversity-averse. Representations continue to be distorted by the ethnocentric assumption that migrants/minorities are really like "us" or secretly want to be like "us" or must aspire to be like "us" if they hope to prosper. Or diversity is marginalized by a Eurocentric commitment to liberal universalism. Admittedly, there is virtue in acknowledging that differences are only skin deep. Too much hatred and killing have reflected taking differences too seriously. But difficulties arise when people want their difference to make a difference; when differences really do matter in shaping experiences, identities, and opportunities; and when differences must be incorporated to ensure an equitable playing field. To date, media have proven capable of surface diversity when framed as a cultural tile in Canada's multicultural mosaic. Yet media lack the ideological resourcefulness or institutional will for addressing the complexities of those deep differences that challenge.

In short, there is a price to pay for failing to engage with difference. Over time, stereotypical and misinformed representations contribute to a mediascape that racializes how information is organized (framed) (Tahmahkera 2008). The refracting of diversities and difference through a monocultural lens imposes a singular and standardized ("one size fits all") framework that controls by virtue of conflating – and confusing – equality with sameness. Consider the following examples of a media gaze that is monoculturally (systemically) biasing because of underlying assumptions:

- In that a pretend pluralism endorsed by mainstream media neither takes difference seriously (except as a problem to be solved) nor takes difference into account (except as a source of conflict and confrontation), a monocultural bias is in play.
- In that news media tend to focus on conflict as newsworthy or to frame issues around a conflict narrative, news media are monoculturally biasing by privileging institutional interests over the public good.
- In that all newscasting defines consensus, order, and social stability as the normative standard by which to judge, while framing protest, rapid social change, and chaos as deviant and newsworthy, a monocultural gaze prevails.
- In that whiteness is routinely privileged as the tacitly assumed norm by which others judge, the news media are systemically biasing.
- In that minorities are invariably stereotyped as problem people who have problems or create problems at odds with Canada's national interests, the whiff of monoculturally biasing coverage is all too real.

The cumulative effect of such systemic one-sidedness is control. Mainstream news media do not set out to control or deceive. Rather, this controlling effect is perpetuated by frames that normalize a particular problem definition, diagnosis (or causal interpretation), judgment or moral evaluation, and solution (Entman 1993). Other frames are simply unthinkable under this mediacentric gaze. Similarly, news media do not set out to demean or demonize diversities and difference – at least not without revoking the principles of a free press and a commitment to objective journalism. This demonization arises from doing what comes naturally to news media – namely, the negative framing (or seeing) of minorities as troublesome constituents in need of control or removal. Under such circumstances, it's difficult to avoid the charge that the representational basis of media-minority relations is colour-coded in ways that privilege some and disprivilege others.

part 2

Media Acting Badly: The Politics of Media Gazes

* * * * * * * * * *

What would we know about our society if we had to know it only through TV programmes? How would it inform us about social (race, class, gender) relations in our present world? (Mace 2005)

A key theme in this book challenges the notion of media neutrality in producing and transmitting information or entertainment. There is no such thing as a neutral media institution, one that is free of biases pertaining to preconceived notions of race, gender, sexuality, age, religiosity, or class. To the contrary, all institutions, including mainstream media, are loaded with values and beliefs (ideologies) that normalize distributions of power and privilege along race, gender, and class lines. These ideologies not only reflect the majority interests and mainstream priorities; they also embody ways of talking about the world that promote powerful agendas at the expense of alternative viewpoints. In other words, as discourses in defence of dominant ideology, mainstream media consist of ideas and ideals that define what is acceptable, inevitable, and desirable with respect to race, gender, sexuality, age, religiosity, and class. Racialized (as well as gendered, etc.) notions of normalcy and acceptability are so deeply embedded in the design, organization, and priorities of media's foundational order that neither institutional actors nor audience members do much about them.

A related theme challenges references to media as passive conveyors of objective information. More accurately, media constitute socially constructed discourses in actively constructing people's lived realities. According to this line of thought, there is nothing natural or normal about how media institutions convey messages. The concepts and narratives conveyed by each of the media sectors (see Chapter 1) are not simply tools of expression, but rather discursive frames that help to construct what eventually is perceived as social reality (Boykoff 2006). In that what is seen, heard, and read in the media reflect the capacity of those with power to impose their imprint on reality, the representational basis of media-society relations tends to bolster dominant interests and priorities. In some cases, these preferences in terms of portraying race, gender, and class, in addition to religiosity, sexuality, and age, are deliberately conveyed; in other cases, a preferred interpretation of reality is conveyed – not by intent but by inference or default.

Part 2 explores the concept of media as socially constructed discourses in defence of dominant ideologies. These ideologies are neither neutral nor value-free but encumbered with ideas and ideals about race, gender, class, age, and sexuality. Chapter 3 begins by exploring the politics of racialized media. Are media racist? On what grounds can such an assertion be justified or rejected?

Two themes prevail. First, insofar as mainstream media are owned and controlled by whitestream interests, media priorities and practices tend to embrace the "palemale" experiences and Eurocentric agendas of those who own or control. Second, how and why do mainstream media portray racialized minorities the way they do?

Just as mainstream media are racialized, so too are they gendered. Chapter 4 demonstrates that mainstream media are gendered because of the foundational principles (namely, androcentric interests and patriarchal structures) that govern the portrayal of genders. Improvements in the portrayal of women are unmistakable; however, the pervasiveness of a gendered media gaze remains largely unchallenged.

Chapter 5 discusses the idea of media as classed. Mainstream media are classed because of ownership and control patterns that privilege images of affluence and influence over those of poverty and powerlessness. Departures from this rule suggest the prevalence of a much more contentious dynamic at play in analyzing the representational basis of media-class relations.

Chapter 6 deals with media representations of gays and lesbians. Mainstream media once portrayed homosexuals as the quintessential problem people who deserved the fate they received. Times have changed, with the result that mainstream media have embraced media gays as legitimate players in the mediascape. But improvements in media gaze notwithstanding, images of homosexuality continue to be filtered (distorted) through a predominantly heterosexist gaze for fear of alienating mainstream audiences and straightstream advertisers.

Chapter 7 addresses ambiguities in media representations of youth and older adults. Media depictions of youth are mixed, with images ranging from a fawning deference (as might be expected for a desired demographic) to a relentless negativity. No less mixed is the portrayal of older adults. That older folk continue to be one of the last demographics to endure discriminatory coverage – despite their status as financially solvent – speaks volumes about an ageist media gaze that denies as it demeans.

3

Racialized Media, Mediated Racism

To say that Canada espouses a commitment to multiculturalism is a truism that borders on the trite. Canada constitutes a multicultural society whose embrace of multiculturalism is expressed in demographic fact and ideological commitment; reflected at the level of government policy, statutory law, and constitutional enshrinement; and put into practice at institutional levels. But commitment has proven to be one thing, consensus quite another. Contrary to popular perception, multiculturalism is not about celebrating differences or promoting minority group rights. Nor is it about fostering separate ethnic enclaves. Rather, as a predominantly political act to achieve political goals in a politically acceptable manner, Canada's official multiculturalism is aimed at realigning Canada along inclusive lines through the removal of discriminatory barriers, thereby ensuring full and equal inclusion for all Canadians, regardless of race or ethnicity (Fleras 2010).

At the heart of Canada's multiculturalism is a commitment to the principle of institutional inclusiveness (Fleras 2003). Public and private institutions are under mounting pressure to be more inclusive, in part by improving workplace access, representation, and equity; in part by creating a workforce that reflects, respects, and is responsive to employee diversity; and in part by providing a community-based service that is available, accessible, and appropriate. Mainstream media are no exception to this inclusivity command. Both print and electronic entertainment media – from TV programming to magazine advertising – have responded to the challenge by expanding the quality and quantity of minority representation (Fleras and Kunz 2001). Initiatives range in scope from more diversity training for journalists to less race tagging (assigning a racial label to victim or perpetrator without good reason) and a reduction in the kind of language that offends minorities. A journalist for a major Canadian paper conveys the lengths that newsrooms will go to to placate minorities, in this case Muslim Canadians:

> News organizations bend over backwards not to provoke and not to general-ize. We walk softly and talk even more softly, though that sometimes ends up – by my estimation – in weirdly reticent and pre-emptively self-censored rep-ortage ... Editors huddle and debate the potential repercussions from all pos-sible angles. I can think of no other constituency that is more respectfully – or hyperobsequiously – treated. (DiManno 2004)

Thanks to its inclusivity commitments, the Canadian mediascape is relatively progressive, especially in comparison to other countries (Hier 2008). Unlike Europe, where a racist tabloid press flourishes, Canada's mainstream media rarely disturb the national consensus underpinning a multicultural coexistence (Masood 2008). But improvements stemming from increased awareness, grow-ing criticism, and minority protest cannot mask the obvious. Significant excep-tions remain, and this chapter explores those barriers and contradictions that unsettle the politics of media inclusiveness.

Of those media institutions that have faltered in the inclusiveness sweep-stakes, mainstream news media appear most guilty (Fleras 2007b; Mahtani, Henry, and Tator 2008). Mainstream news media have displayed a stubborn resistance to improving the quality of minority coverage (including of Aborig-inal peoples, racialized minorities, and refugees and immigrants). The process-ing of news information about diversities along racialized lines perpetuates the framing of minority women and men as troublesome constituents – little more than problem people who are problems, who have problems, and who cre-ate problems involving costs or inconvenience. The cumulative impact of nor-malizing absence while problematizing presence is costly. The reputation, self-esteem, and safety of an entire community are compromised by the negativ-ity of a few. The polarization of minorities into good or bad also glosses over their lives as complex and nuanced, evolving and situational, and reflecting multi-oppositional viewpoints that transcend simplistic scare frames (Simmons 2010). Excessive reliance on the themes of crisis, crime, and conflict tends to exagger-ate the boundaries and social distances between groups, in effect compromising the prospects for living together differently (Macpherson and Spoonley 2004).

A failure to connect is glaringly obvious. On one side of the divide are the principles of Canada's official multiculturalism, including an adherence to reasonable accommodation and institutional inclusiveness. On the other side are exclusionary news media practices that marginalize or problematize. However inexcusable, this disconnect between inclusionary principles and exclusionary practices is neither calculated nor a miscalculation. Instead of deliberate duplicity or organizational collusion, a systemic bias is at play. The framing of minorities as troublesome constituents is shown to reflect a systemically biasing coverage that draws attention to some aspects of reality and away from others. For example, consider how prevailing news frames conditionally endorse diversity as a positive contribution to Canada (Jackson, Nielsen, and Hsu 2011) yet reject the newsworthiness of difference unless framed as conflict or problem. The end result is a news media tendency toward negativity or denial in creating one-dimensional representations.

In short, evidence is compelling: mainstream media constitute sites of racism (Alia 1999; Wilson, Gutiérrez, and Chao 2003; Lambertus 2004; Henry and Tator 2006; Jiwani 2006; Mahtani 2009; but see also Hier 2008, 2010). In some cases, this racism is perceived as deliberate in excluding or problematizing minorities (systematic institutional racism); in other cases, it is largely impersonal, reflects unintended consequences rather than wilful attempts to deny or defame, and is inherent within the normal functioning of the news media (systemic institutionalized racism). Media misrepresentation of diversities and difference are thought to be racist when they normalize invisibility (absence) yet problematize visibility (presence). Paradoxically, even positive coverage can prove negative. A racialized subtext may be invoked in contexts where crime and violence are the norm, so that an occasional positive story may well have the perverse effect of inadvertently drawing negative attention to a stigmatized minority community. After all, as others have noted (Fleras 2003; Richardson 2007), in an industry that abides by the principle that the only good news is bad news, even good news may be contaminated if the story reminds readers that the community under coverage is normally plagued by crime and riddled with social pathologies. For example, coverage of positive community events or self-help activities in the Jane-Finch region of Greater Toronto, when framed as exceptions to the rule, in effect reinforces an already popular perception of how really bad the situation is. (But see the award-winning website Jane-Finch.com as a source for community news, politics, history, and entertainment.)

Positive coverage can prove a paradox in other ways. Minority success stories such as the *Cosby Show* and media authority figures (such as black anchors or talk hosts like Oprah) establish excessively high and often unattainable standards. The message is perversely racist: in promoting the idea that if Cosby or Oprah can do it – proving in the process that racist barriers no longer exist – so can all blacks, the tendency is to blame the victim/individual for failure, thus siphoning attention away from the broader structural context of class and discrimination.

No less contentious is the notion of mainstream media as racialized. The terms "racialized" or "racialization" pertain to a socially constructed activity by which negative racial significance is attached to groups of people or their activities. Or, alternatively, negative social significance is assigned to perceived physical difference. With racialization, individuals and groups are racially coded, that is, identified, named, and categorized, resulting in the imposition of race-based meanings on individuals as inherently dangerous or inferior (Bleich 2006). The implications are significant: in shifting the focus from race as a thing to race as a socially constructed activity (process), attention no longer focuses on the physical attributes of minority groups and their presumed inferiority. Emphasis instead shifts to the politics of process involving the perceptions and motivations of those powerful enough to impose race labels that control, re-strict, or demean (Chan and Mirchandani 2002).

References to racialization challenge the neutrality of media institutions in terms of values, operations, regulations, and priorities. Rather than being value-free and objective, media institutions are racialized because all institu-tions are permeated with certain ideas and ideals about what is acceptable, normal, and desirable with respect to race and race relations. These race-based ideas and ideals are so deeply ingrained within the institutions' structure, func-tioning, and operation that most institutional actors are unaware of how this racialization confers benefits to some and not others. To put this argument to the test, this chapter begins by demonstrating how media routinely frame min-orities as invisible, stereotypes, problem people, and whitewashed. The chapter then addresses news media misrepresentation of minorities as systemically biasing because of prevailing news frames. It concludes by demonstrating strategies to repair the representation. To the extent that this systemic bias is foundational rather than superficial, structural rather than attitudinal, institu-tional rather than personal, and consequential rather than conspiratorial, the prospect of creating positive representations is indeed a formidable challenge.

Portraying Minorities: Normalizing Invisibility, Problematizing Visibility

Depictions of minority women and men can historically be classified into four representational frames: minorities as invisible, stereotyped, problem people, and whitewashed (Fleras and Kunz 2001). This unflattering assessment applies to all mainstream media processes, including newscasting, advertising, film-making, and TV programming. That some of these generalizations persist is puzzling yet worrying.

Invisibility

Numerous studies have confirmed what many regard as obvious: Canada's multicultural diversity is poorly reflected in media processes and outcomes. Racialized (visible) minorities in Canada and the United States are rendered invisible in newscasting. For example, in a major study by the Pew Research Center Project for Excellence in Journalism (2010a) of the 67,000 national news stories that appeared in American media outlets over a one-year period, only 1.9 percent of the total news hole ("space") related to African Americans in a significant way (25 percent of story), even though this demographic comprised 13 percent of the US population. The figures were even more telling for Latinos (1.3 percent of stories but 16 percent of the population) and Asian Americans (0.2 percent of stories but about 5 percent of the population). Even substantial representation in the media may be misleading if racialized women and men are pigeonholed into a relatively small number of news slots related to crime or in programming roles as entertainers or athletes. Consider the plight of African Americans on television. Shows whose casts include blacks are common enough, especially those involving workplace contexts. Yet dramas are rarely constructed around black stories because of the belief that there is no sizable demographic audience for such shows. In contrast to racially mixed workplaces on TV, sitcoms tend to be segregated into all-white casts or all-black casts; in turn, minorities such as Latinos, Asians, and Aboriginal peoples are under-represented compared with their numbers in real life (Kamalipour and Carilli 1998; Wilson, Gutiérrez, and Chao 2003). The fluctuating fortunes of racialized minorities on American television is addressed in the Insight below.

insight

From Black-and-White TV to "Colour" Television?

Until the late 1980s, whiteness was consistently normalized and naturalized in American television programming (Downing 2009). Racialized minorities rarely appeared except to reinforce stereotypes or to play second fiddle to white casts, with few speaking parts of substance. This invisibility coincided to some extent with patterns of residential segregation that continue to inform American society. To be sure, exceptions dotted this generalized absence yet problematized presence, including TV coverage of the abuses endured by civil rights demonstrators during the late 1950s and early 1960s. But improvements did not really materialize until the 1970s and 1980s, with the mini-series *Roots* (1977) and programs like the *Cosby Show* (which ran from 1984 to 1992), along with the proliferation of black newscasters at local levels. Even then, many of the shows that featured blacks on BET (Black Entertainment Television) reflected black reproduction of white televisual tropes, thus reinforcing blackness as acceptable when whitewashed, athleticized, or mocked.

According to a 2008 report by the National Association for the Advancement of Colored People (NAACP) titled "Out of Focus, Out of Sync – Take 4," Hollywood's entertainment empire continues to fumble the diversity sweepstakes. Nearly a decade after the NAACP condemned the virtual "whiteout" on broadcast television that "blackballed" minority lead actors from new shows for the 1999-2000 season, minorities continue to be under-represented in nearly all facets of the film and television industry, including in top positions – in part because of subjective practices, a closed roster system, and potentially discriminatory guild membership practices. Not surprisingly, most TV series seem to revolve around white characters, whereas racialized minorities are either nonexistent or play secondary roles (e.g., someone's best friend).

How to account for the lack of prime-time programming created by, for, and about minorities? Commercial considerations rank high. Networks decide which types of shows are most likely to deliver the right kind of viewers their advertisers want (Weinman 2008). This commercial bias is compounded by the paucity of minorities in high-powered executive positions with the power to green-light new series or make final creative decisions. The shortage of minorities on prime-time TV may also be linked to the disappearance of black programming after the networks UPN and WB merged into one – prompting NAACP president and CEO Benjamin Todd Jealous to point out an interesting contradiction: on one side, a black president of the United States; on the other side, the under-representation of minorities in TV-programming, economics prevailing as usual. For example, the upstart Fox network initially catered to black audiences. By offering racialized programming, nearly 25 percent of its audience by 1995 was black. But with the growing popularity of Fox across all demographic levels, programming adjustments resulted in a decline in the number of black viewers (Zook 1999). This dearth of diversities is not without consequence, as Jealous explains: "This is America: so goes TV, so goes social reality. We don't think it's any accident that before we had a black president in reality, we had a black president on TV [Dennis Haysbert on Fox's *24*]" (quoted in Elber 2008).

To be sure, not all is lost. In response to lobbying pressure in 2000, broadcast-ers agreed to bolster minority recruitment and training programs. They also promised to monitor the progress of minority hiring both in front of and behind the camera. Important strides included the casting of Dennis Haysbert in *The Unit,* Laurence Fishburne in *CSI,* and America Ferrera in *Ugly Betty.* That two of these shows are ratings hits would suggest a mainstream responsiveness to non-white actors in lead roles rather than scattered across ensemble dramas, although *Grey's Anatomy* appears to have done a good job in creating a racial mix. The CBS is also singled out for its record in employing minority executives (see Nordyke 2008).

But other figures look bleak: the number of minority actors in prime-time shows dropped from 333 in 2002-03 to 307 in 2006-07; the number of minority writers dipped as well, from 206 in 2005-06 to 173 in 2006-07 (see Elber 2008; Jhaveri 2008; Nordyke 2008). By the 2009-10 season, even fewer TV shows featured an African American lead. One of the few settings involving a black family is Cleveland, in the animated series *The Cleveland Show,* a *Family Guy* spinoff whose token black character is narrated (voice-over) by a white writer-actor (Mike Henry) (Weinman 2008). Laurence Fishburne remains the only black lead in a hit drama series, while Wanda Sykes is the only black on the long-running sitcom *The New Adventures of Old Christine* (ibid.). As the saying goes, the more things change ...

Critical-Thinking Questions

Why are racialized actors disappearing from prime-time TV despite increased number of minorities in society and growing pressure for institutions to be inclu-sive? What can be done to reverse the decline?

＊ ＊ ＊ ＊ ＊ ＊ ＊ ＊ ＊ ＊ ＊ ＊

It would be inaccurate to say the news media ignore minorities. What pre-vails instead is a "shallows and rapids" treatment; that is, under normal circum-stances, minorities are ignored or rendered irrelevant by the mainstream press (shallows). Otherwise, coverage is guided by the context of crisis or calamity, with the focus on natural catastrophes, civil wars, and colourful insurgents (rapids). When the crisis subsides or persists too long, media interest wanes. Admittedly, some minority communities experience conflicts and problems; nevertheless, the absence of balanced coverage may distort public perceptions of what is normal and routine. This distortion may not be deliberately engineered. Rather, the flamboyant and sensational are accorded disproportionate coverage to satisfy audience needs and to sell copy, without much regard for the effects on those sensationalized (see also Jackson, Nielsen, and Hsu 2011). The media may shun responsibility for their discriminatory impact, arguing that they are reporting only what is newsworthy. Deliberate or not, an exclusive focus on negativity induces the systemically (inadvertent) biasing effect of portraying minorities along one-dimensional lines.

Stereotyping
Minorities have long complained of media stereotyping (Mahtani 2001). People of colour were historically portrayed in a manner that played into prevailing prejudices. Liberties with minority depictions in consumer advertising were especially flagrant. In an industry geared toward image and appeal, the rule of homogeneity and conservatism prevailed. People of colour were rarely depicted in the advertising of beauty care and personal hygiene products. So entrenched was the image of whiteness as the preferred standard of beauty that advertisers wanted their products sanitized and bleached of colour for fear of lost revenue (Bledsloe 1989). Elsewhere, images of racial minorities were steeped in unfounded generalizations that accentuated the comical or grotesque. This stereotyping fell into a pattern. People from the Middle East were portrayed as bombers, belly dancers, and billionaires – little more than tyrannical patriarchs or ruthless fanatics who manipulated Islam for ulterior purposes (Elmasry 1999; Karim 2002; Shaheen 2001, 2009). ("Islamophobia" refers to fear-based hostility toward Islam and Muslims, which tends to demonize not only an entire faith as inherently different, alien, and inferior but also its followers as irrational, intolerant, and violent [Rendall and Macdonald 2008]). Asians have been typecast along several formulaic traditions (sly or smart or rigid) and recurrent stock characters (namely, the yellow peril, Madame Butterfly, Charlie Chan) (Xing 2009); Latinos are typecast as hot-blooded; and blacks in prime-time shows remain stuck as superheroes/athletes or sex-obsessed buffoons, alongside a host of secondary characters such as hipsters, outlaws, and gangstas. Nowhere is stereotyping more striking than in linking racialized minorities with criminal activity, as demonstrated in the Case Study below.

case study

Stereotyping Crime, Criminalizing Stereotypes

Crime reportage on local television news abounds, partly because the twinning of drama with emotion and visuals is a proven winner for attracting audience shares and generating advertising revenues (Benson 2005). A fixation with highly visible crimes tends to focus on the poor, often youth and those of colour, in effect reinforcing recurrent stereotypes that conflate negativity with difference (D. Kelly 2006). Yet media coverage of street crime is paradoxical; that is, the least frequent forms of crime (violent crime) may be exaggerated, whereas the most common (white collar or property crime) tend to be downplayed (Perlmutter 2000; Surette 2004). An obsession with the sordid and sensational produces coverage that disdains the normative and the normal yet exaggerates the deviant and abnormal. Behaviour at the extremes comes to define the norm, in part by labelling an entire community with the actions of a few, thus amplifying anxieties over criminalized types who are out of control and in need of more control (Hirst and Patching 2005). Relying on the emotions of sensationalism to narrate a story can easily distort the parameters of the debate, influence public opinion on social issues, and popularize assumptions about what is normal, desirable, or acceptable (Barker 2005).

Notions of race still tint the lens through which crime and criminality are framed (Henry and Tator 2002; Sveinsson 2008). Violent crime is often framed as endemic to certain racialized communities yet largely unrelated to the structures of society, including those of discrimination, disadvantage, and inequality. The contextual (social and economic) basis of crime is often ignored by news media, thus reinforcing a blaming-the-victim mentality. Newer discourses are no less racialized and deterministic: equating race with crime has been dislodged by reference to culture as the prime mover of criminality. Essentialist notions of culture prevail in linking it with crime – that is, culture as innate, culture as a way of life determined at birth, and culture in compelling people to behave in a predictable way (Fleras 2004b; Sveinsson 2008). The popularity of cultural explanations is understandable in this politically correct era (Fleras 2004a); after all, it's socially unacceptable to say that blacks have an inherent criminal nature. But few have qualms in saying that black culture glorifies crime. And yet, as Sveinsson concludes, both statements are saying the same thing: unlike the law-abiding "us," they are the criminally pathological "them."

The implications are profound yet disturbing: gangs, guns, and drug violence are defined as cultural and attributed to certain ethnic groups, with the result that entire communities are criminalized because of their cultures. But reality is more complex. Particular groups may be responsible for a disproportionate number of reported crimes; nevertheless, most members of that community are rarely involved in criminal activity.

A double standard emerges: white criminal behaviour is excused as an isolated and aberrant act for which the individual alone is responsible. The heinous actions of murderer and serial rapist Colonel Russell Williams (or Paul Bernardo or Robert Pickton or Clifford Olson) have not prompted calls for white males to acknowledge their complicity as accomplices to the crimes. Nor is the white community badgered into doing something about these violent psychopaths. By contrast, black crime remains a group crime or cultural trait for which the entire community must take responsibility (Wortley 2003). By virtue of criminalizing race while racializing crime, the cumulative effect of this stereotyping is controlling (Jiwani 2006).

Critical-Thinking Questions
What is meant by the two sets of expressions "stereotyping crime" and "criminalizing stereotypes," and "racializing crime" and "criminalizing race"?

* * * * * * * * * * *

Why stereotyping? A reliance on the stereotyping of minorities is about advancing media interests. Media are in the business of making profits, not raising social consciousness or fostering social change; as a result, they rely on and purposefully construct stereotypes – defined as mental cookie cutters that impose a simplistic pattern upon a complex mass. Reliance on these simplistic and reductionist images creates readily identifiable themes (or tropes) that advance storylines, plot twists, or character development. Stereotypes are also crucial for processing large amounts of information in a compelling way that makes sense to viewers by meeting their expectations and eliciting anticipated outcomes. Finally, stereotypes simplify the process of representation by providing a convenient shorthand for audiences to relate to because of shared cultural codes. Over time, these stereotypes solidify into definitive statements about "reality." And, while not real in the conventional sense, stereotypes can be very real in their social consequences.

In short, a reliance on stereotyping serves to remind us that media interests are not served by exploring the complexity of characters. Rather than an error in perception or a mistake accidentally created, stereotyping constitutes a normal and structural necessity, involving a pattern of thought control through the internalization of negative images (Churchill 2002). Projecting mainstream fantasies and fears of the racialized "other" serves a dual function: self-fulfilling prophecies are established, and a blame-the-victim mentality (Xing 2009) is secured. Such stereotyping may also contribute to the construction of white identities by privileging the normal "us" over the problematic "them." To the extent that whites have long resorted to projections about the "other" as a basis for collectively defining who they are in relation to the world around them, media images really do say more about the "us" than the "them."

Problem People

Minority women and men are frequently depicted as troublesome constituents who are problems, have problems, or create problems (Jiwani 2001, 2006; Fleras 2004a, 2004b). As problem people they are taken to task by the media for making demands that challenge national unity, identity, or prosperity. People of colour, both foreign and Canadian-born, are targets of negative reporting that dwells on costs, threats, and inconveniences. Media reporting of refugees usually fixates on illegal entries and the associated costs of their processing and integration into Canada. Canada's refugee determination system is repeatedly rebuked for allowing entry of refugees who pose a security. Immigrants are routinely cast as potential troublemakers who steal jobs from Canadians, cheat the welfare system, take advantage of educational opportunities, lack commitment to Canada, engage in illegal activities such as drugs or smuggling, imperil Canada's unity and identity by refusing to discard their culture, and undermine its security by spawning homegrown terrorists (Karim 2006a, 2006b). And although immigrants are portrayed in utilitarian terms because of their contribution to Canada's economy (Roberts and Mahtani 2010), negativity is reinforced when migrants are framed as troublesome constituents.

Whitewashing

Media representations are increasingly diversity-friendly. In contrast to the past, when racialized minorities veered outside the preferred advertising demographic, mainstream media are under pressure from government regulation, minority assertiveness, and commercial imperatives to move over and make space. No more so than in advertising and programming, where the quality and quantity of minority appearances have escalated in recent years. And yet, media acceptance is not unconditional but comes with strings attached. Minority women and men are diminished by reduction to ornamental levels that are meant to amuse, distract, or embellish. This decorative aspect is achieved by casting minorities in stereotypical roles associated with the exotic and sensual – portraying congenial hosts in foreign destinations, enlisted as superstar boosters for athletics and sporting goods, or ghettoized in certain marketing segments related to rap or hip hop. As noted above, minorities on television are often locked into roles as entertainers or athletes. Rarely is there any emphasis on intellectual or professional prowess, much less minorities serving as positive role models to which youth can aspire outside of athletics or entertainment (Edwards 2000).

In short, minorities are rendered acceptable by media if their appearance or actions coincide with mainstream expectations or values. To achieve this goal of acceptability, those minorities whose differences are perceived as problematic are whitewashed by sanitizing them for mainstream palettes. A depoliticizing by whitewashing may prove inherently satisfying to mainstream audiences, who have historically enjoyed laughing at minorities when cast as breezy entertainment. But a depoliticizing by whitewashing is not without consequences. The laugh-tracking of minorities ("playing them for laughs") has the effect of reassuring audiences that all is well because everyone still knows their place. The ethnocentrism of a white superiority complex may not be openly articulated by media whitewashing. Rather, this ethnocentricity is assumed and normalized as the unquestioned norm that communicates (depoliticizes) as it conceals (whitewashes). (See the Case Study in Chapter 2 on *Little Mosque on the Prairie,* and Chapter 6 on sexuality and the media.)

To sum up, media possess a capacity to foster public awareness of diversities and difference yet have an equal ability to withhold and distort information that can reinforce stereotypes, perpetuate misconceptions, and frustrate dialogue. Minority women and men are rendered invisible through media underrepresentation in areas that count. This was particularly the case in the past, when minorities rarely achieved political or economic success. With few exceptions, this conclusion remains valid (Fleras 2007a). Conversely, minorities are visibly overrepresented in areas that don't count or count for less, including tourism, sports, international relief, and entertainment. Double standards prevail that loop into a cultural catch-22: minorities are criticized for being too different yet chided for not being different enough; they are taken to task for aspiring to be the same yet denounced for rejecting their cultures; and they are upbraided for their alleged lack of loyalty and commitment to Canada yet condemned for too eagerly acquiring Canadian citizenship for personal ends.

Insofar as media portrayals focus on "them" as the "other," minorities and migrants are framed as foreigners or outsiders whose lives depend on being defined by their race or religion to the virtual exclusion of other attributes. Do these indictments mean media are racist? The following Debate explores some of the issues associated with making such a claim.

---

debate

Are Media Racist?

Are media racist? Select the best available answer:
- a Yes
- b No
- c Sometimes
- d It depends

The topic of media and racism elicits a variety of responses (van Dijk 2006; Jiwani 2010; Karim 2010). For some, media are racist because of their systematic and systemic tendency to deny or denigrate racialized minorities by isolating race as a factor in negatively defining experiences, identities, and outcomes. Others agree the media are racist but for fundamentally different reasons. Media stand accused of betraying a commitment to journalistic excellence (i.e., objectivity and accuracy) by espousing a pro-diversity position to avoid charges of racism (McGowan 2001). Still others seem to take an intermediate position: media may be racist at times, although much depends on how racism is defined. For still others, any blanket denunciation is unfair when it trivializes the emergence and proliferation of progressive media outputs (Hier 2008). How does the debate play out?

Yes

Many media scholars endorse a racist view of media (Karim 2002; Jiwani 2006; Mahtani 2009). But the nature and scope of media racism have evolved in response to changes in society. Although racism in the media may be widely acknowledged, its expression is neither immediately visible nor explicitly expressed, as once was the case. The monocultural bias that misrepresents or marginalizes is rarely intentional, since news workers generally shun any charges of racism. Rather, racism is the result of institutional constraints, widely internalized news values, and ignorance of diversities and difference. Racism in the media arises from nearly all-white newsrooms that lack diversity in the selection and presentation of news, where minority issues are filtered through a white perspective and news is collected from predominantly white elite institutions (van Dijk 2006). For example, news media portrayals of diversities and difference can be construed as racist because of journalists' choices in articulating and sustaining a racist discourse (Mahtani, Henry, and Tator 2008). A critical discourse analysis demonstrates how journalists unconsciously employ visual and verbal images to racialize and stigmatize ("other-ize" or stereotype) minorities (Henry and Tator 2002). This racialization of minorities is not conveyed in an openly racist way; preferred, instead, are news values and practices that normalize Euro-Canadian values and practices as natural and superior.

No

A few media scholars deny the existence of media racism. To the extent that it's expressed, racism is framed as something that happened in the past, is manipulated by the unscrupulous as an excuse or smokescreen, and reflects pathologies within the majority or the minority community (J. Cohen 1999). Moreover, news media are walking on eggshells and bending over backwards to avoid offending minorities such as Muslims (Asra Nomani in Chuang 2010), with many taking pains to acknowledge the loyalty and industry of most migrants and minorities (Silk 2009). But others argue that the media are perpetrators of reverse racism. In a controversial book, William McGowan (2001) argues that political correctness has corrupted American journalism by whitewashing (or colouring) the news. According to McGowan, journalists are reluctant to write anything negative, judgmental, or critical about either minorities or government diversity programs for fear of being labelled as racists, sexists, or homophobes. A pro-diversity newsroom culture that refracts difference through the politically correct lens of cultural relativism accentuates the positives by (1) ignoring negative stories, (2) putting a positive spin on the negative, or (3) scrutinizing white motives behind even progressive initiatives.

In defence of his argument, McGowan examined media coverage of two grisly murders. The murder of openly gay college student Matthew Shepard (the subject of the film *The Laramie Project*) resulted in some 3,000 stories devoted to the case. The murder of a thirteen-year-old male, Jesse Dirkhising, by two gay pedophiles culminated in only 46 stories in the first month. Although the *New York Times* ran 195 stories about the Shepard case, according to McGowan, no stories about Dirkhising appeared, even during the March 2001 trial in which one suspect was convicted and the other pleaded guilty. For McGowan, the reason was simple. The Shepard murder cast gays into the role of victims, whereas covering the Dirkhising case would cast gays as villains – a position inconsistent with political correctness.

The news media establishment also promulgates what McGowan calls the myth of white racism. According to this myth, all whites are racists, whites alone perpetuate racism, and whites are ultimately responsible for minority problems. Journalists eagerly and exclusively seek out incidents that expose white racism, yet they do so at the expense of objectivity, fairness, and accuracy, relying instead on preconceptions and a tendency to uncritically accept poorly supported accusations (even hoaxes) (e.g., the Duke Rape Scandal). In blaming white racism for the plight and poverty of minorities, McGowan concludes, media downplay or dismiss minority racism toward whites on the assumption that whites can never be victims (only perpetrators) of racial discrimination. Minorities, by contrast, can never be racist because they lack the institutional power to put their prejudices into practice in any meaningful way.

In short, McGowan concludes, the imposition of a politically correct diversity agenda not only restricts debate but also skews coverage of the facts. The end result is a double standard that whitewashes (absolves) racialized minorities of blame or responsibility. Notions of newsworthiness involving minorities or diversity agendas are beyond debate or scrutiny, or, alternatively, unreported if too critical or unsympathetic. Those journalists who transgress the norms of minority-favouritism are subjected to hostility or ostracism. The end result is a kind of *reverse* racism, it is argued, one in which minority differences are positively framed, accorded special treatment, or conveniently ignored when problematic. For McGowan, this kid-glove treatment of minorities reflects a combination of expediency and self-interest. The last thing the average middle-aged white executive wants is a problem about race, especially when salary and promotions may reflect the number of minority hires or expansion into a minority market.

Sometimes

Most media scholars acknowledge patterns of news media racism (Mahtani, Henry, and Tator 2008). Others prefer a somewhat less extreme stance by arguing that the problem lies in focusing exclusively on the negative or sensational, in effect ignoring positive coverage of achievements and developments that contribute to multicultural harmony in Canada (Hier 2008, 2010). But to label media as racist by focusing exclusively on negative coverage of race relations – even if motivated by a business model rather than a sense of injustice – does a disservice. Such an accusation unfairly lumps tabloids with broadsheets and liberal presses while ig-noring how opinion and editorial pieces in print media are more openly racist than the so-called hard news (see van Dijk 2006). As well, positive coverage of diversities and difference can be uncovered with digital media, including Internet sources, so-called alternative mainstream media like the National Film Board, and ethnic and Aboriginal media (Hier 2008). Access to populist media secures access to coverage that reflects a more nuanced and complex reading of race relations in Canada, in effect suggesting that media racism is not nearly as pervasive as widely perceived.

It Depends

In accusing the news media of racism or of being racist, much depends on how racism is defined (Fleras 2010). Media are no longer as blatantly racist in openly condoning white supremacy or minority inferiority. More subtle expressions exist that reflect unconscious biases (subliminal racism). This kind of racism tends to reinforce the saying "In the eye of the beholder." But if racism is defined along structural instead of attitudinal lines, a different picture appears. Media appear to be institutionally racist when racialized ideas and ideals about what is normal and desirable are so firmly embedded in the design, operation, and outcomes of media institutions that a Eurocentric perspective prevails to the exclusion of others. This racism by exclusion does not necessarily arise from intentionally biased coverage. Rather, racism in the media reflects a level of coverage that is systemically biasing because of a relentless one-sidedness that (1) frames minorities as troublesome constituents who are problems or create problems; (2) interprets the world, as seen from a Eurocentric perspective, as normal and desirable; and (3) promotes a preference for a pretend pluralism (superficial diversity) over those deep differen-ces that demand to be taken into account when necessary. In short, instead of labelling media as racist, it may be more accurate to say media produce coverage or programming that is racialized in content and racist in consequences.

Conclusion

Modest improvements notwithstanding, news media messages continue to disdain diversity except as angle, spin, problem, or foil. Media may not intentionally promote racism, although no one should discount the tenacity of prejudice, ignorance, ar-rogance, indifference, ethnocentrism, or laziness. Nevertheless, mainstream media do little to promote intergroup harmony, celebrate non-mainstream successes, or provide news that minorities can use. Thus, although the news hole may expand for migrants and minorities, their presence is framed as problematic (Entman and Rojecki 2001). Migrants and minorities are not necessarily labelled as inferior; rather, they are stigmatized as incompatible with Canadian society because of inappropriate cultural values (Fleras 2004a). Negative news portrayals do not disparage all minorities. Criticism is directed primarily at "bad" minorities whose misdeeds violate national interests or egalitarian principles – in contrast to fawning praise for those migrants who add value to Canadian society. Roberts and Mahtani (2010, 252) address this seeming contradiction:

> What is of interest to us here is the way that the immigrant is effectively positioned as, paradoxically, both the "good guy" and the "bad guy." On the one hand, the immigrant is seen as contributing to a particular segment of the nation's economy. On the other hand, the immigrant is effectively demonized as deviant, criminalized and tarnishing the supposed Canadian way of life. We suggest that we might begin to understand this complex and complicit relationship as being fundamentally shaped by neoliberalism in contemporary Canada.

The framing of minorities as models (good) or as maligned (bad) compromises the possibility of seeing them as complex personalities with multi-dimensional lives. They are stigmatized instead as foreigners or outsiders whose one-dimensional lives revolve around their defining status of race or religion, to the virtual exclusion of other attributes (Keung 2006; Solutions Research Group 2006). Rarely do they appear as actively engaged individuals beyond stereotypical slots or crisis contexts, in effect compromising their acceptance as normal members of society (ter Wal 2004). In other words, each story about minorities as problem people may be valid; nevertheless, if that's the only kind of narrative the mainstream media convey, the net effect is systemically racist.

Critical-Thinking Questions

Do you think mainstream news media are racist or racialized? How and why?

＊ ＊ ＊ ＊ ＊ ＊ ＊ ＊ ＊ ＊

Improving Coverage: Two Steps Forward, One Step Back, Three Steps Sideways

Mainstream media have reacted to these charges of racism and exclusion. Media processes such as advertising have embraced a commitment to inclusiveness in order to capitalize on the marketing muscle of ethnic minorities

(Fleras and Kunz 2001). Blatant stereotypes are no longer tolerated within advertising, except in the most iconic sense of spoofing the past or poking fun at the unwashed. Both film and television have explored and expanded the range of characters, involving minorities across a broader range of contexts (e.g., the hit CBC series *Little Mosque on the Prairie*). Canada's news media have taken steps to improve the representation of migrants and minorities. As noted earlier, initiatives range from more diversity training for journalists to less race tagging (assigning a racial label to victim or perpetrator without good reason) to reduction in the kind of language that minorities find offensive. And racial positives have long infused films, especially the black sensibilities conveyed by Spike Lee, John Singleton, and Tyler Perry. Crossover films, from *Dreamgirls* to *Invictus* and *Precious*, continue to feature predominantly minority casts or minority leads, including Anika Noni Rose as Tiana, Disney's first African American princess, in the *Princess and the Frog* (Barnard 2009).

And yet, each step forward is undermined by one step back (C. Murray 2002). With several exceptions, a business-as-usual mindset prevails in an industry that appears impervious to change or reluctant to accommodate, according to a report titled *Frame Work: Employment in Screen-Based Media – A National Profile* (Women in Film and Television 2005; see also Cavanagh 2004). Both Aboriginal peoples and racialized minorities remain underrepresented in areas that count (success) but overrepresented in areas that don't count (failure) and misrepresented elsewhere except in entertainment or athletics. Negative coverage continues to perpetuate stereotypes or incite hostility – as demonstrated by the controversy over the "Too Asian?" article in the 10 November 2010 issue of *Maclean's*. (The article quoted students who complained that some universities, such as the University of Toronto, the University of British Columbia, and the University of Waterloo, were becoming too academically focused because of Asian students, making it more difficult to compete for grades or to find time and space for fun.) Much of the inertia can be traced to a combination of factors, including fear or ignorance, institutional structures and organizational culture, and the values of negativity and conflict implicit within the prevailing news paradigms. Insofar as they are refracted through the prism of whiteness, racialized minorities are victimized by a Eurocentrism that privileges whiteness as the normative standard of excellence (Benson 2005). Deep differences are difficult to convey because of a Eurocentric commitment to liberal universalism. Not surprisingly, a belief that our commonalities as individuals rather than group differences should prevail for purposes of rewards and recognition may not resonate well with those Canadians who want their differences to be taken seriously in defining who gets what.

The importance of improving the quantity and quality of minority representations is taken as axiomatic. The combination of a growing ethnic market and increased competition for consumer loyalty and dollars has sounded the death knell for monocultural media. But moves to convey a positive minority image generally misfire – sometimes for reasons beyond media control. In their coverage of Aboriginal peoples, news media are encouraged to be fair, accurate, balanced, and culturally sensitive (Wiwchar 2006). Nevertheless, uncertainty prevails in defining these terms, let alone in how to operationalize them for measurement, evaluation, and implementation. Media efforts to improve minority representation may be greeted with disdain or coolness. Positive portrayals and inclusive programming are dismissed as window dressing, condescending, tokenistic, or politically correct. Depictions of minorities in high-status and stable relationships (such as in the *Cosby Show*) are rebuked for creating unrealistic and unattainable expectations that incite resentment. A no-win situation prevails. Media are criticized for failing to mention race and racial identity when deemed crucial to the story (Jiwani 2010), yet inclusion of race when perceived as incidental results in charges of "playing the race card" (introducing race when irrelevant to the story). Too much media emphasis on shared commonalities is criticized as compromising identity; too much emphasis on differences may lead to accusations of stereotyping or needlessly dividing. Bewildered and rebuffed by criticism regardless of what they do or don't do, media workers recoil at the prospect of detonating yet another cultural landmine through negative publicity or a consumer revolt that could impede corporate profits or implode on their personal careers.

Put bluntly, the relationship between media and minorities in a multicultural Canada is sharply contested (Roberts and Mahtani 2010). Do the media have an obligation and responsibility to improve the representation of minorities and migrants? If yes, what role should they play in advancing their acceptance and integration? Since answers are hardly evident, this relationship will remain as racialized and racist as ever – despite demographic changes to the contrary – without a fundamental change in redefining how things are done "around here." The fact that media bias exists is not the problem; after all, bias is inevitable because all social constructions reflect the values and agendas of those doing the creating. To the contrary, the problem lies with media coverage that is so blind to its bias that it cannot admit to this ethnocentrism, preferring instead to cower behind the facade of objectivity and neutrality (Maracle 1996).

Accounting for Media Misrepresentation: Systematic or Systemic?

Reasons for media mistreatment of minorities span the spectrum from the micro to the macro (Alia and Bull 2005): from hard-boiled business decisions that reflect the realities of market forces, to a lack of cultural awareness and deep-seated prejudice among media personnel, to structural barriers that define how things are done. Questions invariably arise: Does media mistreatment of minorities imply the presence of prejudiced personnel or patterns of structural discrimination? Is it a case of unwittingly cramming minority realities into Eurocentric frames for crossover appeal? Are media so pro-white in their content that distortion of the "other" is inevitable? Or do media misrepresentations reflect a preference to act out of self-interest by kowtowing to the dictates of the marketplace, especially during periods of economic uncertainty or corporate restructuring (Roberts and Mahtani 2010)?

Not surprisingly, confusion and uncertainty are the rule rather than the exception. Media personnel may be unsure of how to incorporate Canadians of colour without being accused of paternalism or tokenism. Even sensitive representations must grapple with dilemmas as varied as the following: (1) how to portray other cultures whose practices conflict with Canada's democratic principles without feeding into ethnocentrism; (2) whether to emphasize only positive minority stories or to include both positive and negative, thereby reinforcing stereotypes; and (3) whether cultural differences can be presented without either essentializing group differences or bifurcating reality into the poles of "us" versus "them" (see McAndrew 1992). Unsure of what to do or how to do it, media decision makers may avoid diversity topics for fear of career-curbing miscues.

News media negativizing of diversities and difference is neither random nor accidental. Nor is it something out of the ordinary, a kind of idiosyncratic departure from an otherwise inclusive organizational norm. In that media are anything but neutral but are larded with values and biases, the misrepresentation of diversities and difference is systemic and institutionalized: institutionalized because of coverage that is routine, repetitive, and predictable rather than isolated and haphazard; systemic because of those normative institutional practices that themselves are free of any explicit bias but implicitly biasing by virtue of applying equal standards (from rules to expectations) to unequal contexts. This exclusionary coverage is racialized through the largely unconscious Eurocentric filters that frame "raw facts" into news stories consistent with the prevailing news paradigm (Henry and Tator 2002). The interplay of news values with a mediacentric gaze as the tacitly accepted norm underscores the difficulty of framing diversities and difference except as conflict or problem.

How do media represent an exercise in institutional bias? Is news media coverage of diversity and difference a case of systematic bias because of prejudicial attitudes? Or is it more accurate to say that coverage is systemically biasing because of an implicit institutional bias toward negativity, conflict, and abnormality? An ideal-typical distinction between systemic and systematic bias is critical. A systematic bias involves conscious and deliberate intent by institutional actors who act on behalf of institutions to deny or exclude others. In some cases, systematic bias can involve polite forms, such as coded language or aversive actions; in other cases, open dislike of others is directed through the use of racial slurs or physical attacks; in still other cases, organizational rules and protocols openly discriminate against devalued others. Together, a systematic bias involves an egregious process by which *something* is done by *somebody* to *someone* with an intent to hinder or hurt.

By contrast, a systemic bias is both impersonal and unconscious, yet no less invidious or invasive. Its unobtrusiveness makes it that much more difficult to detect or deter. Unlike its systematic counterpart, with its deliberate slant and explicit agenda (Soroka and Maioni 2006), a systemic bias reflects a biasing so deeply entrenched in the foundational principles and operational processes of an institution that few are even aware of how these rules advantage some, disadvantage others (Fleras 2010). A systemic bias involves the unpremeditated consequences of seemingly neutral institutional rules that, when evenly and equally applied, exert a discriminatory effect on some through no fault of their own. Policy programs and institutional actions are systemically biasing if informed by well-intentioned but ultimately flawed assumptions about what is normal, preferred, or acceptable. As a discrimination without prejudice, the defining feature of systemic bias is its perceived normalcy – that is, a business-as-usual framework. An insistence on applying identical standards to unequal contexts unwittingly but routinely penalizes individuals – even if the controlling actors and institutional routines themselves are free of open prejudice. But a commitment to the seemingly progressive principle of "treating everyone the same around here" when differences demand to be taken seriously is not without consequences in consolidating an unequal status quo.

Consider how news media stereotypes are systemically biasing (Fleras 2010). Media stereotyping of minority women and men is not necessarily a perceptual miscue by prejudiced individuals. Rather, media stereotyping is normal and intrinsic to the operational dynamic of an industry that must simplify information by tapping into a collective portfolio of popular images. In the same way that people depend on stereotyping to simplify everyday reality, media rely on stereotypes to codify reality and process information. Limitations in time and space prevent complex interpretations of reality across the spectrum of human emotion, conflict, or contradiction. Moreover, stereotyping is critical in creating human interest stories, driving plot lines, demarcating boundaries and opposing factions, and developing characterization. But although stereotyping is systemic to newscasting, its impact varies. Unlike the mainstream, which is no less subject to stereotyping, vulnerable minorities lack positive media messages or powerful societal roles to offset news media negativity.

News is systemically biasing in another way. Distortions and omissions are not necessarily the result of deliberate bias or a conscious deviance. To the contrary, these biases reflect the normal processing of information along institutional lines. Rules regarding what is normal and acceptable in coverage and style are deeply entrenched within institutional rules, organizational design, and reward structures. A distinction is critical: in contrast to a systematic bias that deliberately omits or distorts, a systemic bias prevails when the framing of newsworthiness routinely prioritizes the negative over the positive, conflict over cooperation, the sensational over substance, deviance over the normative, and the episodic over the thematic. In that the core values of news media coverage embody negativity, conflict, and abnormality, exaggerated and sensationalized coverage is inevitable. Admittedly, the logic behind this mediacentric (systemic) biasing may not be readily discernible or conscious. Nonetheless, this mediacentric biasing is real and driven by the institutional, not the personal; the consequential, not the intentional; the routine, not the random; the cultural, not the conspiratorial; and the structural, not the attitudinal.

4

A Gendered Media
Male Media Gazes in a Feminist World

Many regard the women's movement as the quintessential transformation of the twentieth century. This transformational moment went beyond simply improving the socio-economic lot of women. The women's movement also challenged the foundational principles of a largely patriarchal constitutional order. By challenging the rules that governed women's relational status in society, this loosely connected social movement not only redefined the very notions of justice and equality along gender lines. Societal institutions also came under pressure to rethink their business-as-usual mindsets and advance a revamped gender agenda commensurate with women's concerns, realities, and aspirations.

Mainstream media were hardly immune to feminist politics (A. Nelson 2010). Historically, mainstream media were institutionally gendered in form and function – designed by, for, and about male interests, experiences, and priorities. An androcentric gaze as normal and necessary prevailed by virtue of framing media images about women from a male point of view (Fleras 2003). With media massaging messages of women as inferior or irrelevant except in their roles as fosterers or fashionistas, female identities, experiences, and aspirations were dismissed accordingly. Women were generally relegated to the maternal-domestic domain, stereotyped by way of mis-/over-/under-representations, objectified to the point of dehumanization, victimized by body images that linked success with sexuality and attractiveness, and typecast as the second sex whose worth lay in appearances or nurturing (Graydon 2001). The relatively small number of media representations that were open to women – namely, as mother, wife, girl next door, spinster, whore, saint, or castrating b/witch – did little to undo a gendered mainstream media (Kanellakis 2007).

In short, images of women were refracted through the prism of a male-dominated media gaze. Media representations of women reflected a gendered gaze that normalized phallocentric fantasies and fears. But is this assessment true in the new millennium? Evidence suggests gender depictions are much more diverse and substantial than in the gendered past (Gauntlett 2008; Douglas 2010). Images of women and their myriad relationships are continually changing and sharply contested across a wide range of media outputs – albeit subject to multiple interpretations and ambiguous readings – thanks to the emergence of women as eager consumers with hefty amounts of disposable income, spending power, and control over financial decisions (Graydon 2001). The combination of shifting demographics, growing economic clout, and viewing patterns is challenging the media's gendered agenda, with the result that women are no longer automatically banished to the outer fringes of programming or newscasting. Paradoxically, it is men who now complain of diminishment as the new second sex, their irrelevance or inferiority being particularly noticeable for lower-class males (Vallis 2009). Finally, the surge in women's Internet involvement is reshaping the social landscape, with women using online communication and social media to expand networks, increase contacts, and enrich relationships (MRTW 2000; Pew Research Center 2009).

But improving the parameters of positive portrayals is not the same as transformation. Nor is there any indication that the pace of change is unfolding according to everyone's satisfaction. Contradictions prevail. On the one hand, women are cresting the wave of power. When she took over from Kevin Newman on Global Television in September 2010, Dawna Friesen became the first full-time female anchor in Canada of a nightly network newscast. Lisa LaFlamme will assume the anchor chair from Lloyd Robertson on CTV News (Houpt 2010). And twenty-five years of Oprah has reinforced her transformative status as a media messiah in a secular age (Lofton 2011). On the other hand, women continue to be evaluated as objects of male fantasy or as mindless subjects in need of constant consumer-driven pampering. As Maureen Dowd (2011) concludes in examining the slew of retrograde images of women in film and on television, "Hollywood is a world ruled by men, and this season, amid economic anxieties, these men want to indulge in some retro fantasies about hot, subservient babes." Or consider the female ideal promoted by so-called laddie magazines like *FHM* or *Maxim*. In both content and advertisements, young men and adolescent boys are encouraged to sexualize their gaze by focusing on the airbrushed smoothness of women's bodies, whose lack of imperfections renders the models as lifeless and interchangeable as store-window mannequins (Marche 2008). Stephen Marche (2008) writes to this effect:

> If you were mugged by any of the women in the top 10 [of *FHM*'s tally of the sexiest women alive], you couldn't pick the perpetrator out of the lineup. They're all white. They all have long hair and they're almost all blonde. They all have the same high cheekbones. Each woman is allowed exactly one deviation from the norm, and that deviation is immediately remarked on – her tattoos ... (An aside: in the June 2009 issue of *Maxim* featuring the 100 hottest and sexiest "babes" in the world, 7 of the top 10 had black hair, 2 were brunettes, and one was blonde. All the women were white, although two could be described as ethnically ambiguous.)

A 2008 report by the Quebec Council on the Status of Women concluded that women are not only increasingly sexualized as objects by the media, they are also stereotyped as "bimbos, birdbrains, submissive, and dedicated to fulfil men's pleasures" – especially in advertising, where suggestive female poses are used to sell everything from beer to boats (Bundale 2008). Or, as pointed out by Jean Kilbourne, co-author of *So Sexy So Soon: The New Sexualized Childhood and What Parents Can Do to Protect Their Kids* (with Diane Levin 2008), advertising increasingly encourages young girls to see themselves as sexualized objects (see also Orenstein 2011). Padded push-up bras and thong underwear for seven-year-olds reinforce this trend toward prepubescent sexualization. And whereas their mothers fought for equal opportunities, empowerment, and non-objectification, daughters have been raised in a hypersexualized media culture where sexual prowess and power are synonymous, where "Snoop Dogg's misogynist *Bitches Ain't Shit* is not an affront but a ring tone," where "slut and bitch are not put-downs but affectionate greetings between female friends," and where "a blowjob is just like shaking hands" (*Maclean's* 2010, 51-52). Nor does age or status seem to make much difference. A blatant sexuality characterizes media attention to "sexy" first ladies – from Carla Bruni (wife of the French president) to Michelle Obama (wife of the American president) – whose gendered status as fashion icons is both celebrated and criticized (Leong 2008).

Like many institutions, mainstream media possess an ambivalent relationship with the genders (Dent 2008). On one side are measured improvements in media representations of women. Representations of gender are more complex and more diverse than in the past, with less stereotyping and objectification – as might be expected in a less scripted era of increasingly fluid and transformative identities (Gauntlett 2008). Although men may be calling the shots in terms of hidden agendas and operating priorities, there is sufficient slack in the patriarchy for oppositional messages to challenge and resist (Douglas 1994). On the other side, however, when it comes to the prevailing gendered agenda, it's still a man's world (Fleras 2003; International Women's Media Foundation 2011; Lunt 2011). Challenges to what structurally remains a patricentric institution make it abundantly clear: mainstream media continue to be gendered in ways that bode poorly for gender relations. Even powerful women – from those who want to kick butt (from Buffy the Vampire Slayer to Hanna, the teenaged assassin with an appetite for vengeance, to Stieg Larsson's *Millennium* series, which includes Lisbeth Salander, the psycho-hacker killer in *The Girl with the Dragon Tattoo* [Quill 2011]) to those who hanker after male butts *(Desperate Housewives)* – cannot dislodge a fundamental mediacentric truth. Unless you conform to rigidly demanding standards of beauty – thin, attractive, fit, firm, and preferably blonde – be prepared for the sniping and the backlash (A. Nelson 2006). Admittedly, there is something misleading in questioning whether the media are good or bad for women. The question implies a falsely dichotomous response; after all, a gendered media can be simultaneously progressive or regressive depending on criteria, context, and consequences. Or phrased differently, when it comes to images and messages, the media can accelerate the pace of progressive change yet simultaneously apply the brakes of reaction and resistance (Douglas 1994).

Such an interplay of mixed messages is proving to be both bracing and intoxicating, yet dispiriting and regressive – in effect confirming Susan Douglas' prescient insight (1994, 294) that mainstream media are simultaneously a woman's best friend in the struggle for recognition and respect and her very worst enemy for pulling the rug out from underneath. In taking a cue for a more nuanced approach to deconstructing a gendered media, in part by acknowledging how media representations appear to be in a state of flux and disarray (Gauntlett 2008), this chapter explores the contested and often contradictory relationship between gender and media. The chapter is premised on the notion that mainstream media are neither neutral nor passive in conveying information about gender and gender relations. To the contrary, mainstream media are shown to be gendered insofar as certain ideas and ideals about women and men are foundationally embedded within organizational designs, assumptions, operations, outputs, and preferred media gazes. By conveying messages about what it means to be male and female within the evolving and contested context of contemporary gender relationships, a gendered media agenda prevails, one whose predominantly male gaze says more about male fantasies and fears than anything about female realities.

To put these assertions and arguments to the test, this chapter analyzes the politics of, debates over, and logic behind a gendered media gaze. It looks at media representations of women in print and programs both in the past and at present, explores the possibilities of challenging the androcentric media gaze, and concludes by discussing the complexities of undoing a prevailing gendered gaze. The central theme is inescapable: the pervasiveness of androcentrism with an ingrained patriarchy continues to undermine the representation of women in newscasting, television programming, advertising, and film. To be sure, evidence points to modest but mixed improvements in realigning media representations of women. Moreover, there is growing awareness that media images of gender cannot be explained in a singular and straightforward manner. Gender representations are too diverse, diffuse, and contradictory to compress into glib generalizations or simplistic formulas. Nevertheless, a gendered media bias persists in terms of double standards and double binds. Or, as Michael Kimmel (2008, 257) writes in articulating the challenges that continue to confront women in what arguably remains a man's world,

> Women can enter men's fields, but then they are on men's turf and play by men's rules. Just as when women enter men's fields in the workplace, or in education, or in the professions, if they succeed too well, they can be seen as insufficiently feminine, have their sexuality called into question, and risk not being taken seriously as women. If they fail, they are seen as very feminine women, demonstrating that inequality is really the result of difference, not its cause. Gender equality in the virtual world of the media, just like the real world, will not come when gender difference disappears, but rather when gender inequality disappears.

Conceptualizing a Gendered Media

Sociologists take as axiomatic the notion that neither manhood nor womanhood qualifies as a purely biological attribute of individuals. Biology may determine whether we are male or female, but culture and society shape the content and conduct of what it means to be a man or a woman (A. Nelson 2010). As socially constructed conventions rather than biological givens, concepts of femininity and masculinity are known to vary spatially (from culture to culture), laterally (within culture), historically (from one period to another), situationally (depending on the context), and longitudinally (throughout a person's lifespan) (Kimmel 2008). The fact that these concepts are cultural and constructed rather than biological and given confirms the socially constructed dynamics that animate male-female relations (ibid.).

No less socially constructed is the notion of a gendered society (Kimmel 2008). All human societies are thought to be gendered inasmuch as the following social patterns appear to be arguably true: (1) a distinction between male and females (among other genders, including transgendered and intersexed); (2) a division of labour, power, and privilege along gender lines; and (3) a devaluation of women's maternal-domestic roles compared with the more public domain roles of men. With time, these distinctions and devaluations become deeply ingrained within the design and dynamics of a society, in addition to its values, priorities, expectations, and reward structures. Two conclusions follow. First, societies are neither gender-neutral nor gender-blind; rather, they are gendered in terms of man-made structures and processes. Second, gendered societies invariably privilege and promote male interests as superior and desirable, whereas female interests, experiences, and realities tend to be dismissed as irrelevant or inferior – at times openly, as was historically the case, or by outcomes that are systemically biasing along gender lines.

A similar line of reasoning can be applied to notions of a gendered media. Like institutions in general, media are neither neutral nor value-free in their design, organization, operations, and reward patterns. Rather, media are social constructions that tend to conceal their constructedness by pretending to be something they are not (i.e., innocent of any bias). They also are sexualized (gendered) in ways that make a distinction between men and women, assign a set of expectations that distinguish men from women, and then devalue the roles and status of women in comparison with that of men. A gendered media constructs gender differences and reproduces gender inequalities by making these differenced inequities seem natural rather than created – in large part by concealing the media's authorship so that its normalness seems to flow from the nature of things (Kimmel 2008, 238). These gendered ideas and ideals become so firmly wired into media's DNA (including structure, function, and processes) that media content are routinely and automatically promoted and normalized as if there were no male perspective or bias. In turn, female interests are ignored or ridiculed unless consistent with the priorities and expectations of a male gaze. How, then, are the media gendered?

- A gendered media is ideologically slanted *toward, by, around,* and *for* men and male realities. Media institutions are infiltrated with ideas and ideals about normalcy, acceptability, and desirability as they relate to male interests, experiences, and aspirations. A phallocentric ideology prevails whose primary purpose – or logical consequence – is that of preserving male power and masculinist privilege.
- Media are gendered because males are the tacitly assumed norm and the reference point by which women as women are defined, assessed, and criticized.
- A gendered media is one that is patriarchal in design, organization, and outcomes. Male agendas, priorities, and interests are advanced – not necessarily deliberately or conspiratorially but logically as a consequence of formulating and framing the world from a male point of view (an androcentric gaze) as natural and normal.
- Men and women stand in a different kind of relation to the media, in large part because the genders benefit disproportionately from an institution that many perceive as patriarchal in structure, androcentric in process, and patricentric in outcomes.
- Media are gendered because women and men use and consume different media – there are women's and men's magazines, "chick flicks" versus "boy flicks," "chick lit" versus "lad lit," guy video games versus girl video games, and so on (Kimmel 2008). A gendered media capitalizes on these marketing demographics by targeting different genders with varying messages.
- Media are gendered because of a prevailing male gaze. Media projections of male fears and masculinist fantasies tend to promote images of women – from mothers to murderers, from passive to manipulative, from weak to powerful – that rarely reflect female realities and experiences. Male perceptions of what is or projections of what ought to be are promoted instead, as if they were inevitable and self-evident rather than constructed and conventional.
- Media are gendered in that women and men tend to have different expectations of the media. They also tend to use media differently so that gender as a variable influences the production, transmission, and interpretation of media messages along the lines of "his" and "her" media (Kimmel 2008).
- Media are gendered insofar as media texts are deeply and persistently encoded in a sexualized way with respect to media structures, priorities, operating procedures, and messages. Moves to ungender a gendered media agenda along regendered lines are fraught with perils and second-guessing

– in part because no one really knows whether an ungendered media is feasible, desirable, or even recognizable.

The politics of a gendered media yield conclusions that are not altogether surprising. Media possess an ambivalent relationship with the genders; as a result, media representations of women continue to be gendered, despite improvements in both the quantity and quality of portrayals (Kimmel 2008). Media are criticized for messages that dwell on gender stereotypes, legitimize gender violence, evaluate women on the basis of appearances, reinforce male projections of female sexuality as the key to social power, and circulate body images that link success with thinness or fitness. Such dehumanization cannot be dismissed as harmless or innocent – at least no more so than the objectification of the enemy by a war propaganda machine can be excused as a frivolous exercise in playful persuasion.

Seeing Like a Gendered Media: Misrepresenting Women

The previous chapter demonstrated how mainstream media have mis-/over-/under-represented racialized minorities by framing them as invisible, stereotyped, problem people, and whitewashed. Media portrayals of women have often paralleled the negative portrayal of minorities (Croteau and Hoynes 2003). Women tended to be marginalized by mainstream media, rendered either decorative or invisible, as the situation demanded. More often than not, they were blatantly stereotyped as the second sex, whose worth and value revolved primarily around appearances or relationships. For example, in a widely covered news story in southern Ontario involving the disappearance and murder of eight-year-old Victoria ("Tori") Stafford, her mother, Tara McDonald, conducted daily press conferences on the front lawn. On one occasion, McDonald was described as "wearing a shiny black-and-white print sundress and what appeared to be freshly painted purple toenails showing in strappy sandals, her long brown hair slicked back in a ponytail" (Blatchford 2009). In addition to the obsession over their looks and likes, women were also pigeonholed into a relatively small number of roles as sinner or saint. This kind of stereotyping may have simplified the media's job. It certainly didn't do much to bolster the self-esteem of women in improving their status in society.

The largely negative media portrayal of women did not escape scrutiny. Mainstream media were criticized for portraying women (and men) in very rigid and often unattainable terms with regard to roles, appearances, and expectations. Flawless fashion models with impeccable skin tones were projected as the norm, in effect ignoring the diversity of women as physical and cultural beings. Women were idealized as white, young, and beautiful; valued for how they looked and what they wore; dependent on men for approval or protection; confined to nurturing and caregiving functions; averse to risk taking or leadership roles; and portrayed as hapless victims of sexual violence. The drudgery of women's domestic maternal roles was romanticized: male-infused images of motherhood pitted the reality of frazzled and exhausted mothers against the schmaltzy serenity of perfectly coiffed wives and cookie-baking moms (Douglas 1994). That reality gap may explain the popularity of Roseanne's famous quip (from the TV series by the same name), "If the kids are alive by five, I've done my job" – a line that resonated with millions of mothers who adore their children yet find motherhood both exhausting and boring (ibid., 284).

That a media double standard once prevailed is beyond dispute (Graydon 2001). Mediated women were generally relegated to the maternal-domestic domain, marginalized by a preoccupation with appearances, objectified as sexual playthings, and gendered by associating self-worth with their relationship to the men in their lives. In advancing the notion of female sexuality and femininity as the key to social power, mainstream media constantly bombarded women with images (fantasies) of perfection that were difficult to achieve without compromising personal health or eroding a positive self-image (Kilbourne 2000). Men, by contrast, tended to be typecast as powerful and successful beings who occupied high-status positions, initiated action, acted rationally, and organized their lives around doing, solving, and achieving. They were depicted as living an exciting and rewarding life; rational and resistant to emotional blackmail; preoccupied with cars, beer, buddies, and weapons; and always under control or in charge. Relationships between women and men were defined accordingly: men as king of the castle and women as lady of the house. Men "did" (act like a man) while women "were" (looking like a lady) – as is nicely captured in an Associated Press release covering the memorial mass in Milan for slain fashion designer Gianni Versace: "Choreographer Maurice Bejart gave the first reading. Sting and Elton John sang a setting of Psalm 23 'The Lord is my Shepherd.' [Princess] Diana wore a black dress and pearls" (Associated Press 1997). Finally, those who did not fit the physical ideal found themselves excluded from mainstream representations. In a industry geared toward the bold (activity) and the beautiful (a rigidly narrow definition of body perfection), women with disabilities were firmly invisibilized (Haller and Ralph 2001).

Media misrepresentations of minority women were no less punitive (hooks 1992; Graydon 2001; Jiwani and Young 2006). Minority women (including Aboriginal women, immigrant and refugee women, and racialized minority women) were vulnerable to misrepresentation as peripheral, stereotypes, problem people, adornments, and the "other" (Kunz and Fleras 1998). If women in general confronted the spectre of sexualization through stereotyping, minority women were doubly victimized through racialized stereotypes that simultaneously pounced on their difference (if different, then inferior) or their sameness (if the same, loss of authenticity). Racialized minority women were shown to occupy domestic(ated) roles, a process that tended to consume the entirety of their lives while reducing life chances to a singular process or a decorative prop. Their bodies were gratuitously paraded about to sell everything from esoteric fashions to sensuous fragrances, with a host of exotic vacation destinations in between. These simplistic articulations trivialized the realities, aspirations, and contributions of minoritized women.

Or consider media coverage of Aboriginal women, especially against a backdrop of the disappearance or murder of some 582 Aboriginal mothers, sisters, and daughters since 1970. News media depictions of off-reserve Aboriginal women appear to oscillate between invisibility/passivity (as victims of crime) and hypervisibility (as owners of deviant bodies, resulting in the criminalization of those women in the sex trade industry) (Jiwani and Young 2006). This criminalization of Aboriginal women draws unnecessary attention to their status as the "other"; it also reinforces the demeaning implications associated with being "otherized," including being perceived as fringe players who deserve to be ignored, insulted or caricaturized, and marginalized. But these unflattering images are being contested, and the next Case Study demonstrates differences in framing minority and Aboriginal women, and how these distinctions are challenged by a Metis filmmaker.

case study

Framing Otherness: Afghani Women (Worthy Victims) versus Aboriginal Women (Unworthy Victims)

News media coverage of minority and foreign women is not entirely consistent. Positive portrayals coexist alongside the negative in ways that may appear to be random. Upon closer reflection, however, a pattern emerges. For example, Aboriginal women in Canada tend to be rendered invisible by the news media; when they appear, contexts of violence or marginalization predominate. Although news coverage of Aboriginal women is minimal, even when violence is involved, the situation differs for racialized immigrant women. Violence against South Asian women may receive more coverage, but only if honour killings are involved (rather than domestic abuse) – in the process invoking stereotypes of South Asian communities as "other," to be pitied or scorned.

Interestingly, news media coverage of women in patriarchal Afghanistan tends toward the positive. Two media discourses prevail about the oppression of Afghani women: their worthiness as victims (innocent, virtuous, and honourable) plus their heroism as resilient survivors (challenging and resisting) (Jiwani 2009). In the first narrative, Afghani women tend to be situated within the context of justifying Western military intervention in Afghanistan (Carastathis 2007). Members of Canadian armed forces are portrayed as chivalrous warriors out to rescue oppressed Third World victims – in part to rationalize the intervention through conventional notions of masculine heroes doing a dirty but necessary job. The second narrative is focused on demonstrating the bravery of women in a context that is unmistakably un-Canadian. Reference to Canada as a progressive (and predominantly white) society is counterposed to the stereotypical constructions of Islam as potentially barbaric in its desultory treatment of women.

Two insights can be gleaned from this assessment. First, the tendency to valorize Afghani women may reflect ulterior motives, rather than a commitment to gender equality. Put bluntly, it's not easy justifying an unpopular war. As Jiwani (2009) observes, the civility of civilized societies like Canada must gloss over their violence by legitimizing and rationalizing the deployment of troops behind a discourse of care, compassion, and rescue. The knights of civilization must also redeem their violence by being good men who rescue helpless victims outside the homeland while protecting vulnerable women within. In other words, references to Afghani women's struggles serve as a proxy for broader issues related to Canada's relational status in the world.

Second, news media coverage posits a distinction between worthy and unworthy victims. The distinction is based on defining what constitutes acceptable lifestyles or occupations through the prism of middle-class values and morality. Insofar as the nature of violent crime coverage depends on the worthiness of the victim, those who are worthy receive sympathetic coverage, whereas those who "deserve" what they get because of lifestyle "choices" are either ignored or framed as unworthy. Yet a counter-discourse can be discerned that not only challenges conventional views but also provides a voice for the hitherto voiceless.

Finding Dawn: Finding Empowerment

Finding Dawn is an award-winning 2006 National Film Board documentary about

= case study

the violence inflicted on Aboriginal women in Canada. Produced and directed by the acclaimed Metis filmmaker Christine Welsh, an associate professor at the University of Victoria who teaches courses in indigenous women studies and indigenous cinema, the film focuses on the fate of three Aboriginal women – Dawn Crey, Ramona Wilson, and Daleen Kay Bosse – of some 580 murdered or missing Aboriginal women in Canada over the past forty years. In addition to honouring those who have passed away, Welsh emphasizes how the living (from survivors of sexual violence to family and community members of the murdered and missing) are taking life-affirming steps to commemorate the forgotten, communicate beyond the silence of the silenced, and construct a society that respects Aboriginal women's rights to dignity and safety. Or, as Welsh comments toward the end of the film, "I set out on this journey to find Dawn. But I also found Faye, I found Janice, I found people who strive, who search and hope."

In an effort to put a human face on this national disgrace, the title itself touches on the story of Dawn Crey, whose remains (numbered twenty-three by the authorities) were found on the property of serial killer Robert Pickton. But in Welsh's hands, Crey becomes more than a number; she's a daughter and sister who, at the time of her murder, was moving beyond a life of drugs and "prostitution." The film moves from Vancouver's Skid Row to British Columbia's Highway 16 – the Highway of Tears – which runs from Prince Rupert to Prince George. Nine women (all but one Aboriginal), including Ramona Wilson, have died or disappeared along this stretch of road since 1990. Filming in Saskatoon focuses on Daleen Kay Bosse, who disappeared in 2004 and whose disappearance and murder are still unresolved (the remains of Daleen were discovered in 2008; court proceedings are underway). Welsh makes it clear that the tragedy of murdered and missing Aboriginal women persists because of (1) societal and institutional indifference toward the poor and Aboriginal, (2) a belief by predators that nobody will miss the weakest and most vulnerable members of society, and (3) the intersection of historical, social, and economic factors that inflame this epidemic of gendered violence.

But the documentary goes beyond a series of depressing vignettes about the dead or disappeared. In challenging a conventional "palemale" media gaze (both male and non-Aboriginal) with its emphasis on female victimhood, the overriding theme is that of empowerment – Aboriginal women and men mobilizing to challenge, resist, and transform. Although painful at times to watch, *Finding Dawn* resonates with messages of resilience and strength. Rather than dwelling on the dark heart of Aboriginal women's experiences in Canada, expressions of courage and outrage are conveyed by Aboriginal rights activists Janice Acoose and Fay Blaney, both of whom are survivors of abuse, violence, and the dangers of life on the streets. Hope and optimism are also demonstrated through the annual Women's Memorial March in Vancouver, community mobilization and vigils along the length of Highway 16, and local family commemorations of missing and murdered daughters and sisters. The film ends with a photo shoot of a large Aboriginal family, with Welsh's voice-over posing the beguiling question, "What is it about numbers?"

Finding Dawn won a Gold Audience Award at the 2006 Amnesty International Film Festival in Vancouver. It was screened for the 2007 International Women's Day celebrations at the United Nations headquarters in New York. This is hardly surprising; *Finding Dawn* is exemplary as a striking testimony to the power of images to inform and reform. Viewers are drawn into a worldwide culture of impunity that allows the murder of women who are poor, indigenous, and in high-risk occupations to go unsolved and unpunished. (The 2009 Mexican film *Backyard* also deals with the femicide of thousands of murdered women in Ciudad Juarez, as does an earlier documentary aired on PBS in 2002 titled *Señorita Extraviada* [Missing Young Women], which, like *Finding Dawn,* focuses on deciphering the silence behind the murders while paying homage to the victims and their families as part of a rallying cry for social justice [Dollarhide 2002]). The worth of *Finding Dawn* as an indictment of society is further sharpened by the eloquent testimonials of strong parents and caring siblings as they struggle to cope with the devastation of lost daughters and sisters. In demonstrating how Aboriginal women (and men) are organizing and demonstrating to combat violence, *Finding Dawn* shatters conventional media stereotypes of Aboriginal women as passive or victims. In the final analysis, however, women can march and demonstrate. But it is men who must change.

Critical-Thinking Question

Once you have watched the film *Finding Dawn,* ask yourself, What is it about the film that provides a fundamentally different way of looking (gazing) at Aboriginal women compared with mainstream media?

* * * * * * * * * * *

Women and Newscasting

News media are known to be influential in advancing a particular rendition of social reality. Socially constructed representations are conveyed through language and image, with an implicit set of ideas and ideals about what is newsworthy. The newsworthiness of newscasting is hardly neutral. As a discourse for manufacturing consent in support of power in capitalist, liberal, and demo-cratic societies, newscasting is transformed into a site of ideological reproduc-tion with respect to (1) consent and common sense, (2) a preferred reading of specific events, and (3) the demonizing of those outside the orbit of normalcy (Wise 2008). This assessment is true across a broad range of news topics, and its application to gender and newscasting is no exception. Women continue to be under-represented as subjects yet subject to news media pitches that un-settle women (as a pitch for sales or a form of social control) in the same way that advertisers hype insecurity about women's appeal and appearances.

There is little doubt that news media were once openly male-centred (A. Nelson 2010). Male-controlled media defined what was newsworthy because of their monopoly of power to make decisions regarding what counts as news and what news counts. Consider the annual Global Media Monitoring Project (2010), which canvassed 1,281 TV, radio, and print media outlets in 108 coun-tries on 10 November 2009, examining 16,734 news items and 35,543 news subjects. (For the first time, national and international Internet sites were in-cluded as a separate category.) The results clearly reinforced the notion of news media as a man's world, with women constituting just 24 percent of news sub-jects (people who are interviewed or about whom the news focuses), up from 17 percent in 1995. Women were a central focus in 13 percent of the stories and experts/spokespeople in 19 percent of the stories, while women reporters ac-counted for 37 percent of news items. Women were least likely to appear in stories about politics and government (14 percent), as experts (17 percent) or spokespersons (14 percent), or as a central focus (10 percent).

The Global Media Monitoring Project concluded that nearly one-half (46 percent) of all news items reinforced gender stereotypes (42 percent of web-based stories proved stereotypical as well). Even coverage of so-called women's issues reflected male readings of women's reality. Many news stories involving gender-based violence tended to be reported in a manner that normalizes such behaviour, renders it largely inconsequential, and sanctions its perpetuation (WACC 2009). Rape myths continue to be framed as predominantly rough sex or tsk-tsked because the victim "deserved it" (Rosalind Gill in Dent 2008). Police remain the authoritative voice in these encounters, with the result that realities are constructed to fit police versions rather than victims' experiences. (The pro-liferation of SlutWalk protest marches since April 2011 reflects a grassroots re-action to a police officer's remark that women should stop dressing like sluts if they do not want to be victimized.) These discourses rarely include any sense of context (of power or exploitation) or long-term consequences. Yet such cover-age silenced women's voices while distorting issues of relevance to women.

Moreover, in an effort to simplify and explain, news media routinely reduce (or frame) complex issues to sloganeering catchphrases (e.g., "All men are rapists"). Women's groups are then expected to defend or debate these issues along the simplistic and confrontational lines established by the media.

Insofar as news content reflects male interests and priorities, it is gendered. Elite white males continue to make, report, or analyze the major news of the day; they also dominate coverage of public affairs. Only a small percentage of news items, either national or international, refer to women as "movers and shakers" (WACC 2009). Unlike depictions of men as active and controlling, women are rarely treated as subjects but rather as objectified victims or survivors. Issues of relevance to women are marginalized or ignored unless grounded in family, health, relationships, or appearance. Not surprisingly, the news still portrays women who attain positions of authority as abnormalities whose status as fish out of water is sufficient to generate the headline or drive a narrative. Sports coverage is particularly prone to under- and misrepresentation (Messner and Cooky 2010). Women in sports continue to be "miniaturized" by conveying the impression that women athletes neither exist nor matter (Markula 2009). They are sexualized by the media's focusing on appearances ("lingerie football"), trivializing (or infantilizing) female athletes and their performances, or delegitimizing their accomplishments as second-rate. And, finally, despite projections that the Internet will prove to be a more gender-friendly news source, women continue to be silenced by even widely read blogging sites, such as the *Huffington Post* (Wakeman 2008). The following Case Study reveals how the concept of a gendered journalism imposes a double standard and double binds on female politicians.

insight

Gendered Journalism and Woman in Politics: Double Standards and Double Binds

> *Facing the press is more difficult than bathing a leper. (Mother Teresa, quoted in Graydon 2001)*

It is generally accepted that journalism and the news media do not hold a mirror to society. Rather than providing an accurate reflection of what is out there, media preselect aspects of society based on perceived audience expectations and institutional values, routines, and priorities. Journalists tend to interpret the world of news through largely unconscious frames that impose conventional meanings on newsworthy experiences (e.g., "Men are breadwinners"; "Women don't belong in business"; "Women are too emotional"). This selectivity is especially evident in news coverage of women in politics. A host of sexist double standards can be discerned that play havoc with taking women seriously in politics, including the following jeopardies (Braden 1996):

- Journalists are known to pose questions of female politicians they would never ask of men. For example, who is going to look after the children or take care of the husband?
- Journalists tend to sexualize women rather than men, and they do so in ways and wording that extol traditional roles or conventional images of femininity.
- Journalists expect women to be aggressive enough to do the job but not so aggressive as to threaten males in general. Assertiveness in men is okay; in women it's seen as pushy, domineering, or unteamlike.
- Journalists often hold women politicians accountable for the actions of their husbands or children; by contrast, men are rarely held to the same standard.
- Journalists may criticize women for behaviour that many regard as acceptable for male politicians. In a August 2009 *Vanity Fair* profile by Todd Purdum, Sarah Palin (the once-governor of Alaska and Republican vice-presidential nominee in 2008 but now author and possible Republican presidential candidate for 2012) is described as having a narcissistic personality disorder (egotistical, fantasies of grandeur) (Purdum 2009). Such an accusation may be true; however, male politicians from Bill Clinton downward also exhibited megalomaniac tendencies without necessarily being criticized for it (Goldberg 2009). Legitimate criticism or double standard?
- Journalists equate two female politicians competing for the same political office with a catfight, suggesting that it's okay to have one woman in a race, but more than one and the claws come out (Goodman 2011).
- Journalists test the newsworthiness of women against a set of traditional (male) news values – for example, conflict and controversy – even though female politicians may be more interested in promoting the more livable (albeit less newsworthy) values of compromise and cooperation.

The evidence is irrefutable: a gendered double standard undermines the credibility and credentials of female politicians. Female politicians are also entrapped by double binds that relentlessly scrutinize and dissect every move (McDonald 2009). Treatment of women in politics reflects a no-win, dammed-if-you-do, dammed-if-you-don't situation that (1) endorses women who are smart but not smarter than the average male politician, (2) rebukes women who are attractive but dismisses those who are preoccupied with appearances, and (3) rebuffs femininity as weak yet rejects too much "masculinity" as "unfeminine." Journalists invariably judge women politicians on the basis of appearance. If a woman "fusses" over her appearance, she is trivialized as superficial or weak. If she disregards her appearance, she is deemed unfeminine and unelectable. Female politicians also become newsworthy when they deviate from the norm of femininity by engaging in "unladylike" behaviour. But being too "ladylike" can also generate the wrong kind of media noise, especially when stereotyping women as shallow, vacillating, and emotionally unfit for the demands of political office. Not surprisingly, female politicians tend to be ensnared in a kind of no (wo)man's land, since the boundaries between acceptable and unacceptable are often unclear, prone to inexplicable shifts, subject to second-guessing, and reflect a lose-lose proposition, regardless of what they do or don't do.

The combination of double standards and double binds that sexualize women in politics is proving difficult to dislodge. Appearances continue to matter for female politicians; for example, consider how the image of Sarah Palin became almost synonymous with spike heels, designer eyeglasses, and glossy lipstick (Rook 2008; see also McKinney, Rill, and Watson 2011). Or consider how the public is reminded that in a rally in Arizona to support John McCain's bid for senate re-election, Palin wore "a trim black leather jacket and pencil skirt" (Halperin 2010). Michelle Obama may be a Harvard-educated lawyer earning a quarter of a million dollars per year as a university vice-president, but media attention focuses on her as a mother and her appearance, including (1) the $148 cotton sundress she wore on *The View*, (2) a reluctance to wear pantyhose, and (3) a willingness to shop at Target (an upscale Walmart) (Harper 2008). The unmarried and childless status of Australia's first female prime minister, Julia Gillard, featured prominently in that country's 2010 federal election campaign and included references to her ever-changing red hair colour, large earlobes, nasal voice, and lack of fashion sense (*The Australian* 2010). Finally, consider a cover story/lead article in the 18 April 2005 issue of *Maclean's* magazine that features Belinda Stronach – the telegenic Conservative MP who many thought possessed the star power to eventually assume party leadership. In the first paragraph, the reader is told that Stronach sashayed into the party's convention wearing a "vivid green Hugo Boss leather jacket," "striped satin skinny pants," "a chunky pearl necklace," and "taupe stilettos." On the third page of the article is a near-full-page photo spread of her and her splashy fashion sense. Toward the end of the article, we are informed that on the second day of the convention she wore "a tailored pinstripe suit," "a crisp white shirt," and "crocodile stilettos." No reference was made to the sartorial splendour of the males in the story. The message is loud and clear: women in the political domain must plan their wardrobe with as much care as they give to policy statements and electoral platforms.

Charges of media sexism were played out during the 2008 Democratic presidential nomination race between Hillary Clinton and Barack Obama (Marsden and Savigny 2009). For some, Clinton was exposed to sexist bias that would never be accorded to male candidates (Gerstel 2008). Quoting Erika Fox, a communications expert at Johns Hopkins University, and based on the analysis of six major papers, Judy Gerstel argued that Clinton was less likely to be addressed by her legislative title than by her name or gender (Ms. or Mrs.). Others argued that she received less attention than Obama on particular issues but greater focus on her persona, including how she dressed, looked, or spoke. As well, Clinton found herself in a double bind: she had to appear tough, as would be expected of a commander-in-chief, without abdicating her cookie-baking feminine side. In other words, in a deeply gendered society, in terms of what is desirable, acceptable, or normal, media routines tended to compound Clinton's campaign mistakes, thus contributing to defeat (Marsden and Savigny 2009).

This assessment was disputed. The news media, for example, acknowledged some mistakes but argued that the Clinton campaign exploited a few egregious examples of sexist coverage to re-energize a faltering campaign (see Seelye and Bosman 2008). Still others, including Candy Crowley (cited in ibid.), concurred with the charge of press sexism, but only in commentary rather than in hard news. Besides, as many noted, it was difficult to untangle what the media may have disliked or criticized: Was it that Clinton was a woman, a particular woman, or the front-runner for much of the campaign?

To be sure, when it comes to politics, it's better to be noticed (even when stereotyped and trivialized) than ignored. Politics in the postmodern media era are inextricably linked with image making (Parry-Giles 2000). This obsession with appearances also applies to men, who too must address image issues. Nevertheless, men generally have more latitude in how they look or behave – thanks to their general acceptance as "natural born" leaders. This sexism in the news media should not be lightly discounted. Not only are women locked into stereotypical images that demean or deter, they are also trivialized by gender-specific putdowns (from "butch" to "bitch") that demonize women as unfit for office. These sexist double standards and gendered double binds are not necessarily blatant; still, the cumulative effect of subtle discrimination may have a controlling effect in marginalizing the legitimacy of women as effective politicians. Both society and mainstream media continue to be uncomfortable with women in power, especially if they don't fit the traditional female norm of being nurturing, conciliatory, and selfless (Bashevkin 2008; Bouw 2010). An image is perpetuated of women politicians as a novelty or anomaly, people who have no business occupying the nation's corridors of power. And to the extent that the news media emphasize gender to the exclusion of other attributes, such unwanted sexualization and relentless dissection will continue to repel women from seeking office or making political noises (Braden 1996; see also Wolf 1993).

Critical-Thinking Question
How do the concepts of double standards and double binds provide insights into the concept of a gendered journalism?

* * * * * * * * * * * *

Programming TV Women: Couched in Compromise
Television is as guilty as other media in misrepresenting women (Lindsey 1997). For the most part, women were largely marginalized or excluded from television programming because of plot inconvenience or dramatic dead weights. But with the feminization of prime-time audiences, women characters, including African American women, are now the central focus of many popular programs. A feminist/feminine sensibility prevails: consider the new breed of "warrior women" (Zerbisias 2010). Popular characters such as Buffy or Xena or Ally or Carrie or Hanna have discarded conventional images of women as vixens or victims, as killed or kept. Adopted instead are images of women as mean, muscular, and motivated. These televised equivalents of rock's riot grrrls don't go around looking for trouble; trouble follows them in their relentless pursuit of justice. Sexuality may be flaunted – not in the classic sense of bimbo or seductress but as an extension of female resources and resourcefulness. They are nobody's appendage, as the stars of *Sex and the City* remind us. Their perspective on relationships and sexuality is that of urban women in their thirties, and their refusal to be domesticated symbolizes a rejection of scripted patriarchy (Weinman 2008).

Yet the range and quality of TV women is not as progressive as appearances may suggest (Douglas 2010). The realities of women are boxed-in and sanitized to meet the commercial and institutional needs of a rectangular screen. Both prime-time TV and film remain downtime for female actors, who remain under-represented (of the 49,662 roles in television and movies in 1999, 62 percent went to men) (MRTW 1996). The portrayal of women in reality TV can prove unflattering when women are framed as stupid, manipulative, untrustworthy, vindictive, and greedy gold diggers who discard all shreds of decency in their obsessive competition for male approval (Pozner 2010). Even the highly acclaimed shows (for example, the HBO series *The Wire*) have endured criticism for ostensibly sexist portrayals of women as little more than foils for advancing storylines or pumping up male egos. Programming reveals an ambiguity when incorporating social trends. A receptivity to new ideas for plot twists or character development is offset by an unwillingness to deviate from proven money-making formulas (Lindsey 1997). That contradiction alone indicates the presence of rules so ingrained within TV programming that simple recognition – never mind the possibility of challenge or reform – is difficult, even when economics dictate otherwise (Wolf 1993).

In cases where women make inroads (trespass) into male domains, TV shows transform these "gutsy" women into something less powerful. Their status as threats is depoliticized by overtly eroticizing them, exaggerating conventional styles of femininity through cleavage galore and lip gloss, reaffirming their availability to or dependency on men, and reinforcing their status as mothers or endowed with career-dampening maternal instincts. If cast occupationally or powerfully, women remain subordinate to males or, alternatively, appear as ruthless manipulators in securing status or success (Lindsey 1997). TV women confront a remarkable range of problems and entanglements, with most woefully incapable of balancing work demands with that of intimacy. Is such a message a coincidence, or is there a dynamic at play that compromises and contradicts even as it empowers and enlightens (Douglas 2010)? Chapter 9, on women and advertising, addresses this issue.

Women and Film

> *No matter how talented a woman is, no matter how many plaudits she has received, how intelligent her reputation, how garlanded she has been for depicting one of the most talented writers of the last century while sporting a huge prosthetic conk on her noggin, at the end of the day, if she wants to stay in the public eye, if she wants*

> *the magazine covers and the leading roles, she has to be willing*
> *to reduce herself to tits and arse. (Kira Cochrane [2007] on why*
> *award-winning actors like Nicole Kidman still have to bare all*
> *for success)*

Films historically portrayed women in multi-dimensional roles, often romanti-cizing women by putting them on a pedestal to admire or to topple. From the onset of moviemaking, films have tended to slot women into a predetermined set of stereotypes, either good or bad, ranging from mom or girl(friend) next door at one end to spinster or butch at the other, with the golden-hearted pros-titute in between. A more blatant dimension gathered momentum from the 1960s onward with the proliferation of films on the seemingly insatiable theme of sexual violence toward women *(Fatal Attraction, American Psycho)* (Lindsey 1997). Films continue to mix regressive stereotypes with positive role models while punishing women who are too old, too unattractive, not deferential to men, and too aggressive in trolling for younger males. Seventyish male actors (from Sean Connery to Robert Redford to Jack Nicholson) can find meaty movie roles, yet women now in their fifties and sixties (from Diane Keaton to Kathleen Turner, from Kim Cattrall to Meryl Streep) struggle for decent roles – in some cases establishing their own production companies to ensure work. Although exceptions exist, including Helen Mirren and Betty White (of tele-vision fame), older women tend to disappear from a medium in which youth, slimness, and beauty are valued. In cases when they do appear, older women come across as crabby or doddering.

The film industry has an ambivalent relationship with women. This am-bivalence can be attributed to a paradox within the industry. On one side, film's ability to control exposure and willingness to tap into certain markets rather than mass audiences put it in a better position to transcend television's limita-tions, the latter having a tendency to sanitize reality by bleaching it of any pro-vocation. The successes of the Julia Roberts, Halle Berrys, and Susan Sarandons suggest a much higher movie profile for women. Consider films of assertive women *(Thelma and Louise)*, women of strength and endurance *(Interrogation)*, women who transcend shallow materialism and obsession with male relation-ships *(Muriel's Wedding)*, women with skills *(A League of Their Own)*, women bent on revenge *(The First Wives Club)*, women who discover themselves *(Once Were Warriors)*, women who love other women *(Jaguar and Aimee)*, women in quest of a goal *(Kandahar)*, women who don't want to be anybody's doormat *(Moscow, Belgium; Take My Eyes)*, and women out for themselves *(Sex and the City: The Movie)*.

On the other side, however, the film industry is more focused on fantasy than reality. Although moviemaking does have a way of seizing the spirit of the times and instinctively repackaging realism into a popular culture format, the film industry is also driven by the pursuit of audiences and profits, with predictable effects on the artistic credibility of filmmakers. Unlike television, which measures success by an ability to attract women between the ages of eighteen and forty-nine years, the hormones of younger men tend to propel the film industry (MRTW 1996). That kind of discrepancy undermines opportunities for women to tell their stories in their own voices. The silencing may intensify as the number of female directors continues to decline – it fell from a high of 11 percent in 2000 to 7 percent in 2006 – and as female writers continue a freefall both in terms of income relative to male writers and involvement in the top films (Walker 2007). According to *New York Times* writer Manohla Dargis in a 13 December 2009 article, women filmmakers directed only 10 percent of 2009's films, with many of them foreign language, documentary, or low-budget fare that went straight to DVD (Schneller 2009). Not surprisingly, only three women – Lina Wertmüller (for *Seven Beauties*), Jane Campion (for *The Piano*), and Sofia Coppola (for *Lost in Translation*) – had ever been nominated for both Best Picture and Best Director at the Academy Awards, though Coppola won the 2004 Oscar for Best Original Screenplay. (Only one African American filmmaker, John Singleton, was nominated for best director, for *Boyz n the Hood.*)

To be sure, this pattern was upended in 2010 with the emergence of major female talent directing critically acclaimed films like *The Hurt Locker* (Kathryn Bigelow) and *An Education* (Lone Scherfig) (Schneller 2009). But as Jane Campion put it, despite *The Hurt Locker*'s capture of Oscars at the eighty-second Academy Awards for Best Picture and Best Director, the power of the ol' boys network remains intact. So while Sofia Coppola's top prize at the Venice Film Festival for *Somewhere* reinforces a trend, the fact that female directors were shut out of the 2011 Academy Awards suggests the risk of a return to Hollywood normal.

Accounting for the Problem: Archaic Attitudes or Gendered Foundations?

How do we account for media's miscasting of women? Are the media *misogynist* toward women, bearing a hatred that reduces women to irrelevance or contempt? Are media *sexist?* Sexism covers that constellation of beliefs and practices that openly assert the superiority of one gender over another, using this rationale to justify discriminatory treatment on the basis of gender. Are media *patriarchal?* Patriarchy may be defined as a system by men, for men, and about men. Society is organized around male privilege and power in ways that normalize male domination across public and private domains while naturalizing the marginalization of women as inferior or irrelevant. Media processes, organization, and priorities continue to be organized around male agendas and experiences. The logical consequences of normal media functioning exert a controlling effect that secures male privilege and power at the expense of female aspirations and realities. The implications are systemically sexist.

Or is it more accurate to describe media as *androcentric?* Androcentrism consists of a set of tacit assumptions by which individuals (and institutions) routinely see and automatically interpret (frame) reality from a male gaze. The male vantage point is implicitly assumed as normal or necessary; conversely, the validity of other perspectives is dismissed as irrelevant or criticized as wrong. The realities of women are subsequently refracted through the prism (gaze) of male androcentrism, in the process creating a gendered media whose patricentric frames come across as reflective of reality itself, rather than as socially constructed and ideologically contested. As Laura Mulvey claimed when introducing the concept of the male gaze in her 1975 article "Visual Pleasure and Narrative Cinema," media in general and cinema in particular produce and reproduce in viewers images of women as objects owned and controlled by male projections of desires, fantasies, and fears. This androcentric media gaze invariably tends to judge female others by a masculinist standard; it also assumes the unquestioned primacy of this perspective in defining what is acceptable and desirable while denying it is a perspective.

The problem is not just in front of the camera. The lack of women behind the camera as gatekeepers and decision makers translates into a dearth of opportunities to exercise power. Exclusion from the creative and decision-making processes culminates in media images of women that reflect male perceptions and fantasies. Women's realities and experiences are shoehorned into male-friendly frameworks, and women are then criticized when they fail to abide by these standards. Compounding the problem is a reluctance to acknowledge those unspoken assumptions that subject gender relations to double standards. Anastasia Higginbotham (1996, 87) underscores this double standard when commenting on the contradictory messages conveyed by teenage magazines: "Be pretty, but not so pretty that you intimidate boys, threaten other girls, or attract inappropriate suitors, such as teachers, bosses, fathers, or rapists; be smart but not so smart that you intimidate boys or that, god forbid, you miss the prom to study for finals; be athletic, but not so athletic that you intimidate boys or lead people to believe that you are aggressive, asexual, or (gasp!) a lesbian or bisexual; be happy with yourself, but not if you're fat, ugly, poor, gay, disabled, antisocial, or can't at least pass as white."

Clearly, then, young and older women are complicit with mainstream media in marginalizing gender. Not only are women under pressure to play a certain role and conform to a rigid standard of beauty (lean and fit), but they may also mistakenly confuse overt sexuality and sexualization with the exercise of choice, freedom, power, and equality. Or as Rosalind Gill (in Dent 2008) puts it, there is a widespread but mistaken media notion that portraying young women as sexual objects is acceptable, especially if couched in irony, in part because women themselves advocate such representations as reflective of being modern, liberated, and independent (see also Douglas 2010). With women in competition with men – and winning – without necessarily forsaking their femininity or appearance, sexuality is being reclaimed not as an object of male desire but in terms of everything that is exciting, interesting, depressing, and challenging about being a contemporary woman (Weinman 2008). But the consequences of sexualized objectification should not be underestimated, especially when hot, young female pop stars in provocative clothing, dancing suggestively and singing openly sexist lyrics, are aggressively marketed to young girls as models to emulate and for young lads to desire (Kilbourne and Levin 2008). To be sure, it's unwise to posit causal links between media and effects, given the complexities of human behaviour. But when women are portrayed as frilly-minded fashion plates in pursuit of unrealistic images of beauty and sexuality, politics are double-edged.

Regendering Media Agendas

Gradual improvements in the representational basis of media-gender relations can be discerned. The emergence of a feminist critique, combined with the growing involvement of women in mainstream media, is exerting pressure to redefine how media do things. Traditional gender roles were shattered by the feisty "girl" power icons of the 1990s (Madonna, Xena, Buffy, Ally, Avril, Carrie, Lisbeth, and so on), with the result that confident, successful, self-reliant, and assertive women are the norm. In newscasting, women are increasingly more prominent as they assume positions of power and authority in the world of business and politics. In the world of television and film, men and women are generally equal in numbers, though men tend to dominate the leading-character role (Gauntlett 2008). TV programming has shown improvement in the quantity and quality of female portrayals, with roles that often supersede those of men in terms of status, intelligence, and social responsibility. In contrast to their husbands, who are depicted as flatulent, lazy shirkers who make a mess of household tasks, women are portrayed as always there, always busy, and always right. Mary Vallis (2009) writes: "In commercial after commercial on TV, the image of the modern husband and father is one of the buffoon – trapped in a shed he built without doors, staring blankly at spilled juice, gorging on dog cookies until his ever capable wife comes to the rescue." A comparable development can be seen on the big screen, where women are shown as being just as capable as men in having attitude, accomplishing goals, having fun, and taking control. For every film that puts women down, there are those that empower, including Disney films that increasingly feature empowered heroines who are challenging the beauty myth (physical beauty = a husband = living happily ever after) by relying on strength and smarts to overcome difficult situations (Gordon 2002).

But improvements are not the same as transformation. Conventional images of female attractiveness remain, including notions that women have to be toned, fit, and made up. In televised sports, there has been notable improvement in the once insulting and overtly sexist treatment of women athletes by sports commentators. Yet coverage of women's sports has shrunk to almost miniscule proportions – from 9 percent of airtime in 1999 to 1.6 percent in 2009 – despite significant improvements in women's athletic skill levels and massive increases in the number of women in college and professional sports (Messner and Cooky 2010). If sports are more than entertainment, if they are stories about who we are and what values we cherish, Messner and Cooky ask, does ignoring women in sports reinforce the myth of male superiority and men's destiny to dominate in politics and the economy?

Young girls in particular are vulnerable to media assaults by the music, fashion, and cosmetic industries, which rattle girls' self-esteem, causing them to internalize anxieties about boyfriends, girlfriends, body images, sexuality, and social status (Sax 2010; Zerbisias 2010; Orenstein 2011). Men, too, comply with conventional frameworks of attractiveness; nevertheless, they can get away with imperfections and remain "attractive" if they possess money or power or can compensate with charm or humour (Gauntlett 2008). Nor is there any suggestion that the transformation is complete or that everyone approves. Rather, the situation appears to be one of transitional flux, with the result that mixed messages are the rule rather than the exception. Yes, there are female police chiefs, surgeons, and lawyers across TV land, yet there are also reality and makeover shows that cast women as absorbed with appearance, shopping, bodies, and men. The end result, according to Susan Douglas (2010), is that women are pulled into messages that they can be anything they want because of full equality, yet they are pushed and pressured by messages to conform to hyper-feminine ideas of hotness and beauty. In that women young and old are encouraged to aspire to the impossible by living the improbable – by rebelling against (feminist) yet submitting to (feminine) prevailing images of worthwhile women (Douglas 1994) – a gendered media gaze could not be more forcefully articulated.

What do women expect from the media? Media Watch, a Canadian voluntary feminist organization opposed to sexism in the media, provides useful guidelines. The organization begins with the assumption that the struggle against media sexism is a human rights concern rather than an issue of morality, censorship, or profitability. It proposes a media environment in which women are neither invisible nor stereotyped but positively depicted, in which women are realistically portrayed as positive and full contributors to society, and in which women are equitably (and proportionately) represented in terms of their physical, social, economic, and cultural diversity. Gender inclusiveness will be the key in closing the gap between what women want and what media deliver. Not surprisingly, media institutions must improve both their representation of and responsiveness to women for expectations to match reality. This passage from Jiwani and Young (2006, 912) captures a sense of the challenges ahead:

> Thus, it appears the war against women will continue until the dominant hegemonic values change to recognize women first and foremost as human beings whose material conditions are determined by interlocking legacies of colonialism and a racialized and sexualized economy of representations that privileges some women over others. Aboriginality, in this instance, constitutes the contested battlefields of meanings that can only be won when society recognizes its complicity in reproducing neo-colonial systems of valuation that position Aboriginal women in the lowest rungs of the social order, thereby making them expendable and invisible, if not disposable. Similarly, and intersecting with Aboriginal status, sex work also needs to be recuperated from the dominant gaze that sees it simply as a degenerate trade characteristic of deviant bodies confined to the realms of disorder and criminality.

5

Media, Classed
Framing the Rich, the Poor, and the Working In-Between

Canada's mainstream media do not exist in a political void or economic vacuum. Mainstream commercial media are situated within a capitalistic economy whose animating logic entails the rational pursuit of profit. The corporatization of mainstream media into larger conglomerates for controlling the information or entertainment package has reinforced their status as intensely competitive business ventures. In that a bottom-line mentality prevails over national interests or social justice, the conglomeration of media industries into turbo-charged money-making machines exposes the conflict of interest between private gain and public good. That mainstream media are increasingly market-driven and profit-oriented also reinforces a perception of audiences not as citizens to inform but as consumers to attract. With a corporate focus on readers or viewers who appeal to advertisers, the words of a retired editor of the *Philadelphia Inquirer* seem especially apropos: "You can't sell many ads when your readers [viewers] don't have credit cards, and thus some readers are worth more than others" (Cunningham 2004).

Mainstream media are classed by virtue of who owns, controls, and distributes content. Commercial imperatives also exert a powerful if largely unarticulated influence in shaping media representations of classes and class relations (Hackett et al. 2000; J. Winter 2001). The representational basis of media-class relations is rarely or poorly addressed, although the relationship between class and media is unmistakable, thanks to the intertwining of corporate agendas with media priorities (Croteau and Hoynes 2003; Benson 2005; Alper and

Leistyna 2006). What little there is has proven wildly inconsistent while re-inforcing what many may suspect: that ownership and control of profit-oriented commercial mass media by the rich and powerful may indirectly in-fluence representations of social class, with the result that business interests prevail over those of common folk. In acknowledging that some people are more valuable than others because of their class status, media content is slant-ed (with exceptions) toward positive depictions of the affluent (including the middle class), whereas references to the working classes, labour unions, and unemployed and poor (with exceptions, of course) tend to be dismissed or de-meaned (Butsch 1992).

In short, mainstream media are classed. And yet, media discourses rarely address debates about class or classes, much less engage with class-related themes, perhaps from fear that any class analysis may draw unnecessary atten-tion to corporate media in reinforcing social inequality. No less puzzling is the erosion of references to class from public discourses and polite company, with the "c" word brushed off as an irrelevant relic from an archaic past. Perhaps the problem lies in mistakenly conflating class with classism (a belief in the innate superiority of some classes) rather than framing class as a set of relations in-volving either control over the means of production or commonalities in family background with respect to power, privilege, and property, including similar life chances in the marketplace. Nevertheless, the contradiction is unmistak-able: whether we approve or disapprove, are aware or unaware, class consti-tutes a critical dimension in people's lives, from wages to issues of health and safety. And yet, people continue to harbour illusions of living in a classless and egalitarian society, partly because of a media tendency to stifle class talk as a permissible topic or thematic trope. In those cases where class-based social inequalities are raised beyond lifestyle statements, media coverage glosses over the social, structural, and systemic nature of class realities, preferring instead to evaluate individuals on the basis of personal merit. The broader context of opportunities and barriers that preclude meritocratic advancement regardless of individual effort is conveniently ignored.

In light of such media antipathy toward class as reality or discourses, many class-based issues are mocked or marginalized. To the extent that class is por-trayed in entertainment media (e.g., the popular sitcom *Frasier*), the focus is not differential access to means of production or control of key resources. Media depictions concentrate instead on themes that conflate class with vari-ations in family background, rather than on ownership and control of pro-ductive property. Or matters of personal taste or individual preferences prevail (Bullock, Wyche, and Williams 2001). Depictions also tend to ignore the societal and structural determinants of inequality and class positions, thus skipping over macro-level causes of inequality such as educational opportunity or underemployment because of economic shifts related to downsizing, relocating, outsourcing, and offshoring. In that a classed media gaze is highly selective in depicting classes and class relations in terms of who is entitled to what because of their class placement in society, the prospects for living together equitably are compromised.

This chapter endorses a belief that the elite mainstream media play an agenda-setting role in influencing people's perceptions and understanding of the world (Chomsky 1997). With increased media concentration and monopolistic control of information, pressure is mounting to expose who owns what, what kind of information they are circulating and why, and their impact in shaping public opinion and influencing people's behaviour (McChesney 1999). This chapter capitalizes on these assertions by analyzing the representational politics of media-class relations. The chapter demonstrates how corporate-driven images reflect, reinforce, and advance stereotypes that justify class relations in a capitalist Canada (Leistyna and Mollen 2008). The interests of those who own, control, or direct mainstream media are aimed at preserving the status quo by co-opting audiences into seeing like a corporatist media. The chapter also emphasizes how class and class differences are framed by a corporate mainstream media, with generally favourable coverage of the rich and powerful but increasingly less flattering coverage farther down the socio-economic ladder. That makes it critical to delve into what is omitted by this selective coverage and how these omissions perform a disservice in understanding social reality. Discussion of recent changes in depicting the working classes are postponed until Part 3, which includes a detailed study of those "testosterodriven" (Chozik 2010) unscripted TV shows in the vanguard of remasculinizing working-class males in blue-collar jobs.

A Corporate Media Gaze: Whose Interests?

The ownership and control of mass media are highly concentrated and controversial, with a small number of media outlets monopolizing both information and entertainment packages primarily for profit-making purposes. Unprecedented political and economic power over media content, production, and distribution resides in the hands of a few (Croteau and Hoynes 2003). About ten corporations dominate the global media market at present, with the Walt Disney Company being the largest, followed by Time Warner, News Corporation, and

Viacom, compared with nearly fifty firms twenty years ago (Kendall 2005). Just as five book publishers control nearly all the market (Ryan and Wentworth 1999), so too do five giant corporations in the United States control cable and over-the-air broadcasting, including the major TV news divisions NBC, ABC, CBS, Fox, and CNN. The film industry is so highly concentrated with the absorption of small firms that seven companies claim nearly 90 percent of the market. The recording industry is no less oligopolistic, with six global corporations controlling just over 80 percent of the market. As with film, these large corporations are buying up smaller companies, though conceding some degree of artistic licence to ensure "authenticity." The situation is no less monopolistic in Canada, where media concentration litters the mediascape: (1) for television, CBC, CTV, Global, and TVA; (2) for radio, Astral, Rogers, and Corus; (3) for film, Alliance Atlantis and Lions Gate; and (4) for print news, Canwest, Quebecor, and CTVglobemedia (see R. Armstrong 2010).

Why worry about the corporatization of media into profit-preening cash cows? Haven't media always been a business preoccupied with the bottom line? Besides, is big always bad? Media processes such as newscasting may even benefit from improved economies of scale and access to scarce resources. Yet criticism of corporate concentration abounds (J. Winter 2001), especially with big business' reliance on the formative power of media to legitimize its presence, logic, and practices as natural and normal (Leistyna 2009). None other than Microsoft – itself accused of monopolizing the PC industry in the 1990s to the detriment of competition and innovation – has warned of the dangers when dominant information technology companies such as Google or Facebook control their respective markets. In a letter about Google that it filed with the US Federal Communications Commission, Microsoft claimed: "When a single entity achieves dominance and thereby becomes a gatekeeper, there is an inherent risk that it may have both the incentive and ability to place its own interests above consumers' interests in access to a broad and diverse range of content, services, and viewpoints" (Did the Microsoft Case Change the World? 2011). Or, as Herman and Chomsky (1988) explain in their criticism of a corporate media gaze, powerful interests can fix the parameters of debate and discourage public opinion; government and the corporate elite will monopolize access to what eventually is defined as news; large advertisers can influence what issues will appear and how, or what will not appear; and media owners possess the power to determine whose voices will be heard or silenced. The next Insight takes its inspiration from *Manufacturing Consent,* a book by Ed Herman and Noam Chomsky (1988) that exposes the class-based realities implicit in a corporate media gaze.

News *as Corporate* Propaganda Lite: A Chomskyan/Herman Gaze

To say media messages are pivotal in moulding individual attitudes and shaping public discourses is trite yet true. Media messages constitute potent socializing agents of social control whose representations of reality are constructed and conventional rather than a mirrored reflection of the world out there. The constructedness of these conventions as natural and normal is largely hidden from view as part of a tacitly assumed media gaze but internalized as values, beliefs, and norms without people's awareness that their attitudes are changing. The seemingly apolitical dynamic of this socialization process both exposes and camouflages the hegemonic process by which dominant ideas are internalized through the pleasures of the media rather than explicit indoctrination (Kellner 1995). In drawing attention to some aspects of reality as desirable and acceptable, while other dimensions are excluded as inferior or irrelevant, media messages may be interpreted as discourses in defence of dominant ideology (Henry and Tator 2002).

The notion that media are ideologically loaded as propaganda "lite" (or soft propaganda) was famously articulated in 1988 when Ed Herman and Noam Chomsky published their landmark book, *Manufacturing Consent*. In indicting news media as little more than institutionalized propaganda in defence of an elite consensus, Herman and Chomsky proposed an explanatory framework to account for how the powerful can regulate the flow of news media messages without appearing to do so. This political economy analysis of news media performance exposes how mainstream news media represent instruments of power that mobilize consensus to advance state and corporate interests (see Klaehn 2002 and Klaehn and Mullen 2010 for additional analysis). In perpetuating an ideological hegemony, news filters are employed that exclude dissenting voices while ensuring the internalization of those norms that control the remaining voices. The agenda-setting news media are known to interlock with other corporate sectors, thus reinforcing their status as agents of thought control by consolidating the ideological underpinnings of a corporate-state nexus.

According to Herman and Chomsky, news is not really about news. More accurately, it's about circulating pre-existing packages of power in the service of ruling elites who orchestrate hegemonic consensus around a preferred agenda (see Hall 1978, 1980; Hier and Greenberg 2002; Klaehn 2002; J. Whyte et al. 2007). The filtering of reality to reflect government and commercial interests reinforces the news media's role in manufacturing consent. News media fix the premises of discourse by circumscribing the terms of acceptable debate while excluding the viability of alternative viewpoints, thus manufacturing consent and marginalizing dissent. For example, news media's complicity in supporting the Coalition's Iraq War is instructive (D. Miller 2004). In uncritically accepting government claims of a pending danger in the Middle East (the presence of weapons of mass destruction), Western news media might have colluded in legitimizing government actions while demonizing any dissent. (See the 2004 award-winning video *Control Room*.) This and other forms of the self-censorship process are accomplished through news filters that (1) suppress information at odds with powerful interests, (2) consolidate the status quo as normal and necessary, and (3) secure an elite bias and ruling-class interests (Herman 2003a, 2003b). These structural filters are so skilfully embedded within the newscasting process that alternative ways of seeing like the media are unthinkable (Herman and Chomsky 2002, 2).

Clearly, then, the root causes of manufacturing consent are structural (Herman 2003b). As an indoctrination under freedom involving an Orwellian use of coded language to confuse or cause discontent, elite news media function as a form of soft (or democratic) propaganda. To be sure, this propaganda "lite" model is neither infallible as an explanatory framework nor universally applicable as a generalizing directive; rather, it is a first approximation that may require modification if facts prove otherwise (Herman and Chomsky 2002). This model is not concerned with measuring media effects, but rather with the behaviour of and logic behind mainstream mass media (see also Klaehn and Mullin 2010). Lastly, the news media do not act in a monolithic collusion when manufacturing consent. News media sources are known to disagree with one another, criticize powerful interests for actions inimical to their best interests, expose government corruption and corporate greed, and bray against measures to restrict free speech and other rights. Yet disagreements are more apparent than real (Herman and Chomsky 2002), often reflecting dissensus within a tacitly accepted framework of assumptions that constitute an elite consensus (Herman 2003b). For example, news media outlets may differ in acknowledging the relevance of more or less government in regulating a market economy. But they never question the legitimacy of the so-called free market as the source of wealth creation – even if it involves exploitation, precarious or dangerous work, and joblessness because of offshoring or outsourcing. The illusion of diversity is fostered, in other words, but the underlying corporate agenda remains largely untouched, resulting in debates that are limited to squabbles over details (the conventions that refer to the rules) rather than substance (the rules upon which conventions are based) (Fleras 2007a).

Critical-Thinking Question

In what ways does Herman and Chomsky's model of mainstream news media reflect, reinforce, and advance corporate interests?

* * * * * * * * * *

The combination of media mergers, convergences, and cross-media ownership poses a problem for a democratic society (J. Winter 2001). The dangers of media concentration are fourfold: first, the blending of editorial with commercial content to create an undemocratic hybrid; second, the advancement of the interests of those who own or control the media to the exclusion of bystanders; third, the ratings-driven media's motivation of generating revenue rather than advancing a public service; and fourth, the narrowing range of media discourses thanks to fewer owners (Bagdikian 2004). But the abuse of monopolistic media power in stifling the spectrum of diverse voices cannot be underestimated. Canadians are betrayed by the privileging of profits over public good, consumerism over citizenship, propaganda over information, and passivity and fear over empowerment and activism (Nesbitt-Larking 2001; Taras 2001). They have also been misled into *seeing like the media* in identifying with a media-driven definition of the good life that many believe is environmentally unsound and socially unsustainable.

Representing Class: The Rich, the Poor, the Working, and the Professionals

The media are classed in their slanted portrayal of classes and class relations (Heider 2004; see also Croteau and Hoynes 2003; Alper and Leistyna 2006). This class bias significantly affects the framing of the rich and the poor and those in-between, partly because of cross-ownership or mutual interests, partly because of fears that unfavourable coverage might alienate advertising, and partly because of the routine nature of most news gathering in soliciting official (elite) sources (Fishman 1980). What appears as news and news sources is likely to rely on government and business representatives rather than labour officials or consumer advocates. Of course, the leaders of the corporate and political world who make decisions that impact people's lives are legitimate news sources (Bagdikian 2004). But working classes are excluded or appear in periodic fragments as human interest stories rather than in systematic or serious fashion. Very few articles feature the working conditions of those in precarious work or the economic problems confronting workers. When addressed, the articles are relatively short and near the back or under the fold, rarely discuss economic alternatives, and are unlikely to use union leaders or workers as primary sources of information, for fear of politicizing the discourses (Kollmeyer 2004). The end result? An unequal status quo is promoted and preserved when the organizational culture of the news media reflects, reinforces, and advances the privileges, power, and priorities of ruling elites.

Of the many social and cultural factors in society, mainstream media may be most influential in moulding personal consciousness and public discourses. After all, media messages don't mirror what is going on in an objective world external to us but actively contribute to influencing our knowledge of its mediated and constructed reality. This media monopoly – either deliberately or inadvertently – influences notions about class, class distinctions, and class relations. The fabulously wealthy have long been heroized by network shows *(Dynasty, Dallas, Falcon Crest, Lifestyles of the Rich and Famous)*, with plots often focusing on the foibles of characters too rich for their own good (Taylor 2007). Although rarely portrayed as a class, the wealthy tend to be depicted as fascinating if flawed, with a few bad apples thrown into the mix. Media are preoccupied with the power and privilege afforded by wealth, even if some members of the pampered classes are shown to behave badly – lying, cheating, and sleeping around – and perversely framed as guilty for any indiscretions till proven innocent (Jonas 2011). And yet, these individuals are so intoxicatingly attractive to the media gaze that they continue to hog the celebrity spotlight as eminently worthwhile, if somewhat flawed (Kendall 2005).

In short, TV networks appear to have a love-hate relationship with wealth and the wealthy: media love money but dislike the moneyed. But this generalization is precisely that: an approximation that can conceal or confuse. Hollywood's vision of class might have portrayed the rich and pampered as villains and vixens, in contrast to honest working folk as heroes battling "corrupt tycoons, arms dealers, environmental rapists, and Wall Street psychopaths" (B. Johnson 2011, 57). But the upper crust also embodied wise repositories of knowledge with impeccable tastes to boot, in contrast to television depictions of working-class men in blue-collar occupations – from Archie and Al to Homer and Raymond – who reinforced counterhegemonic images of blundering buffoons or the hopelessly baffled (Houpt 2010).

The fortunes of the middle classes are much admired albeit increasingly contested (Kendall 2005). Unlike the misfortunes foisted on working-class families, middle-class parents were often defined as intelligent, sensible, mature, calm, and affable. As superparents, they served as moral compasses for guiding their children along the right path (Butsch 2005). Admittedly, the portrayal of middle classes has lost some of its lustre. Once-positive frames are now increasingly displaced by more ambivalent representations as the middle class forfeits its cash and cachet. Middle-class males are no longer as perfect as they once were (e.g., Jim Anderson of *Fathers Knows Best* or Ward Cleaver of *Leave It to Beaver*). Nevertheless, although they are sometimes cast as emotionally confused or socially clueless – even immature to a degree (e.g., Tim Taylor of *Tool Time*) (ibid.) – they continue to be framed as relatively intelligent and successful in comparison with working-class personalities.

Television's fawning over the middle class – from situations to characters – reinforces their superiority and status as the assumed norm (Ohmann and Maher 2008). By contrast, the poor and working classes, including minority women and men, are ignored, caricatured, or mocked (Jhally and Lewis 1992). The poor are rendered largely invisible by mainstream media (Mantsios 2001). When portrayed, the poor and homeless are framed as statistical abstractions (Kendall 2005), as difficult to define (what exactly is poverty, or who precisely are the homeless?), or as outsiders whose moral turpitude leaves everything to be desired (Bullock, Wyche, and Williams 2001). Generally, the poor are aligned in a negative and stereotyped manner – as dependent, passive, responsible for their plight, and lacking both initiative and morality – precisely those features likely to land them on trash talk shows like *The Jerry Springer Show* or reality-based shows like *COPS* (Mantsios 2001). Welfare recipients are framed as people to dislike or disrespect (Bullock, Wyche, and Williams 2001), whereas single welfare mothers (but not single professional mothers) come across as irresponsible yet responsible for their plight. In addition, both the poor and poverty tend to be racialized – framed disproportionately as problems of visible (racialized) minorities (Baumann and Johnston 2008) – thus reinforcing yet another stereotype.

Unflattering representations of the poor reinforce their failure to abide by the principle of meritocracy – you can make it if you (really) try (Leistyna and Mollen 2008). But not all poor are similarly depicted. On the one hand are the deserving poor: the working poor, children, the elderly, and the once middle class but now the nouveau poor because of the economic recession (deMause 2009). These unfortunate individuals who experience poverty through no fault of their own are deserving of sympathy. They may even be framed as happy or cheerfully resigned to their fate, especially when poverty is romanticized as virtuous, noble, or happily coexistent with wealth (the equality of inequality). The end result may normalize elites as morally bankrupt, alongside a naturalizing of the poor as materially poor but spiritually rich (Baumann and Johnston 2008). On the other hand, however, are the so-called undeserving poor – from those unemployed of working age to those able-bodied poor on welfare – who deserve what they get (or don't get) because of laziness, stupidity, incompetence, or irresponsibility (e.g., too many out-of-wedlock babies) (Baumann and Johnston 2008; deMause 2009). This distinction between the deserving and undeserving reinforces the well-established ideological narrative that historically informed government and charitable programs (Kendall 2005).

Portrayals of the working-class on television are generally – but not altogether – negative (Mantsios 2001; Butsch 2003, 2005; Kendall 2005; Leistyna and Mollen 2008). Although the white working classes might have once been portrayed as the proverbial salt of the earth whose authenticity could be milked for laughs, a reversal of fortune can be detected (Manzoor 2008). Working-class males tend to be depicted as dull (even stupid), immature, and irresponsible (thus requiring supervision by their betters); as deviants who must lie and cheat to compensate for personal shortcomings; and as clowns on sitcoms like *Married with Children* (Butsch 2003). They are portrayed in an unflattering light – incompetent, trashy (loud, stupid, and stumbling), and prone to using violence as a problem-solving device (Leistyna and Mollen 2008; see also Vallis 2009). Blue-collar males fight with their partners, plot crazy schemes, act childishly, and are inferior to their obviously smarter children. Or they come across as "uncouth, beer-bellied loudmouths, slovenly in appearance, couch potatoes, wife beaters, racists, and supporters of right-wing causes" (Butsch 2005). Predictably, the families of these dysfunctional males incorporate a host of unhealthy dependencies, from drinking and gambling to philandering. Even changes in both society and TV land have not translated into representational improvements, especially among blue-collar workers in manufacturing jobs (Alliance for American Manufacturing 2011). An analysis of some three hundred domestic sitcoms over a thirty-year period – from *The Honeymooners* (1955-56) to *All in the Family* (1971-79), *Sanford and Son* (1972-77), *Roseanne* (1988-97), *Married with Children* (1987-97), and *The Simpsons* (1990-present) – confirms how the dominant image of the working-class male remains that of a stock character, from a lovable loser to a bumbling buffoon (Butsch 1992).

Nevertheless, media framing of working classes may be confusing, even contradictory. Not all working types are uniformly smeared: those in the "professional" working classes – police, nurses, and firefighters – tend to project positively on the screen, in contrast to the largely negative framing of blue-collar workers in assembly-line jobs as faceless, undeserving, eyesores, down on their luck, with only themselves to blame (Mantsios 2001). Such a range of representations complicates the defining of "working class," despite a tendency

to associate it with people in low-wage occupations, without college education, and struggling to get by economically (Working-Class Perspectives 2008).
Mixed messages proliferate: to one side are the more traditional images of male
masculinity. Privileging power as a determinant of masculinity ensured representations of heterosexual white males as "strong, tough, disciplined, athletic, in control of self and others, stoic, providers for dependents, confidently
secure and self-assured (but not cocky, boastful, or arrogant), virtuous at the
core, and not openly superior or oppressive to others" (Kusz 2008). To the
other side are stereotypes of the "working-class dummies," unmotivated and
unproductive shirkers going nowhere, living relics of an industrialized past
(Working-Class Perspectives 2008). More extreme references and associations
included males as inherently racist, sexist, and homophobic, with a worrying
predilection toward aggression yet equally inclined to ineptness and flaccidity.
To yet another side is a different narrative, namely, an infatuation with the dignity of blue-collar jobs as the physical labour and work ethic that keep the
country pumped (ibid.). From the assembly line to outdoor labour, working-
class jobs are shown to require a resilience and physically demanding toughness that few appreciate (Rose 2009). For example, football commentators
routinely praise football linemen as a "lunch bucket brigade" for "getting down
and dirty" without complaint (Carroll 2008).

A gender divide can also be discerned. The working class may be coded in
gendered terms, with a discernible division of labour and status between
women and men. Working wives tend toward middle-class professionalism
and careers rather than menial or blue-collar occupations, thus exempting
them from blue-collar indignities. Professional mothers are no longer social
pariahs because they are portrayed as choosing to raise kids, are well educated
and relatively affluent, and eager to assume the responsibilities of parenthood
(Haas 2006). But gender status is often inverted when working-class wives are
portrayed as more intelligent and sensible than the putative head of the household and prime breadwinner. Accordingly, as Butsch (1992) argues, working-
class males are demeaned and demasculinized by depicting them as childlike
while their wives act as surrogate authority figures. In short, the subordinate
status of largely emasculated working-class men is boxed in by images of consistently competent, capable, and responsible working-class wives on the one
hand and by predominantly positive images of middle-class males and professional females on the other hand (Cunningham 2004).

However mixed the messages, a backlash has emerged. Programs about the
working classes (from *Trailer Park Boys* to *King of the Hill*) may be filtered
through the prism of a middle-class lens that is disdainful, patronizing, and

mired in cliché (Janzen 2009). But a slew of television shows has emerged that portray working-class men as anything but blunderers. Indeed, they are depicted as heroic. This observation is consistent with Desmond's prescient observation (2009) of a resurgent working-class culture, manifest in the wearing of traditionally working-class garb or consuming working-class beer. According to Desmond (ibid., 71), "What we're experiencing in America today is a dual movement, the simultaneous erosion of blue-collar work and the adulation of blue-collar culture. Celebrating factory work renders the factory worker invisible." The proliferation of extreme sports on film and television constitutes one example of remasculinizing images of real men along heroic lines. But nowhere is this remasculinization of the blue-collar working class more evident than in television programs that not only celebrate these men's virtues and accomplishments but also allow them to tell their own stories as they work under intense pressure in unforgiving environments (Janzen 2009). Chapter 10 in Part 3 explores this new representational dynamic.

Putting into Perspective the Misrepresentational Basis of Media-Class Relations

This chapter has argued that media are classed in three ways: first, by virtue of ownership; second, by depicting classes and class relations through a corporate media gaze; and third, in defining what constitutes newsworthiness. As money-making ventures par excellence, mainstream media are classed by virtue of who owns production, controls distribution, and shapes the dynamics of consumerism. Ownership and control of profit-oriented commercial media by the rich and powerful may indirectly influence how social class is portrayed. In acknowledging that some people are more valuable than others, media content is slanted accordingly. Pampered portrayals of the rich and famous (and professionals) are offset by demeaning depictions of the working classes, labour unions, and unemployed or poor, especially minority women and men who tend to be located among the poor and working classes (Jhally and Lewis 1992). As might be expected in light of a corporate/managerial gaze, trade unions and unionized workers are usually ignored except in times of industrial crisis (Kupu Taea 2007). Or they are portrayed as corrupt or lazy and as overwhelmingly responsible for labour unrest that costs or inconveniences (Alper and Leistyna 2006). As a result, a focus on individual heroism as a way of "sticking it to the Man" reflects a pro-working-class sympathy that remains resolutely anti-labour.

To be sure, the framing of working classes is not absolute. Media messages are neither monolithic nor cast in stone and impervious to the world around them (Bagdikian 2004). The prevailing structural and socio-economic conditions of society may prove a factor in shaping coverage (Moller 2008). In a strong economy, individualistic (blame the victim) frames abound; in a weak economy, media may focus on blaming the system, including economic downturns or corporate decision making. The causes of worker impoverishment are depicted as beyond their control, the direct result of economic and political policies that deprive working classes of jobs, wages, and support through no fault of their own. No less interesting is how, in assigning blame, the media invert reality so that the middle and working classes tend to blame those below rather than the classes above for inequalities. Middle classes may blame unions for allegedly excessive demands, whereas working classes may blame immigrants or racialized workers for stealing jobs or padding welfare rolls. In short, what the media really perpetuate is a perverse social order, one in which power and privilege remain in the hands of a few, while the masses are distracted into savouring the symbolic rewards of working-class heroism.

In sum, the media are neither balanced and objective nor independent and neutral when it comes to covering class. Moreover, what the media don't say about classes is just as important as what they do say. There remain significant omissions in televised portrayals of working-class realities, despite the revival of a working-class hero (see Chapter 10), thus reinforcing the status of television as a fantasy medium more interested in conveying realism than reality. Put bluntly, coverage veers toward the superficial and selective. Little is done to contextualize deprivation or marginalization, let alone the suffering and sacrifices of workers – much less to explain its causes on structural grounds rather than in individualistic terms (Bullock, Wyche, and Williams 2001; Devereux 2006). The working classes are rarely given credit for doing the dirty, tiring, and demeaning work that undergirds an affluent society, yet they are too often blamed for societal problems over which they have little control. A media-centric focus on a blaming-the-victim mentality to justify inequities and individual failures in a so-called meritocracy implicates working-class individuals as personally responsible for their plight (Mantsios 2001). Rarely addressed is the notion that worker alienation is systemic and structural, the direct result of economic dynamics and political policies that deprive working classes of jobs, wages, and support. If true, and TV shows from *Survivor* to *American Idol* and *Dancing with the Stars* continually reinforce the myth of America as a land of endless opportunity where anyone can triumph over obstacles to become whatever they want to be (Drabinski 2009), pressure is mounting for rethinking the representational grounds of a media-class relationship that go beyond the misconceptions of a corporate media gaze.

6

Sexuality in the Media
The New Media Gays

Every year cities across Canada celebrate Pride Week. With its focus on the LGBTTIQQ2S community (lesbian, gay, bisexual, transgendered, transsexed, intersexual, queer, questioning, and two-spirited), the celebration commemorates an important dynamic. In the space of just over one generation, the Pride community has evolved from marginalization and harassment to a phenomenon that is no longer considered remarkable or even newsworthy (de Souza 2009).

Alongside this astonishing cultural shift in public and political acceptance is yet another transformation in visibilizing homosexuality. Once excluded from or vilified by mainstream media, gays and lesbians (and bisexuals and transsexuals to a lesser extent) constitute a prominent component of the twenty-first-century mediascape (Barnhurst 2007; GLAAD 2010). The news media are replete with stories about same-sex marriage; gays and lesbians are prominently featured as main characters in sitcoms and dramas and in talk and reality shows; and marketing is increasingly pitched to gay consumers as a legitimate market niche in a fragmented media world. Broadcast television featured more than a dozen gay, lesbian, and bisexual regular characters in prime-time series in the fall of 2008 (ranging from no new gay/bisexual characters on CBS to seven on ABC, albeit no lesbian characters), accounting for 2.6 percent of all regular roles (Associated Press 2008). The quality of representations is no less impressive: consider this statement by Kurt, the openly gay character on the popular series that celebrates all things different, *Glee:* "I'm proud to be different. It's the best thing about me" (cited in Doyle 2011). In films, the framing of homosexuals is no longer fixated on the flamboyant, hypersexual, and deviant. As proof, the much-hyped *Brokeback Mountain* not only received positive publicity for mainstreaming media gays, it also generated controversy when it failed to win an Oscar for Best Picture. Four years later, Sean Penn won the Best Actor Oscar for his portrayal of Harvey Milk, the first openly gay person to occupy a major public office in the United States.

To say we are living in an era best summed up by the expression "We're here, we're queer, get used to it" is surely an understatement. And yet, as many have noted, appearances are deceiving (Barnhurst 2007; Tatchell 2009). Seemingly emancipatory messages, narratives, and representations may well have the perverse function of reinforcing an assimilationist status quo by parlaying a sanitized version of homosexuality into the dominant discourse. Or, alternatively, by punishing homosexuality for daring to claim public space, the privileging of straightness is normalized. According to Fejes and Petrich (1993), of the thirty-two films between 1961 and 1976 that featured a major homosexual character, the homosexual character was killed in eighteen of them, committed suicide in thirteen, and lived in one – but only after being castrated. And although much progress has been made in the quality of representations, how to explain the deaths of leading characters in the highly acclaimed films *Brokeback Mountain* and *Milk?* Additional problems and paradoxes include intolerance through harmful stereotyping, reinforcing isolation at the expense of activism, trading equality for assimilation and straightstream acceptance, and converting a collective for gay radicalism into a chic commercial commodity for personal consumption.

Clearly, a paradox is in play. Too little visibility hardly advances the cause of media gays. Too much exposure is equally problematic when media coverage is framed and filtered through a heterocentric gaze. For mainstream media, the politics of representation involves the challenge of balancing a heterosexist media gaze with the realities and aspirations of homosexuals. Or to put a not-too-fine spin on it: *How to make media depictions of homosexuality more palatable to the heterosexist sensibilities of straight audiences and sometimes skittish advertisers, without infringing on the legitimacy, identities, and integrity of gays and lesbians?* To date, responses appear to have focused on a superficial inclusion through a process of normalization (Barnhurst 2007). That is, displays of homosexuality are legitimized when they are aligned along a heterocentric media gaze. For some gays and lesbians, however, a defiantly homocentric gaze is critical. A homocentric gaze ensures the identities, realities, and experiences of gays and lesbians are refracted through the prism of homocentricism rather than distorted by the heterocentric lens of a still straight media (Tatchell 2001, 2009).

That we live in an age of diversity and difference is beyond dispute. The combination of mediated technologies with a postmodernist context not only renders patterns of diversities more acceptable to a conventional media gaze, it also intensifies the politics of difference by challenging convention. Oppositional ideals and alternative ideas no longer convey an implied political threat, as they might have in the past. Once-marginalized groups are neither excluded nor vilified to the extent that they once were (Shugart 2003). This chapter explores the changing fortunes of a historically marginalized group whose relationship with the media has proven contradictory at best, destructive at worst, yet hopeful for the future. The chapter also demonstrates how recent improvements in framing media gays and lesbians – however overdue – are often less than what they seem.

Homosexuality in Media History: Gays under a Media Gaze

History offers a bleak picture of media-homosexual relations. Gays and lesbians were rendered invisible by mainstream media, framed as laughs for a comedic break, or demonized as the personification of evil to be dealt with accordingly. Sparse and selective representations (gays as effeminate; lesbians as unattractive man haters) tended toward their victimization as vixens or villains – little more than problem people with deep-seated pathologies (Raymond 2003). Rarely, if ever, were gays and lesbians portrayed as ordinary folk; rather, they were cast in roles that focused on their deviance (sexuality) as a threat to the social and moral order that had to be neutralized by ridicule or physical violence. The Case Study below on homosexuality in the movies explores this negativity.

— case study

Outing the Cinema: Engaging a Gay Gaze

> *In a hundred years of movies, homosexuality has only rarely been depicted on the screen. When it did appear, it was there as something to laugh at ... or something to pity ... or even something to fear. These were fleeting images, but they were unforgettable, and they left a lasting legacy. Hollywood, that greater maker of myths,*

> *taught straight people what to think about gay people ... and gay*
> *people what to think about themselves.* (The Celluloid Closet)

The "outing" of gays and lesbians within films is a work-in-progress. Homo-sexuality in films has undergone a major shift from the fringe to the mainstream, from persecution and suppression to emancipation, tolerance, and growing ac-ceptance (Davies 2008). Gays and lesbians increasingly occupy a common ground with straights on the silver screen. Open sexuality between men and between women is so routinely displayed in films as to barely cause a ripple. As proof, many look no further than the lavishly praised and widely acclaimed films *Milk* and *Brokeback Mountain,* in addition to *Capote, Transamerica,* and *Save Me.* Clearly, then, what once was taboo is increasingly routine, even *de rigueur.* Nevertheless, debate persists as to whether film should focus on specific and distinctive gay/ lesbian sensibility and lived experiences. Or, alternatively, should homosexuality be portrayed as part of the general human condition and accepted accordingly (Callow 2008)?

The degree of acceptance in recent years stands in sharp contrast to the past. A range of depictions, from ambivalence and awkwardness to hostility and hatred, characterized cinematic representations. Framing homosexuality as a problem proved debilitating: gays and lesbians tended to be ignored, vilified, or caricatur-ized by mainstream film representations (Croteau and Hoynes 2003). Early movie depictions of gays and lesbians reflected popular beliefs and assumptions about homosexuality, which in turn helped to shape both public perception and self-image. Film images have rarely flattered gays and lesbians, even if the content of this homophobia has varied over time. Gays were incorporated as comic relief or erotic titillation or to depict deviance, perversion, and decadence (Fejes and Petrich 1993). Even with the 1934 Production Code forbidding overt homosexuality in films, gays and lesbians continued to flourish in the movie industry but resorted to play-ing the "nod-nod, wink-wink" game to circumvent homophobic censors (Abrams 2008). With film censors routinely snipping out any signs of homosexuality, gay and lesbian audiences relied on double entendres ("friends of Dorothy") or telltale symbols to identify the sexuality of the portrayed character.

Initial film depictions (from 1900 to 1950) tended to portray gays as effeminate sissies. These limp-wristed portrayals were exemplified by the fussy sidekick or swishy interior decorator, both of whom provided comic relief or a humorous foil. By contrast, lesbians were stereotyped as sinister, butchy characters whose dor-mant desires caused them to prey upon innocent women. And gender-benders such

case study

as Marlene Dietrich or even Judy Garland simply generated more ambivalence for those seeking multiple interpretations. A new image emerged during the 1950s that persisted until recently. Gay bashing become the norm; the appearance of gays on the screen betrayed a morbid fascination with sexuality and danger. Gays were slotted into largely pathological roles, their subculture resonating with the language of menace, fear, or pity (Davies 2008). The film *Cruising* marked the high point for casting gays as psychopathic killers. They were depicted as secretive, alienated, and confused – tragically self-destructive loners whose sexual orientation was heavily implied but rarely explicitly portrayed. Sal Mineo's role in *Rebel without a Cause* is a prime example of this genre of gay as outcast, unhappy, sick, or evil. Not surprisingly, images of homosexuality as a dirty, shameful secret and homosexuals as emotional wrecks and tormented individuals left a lasting impression in framing perceptions about gays and lesbians (ibid.).

The 1980s saw major improvements in the cinematic treatment of gay and lesbian themes. Realistic themes and positive portrayals of homosexuality gathered momentum in response to societal changes that decriminalized homosexuality between consenting adults (Croteau and Hoynes 2003). Positive portrayals were not unheard of prior to this. For example, the 1970s film *Boys in the Band* portrayed four gay friends as reasonably normal and well adjusted. Once this threshold was crossed, depictions of homosexuality became increasingly normalized. Just as films involving straights have become more graphic and explicit, so too have homosexual portrayals, with gays and lesbians being depicted as complex humans with healthy sexual appetites. The 1971 British film *Sunday Bloody Sunday* dealt with homosexuality in a mature manner, suggesting that the British (more so than Americans) were more comfortable in positively casting homosexuality. With the 1982 film *Making Love,* audiences were exposed to an open if awkward relationship that involved displays of affection and tenderness, including deep kissing and bedroom scenes.

No film in recent memory has created as much buzz as *Brokeback Mountain.* Its claim to three Oscars, four Golden Globes, and four BAFTAs (the British equivalent of Oscars) attests to its popularity and critical appeal (Gauntlett 2008). For possibly the first time in movie history, a film with crossover appeal depicted the social realities of homosexuality through a predominantly gay gaze (Snider 2008). Prior to the critically acclaimed *Brokeback Mountain,* Clifton Snider notes, no major motion picture had focused attention with such frankness of a relationship like that displayed between Ennis and Jack – two unstereotypically gay and attractive young men who from the very beginning are unknowingly objects of each other's gay gaze. Audiences both straight and gay could appreciate the two men for who they were, not just what mainstream media wanted them to be. Homosexuality was dramatized as a largely inherent and immutable identity rather than some aberrant or elective agenda concocted by cultural elites. The impact on gay audiences was overwhelming: as Snider (ibid., 54) writes in extolling a gay gaze, "To look at images that reflect our 'inner selves' is a powerful and profound experience, all the more so for its rarity among gay male viewers" (see also Davies 2008 for unstinting praise).

Similar accolades attended Gus Van Sant's film *Milk,* with its focus on Harvey Milk (played by Sean Penn), who spearheaded a revolution in the struggle for gay rights. In anointing it the "gayest motion picture ever made," Brian Juergens (2008) praises the landmark film as an affecting testament to the courage and complexity of gay men and women at a defining point in gay rights history. Unlike earlier films, which featured coming-out stories or closeted romances, Zant/*Milk* took gay relationships for granted, almost to the point of relegating homosexuality to the background at times, while focusing on the political movement that ignited the cultural wars (Ledger 2008). At the same time, audiences are taken into the world of gay men in unprecedented ways. The screen is rarely without a gay character. Nevertheless, conversations, debates, and activities are not just about discrimination and protest marches; nor are they entirely about being gay. Realities revolve around gay men living their lives – laughing, lounging, loving, squabbling, working, and supporting one another. In other words, Harvey and his friends are neither purely perfect nor entirely blemished, but human. They don't want to hurt anyone; they just want what is fair. Or as Juergens (2008) describes the film, "This isn't about a gay man struggling to come to terms with himself, it's about a gay man struggling to get the world to come to terms with him. That alone makes it like no other."

What can we conclude? Are gays and lesbians truly out of the cinema closet? Or are there still some celluloid skeletons rattling about? Is greater visibility the equivalent of assimilation into a conformist society, or should it be equated with inclusiveness in a transformative society (Tatchell 2009)? What to make of the current fascination with lesbian chic or a gay aesthetic: Is it a sign of fundamental change or of flirting with the trendy and fashionable? How to assess films like Sacha Baron Cohen's *Borat* and *Bruno,* with their outrageously raw portrayals of gay sexuality (Tatchell 2009)? Both films mercilessly ridicule knuckle-dragging homophobes yet also reinforce crude gay stereotypes by a sex obsessed "cockaholic" (ibid.) who uses and abuses everyone around him. By mocking prejudice as a shallow and bitchy queen, does Cohen reinforce or undermine homophobia?

case study

Improvements are evident. Compared with the invisibility of a generation ago, gays and lesbians are now foregrounded as people with lives and loves. They are increasingly portrayed as multi-faceted and emotionally complex individuals rather than as one-dimensional cardboard characters – especially in those media that do not have to pander to mainstream tastes. For example, the film *Aimee and Jaguar* (released in 1999-2000) revolves around a group of women during the Second World War in Berlin in a variety of poses and activities – from dance parties to espionage – with lesbianism but one component that complements their wit, strength of character, and generally complex personas. Lilly (Aimee) and Felice (Jaguar) are never reduced to caricatures; their lived experiences are always open to candid displays of frank emotions, with a focus on survival. They are genuinely in love and desperate for happiness at a time of turmoil (Bendery 2009).

Yet this new visibility does not necessarily represent a significant challenge to entrenched definitions of what is normal or natural. Too often homosexuality is framed as remarkable for its differences from the norm of heterosexuality. Alternatively, images are lifted out of the context of gay and lesbian life and offered up as exemplary of mainstream values, depoliticized, and devoid of political or historical context (Stone 2001). As independent film producer Jan Oxenberg concluded, gender bending still comes with a cost. The gay hero perishes – often as a tragic and misunderstood figure whose death is redemptive (consider the film *Boys Don't Cry*). Even in *Brokeback Mountain,* mixed messages prevail: both males marry and have families, yet one of the gay males dies. And, of course, Harvey Milk is assassinated. It remains to be seen when Hollywood will be ready to accept a gay who is normal and lives to celebrate his homosexuality (but see the films *Save Me* or *Antartica*). Finally, in a classic case of making more palatable the once unthinkable, depictions of homosexuality are often stripped of their transformative powers. Critics may have praised *Brokeback Mountain* for its universality, with its focus on the universal emotions of love, lust, and loss (Snider 2008), but in doing so they confirmed the adage that deep diversities must be scrubbed clean of their naughty bits to ensure audience appeal.

In other words, the greater visibility of gays and lesbians is not the same as social acceptability or greater authenticity. Yes, there is more visibility for attractive (both physically and morally) gay and lesbian characters, but rarely are they shown as politicized or through overtly sexualized gazes that challenge homophobia or racism (Hubert 1999). Media have selectively co-opted images of gays and lesbians by repackaging them for mass consumption and acceptance by the mainstream (both audiences and advertisers). The end result is a sanitized and unidimensional message that not only trivializes their concerns, differences, and individuality but also marginalizes their realities to placate mainstream audiences. Or, as Stone (2001, 62) reminds us, "Sophisticated marketing has created an anti-political trend by selling passivity as social currency, assimilation as success, and superficiality as fashion." With media primed to commodify all cultural forms, including homosexuality, there is a danger of co-optation replacing denial and/or death as the preferred image.

Critical-Thinking Questions

In depicting homosexuality on the big screen, how does a gay gaze differ from a mainstream (or straight) gaze? What are the dangers associated with greater media acceptability of homosexuality in movies if refracted through the prism of a mainstream media gaze?

* * * * * * * * * *

Couched in Compromise: Normalizing Homosexuality?

The emergence of a gay and lesbian aesthetic is challenging the demeaning discourses of the past. Gays and lesbians are increasingly positioned as a visibly chic component of the mediascape, with lives and life chances not unlike those in straight society. Possibly in response to Bill Clinton's open courting of the gay vote in 1992, major news organizations began covering queer political issues more regularly and positively (Barnhurst 2007). No less impressive is the growing visibility of homosexuality in television – keeping in mind that (1) the first gay male lead in prime TV did not appear until 1998-99 with *Will & Grace* (Hart 2000), and (2) it wasn't until May 2000, on the teen soap opera *Dawson's Creek,* that the first male-to-male romantic kiss was featured in American prime-time programming (Gauntlett 2008). In contrast to the commotion created by Ellen DeGeneres, who announced her sexuality on *Oprah* in 1997 and again later in her sitcom series (cancelled shortly afterward), the incorporation of gays and lesbians into TV programming at present barely elicits a peep. TV programs from *Queer Eye* to *The L Word* are more inclined to make homosexuality visible and risqué (within limits) (ibid. 2008) – although gayness is often reduced to a commodity that services heteronormativity while depoliticizing queerness (Berila and Choudhuri 2005).

The numbers are informative. According to David Wyatt (2008), an analysis of television programs in Canada, the United States, Australia, and the United Kingdom incorporating gay, lesbian, and bisexual characters reveals significant increases in the quantity of coverage: in the 1960s, there was one gay character; that number increased to 58 in the 1970s, 89 in the 1980s, 337 in the 1990s, and 475 between 2000 and 2007. In its fourth annual review of fifteen US networks for the representation of gay characters, GLAAD (2010) awarded MTV an excellent rating for content reflecting the lives of lesbians, gays, bisexual, and transgendered (LGBT) people (42 percent of its 208 hours of prime-time programming included such characters), followed by ABC, with 26 percent of its prime-time programming including LGBT impressions. At the other end, CBS, with 7 percent, earned a failing grade. Much of this quantitative shift can be attributed to economics. Gays and lesbians are increasingly profiled positively because of their command of hefty disposable incomes and lavish spending styles (Fleras 2003). These indicators translate into a desired advertising demographic, with a corresponding reluctance to alienate gays and lesbians.

And yet visibility in television media creates its own set of contradictions (Barnhurst 2007). Put bluntly, visibility does not guarantee legitimacy (Shugart 2003). In making gays and lesbians more palatable for audiences and advertisers, the question of authenticity arises: What qualities of gay identity render it both acceptable and popular for the heteronormative sensibilities of a mainstream audience? To date, homosexuality is framed in ways that not only privilege male heterosexuality but also extend its privilege. For example, the pairing of a gay male with a heterosexual female creates a heterocentric whitewashing that legitimizes homosexuality. Shows like *Will & Grace* make homosexuality safe for a mainstream audience, thanks to their status as standard sitcom fare with quirky behaviour, double entendres, silly misunderstandings, and embarrassing peccadilloes. Scenes involving explicit homosexuality tend to be sterilized to avoid offending audiences and advertisers (Barnhurst 2007). In the German film *Light Gradient,* for instance, there is full-frontal male nudity involving two young men when showering, but when the sex scenes start, the camera recoils by panning over to rustling treetops or to farm animals.

The end result is a homosexuality that is (1) desexualized by never depicting gays and lesbians as romantic or passionate, (2) framed as an unrealistic mode of being or a temporary interruption in the march toward heterosexuality (Snider 2008), (3) rendered devoid of gay social and political contexts, and (4) depoliticized to the level of the personal and the interpersonal rather than contesting political contexts. A heterocentric characterization of sexual roles and relations fails to address the complexities of human sexuality and, further, imposes fairly rigid notions of what constitutes acceptable and expected behaviour for gays and lesbians. For example, portrayals of excessively feminized males and masculinized females may generate stereotypes that elicit public ridicule. These gender-bending patterns are normally associated with gays (gay men as effeminate) and lesbians (as butch) then embodied in media expressions that often provide a primary and preliminary source of information about homosexuality. And although broader representations can help to demystify homosexuality, repeated portrayal of gay and lesbian stereotypes that tend to refract homosexual realities, experiences, and identities through the prism of a straight media gaze not only distorts gay/lesbian realities but also misleads the general public.

The conclusion seems inescapable: sympathetic portrayals and greater visibility do not necessarily yield more complexity or less stereotyping. To the contrary, by packaging homosexuality as palatable for the straightstream – for example, by presenting lesbians as conventionally attractive women whose attractiveness softens any defiance of mainstream society – homophobia is reinvented and legitimized by/for/around a more inclusive heteronormativity (norms that naturalize the superiority of heterosexuality) (Shugart 2003). Nor does the solution lie in a commitment to equality or law reform that intends or has the effect of assimilation into a heterosexist consensus. According to Peter Tatchell of OutRage!, a queer liberation group, equal rights for gays and lesbians invariably means parity on straight terms, within a pre-existing framework of media rules and messages devised by, for, and about a heterosexual majority. Instead of a co-optation by consensus (hegemony), what is proposed is a reaffirmation of those queer politics that challenge, emancipate, and transform. Rather than an assimilationist equality, what is advocated is a commitment that celebrates the uniqueness of (homo)sexuality as different yet equal; as socially constructed and as normal as heterosexuality; and as requiring a media space between separation and assimilation both to ensure sexual liberation and to acknowledge the societal contribution of gays and lesbians (Tatchell 2001).

Admittedly, times have changed with respect to expressions of homophobia. As Shugart (2003, 70) writes, while "blatant negative stereotypes of the past no longer consistently occupy daily media content, the more subtle images of heterosexually defined homosexuality are equally damaging to affirmative gay and lesbian identity and politics." This hetero-media whitewashing of homosexuality into something palatable serves to remind us that the politics of sexuality continue to polarize (Barnhurst 2007). It should also serve as a warning of the power of mainstream media to define what counts as difference and which differences count, in the hopes of ensuring that everyone is different in the same way.

7

Engaging Age(ism)
Young Adults, Older Adults

To say we live in interesting times may be clichéd. But like many of its ilk, this cliché yields insights into the paradoxes that prop up contemporary social life. Consider the following paradox: Western societies seemingly worship on the altar of youthfulness as the preferred cultural ideal yet ostensibly detest the young as quintessentially problem people (Barnhurst 2007). Young people (used in the broader sense to incorporate those from tweens to thirty-somethings) are revered as attractive, trendy, energetic, knowledgeable, and a major driving force in advancing societal prosperity and well-being. A cult of youth focuses on the young as vibrant, happy, and beautiful, in contrast to the old, who are perceived as tired, unattractive, and grim (McMullin 2010). Yet society appears to have an equally powerful disdain for youth. They are widely reviled as pampered, spoiled, full of themselves, and wallowing in self-entitlement, as well as prone to violence, crime, and anti-social behaviour in general. This ambivalence toward youth as desirable yet detested is best captured in a fractured howler: "Youth is wasted on the young."

Mainstream media are no less paradoxical when representing youth − revered yet reviled. Youth are deemed to be the preferred demographic; accordingly, media content is designed, organized, and circulated to pander and promote. Advertising in particular is aimed at a youth demographic, despite that older Canadians are more financially disposed to buy and consume. Movies are routinely produced with a youth demographic in mind, for example, coming-of-age stories and romantic comedies for young women; the gross or the gory for young men. In television, it seems ages ago that "parents knew best"; not surprisingly, the young and the precocious now rule the family roost and beyond. Even the news media have hopped aboard this youth band-wagon. In hopes of surviving the challenges of social media and mobile ICTs (information and communication technologies), news media are trolling for a more youthful demographic through more youth-friendly formats and stories.

Nevertheless, the same media that extol the virtues of youthhood display a degree of ambivalence and mistrust that borders on hostility. Judging by news media depictions of youth – especially those marginalized by race, gender, poverty, immigrant status, sexuality, dis/ability, or aboriginality – young people are routinely framed as deviant, problematic, and perpetually in crisis. Young people and teenagers are framed in the negative context of criminality and other risky behaviours rather than in positive contexts related to productive work or community volunteering (Media Monitor 2000). They are portrayed as more problematic than generations in the past because of allegedly higher violence levels (acting like animals), more intense levels of substance abuse, and lower levels of academic achievement (Males 1999; YouthNet 2008). Distorted pictures of youth include images of teenagers who think only about themselves; angry young (black) males immersed in a culture of drugs and guns; out-of-control students in unsafe schools; students sleepwalking (or cheating their way) through postsecondary education; provocatively dressed young women, including teen mothers ("children having children"); young girls as fashion preoccupied and Bieber-obsessed; and me-media youth who disrespect hard work or the value of a dollar (D. Kelly 2006; McKnight Foundation 2008).

To be sure, as the article "Media and Youth" points out, the framing of youth by media can take different vantage points, including debate over what to include (children, teenagers, young adults?), in addition to gender and racialized differences. The advertising media frame youth as potential consumers with hefty disposable incomes. Broadcasters prefer framing youth in a negative light – as threats or as criminals (especially minority youth). Media researchers focus on youth in victim frames. Exposure to media, they argue, culminates in a host of negative attributes and behaviours, with the result that youth need protection from media influences. Differences of emphasis notwithstanding, media framing of youth reinforces their status as problem people in terms of the challenges they pose to media or to society.

By contrast, stories of ordinary youth and positive youth accomplishments receive scant media attention. In acknowledging that "good kids" lack a compelling newsworthiness, an editorial writer for the *Vancouver Sun* (2004, quoted in D. Kelly 2006, 29; see also *Maclean's* 2009) explained why news media dwell on "bad kids'" stories despite a decline in risky behaviour among youth: "The news is about conflict and conflict requires that people break the rules, so we hear, perhaps too often, about teenagers being killed in car accidents, through bullying, or through drug abuse. The news is also about what's new, what's exceptional, and the survey confirms that troubled kids are the exception." And good intentions may not be enough to finesse the frame game. Even if reporters are receptive to marginalized discourses of success, their messages get lost because they have little control over story placement, layout, tone, and spin/angle (D. Kelly 2006). Not surprisingly, youth success stories do little to neutralize the barrage of relentlessly negative narratives that demonize young people as fundamentally anti-social. The fact that youth have minimal pull with the media compounds the marginalization and stigmatizing. However unfortunate, they are not the only demographic susceptible to the bias of ageism, as demonstrated in this Insight on older adults.

---

insight

Invisibilizing Older Adults: Problematizing Their Presence

> *How this country thinks of older people, relates to older people, and how older people think of themselves ... is directly affected by what is put on television. (Jeffrey Sagansky, former CBC entertainment president, 1993, quoted in Donlon, Ashman, and Levy 2005, 307)*

Youth are not the only demographic to be negatively singled out and stigmatized by the media. Although youth are idolized yet deplored, and youthfulness envied yet dismissed, the media appear reluctant to admit the presence of older adults other than as an alien, segregated, and even worthless demographic (Lee, Carpenter, and Meyers 2006; Morgenson 2010). Or, as headlines like to remind us over and again, older adults as senior citizens represent a demographic time bomb (or tsunami, etc.) whose growing numbers and health care costs are likely to bankrupt Canada (Vieira 2011). To be sure, progressive images in television series (e.g., *The Golden Girls, Murder She Wrote, As Time Goes By*) allow older adults to appear as powerful, affluent, active, admired, and sexy (especially older men [Rozanova 2006]). Magazines and advertising aimed at older adults invariably produce positive images (Lumme-Sandt 2011). And films can also positively portray older adults, albeit in a stubborn and curmudgeonly way, including Clint Eastwood in *Gran Torino* (2008) and Hal Holbrooks's acclaimed role in *That Evening Sun* (2009). But nega-tive images of older adults in print, on television, or on the big screen are the rule rather than the exception (Ramirez 2002). Often older adults are boxed into frames that say "difficult, stubborn, eccentric, and foolish" (providing comic relief because of incompetence or incontinence) (McGuire 2008). Paradoxically, both positive and negative portrayals of older adults may be ageist. By advancing normative stan-dards of how seniors should act, mainstream media tend to marginalize those who fail to meet these ideals, while downplaying the institutional discrimination and segregation that curtails such attainment (Rozanova 2006). A soft-focus vision of fun time with adoring grandchildren may also conceal the realities of loss – loss of health, loss of income, loss of vitality, loss of family and friends, and loss of dig-nity (Cann and Dean 2009).

In a world that is rapidly changing because of mind-boggling innovations in the information and technology sector, the wisdom of the aged is increasingly dis-counted. Compounding this disadvantage is their loss of status: older Canadians do not participate in those productive roles (from working to raising a family) that garner value in modern society (McMullin 2010). As a niche market, older Canadians are hardly worth pursuing with any degree of commitment, despite possessing substantial purchasing power. Even when products or services could be profitably marketed toward the older age bracket – for example, pharmaceuticals – the fear of being tainted as an old people's product is tantamount to a commercial death wish (notice how GM no longer manufactures the *Olds*mobile). Television and film are reluctant to incorporate mature themes and content for fear of alienating the profit-able youth demographic. Theatre managers may be even more loath to engage a demographic unlikely to mill about the concession stand. Not surprisingly, empha-sis is on those films with a proven capacity to attract those who think nothing of dropping ten bucks on a box of popcorn and a pop (keep in mind that theatre profits are largely driven by concessionary sales).

Ageism can be defined as the tendency of one age group to frame another age group along negative lines while preferring to define itself as the norm and stan-dard that defines and evaluates. It consists of a tendency to see and interpret real-ity from the perspective of a certain age group (usually directed by youth at the old, but the reverse is true as well) as normal and superior, while other age group per-spectives are ignored or dismissed. In most cases, ageism involves a perception of older people as stereotypes (passive, needy, and frail) and as second-class citizens who do not deserve the same amount of attention, respect, or resources available to the general population; who lack capabilities and even cease to be persons; and who are subject to age-related discrimination (Gray Panthers 1995). To no one's surprise, ageism may be the most common form of discrimination (according to a survey in the United Kingdom involving two thousand adults, 23 percent of the population experiences ageist discrimination compared with 7.5 percent of the population for sexism, 7 percent for racism, and 6 percent for disability [Age Concern 2007]). Compounding this injustice are fears that, unlike racism or sexism, ageism and ageist stereotypes are tolerated by society (Donlon, Ashman, and Levy 2005; Age UK 2011). Age-centrism, with its tendency to see and interpret reality from the perspective of a certain age group (usually directed by youth at the old, but the reverse is true as well), prevails as normal and superior, and other age group perspectives are ignored or dismissed. Worse still, media ageism that demeans youthfulness while demeaning the old can have devastating consequences, ranging from deteriorating mental health and aborted identity development (Ramirez 2002; Donlon, Ashman, and Levy 2005) to elder abuse and health care discrimination (International Longevity Center 2006). As Age UK (2011) concludes in its report on challenging age discrimination:

> As well as strong laws [to ensure that older people have access to goods and services in the private and public sector] we need a change in attitudes. It is time to stop treating older people as second class citizens. We need to look beyond someone's age at their individual strengths and strive for a society which enables older people to remain active and independent.

Can anyone be startled by criticism of media mistreatment of older adults? What kind of message is conveyed about aging by (1) Walmart's decision to market anti-aging creams to tweens between the ages of eight and twelve, (2) headlines that routinely pounce on the looming demographic tsunami and economic burdens posed by a greying population, and (3) stereotypes that tend to equate being old with two characters lampooned on *The Simpsons:* Grandpa Simpson (useless, demented, drooling) and Mr. Burns (creepy, mean-spirited, hateful) (Cann and Dean 2009). Mass longevity may be praised as an indicator of Canada's standard of living, but those who dare to live long are framed as a fiscal calamity because of spiralling health care costs (Roszak 2010). Worse still from a media perspective, society is being inundated with the wrong people – people who have little interest in innovation or the next hot thing on the market. Roszak (ibid., 7) pokes fun at the fears of marketers when he writes, "How can we afford all these people? How are we going to sell them i-phones, HDTV, flashy clothes, news movies, and next American icon?"

Depictions of this demographic leave much to be desired in a media world that simultaneously worships on the alter of youth (at least in advertising, filmmaking, and TV programming) yet demonizes the young as troublesome constituents (in newscasting). Unlike coverage of children who are abducted or are abused by parents or guardians, older adults rarely receive the same sympathetic media treatment (Cann and Dean 2009). Media visibility remains a problem: Hollywood actors bemoan the paucity of stories and characters involving the old (especially older women), culminating in their gradual disappearance from both the public eye and media gaze (McGuire 2008). Admittedly, presence is not always a panacea: consider how Disney's stockpile of villains – from wicked stepmothers to grumpy dwarfs to crazy mad hatters – expose children to negative (even scary) images of older adults (Robinson et al. 2007). Or as was sharply articulated to the US Senate Subcommittee on Aging by Doris Roberts, seventy-one, who plays the role of the mother in the hit TV series *Everyone Loves Raymond,* "When not dismissed as irrelevant, we are portrayed as dependent, helpless, unproductive, and demanding, rather than as deserving" (Ramirez 2002). In other words, there is much to commend in Cann and Dean's insightful quip (2009, 126): "The world wants longevity, but it does not want old age."

Critical-Thinking Questions

Both youth and older adults appear to be victimized by negative media coverage. For youth, the news media are the problem; for older adults, advertising appears the culprit. Why and how is this the case?

* * * * * * * * * * *

Youth advocates lament the bleak and unrealistic framing of youth in media (McKnight Foundation 2008). In an industry propelled by power or problems as newsworthy, young people are rarely covered, and when they are, coverage is negatively framed around crime and violence. Consider a study that examined 1,065 editions of newspapers and 354 television newscasts for topics related to young people. The study found that crime and violence accounted for about one-half of the news coverage. Only about one-quarter included any trend or background information (Kunkel et al. 2002). Other studies tend to support these figures. For example, according to Lori Dorfman (2000), director of the Berkeley Media Studies Group, a study of three major Californian papers found that a full 25 percent of youth coverage is devoted to violence-related themes. An unbalanced picture of youth – especially of minority youth – results in popular understandings of race and crime that influence media coverage, and vice versa. As noted by Vappu Tyyskä (2009, 10),

> There is an unfortunate tendency in the media ... either to vilify youth, or to blame them and/or their families for their plight. The voices of young people themselves are frequently missing. Where youthful voices are presented, they are used to show the lack of concern by adolescents and people in their twenties with their communities, witness their passivity in politics, and their preoccupation with the trivial pursuits presented by the leisure industry. Where young people are associated with action, this tends to be negative. The media fuel this with negative and slanted coverage of youth crime, street youth, youth gangs, and other delinquent or criminal forms of activity, giving the impression of young people running amok in their homes, schools, on the streets, and in our communities. The actions of youths that get attention are portrayed as dangerous and destructive, exemplified in the ongoing reports of "raves," "rap," and "gangsta" music and youth cultural phenomena, or about the large youth-driven demonstrations against the power of global corporations, and the international financial machinery. The views presented in the media both shape and reflect generally accepted public opinions.

In short, media portrayals matter because most Canadians source much of their information about crime, criminality, and control from the media (see McKnight Foundation 2008). Insofar as media coverage of criminal activity often exaggerates the opposite of what happens most frequently in reality (Perlmutter 2000; Surette 2004), its role in exacerbating intergenerational tensions is hardly surprising. Similarly, media play a pivotal role in influencing public awareness of youth-related issues. The consequences of conflating youth with crime (particularly minority crime) are costly: public support for punitive public policies escalates because of the culture of fear engendered by constant emphasis on negative stories (Sveinsson 2008; YouthNet 2008). Conflating crime with youth also reinforces the perception of youth as a liability rather than an asset. After all, if audiences have little contact with young people except through the media, they are likely to perceive youths as threats or problems. And yet there are few alternative representations of youth or positive achievements to offset the negativity (Sveinsson 2008).

Clearly, then, media images of youth reflect a raft of ideological interests except those of the young. Youth are not only associated with social problems, but also blamed for the costs associated with solutions (Males 1999). They may be scapegoated for the ills of society, although there is little evidence for blaming those who are not responsible for conditions largely beyond their control. Common portraits of youth are based on adult anxieties and mainstream panics about the potential risks that young people may encounter or the damage they may inflict on society (Cushion 2004). With such media negativity, is it any wonder that youth are increasingly abandoning the unfriendly gazes of mainstream news media in favour of alternative sources?

part 3

The (Mis)Representational Processes:
Case Studies in Seeing Like the Media

* * * * * * * * * *

A moment's reflection should reveal the obvious: our knowledge of the world is constructed by media who are, themselves, constructed. In the absence of personal experience for peering into social reality, mainstream media provide a preliminary and often primary point of contact with the what, why, and how. Each of us internalizes media messages in terms of how (1) we see and think about ourselves (and how we *think* others see and think of us), (2) we experience the world around us, and (3) we should relate to others. As a result, the world we inhabit is a "mediated" one; that is, in a mind-dependent world, there is no such thing as objective reality or absolute truth (or at least no humanly known way of ascertaining the objective or absolute). Only discourses of reality exist, since nothing can be known except as a representation consisting of narratives, symbols, and images. In short, no one should discount the pervasiveness and persuasiveness of media in constructing and conveying these representational frames within contexts of power and domination.

But Part 2 has made it abundantly clear: mainstream media continue to (mis)inform and mislead because of prevailing media gazes that are embedded in dominance. Messages about what is acceptable or who is desirable in terms of race, gender, class, age, and sexuality are deeply entrenched in media (mis)representations of racialized minorities, women, working classes and the poor, youth and the elderly, and gays and lesbians. In other words, media representations are gendered, raced, classed, and sexualized, yet they conceal their underlying logic and production values to convey the appearance of neutrality or objectivity. Audiences are subsequently absorbed into the media gaze without their awareness of the indoctrination process. Not surprisingly, media-constructed images of diversities and difference – although constructions in their own right – eventually evolve into lived-in realities for racialized minorities.

To be sure, some media processes, such as advertising, have vastly improved the quality of diversity coverage, with once-marginalized minorities positively portrayed or aggressively pursued as consumers – even if the transformation is propelled by a business model instead of social justice concerns. Although women continue to experience mixed media messages, conventional notions of beauty and femininity are increasingly contested. From commercials to TV programming, a broader range of images helps to offset the stereotypical or demeaning, including representations of women in advertising or working-class men in muscular occupations. And yet other media messages about the less privileged or historically disadvantaged are seemingly stuck in a rut:

- Mainstream news media continue to frame immigrants and refugee minorities as troublesome constituents whose activities pose costs or create inconvenience, in part because Canada's immigration program, but especially its refugee determination system, is also framed as broken and in need of a major overhaul.
- Depictions of women in advertising remain mired in double standards. More inclusive messages of physical beauty are offset by equally menacing messages exhorting women to buy and consume, if only to stave off the essential cultural nightmare of a consumerist society – the fear of failure, the envy of success.
- Portrayals of working-class males continue to be couched in compromise – positive narratives alongside negative coverage – despite the proliferation of reality-based programming that extols the manliness of working-class males in risky blue-collar jobs.
- Religions in general, and religious minorities in particular, are disparaged by predominantly secular media gazes, with faith-based groups often linked to security concerns or value incompatibilities.

To untangle these paradoxes in representation, Part 3 explores the misrepresentational process by way of case studies on seeing like the media. Chapter 8 looks at the relationship between newscasting and immigration. This chapter demonstrates how mainstream news media continue to misrepresent immigrants and refugees by racializing newscasting through coverage that is systemically biasing because of excessive negativity. Chapter 9 explores the contested and evolving relationship between women and advertising. Images of women in advertising may have left much to be desired in terms of accuracy or balance. But seemingly more positive developments can be discerned, most notably Dove's Campaign for Real Beauty, in challenging (or so it seems) the rigidly defined representations of beauty in advertising. Chapter 10 addresses recent depictions of working men and their workplaces. A slew of "testostero-driven" reality-based shows on speciality cable channels romanticize the work of men in risky occupations, in the process remasculinizing the representation of blue-collar guys yet concealing the dangerous realities of their lived experiences. Chapter 11 looks at how media gazes frame religion in general, and Islam and Muslims in particular. Damaging in its own right are the effects of negatively framing Islam and Muslims as a religion and a people whose beliefs are perceived as contrary to a secular Canada. This misrepresentation also compromises the very ideals Canadians aspire to – tolerance, equality, and inclusion.

Racializing Immigrants/Refugees
News Framing the Other Within

Canada can be defined as an immigration society. In the parlance of sociologists, four normative criteria define an immigration society: (1) policies and programs exist to regulate the flow of immigrants into society, (2) immigrants are seen as positive contributors toward nation building, (3) immigrants are entitled to permanent residence through attainment of citizenship, and (4) programs are in place to facilitate immigrants' settlement and integration. On the basis of these criteria, Canada qualifies as an immigration society: specific rules are in place to control the intake of approximately 250,000 immigrants per year (the average annual intake over the past fifteen years); immigrants are generally perceived as making an economic and cultural contribution to Canada; they are expected to become citizens (about 85 percent of all immigrants take up citizenship); and programs under the multiculturalism umbrella are designed to improve immigrants' chances of settling down, fitting in, and moving up (Fleras 2010).

Canada is also widely acclaimed as a multicultural society. As a multicultural society, it abides by the principles of multiculturalism as grounds for living together differently, while taking steps to ensure that differences don't get in the way of living together equitably (Fleras 2009). This commitment to multiculturalism as principle and practice can be operationalized at different levels of meaning:

1   Canada is multicultural in terms of demographic fact. According to 2006 Census data, nearly 20 percent of Canada's population is foreign-born (second highest in the world after Australia, at 22 percent), with just over 16 percent identifying as visible minorities, and just under 4 percent identifying as Aboriginal. This multicultural diversity is expected to expand in the foreseeable future, in part because of a robust immigration pattern and high Aboriginal birth rates.

2   Canada is multicultural because of a prevailing ideology that endorses the values of tolerance and respect for diversities and difference (Transatlantic Trends 2010). A commitment to multiculturalism is also embraced as a core value and as an integral component of its national unity and identity (Kymlicka 2008).

3   Canada is multicultural at official levels. A multiculturalism policy originated as an all-party policy agreement in 1971, was subsequently entrenched in the Constitution Act as an interpretive principle (i.e., nothing in the Charter of Rights and Freedoms will be interpreted in a manner that is inconsistent with the enhancement and preservation of Canada's multicultural character), and finally accorded statutory standing with passage of the Canadian Multiculturalism Act in 1988. That Canada remains the world's only official multicultural country (in statutory and constitutional terms) speaks of its commitment and convictions.

4   Canada is multicultural in its commitment to putting multicultural principles into practice. Mainstream institutions are expected to be inclusive of diversity by (1) improving workplaces by making them more respectful, reflective, and responsive to diversities and difference; (2) redefining institutional rules for removal of discriminatory barriers; and (3) ensuring delivery of services that are available, accessible, and appropriate (Fleras 2009).

Canada's mainstream media are also bound by a multicultural commitment to inclusiveness. Until recently, however, mainstream media misfired in responding to diversities and difference. Openly racist and demeaning coverage of minority women and men resulted in defamatory images and derogatory assessments of new and racialized Canadians (Fleras and Kunz 2001; Mahtani 2001). A news media fixation with the sordid and sensational glossed over the normative (normal and routine) by exaggerating the exceptional and pandering to the extremes. Minorities and migrants remained vulnerable to questionable coverage in which they were (1) miniaturized as irrelevant or inferior, (2) demonized as a social menace to society, (3) scapegoated as the source of all problems, (4) "otherized" for being too different or not different enough, (5) refracted through the prism of Eurocentric fears and fantasies, and (6) subjected to double standards that lampoon minorities regardless of what they do or don't do. Glaring inconsistencies prevail because of mixed messages that normalize invisibility and problematize visibility (Henry and Tator 2002): on one side, there is a tendency to normalize the invisibility of highly visible migrants and minorities in domains that count as success (e.g., politics or business); on the other side, there is an inclination to problematize their visibility in areas that count as failures (e.g., crime).

In short, news media's portrayal of immigrants, Aboriginal peoples, and racialized minorities has left much to be desired (Mahtani 2001; J. Miller 2005; Spoonley 2005; Jiwani 2010). Migrants and minorities are not necessarily labelled as inferior but are inferiorized through association with (1) negative news contexts, including crime, public disorder, and deviance; (2) cultural values and religious practices inconsistent with Canada's national interests; and (3) their status as asylum seekers and undocumented immigration, which is seen as a security risk (Bradimore and Bauder 2011). Modest improvements notwithstanding – and there is evidence of more nuanced and sympathetic coverage (Spoonley and Butcher 2009) – news media messages remain polarized. Newcomers who play by the rules or have proven utilitarian value are portrayed positively (Roberts and Mahtani 2010). By contrast, coverage is locked into negativity when both immigration programs and immigrants and refugees compromise Canada's national and vested interests (see Simmons 2010). Comparing similarities and differences in news media coverage of Chinese asylum seekers who landed in British Columbia in 1999 with that of Tamil asylum seekers ten years later yields an inescapable conclusion: the quality of coverage has improved, albeit only modestly because of an ongoing reluctance to challenge the foundational rules that inform the conventions of newsworthiness.

Mainstream News: Discourses in Defence of Mediacentric Ideology

The politics of news remain sharply contested. For some, the news represents an empirically grounded mirror of social reality dispassionately conveyed by impartial journalists who objectively uncover "what's new" (but see J. Miller 2005). For others, instead of something "out there" to be plucked for placement, news is defined as a socially created and culturally specific convention. According to this line of thinking, there is nothing natural or normal about the picking and packaging of news, despite vested-interest efforts to conceal the contrivance. More accurately, what passes for news reflects a socially constructed exercise involving individuals who make choices about what's on and what's not, who's quoted, and what sources and which spin should be used

(Weston 2003; Spoonley 2005). For still others, news content is driven by a dynamic that combines market models (news of interest reported factually to a consumer public) and manipulation models (distortion of facts in advancing vested interests) with organizational models in which newsworthiness is determined by the needs of the industry.

Inasmuch as news coverage represents a socially constituted discourse within contexts of power and inequality, the misrepresentation of diversities and difference is not without consequences. This is especially so since people's understanding of the world out there is shaped by media preconceptions and prejudicial gazes (Ricard and Wilkes 2007). The realization that news is socially constructed rather than uncovered or reported – and that journalists are culturally grounded rather than objectively detached – exposes those dynamics that systemically frame and subliminally distort the daily news routines, a point aptly described by Sari Pietikäinen (2003, 588):

> Journalism is paradoxical. Ideally news should represent a truthful, balanced, impartial and neutral account of the events ... but a good news report has an angle, a striking headline and lead, and an appealing story as a result of dozens of decisions and choices. News should, by definition, be about important recent events in the world, but research across nations and networks shows that events judged important by newsrooms seem to be, above all, about the economy, governmental politics, and crime. News should take various interests into account and do justice to the complexity of matters by representing divergent values, perspectives, and voices, giving equal access to all relevant parties and points of view. In reality, news reports are filled with the opinions of the establishment (usually those groups or individuals who are able to provide information that requires relatively little preparative legwork or in housing editing).

The conclusion seems inescapable: news constitutes a discursively constructed discourse in defence of a dominant ideology. Ideologically driven news media are loaded with ideas and ideals that draw attention to some aspects of reality as natural and normal but frame others as irrelevant or inferior (Henry and Tator 2002; Schuck and de Vreese 2006). Reality is framed in a way that reinforces news media definitions of what is relevant over what may be really *important* (Moeller 2006). In the end, what the news media deem to be newsworthy because of industry standards may not be if judged by more impartial standards related to impact, importance, or scope.

The ideological slant of news media is rarely conveyed to audiences. The net result is a hegemonic gaze that changes people's attitudes even if they don't know their attitudes are changing. News frames not only select, highlight, and interconnect snippets of reality to promote a particular interpretation but also normalize what stories will appear, how issues will be framed, the context in which events will appear, and the selection of approved images. Their agenda-setting functions secure a framework for organizing the news narrative, mainly by advancing a preferred reading about how the world works, what is and isn't acceptable, and who gets what and why. For example, the framing of news as episodic rather than thematic or contextual reinforces shallower coverage that may conceal more than it reveals (Boykoff 2006). A news media focus on the personalistic, the idiosyncratic, and the abnormal – what is surprising and infrequent – prevails over the substantial or the nuanced. Not surprisingly, what passes for news reflects a pattern of institutionalized thought control, sometimes by intent but often as the consequence of a business-as-usual mindset.

A conflict of interests is equally apparent. Whereas everyday life involves the cultivation of trust through the interplay of routines and cooperation, newsworthiness emphasizes breaches of trust by focusing on the disruptive, the abnormal, and conflict. However illogical by conventional norms of morality and justice, a news media commitment to conflict and abnormality is logical by industry standards. The news media are fundamentally mediacentric in framing social reality, inasmuch as what passes for newsworthiness is driven by a prevailing news paradigm rather than the needs of a democratically informed citizenship. A mediacentric bias prevails when newsworthiness advances media interests – often reflecting an interplay of corporate agendas with institutional values and organizational imperatives – over national interests or the common good. With a mediacentric gaze, the principle of newsworthiness is filtered through frames that prioritize the negative over the positive, deviance over normalcy, and conflict over cooperation – especially so in coverage of immigrants and immigration.

Immigration, Immigrants, and Refugees: Troublesome Constituents

As noted earlier, Canada is an immigration society. Canada has a principled framework in place to regulate the intake of newcomers, defines immigrants as assets in society building, expects them to become permanent residents, and has established programs to assist in their settlement and integration (Fleras 2010). Yet Canada is a paradox when it comes to immigrants and immigration.

Canadians appear to harbour mixed feelings, ranging from hostility to acceptance to indifference, over current immigration programs and the presence of immigrants. Expressions of admiration and respect toward model migrants are offset by attitudes of resentment toward those who allegedly cheat to get in, lie about their status, or misbehave once here. Not unexpectedly, perhaps, Canada's immigration program is increasingly rebuked for a variety of reasons, but largely because of a perceived failure to thwart the entry of unwanted newcomers while delaying the arrival of preferred others (S. Gallagher 2008).

Nowhere is this ambivalence more sharply expressed than in news media coverage of immigrants and immigration. News media tend to define the immigration and refugee systems as dysfunctional, prone to abuse, and in need of a major overhaul. "Good" immigrants are framed as positive contributors to Canadian society, whereas "bad" immigrants and refugee claimants are routinely labelled as problem people who create problems that cost money or are an inconvenience (Simmons 2010; see also Roberts and Mahtani 2010). A mediacentric newsworthiness that chides immigrants and refugees for failing to adopt and adapt reinforces their status as the outsiders within (Jiwani 2006). The paradox of polarities is unmistakable: immigrants who are associated with crime, crisis, or controversy generate headlines; those who comply and cooperate receive only token media (in)attention (Suro 2008).

An analysis of the news media's coverage of immigration and immigrants in moments of crisis is timely and relevant (see Olsson 2009). Media spectacles involving the regulation of immigrants and immigration governance have proven critical in socially constructing images of national community, belonging, and (in)security (Vukov 2003). The representational politics of news media-newcomer relations also raises important questions about the news media's role in brokering relations between Canada and immigrants (see Spoonley and Butcher 2009). Do mainstream news media have a responsibility to foster the integration of immigrants in a multicultural Canada that abides by the principle of inclusiveness? If yes, what is the appropriate role for the news media: (1) to facilitate immigrant integration through supportive coverage, (2) to resocialize the mainstream toward positive acceptance, or (3) to offset negative coverage by emphasizing commonalities and/or positives? What constitutes ideal (balanced and impartial) coverage in terms of what stories to cover and how to present information (Geissler and Pöttker 2006)?

To date, responses have varied in assessing the news media's role in setting the immigration agenda. For some, the news media discharge their responsibilities fairly and equitably in advancing public discourses. For others, however, the flames of intolerance are fanned by news narratives that associate irregular newcomers with illegality, crisis and controversy, and program failure (Metropolis Presents 2004; Suro 2008). For still others, its the proverbial mixed bag. According to Rodney Benson (2010), ten recurrent frames capture the range of debate from left to right: three victim frames (global economic injustice, humanitarian, racism/xenophobia), three hero frames (cultural diversity, integration, and good workers), and four threat frames (job threat, public order threat, fiscal threat, and national identity/culture threat). In that neither consensus nor conviction prevail for improving the representational politics of news media-newcomer relations (C. Murray 2009a, 681; DiversiPro 2007), a paralysis by analysis persists.

Framing Immigration/Immigrants/Refugees in Canadian Print Media

News media coverage is prone to paradox. In their coverage of crime, news media are accused of emphasizing the exact opposite of what really happens (Surette 2007). Other critics accuse news media of exaggerating the least common aspects of criminality and criminal justice by making them the most enduring images (Perlmutter 2000; Fleras 2003). This misrepresentation is intensified by the intensely competitive 24/7 news cycles of cable television (see Suro 2009). In misinforming people about the realities out there, news media perform a disservice in articulating national discourses, shaping public policies, and influencing citizen mindsets.

Similarly, the news media have tended to mischaracterize the domain of immigration and immigrants (Geissler and Pöttker 2005; Suro 2008). News coverage routinely disregards that, while contributing to its prosperity, most migrants arrive through legal channels, want to make new lives with little public fanfare, and enjoy success in their new homeland. A preponderance of negative coverage associates immigration with illegality, crisis, controversy, and government failure, in the process fanning the flames of public hostility and distrust (Akdenizli 2008). Dominant narratives fixate on the episodic actions of individuals (especially on human-interest stories involving drama and spectacle), law enforcement, and policy makers at the expense of contextual dynamics that propel the movement of people in search of escape or opportunity. No less dominating because of deeply ingrained foundational principles is the portrayal of sudden immigrant flows as a crisis rather than the structural outcome of globalization and neo-liberal policies (Bauder 2008b; Suro 2009).

Immigrants are harshly lampooned by questionable news media coverage (O'Doherty and Augoustinos 2008). They are routinely framed as troublesome constituents who pose security risks; steal jobs from "real" Canadians; cheat the welfare system; clog up resource-starved social, medical, and municipal services; create congestion and crowding; compromise Canada's highly touted quality of life; take advantage of educational opportunities without making a corresponding commitment to Canada; engage in illegal activities such as drugs or smuggling; and imperil Canada's national unity by refusing to conform or participate (Centre for Immigration Policy Reform 2010; but see Li 2003). Admittedly, compared with the aggressive tabloid presses in Britain that routinely sensationalize hostility toward migrants and minorities in bold headlines, mainstream media in Canada are paragons of virtue, loathe to openly criticize migrants or government minority policy lest they invite an unfavourable reaction by disturbing a national consensus (Masood 2008). Moreover, evidence suggests a growing news media aversion to vilifying immigrants (especially Muslims) while emphasizing the loyalty and law-abidingness of most (Silk 2009; Chuang 2010). Nevertheless, a positive coverage that emphasizes the economic, demographic, and cultural utility of model migrants (Roberts and Mahtani 2010) is offset by media negativity toward "irregular" migrants – not just in the blatant sense of sensationalist coverage but also through politely coded texts.

Asylum seekers and refugees/protected persons are no less negatively framed – although not all refugees, which, of course, prompts the question of how news frames produce positive or negative representations (Steimel 2010). Those who flee repressive regimes (especially ones identified as Islamist or unfriendly to the West) are framed as deserving because they confirm Canada's moral superiority and secure an image of Canada as progressive (see Jenicek, Wong, and Lee 2009). As well, media coverage may frame refugees as human interest stories – escape, hope, and new harsh realities – an emotional angle that personalizes and dramatizes their discursive status as prior and current victims (Steimel 2010). But those asylum seekers perceived as cheating or manipulating their entry into Canada by declaring refugee status are pejoratively labelled as queue jumpers. Their status as problem people is reinforced by a fixation with illegitimacy and illegal entries, security risks, and national and local integrity; with their presence as a contaminant (disease) or criminal, and as an economic threat; and with the associated costs of processing and settling refugee claimants (Hier and Greenberg 2002; see also Breen, Devereux, and Haynes 2005). Moreover, coverage tilts toward the hysterical when asylum seekers can self-select themselves, eroding the state's sovereign authority to define who can come and in what numbers (Simmons 2010). Such effrontery poses both a dilemma and a challenge to a country's authority, security, and sovereignty (Hier and Greenberg 2002).

But news media's preoccupation with undocumented refugees as troublesome constituents is selective (Fleras 2010). Coverage clasps on framing the immediate or precipitating causes behind refugee movements rather than root causes related to global inequality, ethnic conflict, environmental destruction, and human rights abuses. Conveniently ignored by these frames are the traumas of seeking asylum, difficulties in securing a passage to Canada, and the perils of adjusting to a new and complex environment. In reinforcing the adage that what the news media *don't say* may prove more informative than what they *do say,* exaggerated and negative coverage of refugees could well have the effect of stampeding an already edgy public into supporting policies and programs that serve elite interests or intensify state oppression. The next Case Study provides an interpretive look at how the news media frame migrants and minorities by way of racialized discourses.

---

case study

Putting It to the Test: Headlining Migrants and Minorities in Canadian Papers

How do Canada's news media portray racialized minorities, including immigrants and refugees? In a balanced and objective manner as might be expected of a mainstream institution within a multicultural Canada? Or as an endless series of dramatic breaking stories that surge onto the agenda, only to abruptly subside, resulting in even more episodic and crisis-driven frameworks (Suro 2008)? Insofar as most Canadians rarely have meaningful or sustained contact with immigrants but rely on media representations for their information, the impact of news media is incalculable in influencing public attitudes and shaping immigration debates, framing national discourses, and constructing ideologies (Mahtani 2008a).

For one year (from 12 February 2009 to 11 February 2010), I collected data for analyzing news media portrayals of racialized minorities (including Aboriginal peoples and immigrants). The content analysis focused on all newspaper headlines from Canada's two national papers *(Globe and Mail* and *National Post)* that made references to immigrants, Aboriginal peoples, and minorities, as well as to programs or institutions related to diversities and difference. Inclusion of an article header/headline was restricted to those involving (1) an event in Canada related to ethnic, race, or Aboriginal relations; migration and settlement; immigration and multiculturalism; racism and discrimination; and conflict and crime involving minorities;

(2) its placement in the hard news section (rather than entertainment or sports or opinion/editorial sections); and (3) an explicit reference to a minority or diversity dimension in a headline or accompanying photograph. The headlines/photos were then catalogued as positive or negative, with a category of neutral for those stories that failed to fit into either. The use of headlines as a data source can be easily justified not only because headlines are important units of meaning in their own right but also because they create and convey impressions (Hackett and Zhao 1998). As many have noted (van Dijk 1991), headlines are meant to capture the most important information about the article. The words used in headlines communicate opinions and emotions; they also establish the tone by encouraging the reader to think a certain way about the subject (Henry and Tator 2002). To determine reliability in assessing a headline as positive, negative, or neutral, a colleague was asked to evaluate the stories along these lines. The intercoder reliability rate was 80 percent; interestingly, the five items that I had defined as positive or neutral were negatively labelled by the coder. Still, the results of the content analysis should be approached as informational rather than scientific, given the high level of subjectivity in such an exercise.

The results proved interesting, if not altogether unexpected. During this period, the *National Post* published a total of 429 articles related to minorities or diversity. There were 25 positive headlines, another 82 were neutral, and the rest (322) were negative inasmuch as they indicated or implied that minorities were troublesome constituents – that is, problem people who are problems, have problems, or create problems. The *Globe and Mail* published 409 stories involving minorities or diversity, 54 were positive, 91 neutral, and 264 negative. In total, of the 838 headlines in the *Globe* and *National Post,* 586 – about 71 percent of the total – were negative, whereas the 79 positive headlines account for about 8 percent of the total (headlines available on request).

Explicit references to immigrants/refugees and immigration proved a fraction of the total. Of the 828 headers/headlines in the *National Post* and *Globe and Mail,* 72 referred specifically to immigration and immigrants/refugees, with 51 being negative, 5 positive, and 16 neutral. These results compare to those in a *National Post* study by Henry and Tator (2002) conducted between December 1998 and September 2000. According to Henry and Tator, 61 articles (both hard and soft news) dealt with immigration, but only 10 were positive, with more than half of those written by guest columnists. Interestingly, a similar pattern was found on the Canada Immigrant website (http://www.canadaimmigrants.com/news.asp), which claims to offer the most relevant Canadian immigration news, including the best local, provincial, and national coverage of recent events. Of the 152 top immigrant stories for 2009, a total of 105 headlines proved to be negative, 13 were positive, and 34 neutral (see also Fraser Institute 1993; Breen, Devereux, and Haynes 2005).

This study of migrants and minorities reinforces news media's reputation as the "medium of the negative." An industry that thrives on the principle "only bad news is good news" is unlikely to generate positive coverage (Jiwani 2010). No one is suggesting a deliberate bias in advancing such one-sided coverage. Nor is any single headline unlikely to undo what Canada has accomplished to date. Rather, the problem entails the cumulative impact of predominantly negative headlines, reflecting a combination of subliminal Eurocentric assumptions about normalcy and acceptance, with systemic biases that routinely privilege conflict and problems as newsworthy (Fleras 2003). Regardless of who or what is at fault, the impact of such slanted coverage clashes with Canada's multiculturalism ideals to facilitate the settlement and integration of new Canadians.

Critical-Thinking Question
Canada is normally regarded as an immigration society. Numerous surveys demonstrate that, generally, Canadians tend to have largely favourable attitudes toward immigrants and immigration (Transatlantic Trends 2010). How, then, to explain the predominantly negative framing of immigration and immigrants in Canada's news media?

* * * * * * * * * *

News Media Coverage of Massed Asylum Seekers
The sight of a rusting ship berthed at Ogden Point in Victoria, British Columbia, in October 2009 with 76 migrants/asylum seekers on board rekindled memories of a similar incident a decade earlier. In the summer of 1999, four boats carrying 599 migrants/asylum seekers from Fujian province in China arrived on the shores of British Columbia, with the first boat arriving on 20 July, the second on 11 August, the third on 31 August, and the fourth on 8 September. Most of the migrants arrived without proper identification, claiming to be refugees on grounds of political and religious persecution.

The majority of migrants from the first boat were released after a series of interviews and a promise to appear at their refugee hearing dates. Migrants from the other boats were not so fortunate. In response to growing public outrage and ramped-up media hysteria, they were taken into custody, housed in a Canadian Forces barrack, and detained to await the processing of their refugee claim. In addition, nine Korean crew members from the second boat were charged with smuggling but eventually acquitted, and three Chinese crew from another ship were subsequently sentenced to four years in prison. No high-level smugglers were ever convicted (*Province*, 18 October 2009). In the end, about 35 asylum seekers from the last three boats were allowed to stay in Canada, 330 were deported back to China, and the rest simply vanished.

The arrival of smuggled Chinese asylum seekers ignited a media maelstrom that induced near panic among the public (S. Cohen 1972; Hier and Greenberg 2002). Any sense of proportion quickly disappeared in a haze of confusion and uncertainty. Consider the broader context: of the 1,100 asylum seekers who landed at Vancouver International Airport in 1999, including 402 Chinese nationals, all were released almost immediately (Simmons 2010). To be sure, massive coverage of the "crisis" on television and in local and national newspapers was understandable (Greenberg 2000; van der Zon 2000); after all, news decisions had to be made under conditions of great uncertainty and confusion with regard to what happened, how things would unfold, and the magnitude of the crisis (Olsson 2009).

Initial media coverage was sympathetic. Migrants from the first boat were portrayed as victims of international smuggling rings rather than as active agents in human trafficking. Coverage initially focused on the health of the migrants – generally good, despite the ordeal they had endured. But coverage quickly bolted from caution to stridency with awareness that additional boats had evaded federal border authorities. A victim-oriented perspective rapidly faded as news media coverage leapt into the exclusionary, accusatory, and racist (albeit in coded terms or through implicit assumptions made). Events were framed around the generic "bad news" themes of public disorder and conflict, transgression of norms and values, and confrontation (Greenberg 2000). Issues pertaining to sovereignty and security drew considerable attention, as did the need to combat smuggling and trafficking, tighten Canada's lax refugee laws, and secure its unprotected borders against a so-called Asian invAsian. Migrants, in turn, were reframed as active agents in the process, then racialized and dehumanized accordingly as the "other," that is, as illegal, aliens, criminals, dishonest queue jumpers/gatecrashers, threats to health and safety, and a financial drain on existing social and welfare services. A media-hyped hysteria over security threats to Canada's porous borders by "invading aliens" or "illegal migrants" fuelled a panic that resounded with references to floods, waves, deluges, invasion, and boatloads (van der Zon 2000; Vukov 2003) – as these newspaper headlines demonstrate:

"No Name Ship Found Crammed with Asians" (*Globe and Mail,* 21 July 1999).
"Illegal Human Cargo Believed on Ship Heading to BC" (*Globe and Mail,* 11
    August 1999).
"Ship Dumps Human Cargo" (*Globe and Mail,* 12 August 1999).
"A Crate of China Dolls Arrives in the West" (*Globe and Mail,* 7 August 1999).
"A New Shipful of Migrants Will Tax the Already Thinly Stretched Resources
    of Federal Agencies" (*Times Colonist,* 13 August 1999).
"Police Hunt for Fugitive Migrants" (*Times Colonist,* 26 August 1999).

In short, over a period of two months, the Canadian news media hyped a crisis that contested Canada's immigration and refugee determination system (Hier and Greenberg 2002). The fear mongering conveyed by unsympathetic coverage of the 1999 Fujian Chinese landings in British Columbia may well have proved a catalyst for more restrictive controls. Tamara Vukov of Concordia University (2003, 346) explains:

> The media framing of the Chinese migrants as "human cargo" signalled the inauguration of a Canadian public discourse on migrant trafficking that is now being governmentalized in highly repressive ways ... Media myths such as the trope of "human cargo" act as culturally resonant sites of conflicting values and social tensions, as well as focal points of popular and political affect. In the news media such myths further work through the processes of inflation and amplification, focusing on a single case and intensifying it until it takes on a representative or realist status ... Through media spectacles, affective myths around immigration, such as "porous borders" or "floods" become discursive events that serve to frame specific strategies of policy intervention, giving momentum to particular policy agendas and forms of government regulation (i.e., plugging the border).

Perhaps it was no coincidence that rhetoric over passage of the 2002 Immigration and Refugee Protection Act focused more on protecting Canada from unwanted migrants and human smugglers than on securing protection for those more vulnerable. Admittedly, there is no agreement over the role of media in influencing the social context that leads to government policies (Barker 2005). For some, media play an insignificant part in policy-making processes. For others, by determining the focal issues for policy makers, media are pivotal in shaping policy making. For still others, the media's degree of influence varies considerably, is contingent on the issue at hand, and rarely follows a linear and straightforward path – resulting in a powerful role when policy makers are unsure about their actions, but in a weaker role when government priorities are already established or in the hands of established policy makers (ibid.).

Ten years later, in October 2009, a dilapidated freighter with 76 Tamil refugees/asylum seekers aboard was intercepted in Canadian waters and anchored in Vancouver Harbour. (Another ship, the *MV Sun Sea*, carrying 492 Tamils, arrived in August 2010, setting off yet another fierce debate over the porosity of Canada's borders [Whittington 2010].) All 76 were taken into custody for processing to determine their eligibility for refugee status because of danger, displacement, or persecution in Sri Lanka. Virtually all the claimants were detained indefinitely by federal authorities in correctional facilities (jail) on grounds that, without proof of identification, it would be a daunting task to determine who was a legitimate refugee and who was a terrorist to be barred entry into Canada. (It should be noted that Canada accepts about 93 percent of all Sri Lankans who file refugee claims; Canada is also home to more than 300,000 Sri Lankan Tamils, most of whom live in Toronto.) Fears were circulated that more vessels carrying Tamil Tiger (LTTE – Liberation Tigers of Tamil Eelam) gun-running and human-trafficking agents could be headed for Canada as part of a larger network of boats fanning out Tamil asylum seekers to other countries. The federal government also appeared reluctant to release the arrivals on their own recognizance – seemingly out of spite to punish them for paying human smugglers up to $45,000 to gain back-door entry into Canada. Or as Immigration Minister Jason Kenney explained in justifying a tough stand on the issue: "We don't want to develop a reputation of having a two-tier immigration system – one tier for legal law abiding immigrants who patiently wait to come into the country, and a second tier who seek to come through the back door, typically through the asylum system ... We need to do a much better job of shutting the back door of immigration for those who seek to abuse that asylum system" (quoted in J. Armstrong and Ibbitson 2009).

Despite significant differences between the events of 1999 and those of 2009 (most notably, one ship versus four ships), few changes in news media coverage could be detected (see also Suro 2008). For a six-week period, I scanned the headers and headlines from both the *Globe and Mail* and *National Post*, in addition to three BC papers, the *Province, Vancouver Sun*, and *Victoria Times Colonist*. (The *National Post* and the BC dailies are owned by Canwest, with the result that the same story, albeit sometimes with different headlines, appeared in all four papers.) The results proved unsurprising: the *Globe and Mail* carried 10 headlines, 7 of which were negative, 2 neutral, and 1 positive; the *National Post* had 5 headlines, 4 of them negative; and the BC papers had a total of 17 headlines, 8 negative, 8 neutral, and 1 positive. The total for all the papers was 32 items: 19 negative, 11 neutral, and 2 positive. As before, the language that informed the headlines resonated with the menace of negativity or problems.

"Latest Migrant Ship Recalls Waves of 'Refugees' in 1999" (*Province*, 18 October 2009).

"Canada Now Part of the Global Smuggling Pipeline" (*Globe and Mail*, 20 October 2009).

"Deported Toronto Gang Member Found Aboard Migrant Smuggling Ship" (*Vancouver Sun*, 10 November 2009).

"Minister Determined to Fight 'Human Smuggling'" (*Vancouver Sun*, 21 October 2009).

"Sri Lankan Migrant Wanted for Smuggling" (*Times Colonist*, 27 October 2009).

As in 1999, overall coverage was largely negative, with undue emphasis on criminality, security, terrorism, and possible risks, rather than human rights and social justice (Bradimore and Bauder 2011). A key discursive trope focused on the issue of smuggling, with increased reference to the threat of terrorism because of alleged migrant ties to the banned terrorist group the Tamil Tigers (LTTE). This demonization is hardly surprising; after all, news coverage of the Tamil community is routinely couched in terrorist narratives (from Canadian-based organizations that are fronts for international terrorists to fundraising campaigns for supporting homeland terrorism) (Henry and Tator 2002, 123). Such demonizing may play a key role in legitimizing national security discourses while naturalizing state intervention (see Smolash 2009). Equally noticeable were repeated references to the vast sums of money paid to the smugglers, thus undermining the legitimacy of the refugee claimants:

"Ship of Tamils Stirs Fears of Hidden Tigers" (*Globe and Mail*, 22 October 2009).

"Cargo Ship Passengers Wanted in Sri Lanka for Terrorism" (*National Post*, 23 October 2009).

"Expert Claims Migrants Are Tamil Tigers" (*Globe and Mail*, 11 November 2009).

Yet changes in coverage could be discerned despite this continuity, namely, the framing of Tamil asylum seekers through the lens of national security, criminality/smuggling, and terrorism rather than humanitarian issues. Although this alleged breach to Canada's integrity and sovereignty elicited heated reactions, media coverage remained more muted than in the past. Headlines remained relatively restrained and neutrally framed by avoiding inflammatory language. References to "illegal migrants" never appeared in a headline, though some of the coverage did make this reference in the storyline (for example, see "Seeking a Safe Haven, Finding a Closed Door," *Globe and Mail,* 20 October 2009, "Minister Determined to Fight 'Human Smuggling,'" *Vancouver Sun,* 21 October 2009). The pejorative expression "boat people" was also discarded from headlines/headers. Still, questions abound. Why such massive and negative coverage of a relatively small number of migrants, when between thirty and forty thousand asylum seekers unobtrusively arrive in Canada each year at ports, land crossings, and airports? Is it something about the massed spectacle of ocean-going freighters that sensationalizes coverage, in the process transforming negative stereotypes and discourses into a sharpened sense of media-hyped moral panic (Hier and Greenberg 2002)? Is media coverage of government stonewalling intended as a message to the world that Canada is no longer a patsy whose openness and generosity can be mistaken for weakness? Several lessons may be gleaned from both sets of coverage:

1 No one should underestimate the power of the media to whip up public frenzy. Framing matters: for some, debate over smuggled asylum seekers is not an immigration issue related to social justice or human rights (but see Bradimore and Bauder 2011) but about Canada's national interests, namely, fairness, safety, and sovereignty (Crowley 2010). Depending on the frames employed, news media can control public discourses. They can tap into collective anxieties (e.g., lax refugee controls, too many Chinese in Canada)[1] through language that seeks to influence what audiences think about, and how, for defining the problem and corresponding strategies for resolution (Entman 1993; Hier and Greenberg 2002). News media are also adept at rewording racist imagery and racialized assumptions into carefully coded language that obliterates any racist intent (Spoonley and Butcher 2009).

2 Both Canadians and Canada's mainstream news media exhibit deeply conflicted attitudes toward refugee claimants, according to François Crépeau, a professor of international law at McGill University (cited in Scott 2009; see

---

1 On 10 November 2010, the university edition of *Maclean's* magazine published an article titled "Too Asian?" The article tapped into some concerns by unnamed white students that an "Asian invasion" had transformed universities into unfun places. Critical reaction was swift to what some saw as yet another instalment of the so-called yellow peril motif in Canadian history.

also O'Doherty and Augoustinos 2008). "Good" refugees are the conventional types that Canada chooses because they are wanted. Included as well are those escaping evil Communist regimes for the friendly confines of Canada, such as the Hungarians in 1956 and the Vietnamese in 1979. Or as Harald Bauder (2008a) explains, they are the deserving "other" who are worthy of Canada's compassion and rewarded accordingly, namely, with refugee status and permanent residency.

By contrast, there are the "bad" refugees, who began to arrive unannounced in the 1980s. They were framed as queue jumpers who abused both Canada's generosity and refugee system, who rarely possessed the values or skills commensurate with modern Canadian society, and who came from societies plagued with poverty and violence. In representing them as racialized, illegal, and non-belonging, the news media contributed to their rejection while reaffirming a white-o-centric Canadian identity (see Bauder 2008a; Simmons 2010). Worse still, by generating a political frenzy over the policing of Canada's borders, the ensuing crisis could be employed as an excuse to justify draconian anti-refugee measures in the name of national security. On 29 June 2010, a move to streamline the refugee determination process – the Balanced Refugee Reform Act – received Senate assent.

3 Despite improvement in the tone of coverage, there is little evidence of any transformative change that challenges the prevailing news paradigm and its definition of newsworthiness. As Roberto Suro (2008) points out in a different context, news media's approach to immigration and immigrants entails a continuity in change, in some cases exaggerating long-standing tendencies to the point of extremes. For example, journalists' continuing reliance on official sources of information (from police to bureaucrats) ensures negative coverage of the Tamil community in Canada (Henry and Tator 2002). References to Tamil asylum seekers negatively taint Canada's entire Tamil community with the terrorism agenda of a few. In the end, Tamils are "otherized" as the outsiders within. The evidence is overwhelming. Comparable reactions to disparate asylum-seeking spectacles ten years apart reinforces a hoary cliché: that when it comes to covering immigrants and refugees, the more things change *(plus ça change ...)*, the more they stay the same *(... c'est la meme chose)*.[1]

---

1 In August 2010, 492 Tamil asylum seekers arrived by ship and declared refugee status. As before, this alleged breach to Canada's integrity and sovereignty elicited heated reactions. Nevertheless, media coverage in terms of headlines and headers remained relatively restrained and neutrally framed by avoiding inflammatory language.

Advertising Beauty
What Is Dove Really Doing?

Thin is inviolate. Despite the odd fleshy role model or Vogue *issue devoted to "size," female beauty ideals remain impossible ones, as real as fairy tales. After all,* female unhappiness is big business. *(Onstad 2010, emphasis added)*

The advertising media have a love-hate relationship with women. A bimodal pattern of representations may be discerned: on one side, media depictions emphasize the wrinkle-free, poreless, sexualized, and deferential; on the other side, women come across as rebellious, tough, enterprising – and plus-sized. In some cases, the stereotyping of women is as retrograde and offensive as it was in the past. Even the proliferation of progressive images may prove deceiving, since consumerist fantasies can undercut bold proclamations for equality and assertiveness. Yes, the advertising industry may want be as inclusive of women as possible; yet there are fears of moving too quickly for core audiences. Confronted by these conflicting and compromising demands on representational politics, who can be surprised by media depictions of women as bundles of contradictions regarding who they are, what they want, and their proper place in society? Susan Douglas (1994, 17) writes:

Throughout our lives we have been getting profoundly contradictory messages about what it means to be an American woman. Our national mythology teaches us that Americans are supposed to be independent, rugged individuals who are achievement-oriented, competitive, active, shrewd, and assertive go-getters ... Women, however, are supposed to be dependent, passive, nurturing types, uninterested in competition, achievement, or success, who should conform to the wishes of the men in their lives. It doesn't take a rocket scientist to see that these two lists of behavioral traits are mutually exclusive, and that women are stuck right in the middle. What a woman has to do, on her own, is cobble together some compromise.

But improvements in depiction cannot be disengaged from the politics of conspicuous consumption. Advertising has commodified feminism by expanding the choice of must-have goods for those working women who want it all – love, looks, and life. This challenge demands a look both feminine and aerobicized, without sacrificing a satisfying career and contented family. Conventional consumer goods can now be pitched at professional women as products for coping with the demands of career life, although images of success must be secured within a reassuring context of motherhood, household supervisor, nurturing helpmate, and beauty queen. The addition of more labour-saving devices at home seemingly simplifies the challenges of the double shift and a commitment to overcompensate.

The targeting of working women is not by accident or without consequences. Advertising has harnessed the ideological essence of feminism by subverting the message of caring and sharing into the service of commodity relations. As Susan Faludi (1991) puts it when describing how commerce has recast feminism for self-serving purposes: "Feminine happiness equals other women's envy of your purchased glamour. Or in modern terms, who has the better Chanel bag." To be sure, there is no shortage of smart and assertive women who are thin, young, cookie-cutter attractive, and presented in a way that highlights their physical attributes. But one has to look hard to find media attention on a strong and independent woman who is not "hot."

With advertising and gender, reality is rarely what it seems to be. In a patriarchal world, women are continually reminded that their value is connected to what they look like, thus making them more susceptible to advertising and narrow standards of acceptability (She 2007). Women continue to be evaluated as objects of corporate fantasy in constant need of consumer-driven pampering and product enhancement. Not that men are exempt from aggressive marketing. By preying on insecurities they never knew they had, men too are increasingly targeted and exploited for male grooming and beauty products. They too are learning what it's like to assume a constant awareness of continually being looked at as objects of commercial interest. In other words, a regendered media agenda may treat women and men equally, but only by reducing both genders to the same common denominator for instilling the essential cultural nightmare of our society: the fear of failure, and the envy of success.

In short, the growing economic and political clout of women poses an advertising challenge. Blatantly sexist advertising that objectifies and marginalizes no longer carries much cachet with audiences or the industry. Images of women in advertising have become much more complex and nuanced instead, as well as more diffuse and diverse, thus making it difficult to post glib generalizations (Gauntlett 2008). But changes because of these challenges have simply reaffirmed the capacity of media to co-opt and transform the "new" woman for commercial purposes. Despite a shift toward undoing a sexist media, the underlying message remains the same: get the guy, and buy, buy, buy. In recent years, the advertising tack has shifted its course somewhat by employing a bracing mix of conscience and resistance to create brand awareness and product purchase that further intensifies a female disenchantment with the here and now.

Cause Marketing, Gendered Advertising: Fostering "Dove Love" or the "Love of Dove"

The concept of cause marketing has leapt to the forefront of corporate strategies (King 2006; Anderssen 2010). Examples include the gifting by Campbell's of 20 million tomato plant seeds to consumers and students; a commitment by Hellmann's to donate $25,000 for contributions to the local food movement; Pampers' promise of a free tetanus shot for each pregnant American with purchase of every package of specially marked diapers; and The Body Shop's earth-friendly endorsement of issues ranging from saving whales to curbing global sex trafficking (Houpt 2009). More recently, in 2009, Pepsi decided to redirect its massive advertising budget from the annual Super Bowl broadcast into more cause-oriented channels. Finally, there is the proliferation of colour-coded causes. Consumers who feel strongly about the environment often embrace buying "green" or "blue" as an ethical and moral imperative, making a political point along the way (Arnold 2009). Of particular success is pink ribbon cause marketing in which corporations offer merchandise adorned with the pink ribbon symbol, with promises that a portion of the sales will go to breast cancer research or intervention programs (Kozlowski 2007).

Cause Marketing as Corporate Philanthropy or Marketing by Emotional Hijacking?

Cause marketing can be defined as a corporate strategy by which companies openly embrace ethical (honest and transparent) practices or overtly align themselves with humanitarian-oriented causes (Houpt 2009). With cause marketing, corporations utilize their formidable promotion machines to promote positive brand awareness. Studies indicate that cause marketing can generate sales revenues directly – exponentially in some cases – or indirectly, as when securing customer loyalty by reinforcing a wholesome corporate image as socially responsible (Cone 2008). More importantly, a commitment to cause marketing can take the heat off those corporations that pollute, exploit, tamper, or endanger. For example, concerns are mounting over the "ribbonization" of the breast cancer cause as little more than a corporate sales pitch whose spin whitewashes a much darker reality. Even a corporate villain like Nike – once criticized for its use of sweatshop labour – can make amends as a major sponsor by seeding grassroots change in the developing world (Houpt 2009). Clearly, a commitment to corporate philanthropy is not necessarily driven by compassion or justice but for improving sales and market advantage (Anderssen 2010). Samantha King (2006) explains the business of cause marketing:

> Until the 1980s, corporate philanthropy was a relatively random, eclectic, and unscientific activity based largely on the individual preferences of high-ranking executives. Since then, it has been transformed into a highly calculated, quantified, and planned approach, often called "strategic philanthropy" or "charitable investing." Of all the tools that have emerged during this time, cause-related marketing – when a company allies itself with a specific cause, and contributes money, time, or expertise ... is among the most popular and publicly visible. The effect of this transformation has been to place philanthropy at the centre of business activity and to transform it into a revenue-producing mechanism.

This politicization of cause marketing as corporate philanthropy is not surprising. People are positively inclined toward a company or product when it promotes a worthy cause they care about, including the 92 percent of participants who concurred with this notion in an online Cone Cause Evolution Survey conducted in March 2007 (using a sample of 1,066 women and men eighteen years of age and older). Another 83 percent believed companies have a responsibility to support social causes, with many respondents indicating a willingness to switch companies or products for this reason (Cone 2007). More than two-thirds of Americans say they consider a company's business practices when deciding on a purchase, and a substantial number of workers want their company to support a social cause – in the process suggesting a shift in how people perceive the relationship of business (from commitments to operating practices) to society. Of course, consumers hop aboard the cause wagon for self-serving reasons too and not just to help fund research or promote a new corporate-society model. Personal payoffs include making them feel better by linking a purchase with a cause, eliminating guilt over acts of consumerism (saving the world one purchase at a time), conveying an image of progressive citizenship to impress friends, and demonstrating solidarity with those also hugging the high moral ground (King 2006).

The consequences are inescapable. As Carol Cone (2007), chair and founder of the strategy and communications agency Cone, says, "Cause marketing has come of age." And while both The Body Shop and the pink ribbon campaigns have garnered respect and critical acclaim because of their politics, few can match the buzz generated by Dove's Campaign for Real Beauty. For some, it's nothing less than a social revolution transforming society's perception of female beauty (Blotnicky 2008); for others, it's just another clever marketing gimmick full of sound and fury, signifying nothing (Saunders 2008); and for still others, it's the metaphorical equivalent of "same old, same old" – that is, the illusion of change without any fundamental challenge to the rules that inform media conventions about female beauty (Dye 2009). To get some idea of the what, why, and how behind these reactions, this chapter deconstructs Dove's Campaign for Real Beauty by separating *rhetoric* (what it is saying in rethinking female beauty) from *reality* (what it is really saying and doing in rebranding Dove as a politically correct beauty product). Three issues dominate:

1 *Turning a profit by inverting beauty standards* (CBC 2005). The logic behind the Dove campaign is fundamentally aligned with the principles of cause marketing and niche advertising, namely, to target a market niche, attract attention, arouse interest, neutralize doubts (testimonies by ordinary people can be effective, as Tim Hortons knows only too well; see also the Chapter 12 Insight on the demotic turn), and create conviction through images that emotionally connect (Fleras 2003).

2 *Behind the hype: still buying beauty.* Dove's campaign is consistent with the promotion of consumerism by linking beauty with a purchase. Yes, Dove displaces the "fantasy babe" image of female beauty with a more realistic display of natural beauty. Yet the rules of the game remain the same (beauty of any size or shape must be purchased), only the conventions (images) that refer to the rules undergo change. Is it possible for a profit-oriented corporation to credibly promote progressive change (N. Cohen 2005)?

3 *Beauty is still only skin deep.* Despite Dove's promises to democratize the concept of female beauty, its advocacy of natural beauty remains locked into

a narrow definition: that is, firmness and tightness at all costs, because external beauty remains a primary source of self-esteem.

Dove's Campaign for Real Beauty: The Rhetoric

Many have criticized the depiction of women in the media as misogynist (hateful), sexist (inferior to men), or androcentric (reflecting a male perspective – gaze – as normal and normative). This critique is not altogether surprising given the patriarchal principles (structures and values) that inform a mainstream media's foundational order. Of particular note is the critique of advertising images that slot women into a stifling set of stereotypes. As Shari Graydon (2001) and others (Kilbourne 2000) explain, advertising tends to portray women in demeaning ways: as objects, as infantile, as sex ready, as shallow, and as obsessed with beauty. Definitions of beauty are themselves rigidly cast, with advertising images focused on whiteness (blondeness), fitness (toned and firm, but not too muscular), and thinness. The impact in promoting such Eurocentric standards of beauty is thought to be unnatural and unhealthy (Dworkin and Wachs 2009; Dye 2009). Problems proliferate, ranging from diminished self-esteem to a slew of potentially fatal eating disorders. Not surprisingly, perhaps, in a survey conducted by Dove as part of its Campaign for Real Beauty, only 2 percent of three thousand women described themselves as beautiful (the survey included respondents from ten countries where the dominant culture's conception of beauty tends toward Western ideals) (Dove 2004).

Attempts to challenge unrealistic standards of beauty paid dividends when Dove initiated a campaign in 2003 to counter these damaging stereotypes. To reinforce this notion of natural beauty by using *ordinariness* as the selling point, Dove employed non-professional models – that is, "average looking" ("real") women rather than anorexic, unsmiling, and silicon-injected models (*Salon. com* 2005).[1] By marketing itself as an esteem-building brand for enhancing the natural beauty of ordinary women instead of employing the emaciated and unhealthy images associated with professional models, the explicit goal of the

---

1 The original six women who were featured in the first set of American ads became celebrities in their own right, with national television appearances on *The Oprah Winfrey Show* and CNN. But critics indicate these natural women are anything but. Although somewhat plumpish, with paunches and bums, and ranging in size from four to twelve (as an aside, on average, American women are a size fourteen), these women are conventionally attractive, with straight white teeth and not an ounce of cellulite (Garfield 2005). Persisting as well are allegations of retouching, including using professional makeup and airbrushing (see Saunders 2008).

Dove campaign was clearly articulated: to challenge society's stereotypical perception of beauty while inspiring women to take care of themselves (Media Awareness Network 2009). In that sense, Seth Stevenson (2005) writes, the message conveyed by Dove differs from the conventional marketing of beauty products, which historically have been aspirational ("Buying this product will make me look like her"). For Dove, the message tends toward the inspirational ("These women who look like me are happy and contented; if I buy this firming cream, perhaps my self-hating will stop").

The reach and impact of the Campaign for Real Beauty have proven a smashing success – product recognition; buzz to kill for; corporate halo effect; and profits galore (CBC 2005). Admittedly, most people know that Dove is in business to sell products in a socially responsible way. And like The Body Shop's eco- and animal-friendly stand, Dove is equating consumerism with making righteous political noises (Stevenson 2005). Yet there is no denying that Dove is also generating awareness about the objectification of women through beauty stereotyping. For Karen Blotnicky (2008), the selling of a more healthy and democratic (inclusive) image of female beauty has triggered a wave of social change. On the campaign's shifting of the yardstick for defining beauty toward the real, natural, diverse, and attainable, Gloria Steinem, founder of *MS Magazine,* is quoted as saying (in CBC 2005): "It's a change that women – and some men, too – have been agitating for for 35 years. I've spent 15 years of my life pleading for ads that reflected our readers by age, race, ethnicity. We could demonstrate that women responded better to ads that were more inclusive of them, but they just weren't coming."

To capitalize on the buzz, the Dove Self-Esteem Fund in partnership with Girl Scouts was established to help young women put the notion of beauty in perspective. And if imitation is the sincerest form of flattery, consider the following in expanding the marketing niche for "real beauty." According to *Salon. com* (2005), Body & Bath Works launched a line of "Real Beauty Inside and Out" personal care products designed for girls ages eight to twelve to look, feel, and be their best by way of body lotions, splashes, soap, and lip balms in girl-friendly berry colours and festooned with inspirational messages.

What Dove Is Really (Not) Doing: The Reality

> Reform: *changing the endless conventions that refer to the foundational rules.*
> Transformation: *challenging the foundational rules that generate the conventions.*

There is no shortage of criticism directed at Dove's politicization of female beauty as a cause-marketing strategy. Much of the criticism – although legitimate – tends toward the superficial and secondary.

For some, anger is directed at the hypocrisy of Unilever, Dove's parent company, whose marketing of Axe – a male line of hygiene products – conveys blatantly sexist images of ultra-thin hypersexualized women uncontrollably lusting after Axe men (N. Cohen 2005), in the process reinforcing the concept of gendered advertising, with one (real women) aimed at women, the other (fantasy babes) at men (Dye 2009). Other Unilever-related but ostensibly regressive beauty products include Fair & Lovely, a skin-lightening agent, and Slim-Fast, a weight-reducing product.

Others criticize the process Dove employs to bring about progressive social change. Instead of promoting collective resistance in actioning a public good, Dove's campaign tends to foster competition among privatized individuals in determining whose looks are more naturally unique. A reliance on the Internet to establish online communities is commendable, yet such a move cancels the physical connectedness that compels people to act (Dye 2009). That men are not allowed to participate in the campaign is also problematic; after all, male concepts of beauty directly affect the way women see themselves, and men themselves are influenced by prevailing media gazes.

Still others doubt the Dove campaign can revolutionize changes in redefining female beauty standards (Saunders 2008). Instead of a counterhegemonic thrust in challenging the rules governing cultural conventions, the campaign is dismissed as just another marketing ploy (according to Eileen Saunders [2008], the use of non-professional models is an extension of the reality-programming trend), with little impact on the cultural standards by which women are judged and by which they judge themselves.[1]

A more sweeping critique accuses Dove of not doing anything different, despite claims to the contrary. That is, instead of fostering transformative change in thinking about female beauty, Dove is simply reforming the conventional notions of beauty without challenging the rules that link beauty with buying. Rather than redefining the rules of beauty by turning it inward or making it

---

1 According to the campaign website, Dove envisages itself as a catalyst for progressive social change by offering a healthier, broader, and more democratic view of beauty. In reality, the Dove campaign is just another rebranding exercise for escaping the commercial clutter of its competitors. In addition to Dove's entry into hair and skin care products, a significant corporate repositioning was necessary for it to go beyond its image as just a boring soap brand. Accordingly, by transforming its soap into a beauty bar brand, Dove could justify its bona fides as the champion of real beauty (Saunders 2008).

more inclusive, Dove is still selling beauty products by utilizing a feel-good campaign to create a deep brand loyalty that masks an intrinsic contradiction. Put bluntly, Dove's campaign reinforces the very beauty myths that it claims to challenge (Dye 2009). What Dove ads are really saying is that it's cool to be plump and curvy, but only when the skin is taut, toned, firm, cellulite-free, and doesn't jiggle (Stevenson 2005; see also Dworkin and Wachs 2009). Cultural critic Susan Bordo (1993, 191) acknowledged the finality of firmness in defining beauty when she wrote, "It is perfectly permissible in our culture (even for women) to have substantial weight and bulk – so long as it's tightly managed. Simply to be slim is not enough – the flesh must not wiggle." Real women may have real curves, in other words; nevertheless, Dove wants you to buy firming creams to care for those curvy bits. Or as Rebecca Traister puts it in lampooning Dove's mixed message, "Love your ass but not the fat on it" (*Salon.com* 2005). Love your curves as long as they are tight and firm because being beautiful is the most important thing a woman can be. Yes, beauty in any size, but not without a purchase because you are never okay just the way you are. And while you're at it, don't forget the pro-age ointments to *reverse the process of natural aging* or natural glow tanning lotions to create a *healthier-*looking skin.

Let's be upfront about this: instead of a counterhegemony that challenges conventional notions of beauty while enhancing self-esteem through improving self-image and female empowerment, the opposite may be more true when it comes to Dove's campaign. Dove is primarily a product of corporate instrumentalism (invoking good and ethical corporate citizenship and responsibility) that ultimately disempowers women by further commodifying their lives (Dye 2009). Less a shining beacon for social change and more a marketing strategy complicit in the very social problem it is seeking to transform, the Dove campaign co-opts women into yet more commodity fetishism. Or, as Dye (ibid., 124) writes about the fetishism of beauty as a commodity, "Rather, by marketing its 'real beauty' products as emblems for 'self-esteem,' Dove is able to commodify it, constructing 'self esteem' as a fetishized object that can be purchased in the form of make-up and firming creams."

A Dove survey in 2004 inadvertently exposed the contradiction. The survey found that 88 percent of women said being loved was the single most important factor in making them feel beautiful. Instead of focusing on this dimension, however, Dove is substituting commodities for real emotions. As Unilever spokesperson Stacie Bright explained without a hint of irony in defending Dove's promotion of firming cream, "It's about feeling good about yourself. And that's about bringing products that matter to women" (cited in *Salon.com*

2005). But equating Dove with notions of natural beauty and self-esteem creates meaningless associations that entrap women into buying to overcome insecurities (Dye 2009).

In short, what Dove is doing is neither transformative nor emancipatory. And it is not doing anything different in terms of marketing logic and advertising strategy. By hitching its fortunes to contesting beauty conventions rather than challenging conventional rules, Dove is just another exercise in cause marketing. However valuable and valid this exercise is in exorcizing the demons of beauty stereotypes, Dove continues to prey upon women's physical insecurities by reminding women that they have no purpose except aspiring to beauty (Rupp 2008). Looking natural or aging naturally are not options without a product purchase to slay insecurities about intrinsic flaws. In the final analysis, the pitch never changes because nothing is ever done to *challenge women's obsession with altering their bodies and improving appearances through a product purchase in an attempt to bolster self-esteem and empowerment* (see Dye 2009). In other words, neither natural (or real) beauty nor the sense of being comfortable within one's skin comes without a cost. They must be purchased, or as Eileen Saunders (2008, 117) writes, "[The campaign] is not a case of 'celebrating real beauty' so much as telling us where we can purchase it."

To conclude: in some ways, Dove's endorsement of natural beauty is both enlightening and empowering. In other ways, however, the campaign for natural beauty is no different from the false beauty of cosmetics and surgery that amplify insecurities for commercial self-interest. In still other ways, Dove's campaign is a bundle of contradictions. In that the campaign *inspires* by giving with one hand (celebrating natural beauty) yet *constrains* by taking with the other (natural aging must be averted), a conflict of interest is palpable (CBC 2005): "The feel good 'women are ok at any size' message is hopelessly hampered by the underlying attempt to get us to spend, spend, spend to 'correct' those pesky 'problem areas' advertisers have always told us to hate about our bodies" (Pozner 2005).

From a marketing perspective, Dove's campaign as woman-friendly and socially engaged raises thoughtful questions: Is it possible to sell any beauty product without capitalizing on women's insecurities and female unhappiness (Onstad 2010)? After all, if women thought they looked perfect just the way they naturally are, why buy any beauty product to improve appearance (Stevenson 2005)? And if beauty is defined by internal qualities, why pander to the external? And that's a contradiction a consumer-driven economy dare not contemplate, let alone challenge.

10

Reclaiming a Muscular Masculinity
Televising a Working-Class Heroic

WITH THE ASSISTANCE OF DR. SHANE DIXON

It is taken as axiomatic that mainstream media representations are classed. That much is conceded, thanks to the interplay of ownership patterns with commercial imperatives. And yet, inconsistencies prevail in an industry long dominated by men. Although media programming tends to reward male characters by linking masculinity to power, dominance, and control (both self-control and control of others) (Hanke 1998), not all TV males are created equal. As discussed in Chapter 5, on media and class, television depictions of working-class men – from Archie and Al to Homer and Raymond – reinforce images of blundering buffoons or the hopelessly helpless (Vallis 2009). In looking to tap into the buying power of women at the expense of men, advertisers routinely portray males as goofy and gaffe-prone: bumbling husbands, dumb dads, piggish boyfriends, and thuggish adolescents (Krashinsky 2009). But not all males are equally pilloried: professionally employed middle-class males tend to receive more sympathetic media treatment.

The recent emergence of a new working-class culture of muscular masculinity celebrates the unsung heroism of the blue-collar worker (Strauss 2010). Reality-based programming that valorizes the culture of working-class masculinity in blue-collar work is gaining popularity in the aftermath of 9/11 rescue efforts and the common folk appeal of Sarah Palin (Carroll 2008; Nixon 2009; Wente 2009; Malin 2010). Despite the gradual erosion of blue-collar jobs, extreme working-class reality shows (or male docu-soaps [Meltzer 2010]) are proliferating on cable TV, including *Deadliest Catch* (Alaskan fishers), *Ice Road Truckers* (Arctic truck drivers), *Black Gold* (oil rig work in Texas), *Sandhogs* (underground workers in New York City), and *Ax Men* (Oregon loggers). Dubbed by some as testostero-reality shows, ones that celebrate gritty blue-collar jobs, these programs represent a breakthrough in television's ceaseless quest to attract elusive male viewers, in part by tapping into the simple notion that audiences not only long for the physicality of the outdoors but also romanticize those men who brave the elements to do dangerous work (Chozik 2010). These highly charged fantasy sites promote the legitimacy of the working-class virtues of virility and toughness – strikingly at odds with the blandly effete white-collar culture of the knowledge economy or the emotional labour implicit within feminized service work (Kusz 2008; Nixon 2009). In light of the much ballyhooed crisis of masculinity because of global, structural, and cultural changes, these shows on "doing" (digging, harvesting, drilling, driving, and cutting) provide a riveting escapism for remasculinizing manly men by privileging a working-class heroic.

In short, a new breed of reality-based shows has emerged that articulates a fundamentally different narrative: the post-postmodern man of muscular masculinity. Although each of the programs involves different challenges, strategies, and working conditions, content is focused on work that is consistently risky, rugged, and manageable only by those who objectively assess the situation and apply manual skills to achieve tangible outcomes (Dummitt 2007; Crawford 2009a, 2009b). By analyzing a genre of reality-based television programming that focuses on hyper-masculine performance under duress, this chapter explores the symbols and images associated with the remasculinization of working-class males. This heroic working-class culture is shown to reflect select aspects of a hegemonic masculinity: independence, individualism, toughness, rationality, and discipline – in the process offering a counterbalance to the less flattering and often demeaning images of emasculated working-class men who dominated television. The chapter concludes by arguing that a reliance on this genre of macho male programs constitutes a key ideological tool by which hegemonic narratives of straight, white, and manly masculinity are internalized through the "pleasures of the media" rather than by explicit indoctrination (Kellner 1995). Or as Kusz (2008, 99) says in pointing out that a white patriarchal order is symbolically reproduced under a tough new guise (see the film *Tough Guise* [Katz 1999]), "These seemingly 'different' white male protagonists paradoxically function to reproduce white American patriarchy even as they appear, on first glance, to be distanced and disaffiliated with it."

This chapter capitalizes on the televised spectacle of men acting like manly men as a starting point for analyzing the politics of masculinity in the twenty-first century. The chapter argues that the remasculinization of working-class males reflects a reaction to their emasculation by the entertainment media. The reframing of working-class males in these docu-soaps also provides a useful vantage for analyzing the mediated politics of a hegemonic masculinity (Mazzarella 2008; Kimmel 2010). Reliance on such an extreme masculine makeover is not without context or consequences. Understanding the popularity of these reality-based programs necessitates their placement in the broader context of shifting gender and class relations (see also Chapter 5). In threatened response to changes in the social, cultural, and employment context where physicality no longer defines women and men, as Katz and Jhally (1999) assert, a retreat into the muscular masculinity of a more primal gender order (from WWF's *SmackDown!* to the mixed marital arts of UFC) reinforces patterns of power and control through size and strength. Finally, despite representational improvements, significant omissions are shown to persist in portraying the realities of working-class males, thus reinforcing the aphorism that what media omit may be more important than what they include.

Cutting, Driving, Digging, Drilling, and Harvesting: All in a Day's Work

In recent years, a slew of shows has emerged that celebrate the heroism of working-class men – for example, *Deadliest Catch,* which is about Alaskan king crab fishing in the Bering Sea; *Ax Men,* about loggers in the northwestern forests of the United States; *Ice Road Truckers,* about transport in northern Canada; *Black Gold,* about roughnecks on the oil derricks of Texas; and *Sand Hogs,* about miners under New York City streets. These programs are popular, possibly because of the awe and beauty of the work environment, along with the moxie and mettle the men display in coping with the destructive forces of nature (see Desmond 2008). Ratings are one indicator of popularity. Highlighting the fact that some of these shows have gone beyond niche markets, a few cast members of *Deadliest Catch* have been interviewed on national talk shows (including *Larry King Live* on CNN, 17 April 2010). The programs are also supported by interactive websites that allow viewers to learn more about the specific equipment used by the workers, about the workers themselves, and about the industry. Several of the websites also enable people to watch full episodes and download them to their computers, or offer the option of purchasing seasons of the program on DVD. Fans of the television shows can purchase memorabilia such as baseball hats and T-shirts with the program's logo.

These shows are an offshoot of the reality television trend. In line with the inherent competitiveness of these unscripted programs, they focus on companies or individuals who compete to see who can do the most work over a period of time. For example, in *Deadliest Catch*, a crab count records the number of pounds of crab caught; in *Ax Men*, a tally is kept of the number of log loads each company sends to the sawmill; and in *Ice Road Truckers*, the men compete over the number of loads transported. Narrators guide viewers through the shows. The film crews are on location, using handheld video cameras that enable them to get close to the action and speak directly to workers as they carry out their jobs. There are replays of significant events, such as near accidents, and occasionally viewers are given an overview of a piece of equipment or situation using computer-generated imaging. Of particular salience to this transformation is the "triumphantilizing" of the working-class heroic, primarily by fixating on the themes of valour and courage under states of duress, resiliency in the face of danger, the relative autonomy of working outside the cubicle, the interplay of rugged individualism with collective mateship in getting the job done, ultimate success no matter how formidable the natural elements (pitting "man" against nature), the authenticity of hard manual labour ("working with your hands"), and the challenge of conquering new frontiers as pioneers once did. In light of these challenges and risks, several other themes can be discerned that celebrate the authenticity of ordinariness.

Heroism: Unsung and Underappreciated

In their own way, each of the shows discusses what important commodity or service is offered to society. In *Black Gold* it is oil. In *Sandhogs* it is a tunnel for water. In *Ice Road Truckers* it is material for northern communities and mines. What also comes to light in these television shows is (1) that the workers are employed in industries that people depend on for their high living standards, and (2) that the work (and the sacrifices and risks that are so often associated with it) of these largely unsung heroes largely goes unnoticed by the wider population. In other words, not only are the services and commodities that these workers provide the public of crucial importance, but they are typically unacknowledged. Although people are happy to consume what workers toil to produce, few consider the workers who are doing the jobs *and* what it takes – including the risks – to do the job. At times, workers are seen talking about how their occupation is un- or underappreciated. A comment by a driller from *Black Gold* typifies the sentiments of the workers: "It would never register with them [consumers] that the guy digging that hole out there in the ground is the reason you've got gasoline for that vehicle sitting out there in your driveway."

Danger: Risking It All by Rising to the Challenge

Danger predominates in all of these shows. Men are exposed to bodily risks because of their working environment. For the fishers on the Bering Sea, it is the dangers of the high seas. For the loggers of *Ax Men,* hazards lurk in the towering trees they fell, movement across steep slopes, and transportation into sawmills. In reinforcing the common theme of man (men, usually) against nature, the Ax Men risk their lives accessing timber in inaccessible locales because of snapped cables and runaway logs. And for the Sandhogs, it is the threat of rock falls plummeting into the tunnels they excavate or breathing particulate-filled air. The men of *Ice Road Truckers* continually confront danger as they drive their rigs over frozen lakes that double as roads to deliver goods to remote mining communities, all the while coping with notoriously inclement weather conditions, subzero temperatures, and cold-induced equipment breakdowns. Truckers must drive great distances for many hours at monotonously low speeds – forty kilometres per hour – across barren landscapes and through whiteouts, listening intently for the telltale cracks that warn of breaking ice. If the driver attempts to speed up, the risks increase for getting a fine or breaking through the ice. The bearded and burly fishers in *Deadliest Catch* are continually at high risk of injury or death. (Commercial fishing appears to be the most dangerous job based on fatalities per 100,000 of population; see Power 2008.)

The machinery used in these industries can be as deadly as the environmental conditions. As mentioned, the failure of machinery poses hazards. In one episode of *Ax Men,* loggers scramble to avoid errant logs that have been let loose by a broken overhead line. In *Ice Road Truckers,* a driver at risk for frostbite coaxes his truck along after it develops mechanical problems in minus forty degree Fahrenheit temperatures. In *Ax Men,* the uneven, stick-strewn terrain makes it difficult to get around. On the boats featured in *Deadliest Catch,* the pitching decks awash with cold water create problems of footing. In both *Ax Men* and *Deadliest Catch,* viewers are treated to workers tripping and falling while trying to maintain their balance. Inexperienced workers are shown making missteps that threaten to injure themselves or endanger their work crew.

How do these men confront the risk of injury and fatality? Frequently in these shows, the risks of injury and death are portrayed as part and parcel of the job. Workers concede that they worry about potential risks; nevertheless, they do not dwell on them for fear of becoming immobilized ("paralysis by analysis") or, worse still, of incurring the wrath or ridicule of co-workers. In a fashion analogous to media coverage of a sporting event, near misses and close calls are repeated numerous times, dramatizing how a worker dodged certain injury or cheated death. Often, these replays are followed by commentary from the worker(s) involved in the incident, who describe it in harrowing detail. When injuries happen, the audience is exposed to how they are dealt with. In many cases, minor injuries are addressed by the injured party himself or with the assistance of fellow workers. In one instance, a fisher on a crab boat who has jammed his hand in the door of a crab pot is treated by the captain in the boat's galley. With his hand on the table, the fisher relieves the pressure building underneath his fingernail by heating tweezers with a lighter and burning a hole through the nail. As the camera zooms in to capture the blood and ooze flowing from the pierced fingernail, the captain commends the fisher on his toughness.

Manly Masculinity as Rugged Individualism

Another theme emphasizes the distinctiveness that distinguishes these workers from everyday folk (see Chozik 2010). There are continual reminders that the work can be done only by men who are masculine enough to keep pace, endure the pain that the job dishes out, and persevere in the face of long work hours. For instance, in *Ax Men,* when a greenhorn runs into problems unloading timber, a boss attributes this weak performance to his status as a "boy" rather than a man. In an episode near the end of Season One, *Ax Men*'s narrator notes dramatically, "It's either time to give up or man up." In *Deadliest Catch,* this theme is best seen when the crabbers are in the "grind" – an onerous, monotonous setting – unloading and resetting crab pots for up to thirty-six hours at a stretch. Workers must also demonstrate that they have the ability to keep up to speed, and the stamina that that requires. With *Ax Men,* workers are shown running to the logs to ensure they are secured and removed from the bush as quickly as possible. Failure to hustle is often met with derisive yells from other workers. Sometimes these are playful jabs; other times they are commands that clearly highlight the power differences between supervisors and employees. In all of these shows, the theme "time is money" reigns supreme, so that those who falter are seen as being lesser by their workmates and other companies.

Autonomy of Workers, Authenticity of Work

Workers in these programs routinely refer to the freedom of their work. The shows highlight that men are able to escape the alienation that seems to pervade those in the city, in the cube farm, in the office. As a trucker in *Ax Men* notes, motioning to the window of his truck as the camera pans over an unpopulated, heavily forested, steeply sloped valley, "Nice view from my office." In other shows too we are reminded that the work being carried out is not within the concrete confines of the city. Viewers are privy to expansive vistas of the Bering Sea and Alaskan coast in *Deadliest Catch*. Even when the television shows are outside the wilderness, as is *Sandhogs*, they highlight the distance from the constraints of late modernity. The miners featured in *Sandhogs* work beneath one of the busiest cities in the world, but their work underground affords them separation from the rigours (rules) of everyday work in the knowledge economy. Also running through the shows is the idea that "out there" (or in the case of *Sandhogs*, "down here") is a different place – one where hard work is celebrated and men can act in a manly manner. And in many ways they do: there is cursing, yelling, hooting, and playful jousting – as might be expected in a masculinized environment. Of course, as Desmond (2006, 88) notes, this "freedom" does not amount to an absence of rules, but rather a different set of rules that govern a work subculture.

Esprit de Corps: Competition as Camaraderie
Despite the virtues of individualism and autonomy, notions of camaraderie and/as competition are prominently featured. In some of the programs, terms such as "brotherhood" are invoked to describe the relationships between workers who generally work in small groups. At times, it is difficult to discern who has seniority or who is in charge. This is akin to firefighting fraternity or team sport conviviality in which members look out for one another. As a timber cutter from *Ax Men* explains in an episode, "We pick at each other ... But don't try to get between us." Moreover, because of the way several of these shows are set up – as competition between companies – there is an "us versus them" mentality – an identification with the company in its fight with competitors. For example, in *Ice Road Truckers*, there is an annual competition to determine who owns the largest number of runs during the two-month season. But rarely do we see the "us versus them" scenarios that pervade many workplaces, namely, workers' battles with management.

In sum, a new breed of unscripted manly men shows has emerged. Its focus on the working-class hero represents a channel for remasculinizing males through the prism of their working lives (see Chozik 2010). Whether it's *Ice Road Truckers* or *Ax Men* or *Sandhogs*, the theme is unmistakingly similar: the return of machismo through the bravery and courage of real men in risky competition with the forces of nature, co-workers, and management. Each of the shows attempts to resuscitate the prerogatives of a working-class masculinity.

Membership in a working class that embraces manly manual labour not only provides a source of pride, self-esteem, and respectability but also registers a degree of disdain for the squishy middle class as unmasculine because of its rootedness in feminized service work involving emotional/mental labour (Nixon 2009). Matthew Crawford (2009a, 36-37) sings the praises of accomplishing something by "working with your hands" when he writes:

> Most of us do work that feels more surreal than real. Working in an office, you often find it difficult to see any tangible result from your efforts. What exactly have you accomplished at the end of any given day? Where the chain of cause and effect is opaque and responsibility diffuse, the experience of individual agency can be elusive. "Dilbert," "The Office," and similar portrayals of cubicle life attest to the dark absurdism with which many Americans have come to view their white collar jobs.

This valorization of working-class experiences and culture reflects the macho masculinity of skilled manual labour that entails danger, risk, fear of failure, and the ability to stick up for yourself when others are trying to stick it to you. The hegemonic masculinity that privileges a manly masculinity as the preferred ideal reduces the fear of being feminized by office work through participation in working-class heroics (Mumby 1998; Nixon 2009). These docu-soaps also tap into male insecurities. In a world where men are adrift in a sea of anxieties and roles, they provide soothing escapism that fixates on manly ideals (Meltzer 2010).

Crisis in Televised Masculinity: Working-Class Heroic or Hegemony in Action?

> *After years of dutiful, dues-paying obsequiousness, men seem to be coming to the realization that surviving (and even enjoying) the wide-open gestalt of 2010 demands a different response than testicular retraction. In others words, we're witnessing the remasculation of the American man. (Gordinier 2010)*

Hegemonic masculinity has long proven to be a staple of television programming. From sitcoms and westerns to drama and soaps, positive images of male masculinity dominated, images of active and controlling men who used their prowess and power to overcome obstacles in the successful achievement of goals (Mulvey 1975; Fiske 1987). But cultural definitions of manhood and the socially constructed notion of a hegemonic masculinity are sharply contested in response to ideological shifts and structural realities (Connell and Messerschmidt 2005). As a theoretical construct or normative ideal, the concept of of a hegemonic masculinity is neither static nor inevitable (Katz 1999; Connell 2005; Gordinier 2010). Rather, the concept itself is constantly under contestation and construction along the lines of whatever patriarchy wants it to be at a particular point in time, in the process doing whatever is necessary to remain hegemonic, even if this entails incorporating more traditional feminine characteristics – from tears to nurturing (Hanke 1998; Mazzarella 2008). In short, references to masculinity reject any notion of specific and constant ("essentialized") attributes or natural state of being, yet acknowledge that whereas multiple masculinities based on intersecting inequalities may influence male behaviour, the range of masculinities and the relations between them usually revolve around a hegemonic set of ideals held by a society's ruling elites (Connell 2005, 75-78).

In recent years, the erosion of male cultural normativity and social authority has neutered notions of a conventional masculinity (Kimmel 2010). Mass media depictions of masculinity that privileged the hegemonic male wilted under the onslaught of competing masculinities such as those espoused by feminists and gays (Hanke 1998). The masculinist ideal of John Wayne was preempted by Alan Alda of *M*A*S*H* fame during the 1970s and 1980s, then by *Seinfeld* in the 1990s, but never entirely displaced, resulting in a mounting identity crisis ("Who are we?") and a crisis of confidence ("What should we be doing?"). Or as Henry Giroux (2001, 7) writes of the perceived crisis in masculinity: "White, heterosexual men in America have not fared well ... Not only have they been attacked by feminists, gays, lesbians and various subaltern groups for a variety of ideological and material offences, they have also had to endure a rewriting of the very meaning of masculinity." This crisis in masculinity reflects a constellation of economic, cultural, social, and political factors but is sharply symbolized by the proliferation of jobs involving emotional or mental labour – in effect making manual work an anachronism in a knowledge/service-driven economy (Nixon 2009; Wente 2009).

Mainstream media rely on several strategies to revive straight, white, manly masculinities without explicitly declaring an all-out cultural war (Kusz 2008). One way is to encode white males as conventionally masculine, with a corresponding list of traits diametrically opposed to those associated with the effeminate New Age/metrosexual guy (see Vincent 2008). For example, after years of focusing on men's softer side, marketers for Old Spice ("Should your man be an Old Spice man?" or "Bathe yourself in power") or Dockers ("Wear the pants") are cranking up the testosterone level by trumpeting traditional male strengths and the masculinities of yesteryear. Another strategy is to juxtapose these masculinized images with those of affluent white (-collar) males upon which the so-called "evils" of feminism and political correctness are projected and played out. As this chapter has argued, by putting muscular masculinity to the test, the popularity of these testostero-driven male soaps represents one way of symbolically annihilating the competition.

Yet this heroic narrative is not always what it seems to be, largely because appearances can be deceiving. As Desmond (2008) points out in debunking the hypocrisy of labelling wildlife firefighters as heroes, there are two ways to dehumanize: either strip people of all virtue or cleanse them of all vice. Heroicizing workers in risky occupations has had the effect of flattening their humanity. All that remains are mythic creatures – noble, virtuous, manly – whose sacrifices ensure a comfortable standard of living for the population at large. Reactions to this heroism are mixed: at their best, these shows highlight the difficult work and sacrifices made by working-class men so that the affluent can revel in the good life. Valorizing the concept of worker as unsung hero also performs ideological work because the mythology conceals how the professional blue-collar risk-takers generate wealth for the rich and powerful. At their worst, these shows – in their attempts to valorize the working-class heroic by escaping into fantasy – gloss over too much of the men's working lives. In conveying a nostalgia for a fictional North America of frontier myths, wilderness triumphs, and muscular masculinity, they depoliticize and gender the working-class characters, thus allowing audiences to vicariously engage with the masculine adventure and working-class drama without having to deal with prickly issues related to job security, fair wages, or environment despoilation (Kimmel 2010; Lockett 2010).

In short, despite the remasculinization of working-class identities and blue-collar heroics, what is omitted is no less significant. Notwithstanding some focus on the suffering and sacrifices of workers, little is done to contextualize deprivation or marginalization – much less to explain its causes in structural rather than individualistic terms. Often excluded are factors that would expose job hazards that go beyond risks that naturally inhere in nature and technology or are regarded as just "part of the job." That these occupations are dangerous is not in dispute. Transportation, forestry, and commercial fishing rank as some of the most hazardous industries in North America (Krahn, Lowe, and Hughes 2007, 314-15). However, in television's attempts to valorize "dangerous jobs" and the men that do them, what is omitted reflects a medium that seeks to draw in viewers with stories that excite but ultimately may misrepresent the totality of workers' experiences. The omission of injury such as repetitive strain, work hazards, and near-misses reinforces a media's compulsion for material that is enticing to viewers but understates other dangers that, perhaps not as exciting, may be as equal or more devastating than the ones shown to viewers. That makes it doubly important to deconstruct the label of heroism when it involves the lunch-bucket brigade who do the dirty work, shouldering job-related risks in the process. Only when the contradiction between the real (worker) and the ideal (hero) is exposed for what it is – discourses in defence of dominant ideology – can working-class images transcend a media gaze that flatters as it flattens.

11

Framing Religion
Media Blind Spot or Coverage That Blinds?

The relationship between mainstream news media and organized religions has proven awkward at best, hostile at worst (see Haskell 2009). News media coverage tends to dismiss religion as irrelevant, irrational, or an irritant; by contrast, secular world views are defended as normal, necessary, and superior in advancing national interests. References to religion are filtered through contexts of conflict or aberration because of prevailing news values that promote the newsworthiness of negativity and abnormality. Few should be surprised by media negativity toward religion, religiosity, and religious diversities. In an overtly secular society that abides by the logic of science, reason, and technology as grounds for progress, prosperity, and peace, religion is a target for criticism and ridicule – reflecting an elite consensus that portrays religious people as troublemakers or feeble-minded and unworthy of protection or entitlements (Hitchens 2007).

That mainstream news media negatively frame religion in ways that exclude, distort, or demean should come as no shock. This misrepresentation persists across a broad range of mainstream religions. Media expressions like the film *Doubt* or TV episodes of *Law & Order* or newspaper coverage (Lewis 2009) imply every Catholic priest or Protestant pastor is a pedophile (in reality, studies suggest only about 2 to 4 percent have sexual contact with minors, a figure comparable to the percentage of sexual predators in the general population [Friscolanti 2009]). Religious members and faith-based minorities are routinely devalued as problem people, that is, as people who are problems ("stuck in the past") or who create problems through demands that cost or precepts that discriminate (Stein 2007). For example, consider the persistence of four negative images of evangelical Christians since 1970: the psychotic, the naive, the hypocritical, and the insensitive (Rendleman 2008).

Nowhere is the demonization of the divine more evident than in news media's hyping of religious minorities as threats – especially faith-based communities like Sikhs or Muslims, who many believe pose a threat to national security and societal culture (see the Case Study at the end of this chapter). As the lead story in the 4 May 2009 issue of *Maclean's* concludes, based on an adult sample of just over a thousand respondents, Canadians display a worrying level of antipathy toward minority religions, with Islam singled out as a purveyor of violence (Geddes 2009). Not surprisingly, faith-based communities are frequently framed as a threat to be controlled, a problem to be solved, or a nuisance to be contained lest they fan the flames of public panic over real or imagined risks (Bramadat 2009).

Such media negativity poses problems. An anti-religion bias not only disrespects diverse religions and religious experiences but also compromises their positive role in society at large, and in specific groups in particular (Marshall, Gilbert, and Ahmanson 2009). Religion is dismissed as irrelevant in describing (understanding, interpreting, and predicting) reality or in prescribing a preferred way of thinking or doing (Marsden and Savigny 2009). In refusing to "find religion" except as a problem or conflict, Canadians are misled at a time when balanced and unbiased information about the politics of religion is badly needed. After all, as pointed out by a leading figure in the field, Paul Bramadat (2009, 2), religion is inextricably linked to many contemporary dynamics involving migrants and minorities:

> Religions are often intimately involved in conflicts that lead people to flee from one country to another; they are involved in the forms of resistance people employ to articulate political views both in the "homeland" and in the "diaspora"; they are typically foundational features of the social structures of the minority communities in the host countries; they (especially different forms of Christianity) are often the recipients of historic state privileges that are emblematic of entrenched power disparities in immigrant-receiving societies; they help to create institutions that facilitate the transfer of money to family members in receiving countries; and, of course, they inform the moral standards, aesthetic sensibilities, and social institutions that provide migrants with a sense of meaning and purpose both during migration and in their new settings.

Put bluntly, religions matter and religiosity must be taken seriously (Seljak 2009). Little can be gained by uncritically accepting claims that social movements or group dynamics (including violence) have been hijacked by manipulative and evil religious leaders whose alleged real motives are political or economic. Such an excessively narrow interpretation reflects a secular reading of social reality that reduces religion to the level of the private, apolitical, and individualistic. Too often contradictions prevail in framing such coverage: on one side, religion is hyped as threatening the integrity of so-called civilized society; on the other side, references to Muslims or Islam (including Islamist terrorism) often gloss over the religious dimensions of human experiences. Fear of appearing intolerant or fomenting bias makes it easier to focus on social conditions or political motives as causal factors (Marshall, Gilbert, and Ahmanson 2009). A blinkered and politically correct view that strips reality of any religiosity would strike those of a religious bent as absurdly unrealistic.

Of course, not all media representations of religion and religiosity are problematic or stuck in the past. Denominational religions are increasingly mediated (from online sermons to radio crusades), and personal experiences with secular media are frequently described in religious terms (through rituals or sense of community) (Stout and Buddenbaum 2008). Or consider how openly commercial media processes are "finding religion." Advertising increasingly relies on religious imagery to cut through the clutter or to generate a buzz through shock and surprise (Mallia 2009). The popularity of TV shows like *Joan of Arcadia* and *Touched by an Angel* suggests a public willingness to pursue religious experience through the media of popular culture, rather than through traditional congregations (Stout and Buddenbaum 2008). Critics are also acknowledging the emergence of religion-friendly films like *Into Great Silence* or *Of Gods and Men,* which won the Grand Prix at the 2010 Cannes Film Festival (Higgins 2011). Even news media appear to have found religion. According to Vultee, Craft, and Velker (2010), religious coverage was a lively topic in the United States until the recent financial meltdown prompted papers to delete religion columns and eliminate reporters on the religion beat. Finally, online religious communication is increasingly important as both institutionalized religions and religious movements look to leverage the Web to improve their online reach (Dawson and Cowan 2004; H. Campbell 2010; SSRC 2010). In their capacity to transcend barriers and construct communities, social media (including blogs) offer new conversations about religion in public life through exposure, discussion, and critique (Akou 2010; H. Campbell 2010).

In that religion matters even if mainstream media balk at taking religiosity seriously except as marketing, caricature, foil, threat, or angle, this chapter explores the complex and contested relationship between religion and mainstream news media in general. The chapter examines how news media coverage of religion has proven both sensationalistic and misleading: sensationalistic because of episodic coverage that supersedes the thematic or contextual; misleading because of a systemic bias against religiosity unless framed as negative, confrontational, or problematic. The chapter also explores the rationale behind a media reluctance to seriously embrace religion, despite its centrality at personal, national, and international levels. In acknowledging that what the news media omit may prove more informative than what they include, thereby contributing to a relentless one-sidedness by default rather than intent, the chapter demonstrates how news media coverage of religion, religiosity, and faith-based minorities is systemically biasing (coverage that blinds), as well as systematic biasing (blind coverage). Special emphasis on the framing of Islam and Muslims as troublesome religious constituents helps to ground the analysis.

Religion Matters: Finding Religion

The post 9/11 epoch has confirmed what many had suspected: whether of a transcendental nature or corrupted for economic and political purposes, religion embodies a formidable dynamic at both local and individual levels, as well as at the national and the global (Stein 2007; Kunz 2009; Policy Research Initiative 2009; Seljak 2009). To be sure, religion once deeply mattered in terms of people's identities, group affiliation, and national unity. Many had predicted the eclipse of religion in light of scientific and technological advances; after all, was it not synonymous with ignorance and superstition or a reactionary sop to poverty and oppression? But rather than retreating or disappearing, religion remains a powerful and pivotal force in human affairs. Religion is rapidly replacing ideology as a meaning system. As people increasingly crave stability and order in an increasingly unpredictable world, especially as globalization continues to disrupt local cultures, religion provides a bastion of personal identity and a source of group solidarity in times of uncertainty, change, and diversity (Bibby 2011).

Canada is a particularly instructive example of religion's ability to evoke wildly divergent reactions. On one side are the doomsayers who predict the eventual demise of religion. With the possible exception of evangelical Christianity and Roman Catholicism, mainstream religions are waning in popularity (Bibby 2011). Weekly church attendance continues to plummet, dropping from 67 percent of the population in 1946 to 20 percent in 2001. (Monthly and yearly attendances are not nearly as drastic [Eagle 2011].) According to Statistics Canada, more than half of those between the ages of fifteen and twenty-nine years have neither a religious affiliation nor attend a service of worship (Valpy 2010). Only 22 percent say religion is important to them, down from 34 percent in 2002, whereas many dismiss organized religion as illogical and out of touch with reality.

On the other side are the optimists who believe religion and religiosity are growing in public stature (Seljak 2009; Bibby 2011). Many Canadians believe in the existence of God within their midst or have experienced some kind of a religious experience, suggesting a gap between those who believe and those who belong. Gaps such as these have prompted Reginald Bibby (2011) to describe the situation in Canada as neither secular nor revivalist but one of polarization, involving a bimodal pattern of distribution with a durable core of Canadians continuing to value religion (for Bibby, the future looks bright for Roman Catholics, Conservative Protestant groups, and Muslims), alongside a growing number who are leaving in droves. Yes, Canadians may be less inclined toward formal institutional involvement, especially in Quebec, yet regional variations prevail, with church attendance holding steady in the Atlantic provinces (Eagle 2011). In addition to a stable core of formal adherents, many continue to embrace a sense of religiosity at private and personal levels, with just over 10 percent of Canadians saying religion is the most important part of their identity (Policy Research Initiative 2009). This is particularly true among non-Christian faith communities, which remain an area of strong growth in Canada, thanks to the stream of devout immigrants (Bibby 2011), as Table 2 demonstrates:

TABLE 2

Religions in Canada, 2001 and 2017 (est.)

Religion	2001	2017 (est.)
Muslims	579,645	1.4 million
Jews	329,995	375,000
Buddhists	300,345	400,000
Hindus	297,200	600,000
Sikhs	278,415	500,000

And with integration into Canada proving more difficult than many imagined, immigrants and minority communities will increasingly rely on religion to recapture a sense of rootedness, belonging, and attachment (Bramadat and Seljak 2008). In that the intensity and public manifestations of those identities at both individual and group levels are intensifying, a multiculturally secular society like Canada cannot avoid addressing the challenges of growing religiosity ("religious experiences") in a context of diverse religions. David Seljak (2009, 1) captures a sense of the challenge when he writes:

> Those interested in promoting multiculturalism – that is, in making Canada a more diverse, participatory, and just society – should take religion seriously, because Canadians take it seriously. An emerging scholarship is demonstrating the intimate connection between ethnic and religious identity. This connection is so close that members of these communities themselves cannot say with certainty where ethnicity ends and religion begins. One cannot claim to have recognized and honoured the particular identity of an ethnic community when one has refused to acknowledge those religious elements that members of a community see as central to their identity.

Such an attitude has the potential to alienate members of a ethno-religious communities from mainstream society. Consequently, policy makers are beginning to see that a failure to acknowledge how important religious identities are to many Canadians may lead to misunderstandings and injustices that translate into the polarization, ghettoization, and radicalization of certain religion communities – a situation with which many European countries are currently grappling. The challenge lies in living together in common with our deepest religious differences. Paradoxically, secularism may be the answer – not a secularism that is anti-religion or endorses the absence of religion but one in which the public realm is shaped by respect for others and their rights so that deep difference can coexist in free exercise. Or as the editors of *Hedgehog Review* put it in a

FILM CLIP
Muslims in Film: Couched in Compromise

Improvements in movie depictions of Muslims and Islam are widely applauded. Recent films, from *The Kite Runner* and *A Mighty Heart* to *Kingdom of Heaven* and *Days of Glory*, seek to normalize Muslims as ordinary people who range in virtue from good to bad, with shades of humanity in between (Vultee, Craft, and Velker 2010). But even the best-intentioned can boomerang badly – as demonstrated by the reaction and revulsion accompanying the 2008 film *The Stoning of Soraya M.*, based on a true story. The film, in which a Muslim woman (Zahra) narrates her tale to a journalist stranded in a remote Iranian village, revolves around the events leading up to the stoning of her niece (Soraya) a day earlier for being an "inconvenient wife."

Through a series of flashbacks, audiences learn that Soraya was the wife of a powerful and bullying villager, Ali – a nasty piece of work – with deep connections to Iran's revolutionary movement. Ali wants to divorce Soraya and marry a fourteen-year-old, but Soraya refuses his demands, in part because the loss of income would further impoverish her daughters. And therein lies the crux of the story: although Ali is entitled to multiple wives according to the dictates of the ayatollah, he balks at incurring the cost of supporting two families or running the risk of losing his wife's dowry. To get rid of Soraya as expeditiously as possible while concealing his true motives, he falsely accuses her of infidelity; her well-intentioned visits to a recently widowed friend to assist with his housekeeping facilitates the spread of rumour and innuendo. Thanks to the testimony of Ali's cowardly cousin and the complicity of the dastardly village mullah, Soraya is found guilty on the flimsiest of evidence by a sharia court — a system of Islamic law that, according to the film, yields a double standard. That is, if a man is accused of adultery by his wife, she must prove his guilt, whereas if the man accuses his wife, she must prove her innocence.

At one level, the film reinforces conventional stereotypes of Muslims as impulsively violent. Over and again, fundamental Islam is demonized as an essentially backward and unspeakably cruel religion that can be manipulated by the ruthlessly opportunistic for ulterior goals. In using religion for their own selfish gains, the men in the village (including Soraya's eldest son) display a virulent brand of sexism that carries genuine

volume devoted to the politics of religious pluralism, "Secularism in these pages is thus constructed as the friend of all religions, and the foe and champion of none" (Does Religious Pluralism Require Secularism? 2010).

Then there are the pessimistic optimists – optimists who believe religious growth is inevitable; pessimists who frame this growth as problematic. Canadians may be relatively tolerant toward mainstream religions (Geddes 2009); however, they are less amiable toward minority religions that link spirituality to political goals, especially when recourse to extremism is justified in the name of orthodoxy. The expansion of non-mainstream religions can also generate those cultural clashes, from niqabs to turbans to so-called honour killings, that periodically engulf Canadians in debates over where to draw the line. Consider developments in Quebec. It is widely perceived as a socially progressive province, yet its liberal principles appear at odds with seemingly pejorative attitudes toward faith-based minorities. Surveys routinely indicate that a large majority disapprove of open expressions of religion (other than Christianity), suggesting approval of a separation-of-Church-and-state style of secularism that accommodates mainstream Christianity but not religious minorities (Seljak 2009). Fears are driven by a belief that practices that oppose core Quebecer values, such as gender equality, may hide behind a charter-protected freedom of religious expression (which is a charter-protected right) (Reitz et al. 2009). Anxieties about too much accommodation of religious and cultural practices came to a boil with the controversial Herouxville code of conduct aimed at (Muslim) immigrants: this publication of standards to guide immigrant behaviour explained that women shared the same rights as men and therefore "killing women in public beatings or burning them alive are not part of our standards."

But there is another angle. It's quite possible that negative coverage of religious minorities reflects an interplay of sensationalist media with opportunistic politicians. The report of the Bouchard and Taylor Commission in May 2008 accused both English Canadian and Quebec media of conveying a negative impression of Quebecers as intolerant or unreasonable. Yet there is no evidence that Quebecers are less accommodating or more racist or xenophobic than other Canadians. Criticism of Quebecers is constructed and conveyed by a news media that splices together a small number of random and isolated events, thereby hyping the prospect of a looming crisis where none exists. The extent of Quebecers' racism is blown out of proportion by inflammatory and opportunistic coverage hyping moral panics that both media and politicians can manipulate for ulterior purposes (Bouchard and Taylor 2008; Al Hidaya Association 2008). But news media are not the only ones perpetuating anti-Muslim, anti-Islam messages, as revealed by this Case Study of a film that simultaneously challenges yet reinforces stereotypes.

Covering Religion, Uncovering Bias

A paradox prevails: despite this resurgence of religiosity at individual, societal, and global levels, including the centrality of religion in peoples lives around the world and its influence in domestic politics and foreign affairs, news media framing of religion in Canada tends to ignore or distort (see also Marshall, Gilbert, and Ahmanson 2009). Or when religion makes the news, it is often just one element of a much larger story, such as the debate over multiculturalism and reasonable accommodation (see also Pew Research Center Project for Excellence in Journalism 2011). This fixation with negativity, from conflict to scandals, should come as no surprise, especially in a society where news media seem to equate religion and religiosity as something either (1) quaint, myopic,

loathing of women and their sexuality — a misogyny that appears to be stoked by religion and fuelled by feelings of impotence in a rapidly changing world. Not surprisingly, the village men are caricaturized as spineless sycophants who paradoxically invoke the name of Allah ("God is great") during the stoning of Soraya M. Although the stoning of adulterers as a cultural practice that has survived through cultural heritage is arguably a contentious issue within Islam, the twenty minutes devoted to the stoning of Soraya (what some critics have called "torture porn") is viscerally searing in reinforcing stereotypes of Muslims and Islam.

But there is a counterhegemonic message conveyed by this film. In contrast to stereotypes of Muslim women as weak and submissive, Soraya and especially her aunt Zahra are portrayed as strong and outspoken — even fearless — women who are willing to defend their principles and uphold moral integrity against those who want to manipulate Islam to perpetuate misogyny and institutionalize cultural patriarchy. To be sure, there are dangers in polarizing men as bad and women as good (to its credit, the film does expose some women who support the mob mentality). The film can also be criticized for conflating in the public mind all Muslims and Islam as guilty by association. Criticisms notwithstanding, there is much to commend in a film that not only exposes the twisting of religion for self-serving purposes but also refuses to objectify Muslim women as weak and helpless, preferring instead to celebrate the courage of their convictions in the face of seemingly insurmountable odds.

References: Carl M. Cannon, Soraya M. Stoned to Death for Being an Inconvenient Wife, http://www.politicsdaily.com; Safiyyah, The Stoning of Soraya M.: A Review, http://muslimahmediawatch.org; The Stoning of Soraya M., www.popmatters.com; The Stoning of Soraya M., DVD review, www.cinemablend.com; In Good Faith: Portrayal of Islam in the Media, http://blogscritic.org.

and archaic or (2) menacing and subversive. Most news media don't understand religion, much less the religious precepts underlying both political developments and intergroup relations (Vultee, Craft, and Velker 2010). Nor do they take religious motivation very seriously, let alone make an effort to delve into the possibility of religion as a major player in the public domain. The erosion of organized religion as a political force in driving the public agenda also undermines its salience as newsworthy (Bibby 1987).

This biasing of religion involves two dimensions. First, coverage of religion is routinely ignored or marginalized unless spectacular or sordid. Mainstream American media devoted about 2 percent of its coverage in time and space to religion in 2009-10 – an increase of 1 percent from the previous year – with events and controversies involving Islam dominating (Pew Research Center Project for Excellence in Journalism 2011). Should one be surprised by such miniscule coverage? In a world that worships on the altar of science, reason, technology, and evidence-based objectivity, religion is likely to be taken seriously or grossly misunderstood if taken seriously (Marshall, Gilbert, and Ahmanson 2009). Second, incidents involving religion are selected because of their confrontational aspects, thus accentuating the adversarial, the scandalous, or the destructive. Not unexpectedly, news coverage toward the sensational and problematic culminates in a privileging of extremist religious views as newsworthy (Beckford 1999, 107). Cults are sharply negativized as browbeating propaganda, whereas their adherents are dismissed as dupes or dopes (Dawson 2006). Particularly hard hit by negative coverage are those alternative religions whose oppositional stances challenge sanctioned modes of acceptance and desirability (Boykoff 2006).

Is this negative framing of religion justified in a world where religiosity represents a powerful and

central force for many? Of course, religions can be divisive, violent, and patriarchal; religion can also foster liberation, tolerance, community, and inclusion
(Wallis 2005; Marshall, Gilbert, Ahmanson 2009). By offering a vision of social
justice beyond the status quo, religion provides men and women with a source
of support during times of crisis or oppression. But without content or context
to balance the negative with the positive, audiences rarely have the opportunity
to sample information beyond a matrix of boom, gloom, or doom – an omission that is gravely amplified by the absence of voices of moderation. Yes, persons in positions of religious authority have been known to abuse their power
for self-serving purposes. Yet many continue to lead exemplary lives in advancing the spiritual welfare of their parishioners. Clearly, a fundamental conflict
of interest prevails. Religious experiences are complex yet nuanced, evolving,
and situational, involving multi-dimensional viewpoints that resist morselization into visual bits and sound bites. In that the news media rarely do nuance
or context, a combination of factors, from media competition to prevailing
news values, reinforces precisely what religious narratives are not.

Such a negative framing experience does a disservice to religious groups.
The prioritizing of conflict or crisis as news frames transforms faith-based
minorities into troublesome constituents – that is, problem people who have
problems, who are problems, and who create problems that are expensive, inconvenient, or cause conflict. These religious groups are framed (set up) by
such negative coverage, just as people may be falsely framed for something
they didn't do – and the consequences are comparable. Religious minorities are
set up to fall by default or to fail by association because of mediacentric biases
that conspire (however unintentionally) to distort or demean.

Paradoxes prevail. Although many Canadians and Americans remain preoccupied with ethical and existential issues involving religion, mainstream
news rarely addresses the issue of religious faith unless piggybacked onto a
larger story. According to a poll by the Pew Research Center for the People and
the Press, although Americans remain a highly religious population, with the
vast majority professing a belief in God, prayer, and Judgment Day (Beckerman
2004), news media miss the religious angle on any number of significant stories. Journalists seldom penetrate the surface in their coverage of religion because of a preference for scandals or spectacles that emphasize conflict,
extremists, controversy, and caricature. Coverage continues to dwell on the
hard news of religion – from Catholic Church scandals to America's precarious
engagement with the Muslim world and continuing scriptural injunctions over
gay and lesbian marriages. In that even mainstream denominations are ignored

or distorted, the spiritual commitment of believers suffers because of excessively clinical coverage – at the expense of deeper questions about faith and spirituality. Gal Beckerman (2004) writes: "The journalist glances at religious community as if staring through the glass of an ant farm, remarking on what the strange creatures are doing, but missing the motivations behind the actions." Or consider this perspective from Bangladesh, where Islam constitutes a lived reality rather than a media construct:

> Like all religions played out from day to day, it's pretty uneventful. It's not an ideology; it exists in the commitment of miniscule acts of human friendship. It gives people a vocabulary to understand their grief, their moments of elation, their losses, and the pressures they are under. It keeps families together (but doesn't necessarily stop them from bickering or smouldering with resentment; it's a faith, not a magic potion). It works through and around individuals ... It provides, in short, the whole background to the grind and flow of daily life. Islam here is in the air, but not in your face. (Morris 2006)

How to account for this disjuncture between media reality and the realities of religiosity? The conventional response suggests the existence of profoundly different world views. The seemingly secularist bent of journalists makes it difficult to frame reality as religious people see it. The news media and religion represent two institutions that process information in ostensibly different ways. Whereas news media revel in the new and sensational, religions focus on eternal truths and the contemplation associated with people's deepest experiences (Biernatzki 2003). For the news media, the path to enlightenment is paved with objective reality – a belief that everything can be known as long as it can be heard, seen, touched, or smelled. By contrast, as Diane Winston of the University of Southern California concludes (cited in Beckerman 2004), religious enlightenment is largely about mystery, faith, and the unknown – issues that are difficult to quantify by the kind of empirical evidence that news media crave.

A conflict of interest is inevitable. News media dismiss religion as an alternative world view at odds with the values and norms of the prevailing news paradigm. Belief and faith are seen as insufficiently newsworthy to merit coverage unless framed as conflict. Largely fearful of offending anybody or soft-pedalling religious tenets they know little about, news media frame religious coverage in the same way as sports or politics, complete with all the conflict and negativity (Vultee, Craft, and Velker 2010). Non-controversial issues or non-confrontational actions are glossed over as unnewsworthy without the news values of deviance or significance. Not surprisingly, Beckerman reminds us, a story about a homosexual minister is more likely than about the changing nature of Christian doctrine on homosexuality – more about the what and the who, rather than the why. In brief, religion is shortchanged or downgraded not because of a pervasive secularism in the newsroom but because *news media are news media.* Any understanding of religion beyond the superficiality of a conflict frame would entail a fundamental rethinking of what is news. Nowhere is this commitment more compelling than in news media coverage of Muslims and Islam, with its overwhelming focus on events or groups in the Middle East in response to crisis or conflict, as explained in the Case Study below.

_____ case study

Muslims under the Media Gaze: Religion as News Media Hype, Islam as Moral Panic

Particularly vulnerable to media miscasting of religiosity are those faith-based communities whose realities veer outside a preferred Canadian identity or pose a security threat, including Muslims or those of a Middle Eastern appearance (Canadian Islamic Congress 2005; Al Hidaya Association 2008). In a Canada that likes to define itself as a nominally secular society, the challenge of taking Islam seriously poses a problem, with mainstream media conflicted by debates over the separation of church and state (see Kurien 2006). A clash between mainstream Christians and Muslims over the politics of religion is also inevitable. With Islam as the fastest-growing religion in Canada, encompassing 89 percent of Egyptian Canadians and 96 percent of Saudi Canadians (see Bramadat and Seljak 2008), the importance of religion among Muslim groups stands in sharp contrast to the demise of Christianity in everyday life.

News media mistreatment of Muslims and Islam is widely acknowledged (Karim 2002; Raza 2003; Saloojee 2003; Perigoe 2006; Gottschalk and Greenberg 2008; Lewis, Mason, and Moore 2009; Shaheen 2009; Aydin and Hammer 2010). A preoccupation with religious agendas that clash with Western orthodoxies ensures a portrayal of the Muslim world as a perversion of the human experience. Compared with their liberated and freewheeling Western counterparts, Muslim women are portrayed as the burka-clad antithesis of modern women (anti-democracy, anti-freedom, anti-choice). This victimization is further reinforced by sensationalistic media coverage of so-called honour killings and the stoning to death of Muslim women accused of adultery. Muslim men are stereotypically framed as tyrannical patriarchs and ruthless terrorists whose actions transcend the pale of civilization because of religious fanaticism and blatant disregard for human life. Islam is slandered as a violent, backward, and intolerant religion whose adherents must be closely monitored and quickly apprehended (Canadian Islamic Congress 2001). An exclusive focus on Islamist violence is not without consequences. In the words of Dina Ibrahim (2010, 111):

> Muslims living in Europe and the US have become accustomed to the media consistently choosing to perpetuate dominant images of aggression over images of diversity and assimilation. They have become acclimatized to television stations delivering news in the most succinct and narrative manner, focusing on compelling visuals rather than complex narratives that explain the motivation behind violent acts by providing context, background knowledge, and articulate views from multiple perspectives.

In other words, Muslims and Islam are the quintessential outsider or the "other" within – be it smarmy carpet dealers, oily sultans, or bug-eyed hijacker-bombers who don't even pray to the same God (Shaheen 2009). Media hyping of the so-called Islamist menace inflicts damaging consequences in Muslim communities, where virtual states of siege prevail because of insecurities and paranoia (Karim 2002). News media hyping of Muslim Canadians as folk devils within the context of a moral panic discourse also raises questions about national identity (who is a true Canadian?) and national security (who to keep out?) (Hier and Greenberg 2002).

Clearly, there is little in the way of balanced and complex news coverage about the Middle East (but see Silk 2009). Even though Muslims constitute nearly one-quarter of the world's population, including the majority of the population in forty-four countries, they continue to be portrayed as a homogenous mass who suffer at the hands of a seemingly cruel religion (Ramji 2009). In the post-9/11 climate, Islam has become highly racialized; as a result, references to Muslim identity are not about defining Islamic beliefs, but a euphemism for Arabs and Middle Easterners (Carastathis 2007). What little coverage there is rarely shows Muslims or Islam in a positive light, largely because of pervasive Islamophobia – though there are those who believe the news media want to avoid vilifying Islam and Muslim Americans for fear of attracting negative publicity (Silk 2009; Chuang 2010). Negative images persist, however, even if images of violence tend to be associated with overseas Muslims rather than domestic Muslims (D. Ibrahim 2010).

case study

Indeed, a study of British media between 2000 and 2008 exposed the primacy of three recurrent news pegs about Muslims and Islam: terrorism, incompatibility, and extremism (Lewis, Mason, and Moore 2009). The Runneymede Trust, an independent British think tank, has also identified a number of recurrent tropes that demean or demoralize:

- Islam is portrayed as monolithic, static, and unresponsive to change.
- Islam is portrayed as the "other" – remote and removed from core Western values, and incompatible with the principles of tolerance and pluralism.
- Islam is seen as highly gendered in that Muslim women are treated as second-class citizens with fewer rights than their husbands, brothers, and fathers.
- Islam is portrayed as inferior to the West, thus justifying both discrimination and hostility toward Muslims.
- Islam is portrayed as violent, supportive of terrorism, and a catalyst for a clash of civilizations.
- Islam is portrayed as a political ideology manipulated for military advantage.

To sum up, positive and normalizing images of ordinary Muslims and Arabs are almost non-existent in the mainstream media (Alliance of Civilizations 2006; Starck 2007). Coverage of Islam as a stone-age religion and of Muslims as barbaric heathens is heavily skewed toward conflicts in the Middle East, without a shred of historical context to inform and broaden. For news media, the debate over the so-called clash of civilizations – Islamic versus Western – tends to frame their coverage accordingly, that is, protagonists ensnared in a clash of global geopolitics (in the same way the Cold War once aligned all countries and conflicts along an East (Communism)-West (capitalism) axis. Predictably, as Karim (2006b) argues, after every terrorism-driven tragedy, all Muslims tend to be tarred by association as Islamist fundamentalists. References to Islamist terrorism alongside images of people praying at the mosque constructs a generalizing equivalence between the two. A set of visual images immediately triggers negativity about Islam as danger without verbalizing it – thus reinforcing Edward Said's warning that Islamophobia remains a bastion of sanctioned racism, as Karim acknowledges:

> A bearded Middle Eastern-looking man wearing a black cloak and turban can trigger an entire series of images of a fanatical religious movement, of airplane hijackings, of western hostages held helpless in dungeons, of truck bombs killing hundreds of innocent people, of cruel punishment sanctioned by Islamic law,

and of suppression of human rights – in sum of intellectual and moral regres-
sion. (Karim 2006a, 118)

In that minorities often derive much of their self-esteem and acceptance from the
media, the combination of insult and injury fosters resentment over what amounts
to anti-Orientalist propaganda. There is mounting Muslim defensiveness – even outrage – over news media's disrespect of their most cherished beliefs as fair game
for criticism or caricature. As many Pew Research Center (2010) surveys indicate,
Muslims resent the unfairness and stereotyping in news coverage of Islam. Not
surprisingly, then, when ten thousand respondents in predominantly Muslim countries were asked in a Gallup poll what the West could do to improve relations with
the Muslim world, 47 percent (the single largest response) said the mainstream
media must stop disrespecting Islam by demonizing Muslims as inferior or as in-
surrectionists (Alliance of Civilization 2006). However overdue and relevant, it
remains to be seen if the news media can become more religion literate, that is,
take religion seriously because religiosity matters; provide a historical and political context for events and developments with a religious dimension; and critically
reflect on their own beliefs and bias in framing coverage of religion, religiosity, and
faith-based communities (Marshall, Gilbert, and Ahmanson 2009; see also Buddenbaum 2010; D. Ibrahim 2010). Anything less is a recipe for aggravation.

Critical-Thinking Questions
Why do mainstream media appear to possess a pro-secular and anti-religious
gaze? How does this media gaze affect news coverage of Islam and Muslims in
ways that are systemically biasing?

* * * * * * * * * * *

The Case Study makes it abundantly clear: when framed as passive victims of
negative media representations, Muslims tend to be denied agency in the production of media messages (Aydin and Hammer 2010). But however much
media objectify Muslims and demonize Islam, there is another dynamic that
many ignore, namely, the degree to which Muslims of diverse backgrounds
are embracing the Internet and social media to challenge mainstream representations of themselves, debate ideas about the Koran, and exchange shared
experiences (Akou 2010). In acknowledging the possibilities of creatively engaging with digital technologies for religious meaning making in modern society, the implications are far-reaching. From generating new religious spaces

and publics to collapsing old boundaries in defining a religious realm (Dawson and Cowan 2004), a cyberspace that transcends boundaries of time, space, and body exerts a transformational effect on how Muslims practice Islam, how forms of Islam are represented to the world, and how Muslim societies see themselves and others (Akou 2010). An online environment that is relatively difficult to regulate opens windows of opportunity. New voices post views that contest gender and sexuality norms, yet affirm more normative Islamic views, while undermining the authority and influence of traditional media gatekeepers (Aydin and Hammer 2010). Developments that toppled political regimes in Tunisia and Egypt in early 2011 attest to the oppositional possibilities of social media for mobilizing the masses in getting the message out.

part 4

Gazing against the Grain:
Toward an Oppositional Media Gaze

* * * * * * * * * *

P arts 1 to 3 have made it abundantly clear: the concept of a media gaze is real, reflects how media work, and constitutes a powerful force in shaping media outputs and people's perceptions. A media gaze influences what audiences see and interpret; it also massages the audience into seeing reality like the media do because of a mediacentred (mediacentric) perspective that is conveyed as a so-called neutral gaze.

This admission reinforces the importance of recognizing those values, agendas, and myths that inform a mainstream media gaze. In terms of their status as money-making machineries of meaning, mainstream media cannot be disengaged from their role as *institutions of socialization and instruments of social control* (Kimmel 2008). As institutions of socialization, media do more than influence and shape. More accurately, they are reality, because in a media-dependent world, where there is no social reality outside of representations (symbols, images, narratives), media constructions are instrumental in creating those images that circumscribe people's lived realities. As instruments of *control,* media constitute powerful vehicles of persuasion. They *set agendas* for advancing patterns of power and privilege as well as *frame issues* for securing thought control – in the process reinforcing an unequal status quo that empowers some at the expense of others (Fleras 2003).

But not all media are willing to adopt a mainstream media gaze as a preferred metaframe. As noted in Part 1, both populist and online/social media embrace principles, priorities, and practices often at odds with those of private and public media. In acknowledging that the logic behind social media may sharply contrast with that of mainstream media, Part 4 addresses the politics of an oppositional gaze in resisting and contesting a mainstream media gaze. The content here takes its cue from the prescient insights of bell hooks (1992, 116), who promotes an oppositional gaze as an act of resistance in challenging mainstream media's claim to neutrality:

> By courageously looking, we defiantly declared: Not only will I stare. I want my look to change reality. Even in the worst circumstances of domination the ability to manipulate one's gaze in the face of structures of domination that would contain it, opens up the possibility of agency. The oppositional gaze looks to document, looks a certain way in order to assert agency by claiming and cultivating "awareness."
>
> The oppositional gaze stares in the face of domination. It is both subject and verb – "looks" and "looking." By asserting control over the images and structures that attempt to marginalize, dominate and exclude, we can transform the

image. We do not turn away from the one who was lynched, but stare in the faces of the ones who watched.

The first chapter in this part, Chapter 12, looks at social media as an oppositional Web 2.0 gaze. The chapter argues that social media realign how people communicate and connect with one another and a mediated reality in ways that often oppose convention and establish the potential for an oppositional gaze. Chapter 13 explores the notion of Aboriginal/indigenous media as an oppositional gaze. The emergence of Aboriginal (indigenous) media alongside the indigenizing of mainstream media promotes images and voices that reflect and advance Aboriginal realities and experiences instead of non-Aboriginal others. The pervasiveness of Aboriginal online media (from the Internet to social networking sites) in Aboriginal communities reinforces this oppositionality. Chapter 14 addresses the politics of multicultural and ethnic media as a populist media. Conceptualizing ethnic media as social capital secures an analytical framework that demonstrates how mainstream media gazes are challenged through alternative frames and oppositional interpretations. This interplay of bridging and bonding functions also demonstrates how ethnic media, despite their oppositionality, reflect and reinforce a commitment to the principles of an inclusive multiculturalism.

The concluding chapter on media literacy provides a fitting finale to the book. The chapter is anchored around three major themes. First, it provides a set of generalizations that summarize the representation of diversities under all media gazes and across all media domains. Second, the challenges of changing the media gaze are defined in both attitudinal and structural terms, with particular attention paid to the problem of media gaze as soft propaganda. Third, the importance of acquiring critically informed media-proofing skills is endorsed as the best option for re-engaging the media. By withdrawing our consent to be passively drawn into the prevailing media gaze, the chapter emphasizes the necessity of seeing through (deconstructing) a seeing like the media in order to live together with diversities and difference, equitably and with dignity.

12

Social Media as Oppositional Gaze

Forget about the old adage by Marshall McLuhan – "The Medium is the Message." Today and going forward, I think a more appropriate phrase would be "I am the media." (Wacker 2003)

We live inside our media. We are their content. (Edmund Carpenter, The New Languages, *1955)*

The Internet Changes Everything. (Tapscott 2011)

For centuries (five centuries if movable-type books are included), conventional media have ruled the roost. Newspapers and film, together with radio and television, dictated the relationship between media and audiences. Mass media created a product that worked for them, distributed these outputs in ways that suited their convenience, and monopolized the flow of information and entertainment without much resistance or challenge. Big media's relationship with audiences was no less unidirectional and lopsided. Audiences were seen as passive and gullible – little more than empty wheelbarrows that could be loaded up with media content and commercial advertising, then pushed around with relative impunity. Options for averting the media gaze were limited, with the result that audiences – by virtue of being drawn into seeing like the media – rarely got what they wanted but ended up wanting what mainstream media were willing to give.

The introduction of digital and mobile technology has upended this one-sided relationship. A fundamentally different logic prevails with the entrenchment of the Internet and the World Wide Web in the mid-1990s, followed by the spectacular expansion of Web 2.0 social networking media in the twenty-first century. The transformation did not arise immediately. The first websites (Web 1.0) produced content that resembled online extensions of mainstream media. By refusing to link with other sites or provide a comment system for reader feedback, web-based content simply re-created the physical product in a digital format without challenging a gatekeeper mentality in deciding who, what, and why.

With Web 2.0 communication, however, media dynamics have shifted conceptually. No longer a thing or noun (a product for distribution and consumption) but now conceptualized as a process or verb involving communication making largely unfiltered by gatekeepers or prepackaged for passive consumption (Barnes 2010), social media embody a paradigm of their own regarding the ownership, use, and management of communication and information. Insofar as normal rules of communication no longer automatically apply, thanks to the emergence of digital indigenes ("natives") armed with mobile phones and real-time video (Prensky 2001), the authority of conventional media is eroding in ways unimaginable just a generation ago. Blurring the distinction between producer, distributor, and consumer also points to shifts in media-society relations. The possibilities are limitless: realigning the focus away from a mass-mediated society (with its connotation of centralized authority, standardized messages, and mass audiences) to a networking information society that challenges hierarchical patterns of organization and communication is consequential. Social media enable trusted networks of family and friends to negotiate movements within and between fuzzily bounded networks by transforming the basic organizational structures and dynamics of society beyond the confines of the geographical (Castells 2009; Gelerenter and Regev 2010; Howard 2010). Oppositional (or subversive) gazes are evolving that contest orthodox ways of seeing like mainstream media, thanks to the inherently democratizing nature of social media as the bottom-up communication of networked communities on the move and in the making (Tapscott and Williams 2007; Tapscott 2008).

To be sure, neither the Internet nor social media inherently foster civic engagement or democratic reform – as is disingenuously implied by slogans such as the "revolution will be twittered" or "Twitter topples Tunisia" (*National Post,* 22 January 2011). Revolutions are much more complex than a single cause could possibly capture. Authoritarian governments can also employ digital technology to repress and censor through invasive surveillance techniques and cutting-edge propaganda and by pacifying populations with distractive digital entertainment (Morozov 2011). Nevertheless, although each of the social media platforms (blogs, Twitter, and YouTube) appears to have its own personality and function (Pew Research Center Project for Excellence in Journalism 2010b), the emergence of a networking online media has accelerated something of a paradigm shift in connecting, conversing, and community making. If the first phase of the Internet revolution was about creating sites/storefronts, capturing eyeballs, and getting everyone online, the social media phase (dubbed Web 2.0 because of fundamentally different software) capitalizes on the value of connections and interactions to alter how people work, play, relate, mobilize, buy, and learn (Li and Bernoff 2008). Social media are leveraging new patterns of communication by rewriting the rules of engagement and empowerment, (Benkler 2006; Nagourney 2008), while the convergence of digital and wireless technologies offers new ways of collaborating, engaging, and con suming (Y. Ibrahim 2009; Nicholson 2010). Not surprisingly, those digital indigenes who have no memory of a world without Internet or constant communication and who have been networking for most of their lives live in a reality in which everyone is connected but no one is in charge, in a world where there is no there there (see also Prensky 2001).

Unheard of less than a decade ago, the transformative changes brought about by social media are deep in creating, collecting, and storing information; they are structural in transforming the economy, workplaces, and business models; and they dramatically alter the dynamics of communication, conversation, and connection in establishing a flattened information society of networking communities (Benkler 2006; Shade 2010, Part 4). To be sure, most original reporting and news still comes from traditional sources, and online users overwhelmingly rely on so-called legacy media such as the *New York Times* or the *Globe and Mail* or aggregators of traditional news such as Google News. But digital technology enables citizen involvement to influence what stories will appear and their total impact (Pew Research Center Project for Excellence in Journalism 2010b; Rosenstiel 2011). Of those constituencies most affected by doing it differently, Aboriginal peoples and racialized minorities are particularly active in capitalizing on the new social media to advance agendas and priorities. To the extent that both digital platforms in general and Web 2.0 and social media in particular can enlighten and empower historically marginalized audiences, the implications are profound. Both racialized minorities and Aboriginal peoples are constructing oppositional gazes for advancing their individual and collective interests, in part to challenge mainstream media gazes, in part by providing a channel for political advocacy, identity construction, and community mobilization (Geist 2008; Akou 2010; Haythornthwaite and Kendall 2010).

To put these assertions to the test, this chapter explores the dynamics of social media as an oppositional gaze. The chapter examines the concept of social media, compares social media with mainstream media in terms of content and delivery, exposes the continuing digital divide around social media usage, explores the popularity of the "ordinary" as less democratizing or more demotic, and demonstrates the ongoing systemic biases within social media. The chapter also looks at the use of social and online media by immigrant Canadians and Aboriginal peoples, the impact of social media on their communities and communications, and their potential for circumventing the conventional media gaze. Particular attention is devoted to Aboriginal people's use of the Internet and social media as tools for improving community, connections, and communications, especially in those parts of Canada that are remote and removed (Patterson 2010). First, however, an Insight that demonstrates the impact of the Internet as new Canadians negotiate their navigation from "over there" to "in here."

_____ insight

Internet as Resource: Transitioning from "Over There" to "In Here"

In recent years, a fundamentally different category of Internet service has attracted countless users, elicited debate over its market variations, and garnered breathtaking sound bites because of its promise and potential (S. Gallagher 2008). The new services under the umbrella platform Web 2.0 are aimed at harnessing Internet power that empowers users to collaborate, create, and circulate information in fundamentally different ways from the text-based 1.0 sites of transactions (M. Johnson 2010). The Internet revolution has empowered people as citizens – "e the people" – by offering a platform of abundant information and consumer choice (Courchene 2005). Governments and conventional media ("transmitters") can no longer monopolize the information drip as they once did; instead, they must share power with the "receptors" (audiences or users). Citizens as consumers (and vice versa) are calling the shots, with the result that performance standards are often established by those at the cutting edge of innovation rather than by conventional connoisseurs of taste.

The effects of the Internet go beyond simply facilitating the flow of user-generated content. People's relationship to society is affected by access to information and entertainment on a global scale. With the Internet, like-minded citizens networking within and between nations are emerging as dominant players in domestic and global governance (Courchene 2005). Just as ethnic media play a role in the ability of immigrants to live transnational lives (i.e., adjust to life in the new country while remaining attached to what they left behind; Simmons 2010; see also Chapter 14), so too does the Internet enable newcomers to navigate the transition between two or more worlds like never before in real-time space – as nicely pointed out in an article by Navneet Alang in the March/April 2009 issue of *This Magazine* titled "Found in Translation."

Not long ago, one of two options existed for new Canadians wanting broadcast news or entertainment from their homeland: either a small block of minority programming on a multicultural TV channel or ethnic radio, often at an inconvenient time slot, or the rental or purchase of a DVD from a video outlet or corner store. This somewhat cumbersome access to minority media intensified the isolation that immigrants frequently experienced. But with the mainstreaming of the Internet, immigrants now have access to a virtual cornucopia of music, film, and literature. For example, Zip.ca, Canada's most popular online DVD service, possesses a catalogue of over seven hundred Bollywood films, many in high definition. Compare this abundance of riches with the paltry offerings available at Blockbuster or Rogers. Or consider eMusic.com (second only to iTunes as the largest online music seller), which carries about thirty-three thousand artists in its international category. Also accessible is the streaming of current events from Taiwan, poetry from Pakistan, podcasts from Jamaica, and news sites from Somalia.

The implications are twofold. First, a new business model is in place. Unlike the old media days, which relied on selling large quantities of a few bestsellers, online sites can flourish by selling just a few units of a huge catalogue, thanks to the Internet's massive carrying capacity complementing its relatively inexpensive distribution network. The Internet provides a greater variety of content than bricks-and-mortar enterprises because the economies of scale are working in its favour. Second, the very notion of an immigrant lived-experience is changing. In contrast to the past, when most immigrants lived in a kind of cultural limbo – simultaneously culturally cut off from their homeland and unable to connect culturally with mainstream culture – immigrants now have unmatched access to a range of cultural products (Fleras 2011). By easing the transition process, both the Internet and social media serve as a bridging and bonding devices (see discussion in Multicultural/

ethnic media), thus allowing new Canadians to negotiate their transition from "there" to "here" at a pace consistent with their realities and experiences.

To be sure, there are dangers associated with staying connected to the "over there." Of particular worry is the risk of creating ethnic enclaves or cultural ghetto-ization – social trends seemingly at odds with the inclusive principles of Canada's official multiculturalism. And yet, access to the Internet may bolster participation, belonging, and commitment on the multicultural assumption that those secure in their ethnocultural background are more likely to be contented Canadians, with a corresponding commitment toward the tolerance of others. The choice between as-similation or traditionalism is no longer one of either/or because of very real op-tions. Or as Alang (2009, 41-42) writes, "[When] one is no longer forced to cling to an imaginary past but can instead engage the cutting edge of both cultures, the movement to contemporary Canada becomes degrees easier and less threatening ... When immigrants are neither asked to constantly look back, nor entirely conform to an alien present, perhaps the ideal of multiculturalism has found a practical friend in the long tail of the internet."

To sum up, the Internet provides a unique set of tools for integrating immigrants into Canada. By facilitating the transition from homeland to host country, the Internet is proving its worth in fostering a climate for living together with differen-ces. But there are consequences in creating a context that encourages transnation-al connections and hybrid ethnicities. Put bluntly, the over there is now in here and vice versa, and the social contract that once defined the relationship between Canada and new Canadians is shifting as migrants increasingly capitalize on the transnational identities in a glocalized world (Fleras 2010). Regardless of whether we approve or disapprove, like it or not, the very concept of a multicultural and in-clusive Canada will undergo further changes in response to Internet-based gazes that challenge conventional ways of living like Canadians.

Critical-Thinking Question
What is meant by the statement "The Internet provides a unique set of tools for immigrant integration into Canada"?

* * * * * * * * * *

A Social Media Gaze: Shifting the Balance of Seeing

> *In Web 1.0, it was said that content was king. In social media, one could argue that context is now king. (Solis 2010a)*

The popularity of the Internet has spiralled exponentially (Thussu 2008). In 1995, 3 percent of the world's population was online; by 2005, the figure had quintupled to 15 percent, with 90 percent of users in the industrialized countries of Europe, North America, and Asia Pacific. No less astonishing is the remarkable expansion of social media systems both highly interactive ("fast connections") and people enabling ("constantly connected") (Li and Bernoff 2008; Winograd 2008). Upward to one-third of new Web content is loosely defined as social media, including Onternet/online forums, weblogs/vlogs, wikis/Wikipedia (reference), podcasts, email, Google (reference), Facebook (networking), YouTube (video sharing, including television shows and films), and Twitter (microblogging) (Anupam et al. 2007). A shared and connected experience is driving a new digital lifestyle, one in which social media increasingly permeate people's lived experiences in a Twittered universe (Twitterverse). (According to Social Media Today, one in seven people watching the opening Olympic ceremonies in January 2010 and the Super Bowl in February 2010 were online at the same time, suggesting a multi-tasking trend toward interactivity and connectivity in real-time conversation [Solis 2010b].) Clearly, then, computer-generated interactions of social media have evolved into a defining feature of people's everyday lives in seeking out a more participatory and interactive experience (Pare 2010; G. Turner 2010).

Social media can be defined as those Web-based applications (including tools, spaces, and practices) for sharing information online (communication), constructing online personality spaces (interaction, identity, and connection), or establishing virtual networks of loosely connected netizens (community making) (K. Anderson 2009; Watkins 2009). "Second-generation Web content" refers to any online content or activity – from posting a video to writing a blog to connecting with friends through electronic networks – that establishes an interactive partnership (P2P) with the consumer/citizen (Pew Research Center Project for Excellence in Journalism 2008). Social media (or Web 2.0) differ from other Internet sources by their interconnectivity with networked data. Peer-produced services like BitTorrent foster peer production by leveraging user computers instead of a central IT source to authorize and secure service delivery (S. Gallagher 2008). So too with social media: instead of a single authority that intervenes to prepare one file for transfer to another, social media work on the principle that computers can tap into each other because of their direct links as virtually one computing device (Thussu 2008). The end result is a networking information society, with a corresponding capacity to quickly download content and connections to their digital device, reflecting the shift from command-and-control hierarchies to more flexible social networks and participatory arrangements (Benkler 2006; Castells 2009).

Interestingly, there is as much of a divide within the Internet – Web 1.0 versus Web 2.0 – as there is between new media and conventional media (Palfrey and Gasser 2008; M. Johnson 2010). Initially designed to facilitate scientific collaboration through emails and message boards, and eventually evolving into the first true Internet service, Usenet, and the World Wide Web, Web 1.0 shared much in common with conventional media – namely, it was a tool to source information that involved a disruption known as getting online ("dial up") and a tool to "capture eyeballs" to improve sales and services (S. Gallagher 2008). Web 2.0, as the second Internet generation – that is, any online media in partnership with the user – is more like a constant and trusted companion than a convenience to switch on and off. The reality of staying connected and in contact through social networking infiltrates people's lives in fundamentally different ways than in the days when media (from TVs to computers) consisted largely of blankly immobile fixtures. In other words, people's use of the Net changes when they have continuous access to the always-on feature of broadband – changes for users that are almost as significant as the difference between Internet access and no access.

Of particular note is the astonishing growth and popularity of Facebook, resulting in what is tantamount to a digital revolution (M. Johnson 2010). Those who embraced the Internet after the introduction of Facebook are more inclined to process information differently than older online users (Palfrey and Gasser 2008). The distinguishing feature lies in the nature of the socialization. Earlier online environments were generally organized into forums based on common interests and posted accordingly. Such an organizational format proved both atomizing and exclusionary: atomizing in reflecting a place to find like-minded people with similar interests; exclusionary in making it difficult to navigate the labyrinth without a guide. For Facebook users, however, connections are primarily fan-based or instigated through friends or acquaintances. Rather than a neutral ground where users meet in common space, Facebook connections are directly based on access to each other's profile. In dispensing with intermediaries, in the same way that Expedia has rendered travel agencies all but obsolete, Web 2.0 technologies improve information flows that are inherently more decentralizing (democratizing) by virtue of being less hierarchical. Even the how and why of communication differs. Whereas early online communication focused on talking about something (content), social networking media is about community and connection through communication (context) (Watkins 2009).

As primarily a social activity of choice for most young adults in sharing their lives, Facebook use is proving intensely participatory – more a process of talking to significant others than of talking about something. Or as Matthew Johnson (2010) describes it, if the Internet is compared to a high school, using Web 1.0 is like belonging to the chess club, whereas being on Facebook is akin to hanging out in the student lounge.

A generational digital divide persists: adults tend to think of the Internet in Web 1.0 (Usenet) terms; as a result, even Facebook is seen as a collection of destinations for particular purposes (including monitoring their children's online behaviour). But for young adults, Facebook communication is about being plugged into a steady stream of chatter (literally online all the time). As might be expected, those immersed in social media possess norms and values that differentiate them from persons weaned on Web 1.0 platforms (M. Johnson 2010). In a twitterverse of digital media and mobile platforms, young people capitalize on the constancy of this connectivity to define identities, share ideas and creativity, and participate in networks large and small, near yet far, focused yet diffuse (Tapscott 2008; Watkins 2009). The implications are far-reaching as institutions from the workplace to the marketplace, from education to family, are undergoing a (trans)normative shift from a culture of control to a culture of engagement and empowerment (Tapscott 2008). But the popularity and privilege of the empowering "me" as "ordinary media celebrity" raises provocative issues, explored below in the Insight.

insight

From the Authority of Elites to the Authenticity of Ordinariness: Democracy or Demotic?

In an era of interactive and participatory me-media, ordinary people are increasingly acknowledged and revered as the "new celebrities." As Nick Couldry (2003) writes, ordinariness has never been more desired or visible, nor have the statements or presence of these "ordinary celebrities" ever been more faithfully and accurately reproduced. The media's demand for ordinary people is insatiable: consider their visibility in reality TV, confessional talk formats, docu-soaps, reality-based game shows, local talk radio, Facebook and YouTube, citizen journalism and blogs, and as Webcam-girls *(Girls Gone Wild)*. Earlier chapters focused on Dove's use of ordinary women as models to bolster the legitimacy of its Campaign for Real Beauty; the chapter on remasculinizing working-class men in blue-collar jobs also emphasized real men doing ordinary (if risky) work. This move toward the authenticity of the ordinary can be attributed to many causes: the pervasiveness of celebrity, a shift in TV programming toward live (unscripted) formats as a cheaper alternative to scripted programs, and the interactivity of Web 2.0 social media. Regardless of the reasons, this unprecedented era of networked information has proven transformative in prompting a key question. To what extent is the celebration of the ordinary and the real a democratizing trend or, alternatively, a celebration of the narcissistic me (see G. Turner 2010)?

For some, the privileging of the ordinary as both producer and consumer is pivotal in advancing media democraticization. John Hartley (1999) uses the term "democratainment" to capture this notion of a democratizing media by (1) reducing elite formations of media programming because of user-generated content, (2) rejecting the authority of the elites in defining information, (3) ensuring greater inclusiveness for historically marginalized groups, resulting in greater powers of self-determination, and (4) providing a greater focus on the construction of cultural identities along oppositional lines. By contrast, mainstream media as elite formations are losing their cachet because they no longer resonate with the authority or authenticity to communicate or connect like social media.

Others are more skeptical of such grand aspirations (G. Turner 2010). The emancipatory potential of the new mediascape, with its rallying cry of "power to the people," may offer greater media visibility for ordinary people. But instead of any broad-based consensus, this democratic potential can easily morph into anti-democratic trends, ranging from extremism and exploitation (porn) to the abuse of power and divisiveness (ibid.). For critics, multiplying the range of choices may prove more paralyzing than democratizing. Nor does the ordinariness on talk shows or reality TV appreciably alter an inescapable truth: that media industries continue to control the airwaves by operating this symbolic economy in the service of their own interests rather than advancing democracy (ibid.).

In short, celebrating ordinariness is not necessarily about democratization; it may more accurately reflect an almost inexhaustible supply of new and diverse content for familiar formats. What emerges is not necessarily a democratizing process as mainstream media hone their production techniques in mining the rich seam of ordinariness. Emergent instead is what Graeme Turner calls a demotic turn (defined as by, for, and about the common person) that celebrates the "me" over the "we" to the detriment of the "us." But this demotic turn is not without implications

(G. Turner 2010). A bit of playfulness at Marx's expense is helpful here: just as workers' control of the means of production would prove revolutionary, so too would the "ordinary masses" controlling the means of media production likely initiate a new world order.

Critical-Thinking Question

According to the last sentence of this Case Study, the Internet changes everything. What are the implications for society and individuals when the masses control the means of social media production?

* * * * * * * * * *

Conventional Media versus Digital Media: Seeing in the Same Old Way?

The transformative power of digital platforms and social media are profound. Insofar as they reflect a voluminous amount of user-generated content whose reach and impact extends around the world, these networking sites are convenient vehicles for publishing information (such as wiki), engaging in discussion, and establishing online communities by linking up to one another while bypassing traditional institutions (Akou 2010; see also Li and Bernoff 2008). Governments and corporations (including conventional media companies) are searching for ways to employ social media to promote agendas. Advertisers are looking for ways to capture the time spent online and translate that attention into advertising power – and even more so as companies drift away from expensive conventional media advertising toward social media like blogs that encourage speedy reaction to public criticisms or to capitalize on constructive feedback. And citizens both young and old are discovering that social media can improve their lives by securing a voice in this world, in the process shifting the balance of power from a top-down gaze to a bottom-up way of seeing. A brief overview of ideal-typical differences between mainstream/conventional media and social/participatory media draws attention to their distinctiveness:

1 Conventional media require staggering amounts of resources and clearance (including a government-granted spectrum licence to broadcast). By contrast, social media are relatively inexpensive and accessible, enabling most individuals to publish or access information. Not surprisingly, digital "natives" see media content as something for free, whereas those with vested interests in conventional media believe in a price tag.

2   Unlike conventional media, which require specialized skills and training, almost anyone can produce, distribute, and access social media. The logic behind social media is user-generated and bottom-up content, rather than elite-driven and top-down content. The technology of Web 2.0 challenges the field of journalism as citizens assume roles as publishers without editors, thus allowing visitors to choose and share what *they* define as news (Pew Research Center Project for Excellence in Journalism 2008).

3   Conventional media processes involve a significant time lag in producing and accessing communication. By contrast, social media instantaneously compress the distance between production and consumption, producer and consumer (A. Chan 2008). Not surprisingly, conventional media outputs tend to be permanent, whereas social media content can be easily altered by comments or editing.

4   Conventional broadcast media reflect centralized control over production and distribution of content rather than the decentralized user-driven structure of social media (Winograd 2008). In contrast to the conventional media world of centralized production and standardized consumption (K. Anderson 2009), participatory media are highly interactive or dialogical because, in a post-information me-media world, everyone is connected while no one is in charge.

5   Whereas the logic behind conventional media emphasizes a communication from one to many, social media can capitalize on digital and mobile technology to communicate from many to one and from many to many.

6   Unlike conventional media, whose primary functions involve informing or persuading, social media consumption is geared toward communication, connection, and communities. People's lives and identities are defined by networks of communication that connect people through shared content (Wacker 2003; Castells 2009; Watkins 2009; G. Turner 2010).

7   In contrast to conventional media, which tend toward the conservative (see below), social media can prove potentially counterhegemonic. As a new modality of power that challenges the nature of sovereignty in a globalizing world (Kumar 2010), social media are adept at mobilizing the masses into challenging authority, contesting the conventional, and circumventing ruling elites (as demonstrated in the uprisings in North Africa – Tunisia, Egypt, Libya – in early 2011).

An expansive and expanding mediascape raises many questions: Will the digital revolution signal the death of conventional media and their replacement by variations of Web 2.0, 3.0, and so on? Is there a rapprochement in the making between digital indigenes (those born into a language and weaned on a digital and mobile platform) and digital immigrants, who continue to speak with an accent because they can't completely discard the authoritative and top-down mindset of a broadcast mentality (Prensky 2001)? Can the oppositional gazes implicit in the social media's DNA eclipse the conventionality of mass media gazes? Perhaps not, as many concede, including Thorburn and Jenkins (2003). The emergence of new media often sets into motion a complex process of technological and social change, resulting in a dynamic hybrid of collaborative forms that interact, shift, collide, or collude. Established media embrace the new media and digital technologies in the hopes of consolidating their consumer base. Newer media, in turn, may initially model themselves on conventional media models, until they figure out their distinctiveness as a strength to capitalize on. Thorburn and Jenkins (2003, 7) put it aptly in acknowledging the tenacity of the old: "If emerging media are often experimental and self-reflexive, they are also inevitably and centrally imitative, rooted in the past, in the practices, formats, and deep assumptions of their predecessor." The Case Study below puts the slogan of "continuity in change" to the test by showing how, when it comes to new media, the more things change, the more they stay the same.

case study

Net Impartiality? Deconstructing the Wiki Gaze

It's been said that audiences would be better off if communication media dropped their facade of neutrality and objectivity by acknowledging their biases and priorities up front. In this way both viewers and readers can control for biases when deconstructing the politics of seeing like the media. But not all biases are created equal. Some are relatively open and easy to detect and isolate. Others require prolonged critical reflection because they are deeply embedded and carefully concealed behind a cloak of impartiality. These systemic biases are pivotal in creating a media gaze that many perceive as natural and normal. The challenge lies in deconstructing these mediacentric biases in order to understand the what, how, and why.

In the spirit of putting this challenge to the test, the oft-cited and frequently consulted free online and open-sourced encyclopedia Wikipedia embarked on a study in which it sought to deconstruct its own biases (see Wikipedia: WikiProject Countering Systemic Bias at http://testserver.semantic-mediawiki.org). A wiki (of which Wikipedia is the largest of hundreds of equivalents) consists of a social media website that anyone with user edit access can input or modify (S. Gallagher 2008). Perhaps no social media reflects the Web 2.0 participatory nature better than Wikipedia, which relies on hundreds of volunteer administrators to create, edit, and maintain content – by January 2011 the wiki boasted 17 million entries, including 3.5 million English-language articles, making it the largest encyclopedia in the history of encyclopedias (Hesse 2011). The content of Wikipedia is generated not by experts per se but by editors and contributors who voluntarily submit or revise information in hopes of duplicating an online and bottom-up version of the *Encyclopedia Britannica* (according to some sources, the error ratio between the *Britannica* and Wikipedia is minimal). By analyzing who contributes what in terms of subjects and perspectives, this study sought to uncover evidences of a systemic (mediacentric) bias.

According to Wikipedia, a demographic trend has emerged. The average Wikipedian is male, technically inclined, formally educated, generally proficient in English, white, relatively young (aged from fifteen to forty-nine years), originally from a predominantly Christian and industrialized country, and more likely to use ICT (information and communication technologies) skills for employment rather than physical labour. The fact that the majority of contributors tend to be what Monica Hesse (2011) labels young, male, and "nerdy" may explain why the length of the entry for actor Megan Fox is the same as that for American president Millard Fillmore. Furthermore, Wikipedia acknowledges additional factors in controlling who sees and contributes what, namely, the importance of having access to a computer and broadband connection; the prevalence of English-speaking contributors and editors; the presence of those with either wealth or time on their hands to participate in the project; the predominance of intellectuals and computer programmers as contributors; and the domination by contributors who lean toward stronger religious beliefs or political ideologies. In short, two major biases can be detected: (1) a preference for certain topics and a neglect of others (reflecting the nature of contributors) and (2) a slanted geographic bias (i.e., many parts of the world do not contribute).

The conclusions are compelling. Wikipedia admits to a systemic bias because of its tendency to refract reality through the prism (filter or lens) of the average Wikipedian. The Wikipedia site is so loaded with biases because of its contributor base that it can hardly claim to be neutral in the collection, content, and dissemination of knowledge. Certain ideas and ideals that define what is desirable and acceptable as well as accurate and worthwhile are deeply embedded in Wikipedia's design, organization, content, and operation. Readers who are unaware of these biases and distortions may unconsciously internalize a Wikipedia gaze as a neutral gaze. To be sure, no one is objecting to the contribution of articles based on individual interests and knowledge. But the cumulative effect when multiplied across the entire body of contributors and editors results in an unbalanced and slanted coverage of topics. And until the demographic of English-speaking Wikipedians corresponds more closely to global demographics, the Wikipedia gaze reflects coverage that is systemically biasing.

In short, the Internet is hardly a bias-free zone. Nor is it entirely free of conventional media gazes. Just as mainstream media are loaded with values that encourage a preferred reading, so is the Internet ideologically bound despite claims to net neutrality. In the case of Wikipedia and project contributors, the potential for an androcentric, Eurocentric, and class-based gaze reflects a business-as-usual mindset. How could it be otherwise in light of the skewed corpus of editors and contributors, in addition to the slant in topics and coverage? Worse still, as the authors of the project concede, the idea of systemic bias as a factor in undermining Wikipedia impartiality or neutrality is far more troubling than deliberate bias. After all, intentional bias can be detected, isolated, and removed. Systemic bias, by contrast, is so deeply rooted in the process and content that it not only conceals how Wikipedia works but also shapes how Wikipedia audiences gaze upon social reality without an awareness that they are seeing like a social media; indeed, they assume they have no perspective at all.

Critical-Thinking Question

The Internet is neither a bias-free zone nor entirely free of conventional media gazes. Just as mainstream media are loaded with values that encourage a preferred reading, so too is the Internet ideologically bound despite claims to net impartiality. What is meant by this claim, particularly in the context of the Wikipedia project?

* * * * * * * * * *

Indigenizing the Internet: Empowering the Local by Engaging the Global

Canada's Aboriginal media are increasingly immersed in a process of cultural and social networking involving both national and global venues of public access and participation (Roth 2010a). They, like other indigenous peoples around the world, are relying on traditional communication patterns (storytelling traditions) and new media technologies to challenge misrepresentations by outsiders and, further, to amplify Aboriginal voices, disseminate information, and expand their power (Alia 2009, 2010). Media outputs, from indigenous film production to digital media Aboriginal arts, have strongly influenced the imaginations of Aboriginal people, especially youth who no longer identify with their parents' objectives of preserving Aboriginal languages and culture through mainstream media.

More importantly, perhaps, is how social (digital and mobile) media like broadband or Web 2.0 have altered Aboriginal mediascapes (Patterson 2010). Although the elderly and children may look to Aboriginal broadcasting as a source of information and entertainment, young people watch it only sporadically, preferring instead to do their identity building through various social networking sites like Facebook or Flickr. For Aboriginal youth, the Internet provides a way of joining the global world by constructing virtual social networks across vast spaces. As the Internet becomes more accessible and less costly, independently funded Aboriginal media sites are producing videos or films or music that (1) can be posted online (from YouTube to tweets), (2) satisfy a hunger for creativity and stimulation and "identiplay," and (3) identify more with independent media initiatives than with existing broadcasting services.

This social and cultural shift has not only reshaped the Aboriginal mediascape. The implications of being out there with others have been realigned as well by virtue of the Internet's potential as a medium of global mass communication (Roth 2010a, 237; see also Niezen 2005). Indigenous digital media offer an alternative model of grounded yet increasingly global interconnectedness created by, for, and about Aboriginal peoples' lives. In turn, Aboriginal peoples and communities establish their own identities and social and professional networks, enhancing the dynamics of intergroup cooperation, securing access to knowledge for dealing with state administration, and fostering an international personae in new and imaginative ways (Meadows and Molnar 2001; Niezen 2005; Wilson and Stewart 2008).

To what extent have Aboriginal peoples (and indigenous peoples in general) embraced the information superhighway to bridge and to bond? In response to the question, what can the electronic frontier deliver to a people on the fringes of power and remote from the centres of influence? the answer is increasingly clear: greater empowerment by challenging and changing their marginalization or exclusion by mainstream media (Landzelius 2006). This transformation goes beyond debates over new media effects. Emphasis instead focuses on how community members are making themselves a(t) home in a global communicative environment. Four patterns can be discerned, according to Kyra Landzelius: Aboriginal/indigenous peoples are appropriating and moulding ICTs (information and communication technologies) (1) to reflect, reinforce, and advance their needs, interests, and identities – including the use of cyberactivism to overcome poverty and construct more viable economies through education and skills training (A. Chan 2008); (2) as a forum for making claims in the name of ethnicity (or indigeneity or aboriginality); (3) for naming ethnicity or claiming ethnicity (or aboriginality); and (4) for shifting the boundaries by which the politics of ethnicity/aboriginality are rethought, reworked, and revitalized.

To date, Aboriginal peoples' engagement with ICTs encompasses two directional pulls: *inreach* (bonding) and *outreach* (bridging) (Landzelius 2006; see also Chapter 14). Inreach orientations range from promoting localized interests and community services, including the dissemination of ingroup information, to the importation of expert knowledge for community use. Aboriginal leaders are turning to ICTs to deliver high-quality health care to remote Canadian communities. Telemedicine enables medical specialists to observe patients via real-time links, thus providing an affordable way to defeat the tyranny of distance across Canada's vast expanses while balancing Western medical knowledge with Aboriginal health beliefs and practices. As well as protecting the rights of indigenous peoples, ICTs are proving important for building economies through e-commerce, establishing workable governance patterns, and preserving language and culture (C. Chan 2009).

Outreach orientations focus on building bridges with the outside world, including making connections between Aboriginal communities. For example, in 1994, a group of remote First Nations communities in northern Ontario launched an electronic bulletin board that culminated in Canada's largest Aboriginal broadband network and a model network for indigenous communications worldwide (C. Chan 2009). The bulletin board system (BBS) sought to establish lines of communication with the communities' children who were living away from home by providing them with the tools to stay in school at a time when many were dropping out. In less than a decade, the BBS expanded into a telecommunications network known as K-Net (from the Oji-Cree word "kukkenah," meaning everyone, everywhere). Through a satellite network, K-Net links about seventy Aboriginal communities in northern Ontario, Quebec, and Manitoba with communities around the world, in addition to regional networks, to form a national broadband network that provides video conferencing and other applications across Canada. Throughout its evolutionary growth, however, the primary objective has always been addressing local communication needs. A grounded K-Net constitutes an Aboriginal success story in which even isolated communities seek out partnerships, leverage support, harness funding, and use ICTs to address local economic and social needs (C. Chan 2009).

In light of wider debates about the benefits or costs of the Internet in preserving indigenous cultures and promoting their concerns, the conclusion is reassuringly positive. The Internet and social media are more than just mediums that challenge mainstream gazes by de-emphasizing those hierarchical political associations, ethnic designations, and rigid class relationships associated with geographically bound communications (Ebo 1998). For example, the uprising of the indigenous and mestizo peasants of Chiapas in their resistance against the Mexican government exemplifies one of the more spectacular examples of an indigenous cybercampaign against established authorities – thus reinforcing the Web's potential for local empowerment. Online communication also possesses the potential to create meaningful and egalitarian communities by neutralizing the potential divisiveness of race, gender, and class barriers (Arnold and Plymire 2004). In short, far from being at odds with each other or cancelling each other out, the inreach and outreach functions of Aboriginal social media are mutually reinforcing. The local is embedded within the global without compromising the articulation of identities, experiences, and outcomes (Landzelius 2006). The end result promises a new media gaze – a seeing like the Aboriginal media – both enlightening and empowering.

13

Unsilencing Aboriginal Voices
Toward an Indigenous Media Gaze

Most Canadians are largely uninformed (and misinformed) about Aboriginal peoples. Surveys indicate that many Canadian know little about the history, circumstances, issues, and challenges confronting the descendants of the country's original inhabitants. They also lack any meaningful contact with which to make informed decision making. What little they know about Aboriginal peoples is gleaned largely from the mainstream media. For many, the combination of newscasting, television programming, and film constitutes a preliminary and often primary point of contact with the Aboriginal world. In light of such agenda-setting powers, the framing of Aboriginal peoples and issues by mainstream media will profoundly influence and shape public discourses, political debates, and policy developments.

But ideals are one thing, realities quite another. Mainstream media have historically portrayed (and continue to portray) Canada's First Peoples as problem people who have problems or create problems involving costs or inconveniences rather than as peoples with rights who live complex lives within a globalized context (Harvard Project on American Indian Economic Development 2008). Historical context and structural constraints imposed by colonialism are largely absent from coverage, with the result that most news reports and opinion pieces are framed in ways unsympathetic to Aboriginal interests (Harding 2010). Admittedly, positive news stories exist, including coverage that romanticizes traditional culture or celebrates those ruggedly individualistic types who overcome obstacles to become mainstream successes. But exceptions aside, the cumulative impact of negatively framing Aboriginal peoples within decontextual frameworks of crime, crisis, or conflict is not without consequences. As Robert Berkhofer (1979) explains in *The White Man's Indian*, invented images of Aboriginal peoples have long influenced policy makers in providing both moral and intellectual justification for managing the so-called Indian problem.

However inexcusable, this disconnect between inclusionary principles and exclusionary practices is neither calculated (deliberate duplicity) nor a miscalculation (organizational collusion). Gaps between the ideal and reality reflect an institutionalized bias in news media coverage of Aboriginal peoples – in part because of (1) a pro-white news paradigm that normalizes (privileges) whiteness as the normative standard, (2) conventional news norms that focus on negativity and conflict as preferred frames, and (3) commitment to liberal universalism that diminishes aboriginality by downplaying Aboriginal difference as inferior, irrelevant, or threatening. In reaction to this demeaning and exclusionary process, flourishing Aboriginal media offer an alternative to mainstream media negativity (Roth 2010a). The central role played by Aboriginal (or the more generic term, "indigenous") media is increasingly evident in negotiating community relations, social power, and cultural survival, while unsettling patterns of hegemony (Ginsberg 2000; Smith and Abel 2008). So too are moves to combat discrimination, advocate rights, protect language and culture, forge international solidarity movements, challenge misleading mainstream representations and politics of identity, bring human rights violations to the international fore, and advance a sense of aboriginality by linking the local with the global in ways mainstream media can't or won't (Wilson and Stewart 2008). The following passage explains how indigenous media serve as self-conscious instruments of cultural preservation and political mobilization in advancing self-determination and resistance to cultural imperialism at both national and international levels:

> Indigenous people participate in and compete for a place within the new international information order, negotiating with the settler nation, and voicing their concerns with the help of the media. Indigenous media are considered a new dynamic in social movements and help generate a critique of the democratic deficits of mainstream media. Some media scholars suggest that indigenous people are now producing, using, and consuming media to trigger political, social, and cultural change, taking the initiative to represent

themselves and address issues that mainstream media neglect. The rise of indigenous media occurs in a larger global context where, as media theorists argue, developments in international communication place national sovereignty and nation states under new cultural and social pressures. (Bredin and Hafsteinsson 2010, 1)

To put these assertions to the test, this chapter explores the concept of Aboriginal media as an integral component of Canada's expanding media-scape. The chapter demonstrates how mainstream media have generally fumbled the challenge of portraying Aboriginal peoples as peoples with rights, preferring, instead, to see them as problems with needs (Maaka and Fleras 2005). The emergence and expansion of populist Aboriginal media, including news, film, and television, has helped to unsilence Aboriginal voices – too long silenced by a racialized mainstream media – in advancing their interests and the principle of aboriginality (M.J. Miller 2008). And as noted in Chapter 12, Aboriginal peoples' use of the Internet and social media has also proven pivotal in overcoming marginalization and resisting colonization (Patterson 2010). To the degree that Aboriginal media have proven both inward and outward-looking, as well as proactive and reactive in orientation, an oppositional gaze is reinforced.

Aboriginality and News: The Only Good Indian Is a Problem Indian

News media's mistreatment and neglect of Canada's Aboriginal peoples is widely acknowledged (Ricard and Wilkes 2007). Images of Aboriginal peoples as the "other" within are refracted through the prism (prison) of Eurocentric lenses (Lambertus 2004). Representations span the spectrum, ranging from their valorization as noble savage and primitive romantic (including spiritual mystics and environmental custodians) to their debasement as villain or victim, with the stigma of problem people or menacing subversives sandwiched in-between (Alia and Bull 2005). Aboriginal women and men are rendered invisible – a kind of negligence by default – except in contexts of resentment (because of scandals or social problems), rejection (because of Aboriginal peoples' demands and claims), or resistance (ranging from blockades to stand-offs to protests) (Harding 2005; J. Miller 2005). Compounding this negativity is criticism of Aboriginal peoples as social problems because of a seeming dependency on welfare, predilection for alcohol and other substance abuse, abusive violence toward one another or turned inward as suicides, pervasive laziness and lack of ambition, and tendency to mismanage what little they have by hiding behind the smokescreen of Aboriginal rights (or victimhood) to jus-tify illegal activities or rationalize shortcomings.

Alternatively, Aboriginal peoples are portrayed as threats or victims. A standard narrative (or story) is constructed from the conventional building blocks of Aboriginal peoples as dangerous and lawless outlaws/warriors, as pathological problems (victims), and as remote and unknowable (Lambertus 2004; McCreanor 2006). News stories involving Aboriginal assertiveness are framed as a clash between the opposing forces of mayhem and stability (Abel 1997). Aboriginal activism is packaged as a departure from established norms because of its propensity for violence, volatility, and emotionality, and protest-ers are reduced to dangerous militants or irrational ideologues (J. Miller 2005). The combined impact of this negativity borders on propaganda: Canada's First Peoples are villainized as troublesome constituents whose demands for self-determining autonomy pose a threat to society. Success stories are rarely re-ported; the few exceptions that slip into the news hole simply confirm the rule (see the Case Study titled "Framing Aboriginal Protest" in Chapter 1).

To be sure, news media coverage of aboriginality has improved in recent years (Fleras and Kunz 2001). Crude stereotyping of Aboriginal peoples as pa-thetic victims, angry warriors, and noble ecologists (RCAP 1996) has given way to more positive portrayals of "good Natives," especially in editorials, opin-ion columns, and investigative journalism (Spoonley and Trlin 2004). Even in the hard news department, where overall improvement lags, promising shifts can be discerned, including less race/Aboriginal tagging (assigning a racial/Aboriginal label to victim or perpetrator without good reason). Editors increas-ingly pay more attention to the kind of language that may offend Aboriginal sensibilities (e.g., rejecting the use of the term "Indian"). Yet paradoxically, news messages continue to negatively frame aboriginality and Aboriginal peoples, despite a growing reluctance to say anything negative for fear of being branded as racist and attracting the wrong kind of publicity. Aboriginal peoples are routinely portrayed as people out of control and in need of constraint; al-ternatively, they are depicted as passive recipients of actions or events beyond their control (compared with non-Aboriginal actors, who are overwhelmingly portrayed as active agents). The consequences of such negativity are debilitat-ing; namely, a perceived inability to exercise control over themselves and their lives is widely circulated (Harding 2005).

In other words, negative news portrayals do not openly disparage Aboriginal peoples per se. What appears instead are two opposing news constructs: first, a depiction of Aboriginal peoples as positive ("good Indians"), who work within the system, yet are vulnerable to forces beyond their control or susceptible to victimization; second, Aboriginal peoples as problem people ("bad Indians") in need of containment – by force if necessary (Saunders 2006; Harding 2010). Particular censure is directed at those incompetent or corrupt financial managers who are taking advantage of the system for self-serving purposes, thereby violating national interests, principles of good governance, or egalitarian principles – all at the expense of those they are expected to protect and serve. The framing of Aboriginal peoples as model (good) or immoral (bad) compromises the possibility of seeing them as complex personalities with multi-dimensional lives (Roberts and Mahtani 2010). They are stigmatized instead as foreigners or outsiders whose unidimensional lives are defined by their status as pathetic victims, belligerent warriors, and quixotic tree huggers (see also Keung 2006; Solutions Research Group 2006). Rarely do they appear as actively engaged and "normal" individuals in everyday life beyond stereotypical slots or crisis contexts (ter Wal 2004). Even coverage that is positive may prove so excessively sanitized and standardized that Aboriginal identities and realities are simplified to the point of being simplistic.

In short, the representational basis of news media–Aboriginal peoples relations can be summed up in one word: dysfunctional. A conflict of interest is glaring: on the one hand, Aboriginal peoples are framed as troublesome constituents who have problems or who are problems – the politics of aboriginality. On the other hand, the politics of aboriginality focus on Aboriginal rights to indigenous models of self-determining autonomy over land, identity, and political voice (Maaka and Fleras 2008). A robust Aboriginal print media has emerged in hopes of resolving this conflict of interest and overcoming negative coverage that not only glosses over issues of relevance to Aboriginal peoples but also ignores or distorts Aboriginal perspectives. Aboriginal print media and newspapers have played and continue to play a key role in the symbolic reclamation of space for Aboriginal peoples, in part by rejecting negative media depictions, promoting positive stories, challenging Canadian society to acknowledge its rights and responsibilities to Aboriginal peoples, and encouraging Aboriginal involvement in promoting Aboriginal issues at local, regional, and national levels. Below is a partial list of Canadian-based Aboriginal print media that range in scope and readership from the national to the regional and the tribal.

Aboriginal Voices: A magazine that publishes news and perspectives bimonthly about the lives and experiences of indigenous peoples of North America.

For distribution in Canada and the United States, *Aboriginal Voices* works on the assumption that Aboriginal peoples should have a voice in the North American context.

First Perspective News: Published monthly in Manitoba, *First Perspective News,* as Canada's national Aboriginal voice, reports on news and Native law cases and provides First Peoples' event and powwow listings, education and employment listings, and commentary by indigenous writers and contributors.

Windspeaker: Canada's "national Aboriginal news source" is published by the Aboriginal Multi-Media Society of Alberta for both Aboriginal and non-Aboriginal readers. The monthly paper endorses a relevant, independent, and objective commitment to reporting news through information, current affairs, and entertainment.

Weetamah News: This monthly paper has a circulation of about ten thousand and is distributed to many First Nations and Metis communities, tribal councils, and Aboriginal and non-Aboriginal businesses and organizations throughout the prairie provinces and northern Ontario. Since 1990, the paper has provided a forum for Aboriginal voices in which to convey their distinctly Aboriginal perspective to both Aboriginal and non-Aboriginal audiences. The paper is financed wholly through advertising revenues.

Nunatsiaq News: Published in Iqaluit every Friday and distributed throughout Nunavut.

Raven's Eye: Distributed to all First Nations and Metis communities, including friendship centres, in British Columbia and Yukon.

Alberta Sweetgrass: Since 1993, this monthly paper has served the Aboriginal communities in rural areas of Alberta. A monthly circulation of over seven thousand makes it one of Alberta's most popular papers.

Wawatay News: This northern Ontario paper has served the Nishnawbe Aski Nation, Treaty 3 area, and Robinson Superior Treaty area since 1974. It publishes biweekly, in English, Ojibwa/Oji-Cree, and Cree, and reaches eighty-one communities.

In addition to these papers are online publications, including *First Nations Drum,* which provides Canada-wide news on Aboriginal peoples, and the *Headwater News,* with its daily synopsis of news and commentary for Native residents of western Canada and the United States. As well, there is *Dibaud-jimoh Nawash,* news from the Chippewas of the Nawash Unceded First Nation of the Bruce Peninsula in southern Ontario. (The above information is drawn from two websites: http://www.johnco.com and http://www.nativeweb.org.)

Aboriginality and Film: From Tinseltown Indians to Indigenous Storytelling

> *The movies loom so large for Indians because they have defined our self-image as well as told the entire planet how we live, look, scream, and kill. (Comanche writer Paul Chaat Smith, quoted in Wood 2008, 73)*

Media portrayals of Canada's Aboriginal peoples are not altogether different from their portrayals of immigrants and racialized minorities. But although print media continue to misrepresent Aboriginals peoples, visual media such as film have proven more sympathetic in recent years. Such a shift is timely and overdue: to an extent perhaps unsurpassed elsewhere, images of Aboriginal/ indigenous peoples reflect the picture-based storytelling media of film or movies (Rollins and O'Connor 2003; Darian-Smith 2004; Wood 2008). Such an assertion should come as no surprise: although all ethnic groups were stereotyped or demeaned by Hollywood storytelling, Aboriginal peoples were particularly movie-worthy. Proof that Native Americans represent the longest-running subject of films: none other than Thomas Edison employed film images of a Pueblo village in the early 1890s to demonstrate the marvels of his kinetoscope (considered the first motion picture viewer) (Abourezk 2004). Early cinema portrayals of aboriginality swung between the poles of hostility and admiration: on one side, the Enlightenment ideal of the noble savage whose near disappearance signalled the demise of a seemingly pristine era; on the other side, the ignoble and bloodthirsty savage who either harassed white settlers or proved to be hapless victims of white encroachment (Darian-Smith 2004).

This ideal-typical dichotomy underscored the nature of the movie business, namely, a distinction between A films and B films. A films – major studio releases that had big production budgets – tended toward more sympathetic depictions (Aleiss 2005). For example, the Disney production of *Davy Crockett* in 1954 starring Fess Parker acknowledged the reckless bravery of the "redskins" (as Natives were referred to in the film) while conceding their victimization by manipulative white interests – even if these "injuns" (again, as per the film) were thought to lack any sense of property or ownership. But even positive portrayals of Aboriginal peoples were compromised by conventional ideologies of the day, including social Darwinism, with its notion of a struggle for survival and survival of the fittest (Rollins and O'Connor 2003). However noble and admired, Aboriginal peoples were doomed to extinction, in part because of white need or greed, in part because of evolutionary progress. (See

Neil Diamond's *Reel Injuns* for a searing indictment of mainstream media's historical depiction of North American indigenous peoples.)

By contrast, B movies were cheaply and quickly made to satisfy the bottom half of a double bill. They tended to demean or caricaturize by relying on simple formulaic plots, stock villains, shopworn stereotypes, recycled stunt footage, and minimal dialogue. Hollywood's Indians attacked towns (in reality, rarely) and engaged in hand-to-hand combat with settlers, often in ravines (again, a rarity), after encircling fortifications or wagon trains as a combat strategy (apparently only one wagon train ever formed that classic circle under an Indian attack) (Herzberg 2008). Movie themes focused on the heroic feats of pioneers who bravely domesticated an "empty" West in the face of stubborn indigenous resistance to America's manifest destiny (Rollins and O'Connor 2003). Aboriginal women suffered even greater indignities, as might be expected during the B film era. They often were depicted as celluloid princesses, oppressed "beasts of burden," and hot-blooded spitfires whose sexual promiscuity invariably resulted in punishment – even death – for such indiscretions (Berton 1975; Marubbio 2006).

Hollywood may well have proven a dream factory for many, but film proved to be a nightmare for Aboriginal peoples who were routinely chronicled along stereotypical and racist lines. In reflecting "fantasies of the master race" (Churchill 2000), movie portrayals of aboriginality were projections of white fears or fantasies on the silver screen that really had little to do with Aboriginal realities but were more about prevailing white perceptions and prejudices. In the early days of film, for example, Aboriginal people were portrayed as simple folk who lacked complexity, intellect, or ambition – that is, less than human and closer to nature, with depictions ranging from bloodthirsty savages to nymph-like children (Aleiss 2005; Wood 2008). Of the hundred or so silent films about Native Americans between 1910 and 1913, most romanticized the "noble red man" as naive and childlike. In contrast to this, westerns between the 1930s and 1950s employed non-Native actors to portray bloodthirsty savages, hell-bent on killing pioneers and capturing white women (Abourezk 2004). Or alternatively, they were also portrayed as misunderstood yet sincere people who only wanted peace and their land. Adding to the invisibility was a reluctance to assign dialogue, thus reinforcing people's perceptions of (Hollywood) Indians as "very stoic, [having] just one or two lines, no blink, no expression" (Rakauskas 2006).

Over time, however, popular images shifted in response to evolving ideas and ideals. Positive portrayals increasingly proved to be the rule rather than the exception following the inception of the civil rights movement and the ideological shifts associated with the 1960s counterculture era. Instead of insulting their cultures as archaic or debased, Native Americans were portrayed as gentle and peaceful unless provoked, in which case the violence was justified as an act of self-defence (Herzberg 2008). *Little Big Man,* released in 1970, was one of the first blockbusters to demonstrate sympathy in its treatment of Native Americans while questioning the bona fides of Western society as a more progressive alternative. The 1975 TV movie *I Will Fight No More Forever* featured the Chumacha Indian Ned Romero as Chief Joseph, thus signalling the arrival of Native Americans as first-class citizens (Rakauskas 2006). Or consider how the 1990 film *Dances with Wolves* captured the zeitgeist of this celluloid shift – although it still took an enlightened white saviour to salvage a dying Sioux culture (Abourezk 2004). The 1995 Canadian film *Dance Me Outside,* directed and co-written by Bruce McDonald, unflinchingly portrays life on the reserve in the round – that is, gritty and painful yet hopeful and funny. Twenty-first-century films like *Windtalkers* and *Flags of Our Fathers* celebrated Native Americans as proud and loyal heroes willing to make the ultimate sacrifice in advancing the American war effort.

In short, film images no longer disparage America's First Peoples as heathen savages remote in time and place, and without a shred of decency. Paradoxically, it is whites who now are portrayed as murderous savages whose rapacious greed knew no boundaries; by contrast, Native American are the new victims, even if facts do not always support this interpretation (Abourezk 2004). But displacing one set of stereotypes for another is not without consequences. For example, in the blockbuster film *Avatar,* the Na'vi aliens on Pandora are patterned after Hollywood stereotypes of North American Indians – noble savages in braids riding bareback with bows and arrows, yet rescued by a white messiah (B. Johnson 2010). In other words, challenging stereotypes can be tricky, since new ones easily replenish the void (Rollins and O'Connor 2003). Herzberg (2008, 1) writes about the dangers in going from one extreme to the other: "Tribes that had been among those responsible for some of the most vicious massacres in American history suddenly become lovable Teddy bears who helped lost white children and were more pro-environment than Ralph Nader."

Another major trend entails an indigenizing of film (Abourezk 2004). The industry is becoming increasingly indigenized by virtue of a growing number of indigenous actors in front of the camera and indigenous filmmakers behind the camera (Brown 2004). This shift is a reaction to an era when whites rather than Natives were expected to narrate stories about everything from indigenous-white relations to indigenous experiences (M.J. Miller 2008). White actors in bronzed body paint, with often ill-fitting wigs and headdresses, routinely played indigenous roles ("playing Indian"). Hollywood stars included Burt Lancaster in *Apache,* Chuck Connors in *Geronimo,* Anthony Quinn in *The Plainsman,* and Elvis Presley as a Kiowa in *Flaming Star* (Aleiss 2005; Diamond 2010). Depictions of indigeneity were filtered through Eurocentric lenses and the imperatives of the film industry, in the process framing indigenous peoples in terms of their impact on society and according to mainstream needs. The net effect reflects a polarized climate of "us versus them" that is hostile or indifferent toward the "other" (van Dijk 1995; Glynn and Tyson 2007; Burnett 2011). As Lauren Brown (2004) aptly demonstrates:

> Filmmakers are an example of non Indians who have created an Indian identity. Indians in films are generally shown as inferior people who will disappear with the onset of civilized European settlement. They are imagined to be very spiritual, perhaps magical, and to have a close relationship with nature. The classic Hollywood image of an American Indian is one with red skin, a small loin cloth for clothes, moccasin shoes, long straight dark hair, a feather headdress, a tomahawk or arrows in hand, and warpaint on the face who lives in a teepee on the plains of North America. Indians have been historicized and their roles in contemporary society are usually left out of non Indian made films.

Instead of relying on Hollywood to soften its stance, Aboriginal and indigenous writers, producers, and directors have taken control of the process. From the American *Smoke Signals* to the Canadian *Atanarjuat (The Fast Runner),* indigenous filmmakers increasingly rely on formats and content that not only unsettle Hollywood's business-as-usual framework but also advance an indigenous film gaze (Takeuchi 2006; Tweedy and Perry 2006).

Admittedly, difficulties persist in defining what constitutes an Aboriginal/indigenous feature film. In theory, four attributes are thought to be critical (Wood 2008; Columpar 2010): (1) indigenous peoples who make these films live under conditions that reflect asymmetries of power; (2) indigenous films are made by filmmakers who define themselves as indigenous or are defined by others as indigenous; (3) indigenous films are based on cultures that differ to a recognizable degree from mainstream culture, including distinctive storytelling techniques; and (4) indigenous films are made by those with linkages to an ancestral homeland. However valid these defining characteristics, any sharp distinction between indigenous and non-indigenous films should be cautiously approached as loosely defined labels along a very fluid continuum. Films at the indigenous end of the continuum include *The Journals of Knud Rasmussen* (directed by the Inuit filmmaker Zacharias Kunuk).[1] Similarly, *Smoke Signals* was the first feature film written, directed, acted, and co-produced by a Native American. Albeit with a low budget and starring several unknowns, this road-trip/buddy movie depicted contemporary life both on and off the reserve (Abourezk 2004). In the case of *Powwow Highway* (another road-trip/buddy film), the director broke ground in two ways: first, the film involved indigenous protagonists rather than typecasting indigenous peoples as enemies, sidekicks, or love interests; second, it portrayed Native Americans as complex three-dimensional characters rather than as cardboard cut-outs.

By comparison, antipodean films such as *Rabbit-Proof Fence* (2002) and *Whale Rider* (2002) are seen as non-indigenous films. So too are Hollywood films, including *Soldier Blue* (1970), *Little Big Man* (1970), *Dances with Wolves* (1990), *Apocalypto* (2006), and *Avatar* (2009). Yes, each of the films employs some indigenous actors and aspects of their language and culture. And, generally, the indigenes are shown in a more favourable light in contrast to the evil that whites do. But because these films employ white directors who generally impose a Eurocentric/white gaze on the characters and context, resulting in what might be called cultural appropriation (Huijser 2007), each of these films embraces "invader" (Barry Barclay in Columpar 2010, xi) storytelling forms. Storylines are framed to reflect classic narratives that allow viewers to juxtapose the thrill of exotic authenticity with assurances of universal qualities of the story (Siebert 2006). Vincent Ward's *River Queen* (New Zealand, 2005) is a good example of such a trope.

Does the aboriginality in Aboriginal films make a difference? Is it possible for an oral storytelling tradition to coexist as an authentic alternative within a revenue-driven cinematic narrative (picture-based storytelling) without creating distortion in the process? Media theorists like Marshall McLuhan have argued that the indigeneity of films is irrelevant; after all, the structure of films and the very act of processing movie information similarly transforms all audiences more profoundly than the specific images per se. For example, even

---

1 The film *Before Tomorrow*, co-directed by the actor Madeline Ivalu and Marie-Hélène Cousineau, completes the historical triptych of Inuit cinema that began with *Atanarjuat (The Fast Runner)* and *The Journals* (Morrow 2009).

highly acclaimed indigenous films like *Powwow Highway* and *Smoke Signals* have come under criticism on grounds that the storytelling (from indigenous characters to plot lines) is largely mainstream. Insofar as they reflect Western ways of seeing (gaze), indigenous films are, first and foremost, films (Wood 2008). Others disagree with this interpretation. As far as they are concerned, indigeneity matters because it empowers by challenging conventional gazes (Brown 2004). Indigenous filmmakers produce films that not only correct misrepresentations by non-indigenous filmmakers in shaping both whites' and non-whites' perceptions of indigeneity. Indigenous forms of storytelling are also utilized to promote the survival of indigenous cultures and traditions (Wood 2008).

To be sure, the politics of indigenous storytelling can be problematic. Should indigenous differences be emphasized at the expense of glossing over commonalities as humans, and vice versa? Dangers lurk in exaggerating differences by distorting people's expectations of aboriginality as exotic (as well as remote and removed). The expectation of difference leads to audience disappointments when indigenous actors act of out character. But more importantly, indigenous directors are robbed of the right to make films that reflect indigenous lives and experiences (Wood 2008), despite the fact that some cultural differences are deep and fundamental, perhaps even unbridgeable. Regardless of the merits or benefits, greater involvement and indigenous empowerment in film production is beyond dispute. The American Indian Film Institute festival's receipt of over a hundred submissions attests to the growing power of indigenous control over images (Abourezk 2004). With the mesmerizing power of the cinema to viscerally affect audiences, the indigenization of film cannot come too soon.

Aboriginalizing the Airwaves in Canada

Aboriginal peoples have increasingly capitalized on media institutions as a tool of empowerment (Meadows and Molnar 2001; Roth 2006). As noted in the previous chapter, both the federal government and Canada's First Nations peoples have colluded on a range of policies and programs to close the digital divide, especially in remote and rural areas, by promoting Internet accessibility, education, and locally produced content development (Howard, Busch, and Sheets 2010). Nowhere is this linking of the past with pathways into a globally integrated future more evident than in broadcasting. Canada's Aboriginal peoples may possibly possess one of the most advanced broadcasting systems in the world (Roth 2006; see also Zimmerman, Zimmerman, and Bruguier 2000). In northern Canada, Aboriginal communities have exercised control over the local media since the 1970s, largely by appropriating satellite technology to meet social and cultural needs (Meadows and Molnar 2001). The CBC established the Frontier Coverage Package as early as the 1960s. This package consisted of four hours per day of prerecorded videotapes of select southern programming that circulated by air on a weekly basis from community to community (Roth 2010a). The operationalizing of domestic satellite service in 1973 improved the quality and access of telecom services across northern Canada. But programming continued to originate in the south on the assumption that what was good for the rest of Canada was good for the North.

The Broadcasting Act of 1991 proved pivotal in aboriginalizing the airwaves. The act enshrined an Aboriginal right to control over their own communications, while instructing mainstream broadcasting to ensure "the special place of aboriginal peoples" in its programming and employment. In keeping with the spirit of the Broadcasting Act and the introduction of the first Native television network (Television Northern Canada) in the world (Roth 2005), the Canadian Radio-Television and Telecommunications Commission (CRTC) approved the creation of the nationwide Aboriginal Peoples Television Network (APTN) in 1999 – the world's first national network operated by, for, and about Aboriginal peoples with predominantly Aboriginal content built on an extensive history of Aboriginal media use and television production (Roth 2010b). APTN provides a platform on which to produce culturally and linguistically relevant programming for Aboriginal men, women, and children, in addition to providing Canadians with a window into the Aboriginal world.

In structural terms, APTN represents a hybrid service under CRTC regulations that carries advertising (and receives no government funding) yet models itself after public-model TV with its commitment to service rather than profit per se (Roth 2010a). All cable companies must carry APTN as part of their basic consumer package; subscription proceeds are allocated to APTN to complement revenues generated through advertising sales, strategic partnerships, and subscriber fees. APTN produces little in the way of original programming (the acclaimed series *Moccassin Flats* being an exception [Ramsay 2010]), preferring instead to collaborate on an ad hoc basis with independent producers, including the National Film Board (Knopf 2010). Programming from the North is complemented by southern fare, including an expanded range of international programs, from documentaries to talk shows to children programs.

In 2000, APTN introduced live news and current affairs programs that span the globe by incorporating regional, national, and international affairs. On the tenth anniversary of its launch, APTN was available in approximately 10 million Canadian homes and commercial establishments through various providers (mostly cable and DTH – direct-to-home television), with 56 percent of programming in English, 16 percent in French, and 28 percent in Aboriginal languages (Nation Talk 2009).

APTN is generally regarded as a Canadian and Aboriginal success story (Hafsteinsson and Bredin 2010). Benefits are widely touted: it presents contemporary society from an Aboriginal perspective, it promotes a deep democracy by fostering transgressive practices that are simultaneously local yet global, it offers a media discourse that enlightens and that Aboriginal peoples can identify with, and it seeks to undo the effect of exposure to mainstream colonial media (Haftsteinsson 2010; Knopf 2010; Patterson 2010). But such a glowing assessment is likely to attract criticism. According to Kerstin Knopf (2010), who acknowledges the ambivalence of indigenizing the mediascape, APTN may strive to decolonize the Canadian airwaves, but the shortage of quality indigenous content results in program choices whose stereotyping contradicts the decolonizing process. The fact that a Eurocentric hegemony is legitimized through an Aboriginal gaze serves to intensify the ambiguity.

Still, the distribution of locally and regionally produced programming to a national audience allows APTN to counteract mainstream miscasting by promoting a positive and realistic portrayal of Canada's First Peoples across a broad range of topics (Meadows and Molnar 2001; Baltruschat 2004, 2010; M.J. Miller 2008; see also Rahoi-Gilchrist 2010). The sharing of stories with all Canadians by projecting Aboriginal images and ideas through indigenous media also proves effective in influencing public and public policy (Harding 2010). As Lorna Roth (2010a, 237) puts it into perspective when describing APTN as a symbolic meeting place for Aboriginal peoples and non-Aboriginals to communicate their common interests, "APTN has enabled indigenous messages to be heard by constituency groups that might have never had access to a live person of Aboriginal descent; it provides an opportunity to share national imageries and histories, to build bridges of understanding, and to bridge cultural borders."[1]

---

1   The introduction of Māori Television in 2004 has also proven counterhegemonic (Smith and Abel 2008). Māori Television not only poses a threat to established television culture, it also exerts pressure on non-Māori to take seriously Māori viewpoints, nurtures a sense of community and connection with other Māori communities, links Māori issues with global developments, and throws into relief the monocultural offerings of mainstream fare.

14

Ethnic Media
"Empowering the People"

Canada constitutes a multicultural society whose multiculturality reflects different layers of meaning. Four levels of multicultural meaning can be discerned: as demographic fact, as ideology, as practice, and as official government policy and programs (Fleras 2009, 2010). At the core of Canada's official multiculturalism is a commitment to the principles and practice of institutional inclusiveness. According to the Canadian Multiculturalism Act of 1988, all institutions, but especially federal institutions, have a responsibility to proactively engage diversity through initiatives that are reflective of the community they serve, respectful of cultural identities, and responsive to minority needs and concerns. Both public and private institutions have taken steps toward improving levels of responsiveness, including removal of the most egregious forms of racial discrimination in service delivery, modification of institutional structures to ensure equitable treatment, and creation of positive programs to improve access and equity.

However well intentioned, a commitment to inclusiveness is not always doable. Ideas and ideals about the primacy of whiteness and Eurocentrism are deeply embedded within institutional design, organization, foundational principles, and reward structures. So structured are mainstream institutions around racialized discourses of white domination that minorities are routinely and systemically denied or excluded through no fault of their own (Henry and Tator 2006). This institutionalized exclusion is particularly evident in news media coverage of racialized (minority) women and men. Despite modest moves toward improving diversity depictions, the news values of a conventional news paradigm continue to frame racialized minorities as troublesome constituents, that is, as problem people who are problems, who have problems, or who create problems. In terms of coverage, they continue to be rendered invisible except in contexts of crisis or conflict, in the process reinforcing their precarious status as the "other" within.

This framing of racialized diversity around a conflict/problem/negativity nexus is neither intentional nor personal. To the contrary, the unintended yet logical consequences of largely one-sided misrepresentations are systemically biasing by virtue of drawing negative attention to diversities and difference. Embedded values and Eurocentric conventions are so invasive in shaping the selection, construction, and presentation of news as to consistently produce distorted coverage of migrants and minorities. As a result, whites and non-whites stand in a different relationship to mainstream media: whites see themselves painted into the media picture as normal or superior, whereas minorities find themselves racialized and excluded by Eurocentric discourses that demean, deny, and diminish. In that the cumulative effect of such monocultural coverage imposes a controlling effect without much public fanfare about what's going on, debates over the representational basis of media-minority relations are intensely political.

To circumvent the effects of this systemically biasing coverage, ethnic (or racialized) minorities have turned to alternative media institutions. In reflecting minority experiences, identities, and priorities, ethnic (or multicultural) media have proliferated to the point of constituting a robust component of Canada's mediascape (C. Murray 2008a, 2008b).[1] Reaction has varied as well. For some, the expansion of ethnic media is commensurate with Canada's inclusivity commitments; for others, ethnic media are essentially manipulative advocates for special interest groups; for yet others, ethnic media are regressive because they disrupt immigrant integration (i.e., heavier users of ethnic media tend to identify with the ethnic community [Chen and Thorson 2009; see also Spoonley and Trlin 2004]); and for still others, ethnic media are more complex and nuanced than simplistic pigeonholing into good or bad allows. Not surprisingly, debates over the pros and cons of ethnic media resonate with overtones of ambiguity and contradiction, and there are few signs

---

1 The term "ethnic media" is widely used in North America. In Europe, the expression "minority community media" is preferred, "diasporic media" in Britain, "community language media" in Australia. This chapter uses the expression "ethnic media," although the term "multicultural media" is employed as well.

that this debate will abate or resolve itself soon (Geissler and Pöttker 2005, 2006; Will 2005; Murray, Yu, and Ahadi 2007).

Canada possesses an energetic and possibly unmatched ethnic media. Ethnic media abound, from hundreds of ethnic newspapers to radio stations and television programs that inform and enlighten new and racialized Canadians. And yet, despite their centrality to society, references to ethnic media are mired in confusion and marred by misunderstanding. Do ethnic media contribute to or detract from the challenges of living together differently? Do ethnic media play an integrative role in advancing a cooperative coexistence? Are ethnic media critical in engaging immigrant populations in the civic life of society (Chen and Thorson 2009)? Are ethnic media inclusive or insular with respect to outcomes? How does their governing logic differ from mainstream media? How does seeing like the ethnic media differ from a mainstream media gaze? Integration or separatist? Insular or isolationist? Inclusive or exclusive? Divisive or unifying? Bridges or barriers? Outward looking (outreach) or inward looking (enclave)? Progressive or regressive? Society building or society bashing? In exploring the promises and perils of Canada's ethnic media, as well as their politics and paradoxes, this chapter argues that ethnic media constitute an integrative component of an inclusive Canada-building project by doing the following:

1 Advancing Canada's democratic dividend beyond the parameters of mainstream news media.
2 Improving the sectoral interests of immigrants and racialized minorities through alternative media discourses (DeSouza and Williamson 2006).
3 Facilitating the integration of new Canadians. Ethnic media as multicultural social capital provide a bonding device for consolidating a sense of community, in addition to a bridging device for promoting intercultural awareness and exchanges.
4 Circumventing conventional media gazes by offering an alternative or oppositional way of seeing that empowers rather than diminishes.

In promoting ethnocultural vitality without sacrificing a commitment to community or to Canada, ethnic media are shown to embrace both an inward- and outward-looking orientation, as well as a reactive and proactive dynamic. Ethnic media embody the dynamics of bridging and bonding; accordingly, their status as pockets of insularity and as pathways into integration has proven mutually reinforcing. The end result? Ethnic media embody and embrace the inclusivity principle at the heart of Canada's official multiculturalism.

Multicultural Mediascape in Canada

Canada has long campaigned to respect and protect its cultural diversity. In the face of globalization, trade liberalization, and border-busting technology, the media have been entrusted with this responsibility in three ways: first through the promotion of ethnic or third-language broadcasting within the framework of the Canadian broadcasting system (Lincoln, Tasse, and Cianciotta 2005); second, through the mainstreaming of diversities into private and public media; and third, by acknowledging the legitimacy of ethnic media. Yet neither its popularity nor profusion appear to have secured clarity or consensus. There is no agreement over the definition, magnitude, or impact of ethnic media, despite a long history in Canada. Assessing the number of ethnic media is problematic, since start-ups disappear as quickly as they appear because of costs, competition, and local politics. Even the expression "ethnic" in ethnic media is problematic. Does "ethnic" refer to new Canadians or Canadian-born? To visibilized minorities or white European ethnics? Are ethnic media a healthy expression of multiculturalism (pulling together), or an exercise in cultural apartheid (pushing apart), or little more than a tribally driven business opportunity? Despite these uncertainties and confusion, ethnic media can be divided into three main categories: ethnic print publications, ethnic broadcasting, and ethnic mainstreaming. But first, a brief overview of Canada's mediascape.

The Lay of Canada's Media Terrain

Canada is widely regarded as a media-rich society whose impressive achievements are particularly striking despite daunting geographic, demographic, cultural, and historical obstacles (Attalah and Shade 2006; Shade 2010). In articulating the principles and objectives of the country's broadcast system, the Broadcasting Act establishes several priorities for Canadian broadcasting, including an emphasis on Canadian-owned and -controlled media, responsiveness to the needs of all Canadians, and a commitment to expand language diversity without losing sight of Canada's official language duality. Although operating primarily in English and French to ensure the integration of immigrants into Canadian society, broadcasting in Canada is expected "through its programming and the employment opportunities arising out of its operations [to] serve the needs and interests, and reflect the circumstances and aspirations, of Canadian men, women, and children, including equal rights, the linguistic duality and multicultural and multiracial nature of Canadian society and the special place of Aboriginal peoples within that society" (Broadcasting Act 1991, s. 3 (1) (d) (iii)). This diversity agenda has culminated in the development of a sophisticated and complex broadcasting system that serves both

English and French Canadians as well as Aboriginal peoples, and which in addition has a range of third-language services that now constitute an important tile in Canada's media mosaic (Lincoln, Tasse, and Cianciotta 2005). Canada's system of mixed private-public-populist arrangements comprises nearly 700 private and public television services (511 English, 115 French, and 53 third language), alongside 1,158 radio services (867 English, 253 French, and 38 third language).

Canada also possesses a significant if increasingly beleaguered print media. Currently, there are 96 paid-for daily papers across Canada, down from a peak of 138 in 1938, but up from 87 in 1945. Ownership of newspapers continues to be reshuffled among several major chains, including Postmedia Network (formerly Canwest Global), CTVglobemedia, Torstar, Quebecor/Sun Media/Osprey Media, Transcontinental, and Power Corporation (Newspapers Canada 2010b). Equally impressive is the growth of free daily papers (eighteen are currently distributed across Canada) that appeal to new young readers (Newspapers Canada 2010b). Still, the outlook for newspapers appears bleak: readership remains stagnant, with daily paid circulation at 4.1 million on an average publishing day in 2009, down from 5.7 million in 1989, despite immigrant-driven population growth in major cities (Newspapers Canada 2010b). The problem for mainstream papers is not readership per se, which is holding steady (especially if readers of online versions are included in the overall count). More accurately, what is worrying is the spiralling decline in advertising revenues because of the Internet (from Craigslist to pop-up ads) (see also Rosenstiel 2011). Compounding mainstream media's woes is their seeming inability or disinterest in cracking the ethnic market. Despite Canada's commitment to an inclusive multiculturalism in addition to the ethnic policy provisions of the Broadcasting Act, news media remain divided along a colour line between the white-o-centric "we" and the racialized "other" – in the process forfeiting an opportunity to connect with a largely untapped demographic. Under the circumstances, can anyone be surprised by the expansion of ethnic media?

Ethnic Media

Ethnic media grew significantly over the last decade, playing a much larger role than mainstream media in the lives of the fastest-growing ethnic groups – Chinese and South Asian Canadians (Karim 2006a, 2006b). These media range in size from small newspapers printed in home basements to well-established and professionally run broadcast stations, some of which are partly bankrolled by overseas interests (Murray, Yu, and Ahadi 2007). Hundreds of ethnic newspapers publish on a daily, weekly, or monthly cycle, including some that are sufficiently capable of competing with non-ethnic papers. There are those that speak to specific groups (e.g., *Share* – Caribbean and African), and those directed at immigrants in general *(Canadian Immigrant.ca)*. Some are printed in English, many in heritage languages, others in both. Migrant or diasporic media serve the needs of immigrants who wish to maintain transnational ties to their country of origin through print, satellite television and, increasingly, the Internet (Karim 2003). Out of necessity, ethnic media are adapting quickly to new communication technologies, thereby securing access to small and often scattered audiences (ibid.). Of particular note is the emergence of the Internet as a vital media option and communication tool in creating virtual ethnic communities that provide social solidarity and cultural renewal both at home and abroad (Solutions Research Group 2006).

Of course, Canada is not alone in the ethnic media sweepstakes. The United States has also witnessed a major spike in the number of ethnic radio stations (both local and national), newspapers, magazines, Web portals, and public and cable television stations (Hsu 2002). In contrast to mainstream news media, which are experiencing a decline in readership, revenues, and stock prices – especially with the popularity of online news and blogmeisters – ethnic media continue to expand. According to the Pew Research Center Project for Excellence in Journalism (2006), a Californian study estimated that 84 percent of Asian Americans, blacks, and Latinos consumed ethnic media, more than 50 percent indicated a preference for ethnic broadcasts or publications over English-language sources, and 40 percent said they paid more attention to ads in ethnic publications than to those in mainstream media. As in Canada, coverage in the US ethnic media tends to polarize around the local and the global rather than the regional or national, thus reinforcing the role of ethnic media in bridging the gap between the there and the here (Murray, Yu, and Ahadi 2007). The conclusion is now apparent. With ethnic minority audiences accounting for nearly a third of the purchasing power in America, advertisers no longer dismiss this demographic as too inconsequential. To the contrary, these niches are pitched to as vigorously as to the mainstream (Lieberman 2006).

Ethnic Print Publications
Ethnic newspapers are no stranger to Canada's mediascape. From the first ethnic papers written in German at the end of the eighteenth century to the publication of African Canadian papers in the 1850s (including, in Ontario, *Provincial Freeman* and *Voice of the Fugitive*), ethnic media have proven an enduring presence in Canada's mediascape. Estimates at present suggest there

are up to 350 ethnic papers (including about 200 third-language publications) that cater to their audiences on a daily, weekly, monthly, quarterly, or biannual basis. Most of these papers are local in scope and circulation; a few, however, are national publications, including the Chinese-language version of Canada's national newsmagazine, *Maclean's*. In British Columbia, the Indo-Canadian *Punjab Times* competes with three English-language weeklies and four Punjabi weeklies that address Indo-Canadian issues; in southern Ontario, there are seven Punjabi weeklies and a twice-monthly English newspaper catering to the same audience.

Ethnic Broadcasting

No less significant in advancing a multicultural Canada is ethnic broadcasting. The Ethnic Broadcasting Policy outlines the criteria for an over-the-air radio or TV service, such as the minimum amount of time for ethnic and third-language programming (CRTC 2011). At present, licensed ethnic and third-language services consist of six ethnic television stations in Montreal, Toronto, and Vancouver and twenty-one ethnic radio stations that together offer nearly two thousand hours of third-language programming each week. In addition, over 190 ethnic pay and specialty services have been approved for digital distribution, including 10 specialty audio services that require special receivers, 5 analog specialty services, 11 launched Category 2 digital specialty services, and 50 that have been approved but not yet launched (cited in Lincoln, Tasse, and Cianciotta 2005; see also Cardozo 2005). (Category 2 services are digital, pay, and specialty services that are not necessarily carried by cable or satellite distributors [Kular 2006].) OMNI.1 and OMNI.2 are world leaders in producing in excess of twenty hours of original programming per week, including 60 percent in languages other than French or English. VisionTV, a national broadcaster, also features thirty programs about different religious faiths and practices. Finally, the private sector is coming on board too. Multicultural issues have been addressed by Toronto's Citytv station since 1984 through blocks of non-English, non-French programming. Foreign-based services are available as well, either through specialty cable channels or via the Internet and satellite television. A last example of ethnic media includes the world's first national indigenous TV network, Aboriginal People's Television Network (APTN) – discussed in the next chapter. In promoting Aboriginal broadcasting for preserving the languages and cultures of Canada's First Peoples, the creation of APTN represents an example of alternative media by, for, and about an ethnic community (CRTC 2011).

The collective impact of ethnic broadcasting (radio/television) and ethnic print is immeasurable. Argues Ben Viccari (2007), past president of the Canadian Ethnic Media Association (formerly the Canadian Ethnic Journalists and Writers Club): "These media keep their readers and audiences informed about Canada as well as providing a vehicle for expression of freedom of thought that many editors and broadcasters never found in their country of origins." Ethnic broadcasting and print differ in what they can do and how. In contrast to print media, which are relatively free to come and go as they please, ethnic broadcasting in Canada is tightly micromanaged. On the assumption that airwaves belong to the public and must serve public interests, the Canadian Broadcasting Act (1991) asserts the importance of diversity within the broadcast system in the context of ethnic broadcasting. The CRTC stipulates how to put these principles into practice by specifying the conditions for the dissemination of ethnic and multilingual programming (CRTC 2011).

Ethnicizing Mainstream Media

Representing people from diverse backgrounds is not just the responsibility of ethnic media. Mainstream media are also under pressure by law to incorporate ethnic differences on both sides of the camera so that all Canadians can see themselves portrayed accurately, fairly, and without stereotyping (CRTC 2011). The federal government's Task Force on Broadcasting Policy, co-chaired by Gerald Caplan and Florian Sauvageau in 1986, addressed the need to include Aboriginal peoples and racial minorities (Raboy 1988). The Broadcasting Act of 1991 made provisions for Canadian broadcasting, in terms of both programming and employment opportunities, "to serve the needs of a diverse society and reflect the multicultural and multiracial character of Canada." The act not only reinforced the case for "cultural expression" by expanding air time for racialized ethnic minorities; it also insisted on sensitivity training for program and production staff, language guidelines to reduce race-role stereotypes, and monitoring of the on-air representation of racial minorities (CRTC 2011). The institutionalization of the Ethnic Broadcasting Policy led to guidelines for the portrayal of minorities. A regulatory body, the CRTC, was established and charged with the responsibility of developing broadcasting services that reflect Canada's diversity. The CRTC requires all television and radio broadcasters to file seven-year plans on how they will reflect diversity in their programming and operations, and report annually on their progress (Cardozo 2005).

The mainstreaming of diversities is a win-win situation. According to Madeline Ziniak, co-chair of the Task Force for Cultural Diversity on Television and vice-president at OMNI Television, advertisers are waking up to the advantages of advertising to minorities (cited in Prashad 2006). Demographics are propelling the changes: when newcomers and racialized minorities compose nearly half of the populations in Vancouver and Toronto, mainstream media have little option except to acknowledge that "diversity sells." And yet, a more responsive social climate for institutional inclusiveness eludes commercial mainstream media. Hardly surprising: commercial media do not see themselves as reform agencies to promote progressive change or to accommodate diversities, despite a social responsibility to do so because of the power they wield. They are first and foremost a business whose raison d'être is simple: to make money by connecting audiences to advertisers through ratings. Institutional practices such as stereotyping that generate revenues will be retained; those that don't will be discarded. Such a bottom-line mentality will invariably clash with minority demands for balanced and contextual coverage, given media preference for morselization over context, conflict over cooperation, the episodic over the contextual, and personalities over issues (see J. Atkinson 1994). That competing agendas are at play is no less detrimental. The very changes that minorities want of the news media (responsible coverage of minority interests, less sensationalism, more context, toned-down language, and less stereotyping) are precisely the news norms that media define as newsworthy.

Regulating the Ethnic Airwaves

The CRTC drafted its first ethnic broadcasting policy in 1985. The policy was predicated on the multicultural premise that new Canadians would express a stronger sense of belonging if provided with programming from within their community and in their own language (Whyte 2006). Since the CRTC issued Canada's first licence for ethnic broadcasting to CHIN Radio in 1966, the number of licensed ethnic radio and television services has proliferated. For the CRTC, ethnic programming is defined as any radio or television programming aimed at an ethnically or racially distinct group other than Aboriginal peoples. The programming may be in any language, including English or French, or a combination of languages. Depending on the size of the target group and the resources available, stations that feature ethnic programming must incorporate several ethnic groups within their service catchment area. As the CRTC's Ethnic Broadcasting Policy (CRTC 1999) puts it: "Ethnic stations are required to serve a range of ethnic groups in a variety of languages. This is because the scarcity of broadcast frequencies may not permit the licensing of an over-the-air single-language service for each ethnic in a given market. This approach also allows for the provision of service to groups that would not otherwise be able to afford their own single-language service."

Other restrictions apply as part of the mandatory licensing arrangement. According to CRTC regulations, ethnic radio and television stations must devote at least 60 percent of their schedule to ethnic programming. The other 40 percent of the schedule allows for alternative programming to establish a business model for generating revenues in support of ethnic programming. To reflect Canada's linguistic diversity, 50 percent of their programming schedule must be in third languages, that is, languages other than French, English, or the many Aboriginal languages. Ethnic radio stations must fulfill this requirement each broadcast week. Compliance with this requirement for ethnic television stations are measured monthly. Although non-ethnic radio and television stations may air unlimited amounts of ethnic programming in French or English, only 15 percent of their schedules may be in third languages unless they obtain commission approval for an increase of up to 40 percent. Campus radio stations and some community radio stations are allowed to produce up to 40 percent of their schedules in the form of third-language programming (R. Armstrong 2010).

Such micromanagement may appear excessively bureaucratic. Nonetheless, there are rationales: first, to protect ethnic broadcasting from undue competition in the search for much-needed revenue; second, to give non-ethnic stations the flexibility to reflect local diversity. Canadian content requirements apply to ethnic radio and television stations just as they do to mainstream broadcasting: generally, radio programming must produce 35 percent Canadian content for Category 2 general music, but only 7 percent for Category 1 ethnic music; television programming must carry 60 percent Canadian content, including 50 percent during the evening (prime time) broadcast slot.

Theorizing Ethnic Media: Transcending Borders, Constructing Buffers, Creating Bonds, Building Bridges

They respond to the needs of ethnic and racialized minorities; they provide a voice in advancing the welfare of the community; they challenge social injustices; they foster a sense of cultural pride; and they articulate the essence of their communities (Gonzales 2001). Their popularity and success reflect part of a broader worldwide trend toward "people becoming the media" – thanks to greater ease in publishing through alternative and personal media (Deuze 2006; Niles 2008). The "they" here refers to ethnic/multicultural media, whose collective objectives address the informational, integrative, and advocacy needs of those marginalized by mainstream media. In a global context where the local and the global are in constant interplay, yet people's understanding of international and intercultural relations is woefully lacking, references to ethnic media provide fresh insights into the dynamics of cultural multi-belongings and spatial interdependencies (Mediam'Rad 2009). This multi-dimensionality is crucial in clarifying the origins and rationale behind ethnic media; the role they play in society at large, and in minority communities in particular; the challenges in navigating media space; and their growing popularity despite mounting competition and numerous distractions.

Mapping Multicultural Media: A Cornucopia of Riches
Ethnic media come in different shapes and sizes. As a rule, they consist of mostly small broadcasters (radio and TV), cable channels, newspapers, and magazines that target racial and ethnic minority audiences, including Aboriginal peoples, racialized women and men, and immigrants and refugees (Lieberman 2006; Murray, Yu, and Ahadi 2007). Often local but sometimes regional, national, or transnational in scope or circulation, many ethnic media are mom-and-pop start-ups, published on a weekly or intermittent basis in languages other than English or French and distributed free of charge, reflecting commercial or community orientation, or providing their readers with entertainment or essential information for survival or participation as citizens in their country of residence. Other ethnic media resemble mainstream media in form and function; that is, they are sophisticated in operation, content, and distribution, employing sufficient resources to publish on a daily basis for profit (Lin and Song 2006).

As well, ethnic media can be classified according to origins. On one side are homegrown ethnic media that are conveyed in either the native tongue or host country language or a combination of both. On the other side are ethnic media produced abroad but circulated in the host country and incorporating three types of multicultural media content: news events covered by mainstream media, mainstream news events from a minority perspective, and news from within the ethnic community (Weber-Menges 2005; Chen and Thorson 2009). Finally, new technologies are having a direct impact on multicultural media (Georgiou 2002). From multi-channel digital television packages to the Internet and online text and video, digitalization has opened up new possibilities for disseminating multicultural media throughout local, national, and transnational transmission. In other words, insofar as ethnic media may be characterized by a perfect if chaotic ideal of multicultural diversity, it is nearly impossible to construct a single typology (Murray, Yu, and Ahadi 2007).

Targeted audiences are no less variable. Although some ethnic media embrace a commitment to interculturalism in the sense of generating dialogue between minority and majority audiences, many cater to a preferred niche. Even here, internal variations prevail, with some ethnic media directed at the distinctive needs and concerns of immigrants, whereas others target Canadian-born minorities, and still others address different demographics within each category. Audience use is varied as well: first- and second-generation immigrants may rely on multicultural media for information about the homeland; the third generation, as a basis for dialoguing with parents or grandparents; and the fourth generation, in a search for roots (Deuze 2006). Degrees of politicization may vary also; for example, Vancouver-based (but linked to parent companies in Asia) Chinese-language papers – *Ming Pao Daily News, Sing Tao Daily,* and *World Journal* – are largely apolitical in an effort to draw a diverse Chinese Canadian West Coast readership. By contrast, the Punjabi-language press is overtly political, with explicit editorial opinions that probe or provoke (Will 2005). Lastly, ethnic media are proving of value in their role as bulletin boards for announcing upcoming events. Governments often rely on ethnic media to convey information (e.g., advertising of job openings) or to change attitudes, whereas commercial interests rely on them to expand their market penetration (Wu 2005; MacCharles 2008).

No one should be surprised by the role of ethnic media as information-providers, both community-based and culturally sensitive, as well as communication responsive and locally relevant. Mainstream media want to be all things to all people by pursuing the lowest common denominator in hopes of building the largest possible audience – in effect, tuning out audiences because of their generality and superficiality. By contrast, ethnic media focus on the needs of their target community by securing a sound marketing strategy based on "knowing your audience" (Niles 2008). As a clearinghouse for information that connects the there with the here by way of the in-between, ethnic media specialize in those stories that the mainstream ignores by imparting a perspective in a language that resonates (Hsu 2002). Ethnic media offer an alternative to those national news media that are increasingly centralized, standardized, and preoccupied with the trivial or sensational, thereby resulting in myopic and distorted coverage of global issues (Karim 2006a, 2006b). According to Ojo (2006, 351), ethnic media reflect minority attempts to sustain their cultural heritage by way of community-based news and events of interest or relevance to community members. Ethnic media also play an intermediary role;

they connect community with society while securing a strong migrant identity for making the transition into society (Cheng 2005). The advocacy role played by populist media is no less critical in helping to construct notions of identity and community (Georgiou 2002). In crusading for justice and equality, ethnic media may pose those awkward questions that mainstream media spurn for fear of censure or reprisals.

In light of such a (dis)array of functions, styles, and outputs, a theorizing of ethnic media is problematic. In general, ethnic media must be viewed as dynamic in their own right, as well as a domain for challenging the monoculturalism of a mainstream mediated world. But ethnic media differ among themselves in tone, style, and content. Perhaps the only characteristic in common is a propensity to see themselves as "anti-mainstream media while embracing an audience with a shared ethnicity and sense of community" (Georgiou 2002). To the extent that definitions exist, questions arise, including what should be subsumed under the category of ethnic media – as demonstrated in the Insight below.

insight

Mainstream Media as White Ethnic Media?

In theory, the distinction between mainstream and ethnic media is clear-cut. Mainstream media consist of those private or public outlets that cater to the general public; by contrast, ethnic media are thought to specifically target a specific ethnic minority. In reality, however, this intuitive divide is fuzzy. Where exactly do mainstream media end and ethnic media begin? What about global media giants like Al Jazeera, with its 50 million viewers worldwide – ethnic or mainstream? The distinction may be contested because ethnic media may be more mainstream than some would think, whereas mainstream media are more "ethnic" than is often thought. Or consider the seemingly counterintuitive possibility that mainstream media may be *interpreted as* ethnic media that are pro-white in catering to a predominantly white constituency. In the words of Stephen Riggins (1992, 2), "All mass media content could be analyzed from the experience of what is revealed about ethnicity. The *New York Times,* for example, could be read as an ethnic newspaper, although it is not explicitly or consciously so."

The consequences of this inversion are revelatory. In reminding us that all news media are ethnically located, whether conscious of this placement or not, media institutions and texts are neither neutral nor value-free but encoded in a fundamentally racialized (or ethnicized) way. Mainstream media are owned and controlled by corporate interests; as a result, they are organized by, for, and around the values, experiences, realities, and priorities of mainstream ethnic whites (Jiwani 2006). However unintentionally or incidentally, content is designed to promote and normalize Eurocentric norms, while alternative discourses are discredited as inferior or irrelevant. This Eurocentric whiteness not only serves as the normative standard by which others are judged, evaluated, and criticized, but also embeds the ideas and ideals of whiteness into institutional structures, processes, and outcomes, in effect generating a "palemale" gaze that projects white-o-centric fantasies or fears on racialized others. Admittedly, media decision makers and gatekeepers may not be consciously biased toward non-whites. Nevertheless, they unconsciously frame their narratives in a way that selects, highlights, and imposes a preferred Eurocentric gaze as unproblematic.

Parallels between ethnic and mainstream news media are unmistakable: both serve the information needs of their primary consumers and advertising targets. Each is also tribal in orientation, targets a specific audience, relies on advertising and a subscription base for survival, and adjusts its content accordingly. A commitment to the bottom line is a constant for both. Ethnic media are *not* nearly as unsullied by crass business concerns as many believe – in effect blurring the boundaries between ideal-typical distinctions. Publishers and producers are known to follow a time-proven mainstream trajectory: track what is profitable and repackage it as authentic to bolster the bottom line (Jeff Yang in Hsu 2002; Will 2005). They may even share common content (including a shared tendency toward sensational news items), although ethnic media cover more "news you can use" (including stories on immigration laws, health care, and social policies) to help minorities and immigrants adapt to Canada (Murray, Yu, and Ahadi 2007). In other words, many ethnic media differ from mainstream media by carrying additional rather than different content (Will 2005).

However tantalizing it is to equate the two media streams, the parallel breaks down because of a key difference – institutional power. Unlike ethnic media, who are largely powerless outside their communities, mainstream news media possess the resources and resourcefulness ("legitimacy") to make a difference in agenda setting, defining public discourses, and advancing national interests. That fact alone reinforces a need to be cautious in equating mainstream media with ethnic media except for purposes of analysis by way of inversion.

Critical-Thinking Question
What are the benefits and costs of analyzing mainstream news media as ethnic media in their portrayal of diversities and difference?

* * * * * * * * * *

Reactions to ethnic media vary as well. For some, there is much to commend in processes that reflect the community, act as a political mouthpiece, foster a collective purpose, and create a sense of community consensus. For others, this advocacy commitment inspires a softer journalism that ultimately privileges ideology over balanced coverage (Hsu 2002). For others still, the inward-looking nature of ethnic media not only delays the integration of migrants into their adopted homeland; worse still, it sabotages a shared living together by reinforcing an unhealthy inwardness. Critics argue that ethnic media may further dampen integration; after all, the inception of satellite TV and the Internet allows diasporic migrants to easily retain their homeland roots by tapping into the latest news, fashions, and trends. Once engrossed in their own media world, it is argued, immigrants no longer need to communicate or interact with others, resulting in the fragmentation of society into self-contained and inward-looking enclaves (Husband 2005; Weber-Menges 2005). For yet others, the persistence and popularity of ethnic media attest to the multiculturality and multi-locality that underpin our rapidly changing and increasingly diverse democratic societies within a globalizing world (Will 2005; Murray, Yu, and Ahadi 2007; Fleras 2011).

Toward an Explanatory Framework of Ethnic Media
Ethnic media originated and continue to flourish for a variety of reasons, both *reactive* and *proactive,* as well as *outward* and *inward.* On the reactive side, ethnic and racialized minorities resent their exclusion from the mainstream news media (Husband 2005). Media (mis)treatment of Aboriginal peoples, immigrants, and racialized ethnic minorities reflected their placement into one of four frames: as invisible, problems, stereotypes, or whitewashed (Fleras and Kunz 2001). In an industry enamoured by the logic that only bad news is good news, the framing of minorities as troublemakers resulted in one-sided coverage that demonized or dismissed (Butterwege 2001). Tuen A. van Dijk (1991) writes: "The strategies, structures, and procedures of reporting, the

choice of themes, the perspective, the transfer of opinions, style and rhetoric, are directed at presenting 'us' positively and 'them' negatively ... Their cause is only worth reporting when they cause problems, are caught in criminality or violence or can be represented as a threat to white hegemony." Or consider *Vancouver Sun* managing editor Kirk Lapointe's concession that his paper's coverage of Chinese Canadians is restricted to stories about the Chinese New Year and Chinese criminals, with little in between (cited in Will 2005). In other words, by framing diversity around conflict or celebration as its basis for newsworthiness, news media coverage of minorities is systemically biasing because of negative consequences (Everitt 2005). Who, then, can be surprised by the success and popularity of ethnic and Aboriginal media?

News media's mistreatment of minorities is widely acknowledged – ranging from ambivalence to antipathy (Jiwani 2006; Mahtani 2009). A Eurocentric media may have once openly vilified minorities as unwelcome aliens in a white man's country, but more polite discourses are emerging because of media reluctance to say anything negative about minorities for fear of losing subscriptions or being branded as racists (McGowan 2001). Rather than problematizing minorities as inherently inferior, they are negativized instead by association or by inference: for example, (1) minorities are criticized for not fitting into the framework of society as they should (minorities are okay if they are useful or know their place, otherwise they are dismissed as the outsiders within); (2) minorities are associated with negative contexts related to crime or terrorism; (3) minorities' cultural values and practices are repudiated as incommensurate with contemporary secular society; (4) a refusal to depict minorities within a holistic context of normalcy or acceptability as individuals reduces them to a faceless and unruly mob (Weber-Menges 2005); (5) diversities within minority communities are either glossed over or manipulated as a wedge that drives destructive divisions (Bharma 2008); and (6) minority realities and concerns are filtered through a pro-white gaze that invariably diminishes as it distorts (Sveinsson 2008).

News media mispresentation of Canada's multicultural realities remains as serious today as it was in the past (C. Murray 2008a, 2008b). Not surprisingly, awareness is growing that racialized minorities must do it themselves if they want their voices heard and stories told through representations they can relate to (Campion 2006; Haniff 2009). Ethnic media offer an alternative to simply adding a "dash of colour" through mainstream media quotas and targets. In providing racialized audiences with a culturally relevant space to see themselves beyond that of festivals or victimization (Mahtani 2008b), ethnic media reflect the lived realities of racialized minorities, in a familiar language, with a style that taps into their experiences (Ahmad 2006). A different set of news values is employed that promotes the self-construction of a community's own identity – in contrast to the faux-framed identities imposed by mainstream media (Ojo 2006). Even coverage of negative news is framed differently. Unlike the mainstream propensity for negativity and pathology, ethnic media cover a gamut of feel-good stories, including school successes, community cleanup campaigns, and local business and entrepreneurial achievements (J. Cohen 1999). When addressed, intergroup conflict and community problems tend be situated within a broader context that apportions blame to the system rather than to minority individuals (Lin and Song 2006; Ojo 2006).

Ethnic media also convey a positive outlook. By refracting reality through the prism of minority experiences, realities, and aspirations, ethnic media *proactively* strive to celebrate minority successes, accomplishments, and aspirations. Instead of framing minorities as potentially troublesome constituents, ethnic media foreground profiles of success to promote a positive self-image that helps foster a collective self-confidence. In hoping to avoid assimilation while preserving their cultural identity, ethnic media assist in framing minorities in assertive postures – as active agents of change rather than as passive victims of someone else's agency (Riggins 1992). They are also positioned to operate in a counterhegemonic manner by providing a social and cultural context for understanding the complex social realities that minorities must endure. In that people pay attention to media that pay attention to them, a dedication to community service secures the credibility and popularity of ethnic media (Husband 2005).

In addition to reactive-proactive dimensions, ethnic media are *outward* and *inward* looking (or outreach and inreach). They are inward by supplying information of relevance and immediacy to the intended demographic, including how to navigate the sometimes Byzantine labyrinth of a strange new world. Ethnic media serve a practical purpose by meeting specific information needs for adaptation and survival, including information about settling down, fitting in, and moving up (Whyte 2006). The benefits are inescapable: ethnic media may prove more accessible than mainstream outlets when publicizing free services and fundraising events, as well as when providing information about other upcoming events and visits from overseas dignitaries; in-depth stories about their communities; advice on booking a vacation, sending remittances, and finding legal representation; and a window for catching up on the latest cricket or rugby scores. Of particular importance are the information tip sheets for navigating through the maze of government bureaucracies (Georgiou 2002). Finally, ethnic media provide communities with a voice to articulate their concerns with the wider public while providing a counterweight to an increasingly corporate mainstream news media (Hsu 2002). This building of bridges across communities for fostering the civic participation of minorities and prompting their integration into society should not be underestimated.

Ethnic media are also outward looking. They report international news of relevance to the community through a perspective and tone that resonate more meaningfully with these audiences. They constitute an information system about the homeland that is crucial to adaptation; after all, news from or about home has a special status and value in reflecting a transmigrational/diasporic longing for information about the "there" as a basis for fitting in "here" (C. Murray 2009b; Lin and Song 2006). Homeland news in the immigrants' native language helps to strengthen identities, cultural heritage, and a centred sense of community; by contrast, mainstream media tend to ignore minority issues or relentlessly problematize them. Fostering a sense of bonding provides community members with an esprit de corps to mobilize residents to act upon injustices within the community (Lin and Song 2006).

In advancing an inward-outward and reactive-proactive orientation, ethnic media embody a form of empowerment known as social capital. As Robert Putnam explains in his landmark book *Bowling Alone* (2001), the quality of people's lives within society/community depends on establishing reserves of social capital with respect to trust, friendship, involvement, cooperation, life satisfaction, volunteerism, and sense of community ("neighbourhood") and commitment. Two dimensions inform the concept of social capital: bonding ("within") and bridging ("between"). Bonding social capital consists of those dense social ties and intense patterns of trust that secure strong mutual support and high levels of involvement. Bridging social capital entails more generalized trust in an open community, with greater individual initiative, tolerance of difference, and participation in society (Putnam 2001; Chen and Thorson 2009). To be sure, the more ethnically diverse a community, as Putnam (2007) concedes, the less likely are people to connect or to display trustworthiness (at least in the short run). The potential loss of social capital puts the onus on ethnic media to neutralize this disconnect and distrust, in part by providing both the bridging capital between different groups (ties to people unlike you), in part by way of bonding capital within one's own group (ties to people like you). Or as Madeleine Bunting (2007) writes, linking the bonding with the bridging, "A strong community identity gives them the confidence and the self-respect to establish themselves and get on" (see Riggins 1992; Lam 1996).

In short, ethnic media can be analyzed and classified along two dimensions: a reactive-proactive (defensive-affirmative) dimension plus an outward-inward

TABLE 3

Typology of ethnic media

	Reactive (defensive)	Proactive (affirmative)
Inward (Bonding/insular)	"Constructing buffers" React to media negativity/ invisibility by offering a minority perspective, including access to local and homeland information.	"Creating bonds" Focus on celebrating both personal and community accomplishments to foster community cohesion and culture pride.
Outward (Bridging/integrative)	"Crossing borders" Counteract social injustice (prejudice, discrimination) by advocating for positive changes and levelling the playing field.	"Building bridges" Utilize positive images of minority success for bolstering minority civic participation in an inclusive society.

(bridging-bonding) dimension. If these dimensions are aligned on separate continua and intersected at right angles, a four-cell table is created – reactive inward, proactive inward, reactive outward, and proactive outward – that acknowledges the dynamics and complexity of ethnic media. In theory, all ethnic media should fit into one of these analytical categories; in reality, because most ethnic media are multi-dimensional (reactive + proactive + inward + outward), such a typology may possess heuristic value only for theorizing ethnic and Aboriginal media. An integrative and inclusive dynamic can coexist alongside the insular and exclusive, in the process reinforcing Catherine Murray's prescient insight (2009a) that third-language ethnic media are neither recipes for separate enclaves nor celebrations of conjoining cultures. To the extent that they constitute hybrids that fuse without loss of particulars, ethnic media typify Canada's commitment to multicultural inclusiveness. Table 3 demonstrates how the intersection of these dimensions yields different types of ethnic media institutions or, alternatively, reflects concurrent dimensions of many ethnic media.

Summing up: ethnic media concurrently promote cultural preservation and societal incorporation. Their mutually reciprocating status as pockets of insularity yet pathways to integration cannot be underestimated – especially not in

Canada, where the popularity of ethnic media may well constitute the quint-essential expression of an inclusive multiculturalism. A rethinking is in order, one that neither canonizes nor demonizes ethnic media as either divisive or integrative. A dialectical dynamic is at play: the interplay of the reactive-proactive with the inward-outward generates an insular and integrative pro-cess that pushes as it pulls – bonding and buffering as well as transcending borders and building and bridging. The interplay of this duality function pro-vides entry portals into society by capitalizing on an ethnicity-based infor-mation niche (Will 2005). Admittedly, a preoccupation with transnational links may delay incorporation into society at large (Lin and Song 2006). Or coverage of homeland and local news of direct relevance ("news they can use") may be at the expense of provincial and national coverage (C. Murray 2008a, 2008b). Nevertheless, the emergence of a crossover and hybridic media culture does not necessarily preclude integration. By creating a comfort zone that bridges as it bonds, ethnic media insulate migrants and minorities from the harshness of adapting to a new society and culture, thereby providing a buffer between the here and the there by bridging the in-between.

Ethnic Media: An Inclusive Blueprint for Living Together Multiculturally

What is the role of ethnic media in society? How do Canada's ethnic media relate to an official multiculturalism? Do they contribute to or detract from Canada's multicultural project of inclusiveness? On one side, ethnic media con-form to a modernist notion for living together with differences. Acknowledged is the need for new and racialized Canadians to be treated equally as a matter of routine, regardless of their differences. On the other side, ethnic media by definition embody the principles of postmodern coexistence. Cultural differ-ences may have to be taken into account when necessary to ensure the healthy integration of new and racialized Canadians into society. Fusing both modern and postmodern sensibilities puts ethnic media in a position to reflect, re-inforce, and advance a core multiculturalism principle: that is, a Canada of many cultures is possible as long as people's cultural differences don't get in the way of living together (though differences may be incorporated to ensure a more level playing field). Confirmed as well is the need for respecting cultural diversity and ethnic community while pursuing the goals of institutional inclu-siveness and social justice (Alliance of Civilizations 2006).

Clearly, then, ethnic media remain in the forefront as catalysts in building an inclusive Canada. Their status as an oppositional gaze to mainstream media paradoxically puts ethnic media at the forefront of a global/local nexus unique-ly suited to Canada's inclusive multiculturalism (see Murray, Yu, and Ahadi

2007). By reflecting, reinforcing, and advancing the inclusiveness principles of Canada's multicultural model, ethnic media play an integrative role for advancing a constructive engagement and cooperative coexistence. With ethnic media, community members take advantage of a venue that provides a social network, offers tangible services, ensures immigrant resocialization and settlement, and serves as an organized point of contact and coordination between newcomers and government bodies (Somerville, Durana, and Terrazas 2008). Ethnic media are simultaneously inclusive and insular: insofar as they concurrently promote social integration and cultural insularity without sacrificing a commitment to community or to Canada, ethnic media are both inward and outward looking. They also reflect a reactive and proactive dynamic: reactive, in buffering minorities from the negativity of mainstream media; proactive, in building bridges and crossing borders to take advantage of what the outside world offers. In securing a normative blueprint that buffers, bonds, bolsters, and builds, that insulates as it integrates, ethnic media are proving pivotal in transcending an "us versus them" mentality in exchange for a collaborative "we" in the art of living together with differences.

Conclusion
Re-engaging the Media Gaze

It's trite but true: ours is truly a media age. Media are no longer a device to pick up or an object to turn on, as was the case with immobile technologies. Nor is there much option in weighing whether to embrace or reject media – unless, of course, one is inclined toward a social death wish. Media are more indispensable than ever in a diverse and information-rich mediascape, where everyone seems to be connected – downloading, texting, browsing, blogging, and tweeting – yet no one appears to be in charge. Social media are such a ubiquitous feature in the ever-connected world of Twitter, Facebook, and YouTube that the social lives of many young Canadians would atrophy without "a constant stream of chatter" (M. Johnson 2010). The consequences and implications have been amply documented: social-networking links are transforming people's access to information and communication, from passive consumers to active creators and conveyors, thus creating the potential for a new generation of bottom-up newsmakers with the talent and technology to monitor, disseminate, and mobilize ("citizen journalism" [Pew Research Center Project for Excellence in Journalism 2010b]).

The expansion of the mediascape is incontrovertible. Proof is no further away than in the astonishing growth of social media in less than a decade. Even conventional media remain powerful players in contesting for media space. Despite losing their corporate lustre because of technological changes and shifting discourses, "legacy" media institutions remain agenda-setters in defining what's acceptable, normal, and desirable. The degree to which the blogosphere and Twitterverse continue to rely on mainstream media as sources of information attests to the importance of this dependency (Pew Research Center Project for Excellence in Journalism 2010b). Synergies also arise when institutions leverage the networking power of social media so that they themselves *become the media*, with the tools to stay relevant and directly connected by way of engaged content (Solis 2010a). Clearly, a symbiosis is at play: instead of displacement of one by the other, conventional media combine with new media in an interplay that expands the parameters of our mediated world.

But there is a downside to this mediafication of social reality. As audiences (in both the consuming and creating sense) become more media savvy, conventional and new media are finding new ways of subverting this citizen strength into a consumer weakness. The desperate search for profitable business models in a digital era reinforces the importance of advertising as the mainstay for both new and conventional media. Fierce competition for consumer attention from product placement in films to pop-up ads on television and the Internet eliminates any possibility of advertising-free zones in our fractured reality. The consequences of this cat-and-mouse game are hardly immaterial: those who allow media to dictate their understanding of social reality may find themselves co-opted along corporate lines, with little to show for their efforts. That alone puts an onus on media proofing (acquiring media literacy skills) as an essential survival skill in deconstructing those powerful dynamics that define and distract, conceal and evade, or shape and control. Increased media concentration and monopolistic control of information exert even greater pressure for unpacking questions of who controls what, what kind of information they are circulating or excluding, why and how, and their impact in shaping public opinion and influencing people's behaviour (McChesney 1999; Hackett and Anderson 2010). A critically informed audience must recognize how discursive media frames embody values and myths that simultaneously privilege yet cloak aspects of social reality, thus empowering some at the expense of others. They must also acquire the intuition for decoding those media gazes that coax people into seeing like the media, in the process robbing Canadians of the autonomy and incentive to take democratic action (Hackett and Anderson 2011).

In short, mainstream media must be exposed for what they really are: money-making machineries of meaning structured in ideological dominance. As hegemonic discourses of thought control, media are powerful dynamics in transmitting images, ideas, myths, and symbols that reflect and reinforce collective beliefs and core values of a predominantly unequal society (Henry and Tator 2002). To be sure, most people think they are reasonably media literate; after all, those weaned on iPods, BlackBerry, YouTube, and Facebook are conversant in the know-how of downloading music, uploading video, staying connected 24/7, texting and posting tweets, and microblogging. And yet, the very individuals with an endless propensity toward technological wizardry and media savvy are precisely the ones who may be misinformed about what is really going on, and why. True, there is widespread knowledge about the "gee whiz" aspects of digital media technology. There is less wisdom about how media messages are produced and consumed, who controls the media, the economics of the industry, hidden agendas, and the often subtle ways that media influence attitudes and behaviour (Potter 2005).

This final chapter makes it abundantly clear: media are socially constructed and socially constructing, but neither the process nor the impact can be readily discerned. First, rather than something natural or normal or neutral, media content and structure are human accomplishments that skilfully conceal their constructedness behind a media gaze. Second, as sociologists have long claimed, people's lived realities are socially constructed; accordingly, individuals become social(ized) beings through interactions and communication with the world out there. That alone makes it doubly important for critically informed citizens to deconstruct the dual process – constructed and constructing – so that, rather than acquiescing unknowingly to media gazes, they can see *through* a seeing like the media. But to fully appreciate the implications of media proofing in advancing critical awareness, it is important to first recap what this book has achieved in analyzing the media gaze as description and explanation.

The Media Gaze: An Explanatory Framework

The journey through fourteen chapters of this book should yield some concluding questions. What generalizations can be formulated about the politics of media representations of diversities and difference in Canada? Are there patterns that apply to media representations across all media domains? Are there common themes that thread their way through each chapter, thus yielding a bigger picture?

To this point, the chapters in *The Media Gaze* have addressed media (mis)representations of diversities as they pertain to race or gender or class or sexuality or age or religion. This chapter-by-chapter treatment provides specific insights into the how and why behind media framing of women, working classes, gays and lesbians, youth and older adults, religious diversities, racialized minorities, immigrants and refugees, and Aboriginal peoples. But such an approach suffers from inherent limitations, not the least of which is a failure to uncover generalized patterns that apply throughout.

To address this lacunae in our knowledge, this section produces a set of unifying themes about the media gaze. This commitment not only provides an overview of the book's main arguments but also furnishes an explanatory framework to account for media representations of Canada's diversities and difference. To be sure, this inventory of common themes is neither intended to be final nor expected to be definitive. Rather, the focus is on securing generalized insights and recurrent patterns in the media's framing of race, class, gender, age, sexuality, and religion across all media domains. In other words, these generalizations are precisely that: approximations that serve as heuristic devices for analysis, rather than accurate appraisals of media reality. There are too many media in terms of content and change to expect otherwise.

1 *Invisibilizing diversities.* Generally, mainstream media prefer to ignore representations of diversities and differences unless there is compelling reason to do otherwise. The degree of invisibility varies by media process. Diversities are often rendered invisible by news media unless framed as conflict or abnormality; other media processes, from film to advertising, increasingly realize the value of tapping into a diversity demographic and respond accordingly. But even in situations where diversity is positively incorporated (for example, the depiction of women either in advertising or television programming), these differences are invariably filtered through a mainstream media gaze (i.e., whitewashed) to make representations more palatable to skittish advertisers and those demographics who prefer their media content to be safe, simple, and familiar.

2 *Problematizing diversities.* When rendered visible, diversities tend to be framed as troublesome constituents. As problem people, especially when it pertains to racialized or religious minorities, as well as youth and the elderly, they are seen as having problems or creating problems that involve cost or pose an inconvenience. This focus on negativity as media worthy is largely structural rather than attitudinal, especially in a news media that glorifies the negative/abnormal as newsworthy ("only bad news is good news"), as well as in the entertainment media, where giving priority to conflict and protagonists ("bad guys") propels most storytelling.

3 *Stereotypying diversities.* Media invariably stereotype diversities and difference. These generalizations are not necessarily the result of deliberate bias. More accurately, the stereotyping is systemic in that it reflects an institutional imperative for reducing a welter of often complex information into digestible bits for facilitating audience consumption. The consequences of this systemic stereotyping are uneven; vulnerable minorities who lack offsetting narratives of power in a mediated world are more victimized by stereotyping than the privileged mainstream.

4 *Systemically biasing diversities.* Is a misrepresenting of diversities a case of systematic bias, or do we have a case of coverage that is systemically biasing because of slanted outcomes? In the past when societal biases were openly flaunted, mainstream media gazes deliberately (systematically) framed minorities as inferior or troublesome. At present, openly negative representations are no longer socially acceptable. To the degree that they continue, however, misrepresentations tend to reflect media gazes that inadvertently if negatively frame diversities in three ways: (1) by coded language whose inferences reside in-between the lines; (2) by associating differences with negative contexts like crime; or (3) by implying their actions are incompatible with mainstream values (Sveinsson 2008). Such one-sided coverage of diversities is systemically biasing by consequences rather than intent.

5 *Depoliticizing diversities.* Coverage of diversities is invariably superficial or lacking in context. Focusing on the glossier aspects, such as festivals or lifestyles, reinforces an aversion to deep differences that challenge convention, in part because media, as businesses, are generally conservative, in part because a widespread value commitment to the principle of liberal universalism (commonalities as individuals supersede differences between groups). Or alternatively, deep differences are framed as a problem that yields conflict or poses a threat to society. Borrowing from Sandra Bem's prescient article in the *Chronicle of Higher Education* (Bem 1994), a similar line of reasoning may apply to a media gaze: in a media-centred world that is structured in dominance, differences that do not conform with the prevailing media gaze are reframed as problems (or as disadvantaging). This depoliticizing of diversities results in the neutralizing (or whitewashing) of these differences to make them more advertising- and audience-friendly.

6 *Tweaking, not transforming.* In reaction to criticism, protest, and concerns over a deteriorating bottom line, mainstream media have significantly improved their representations of diversities. Yet these improvements are less than what they appear. As long as mainstream media continue to reflect a predominantly mainstream media gaze (i.e., pro-white, androcentric, classed by virtue of ownership and control, ageist, secularist, and straight), any changes should be framed as reforms (changing the conventions that refer to the rules) rather than as transformations (changing the rules that inform conventions).

There is considerable value in pointing out recurrent patterns in media's misrepresenting of diversities and difference. But it is no less important to ask why. Why do mainstream media continue to ignore, distort, problematize, or whitewash diversities despite the interplay of ideological changes (toward inclusiveness) with new communication technologies and social transformations in Canada's demographic composition? What is it about the media gaze that precludes it from fully embracing the existence of diversities and minorities grounded in race, gender, class, age, sexuality, and religion? Mindful of the complexities and inconsistencies of such an endeavour, the next constellation of general patterns attempts to provide an explanatory framework to account for the misrepresentation of diversities – seemingly at odds with the industry's best interests and those of Canada at large.

1 *Media gaze as media gazes.* Conceptualizing the media gaze in the singular is misleading. Simply put, there are numerous media gazes, each of which alone and in combination with others will influence the framing of diversities and the representation of difference. Consider the following range of media gazes associated with different media types, including (a) sectoral differences as set out in Chapter 1, that is, the commercial gaze (audiences targeted as consumers), the public service gaze (audience as citizens), the populist gaze (audience as marginal community), and the participatory or social/online gaze (audiences as creators/distributors of "oppositional" messages); (b) media gazes that assume the following dimensions: corporate, racialized, Eurocentric, gendered or androcentric, classed, ageist, and secular; and (c) variations in media gazes that stem from of diverse media institutions and processes such as newscasting, broadcasting (TV and radio), advertising, film, and magazines and books.

2 *Intersectionality of media gazes.* Each of these media gazes can be separately analyzed. In actuality, however, these media gazes simultaneously converge in misrepresenting diversities, thus creating intersecting patterns that amplify the exclusion or distortion. To the extent that a racialized media gaze intersects with a gendered media gaze, which in turn intersects with a classed media gaze, and so on, a multiplier effect prevails.

3 *The bad, the good, and the conditional.* Media gazes cannot be simply assessed as positive or negative – some are, some aren't, and some may be, depending on context, criteria, and consequences. News media gazes continue to negatively frame diversities and minorities as troublesome (although even here we should acknowledge a distinction between hard news and editorials/opinion), whereas advertising endorses a much more positive framing of diversities and difference. Television programming and film may

well fall in between these poles of interpretation. Nevertheless, media messages continue to privilege a corporatized whiteness, maleness, and middle classness as the default option in establishing the normative standard by which others are defined or judged.

4   *A constructed mediacentrism.* Media gazes are socially constructed and mediacentric. As social constructions, media gazes consist of conventions that are created by those in positions of power who conceal this constructedness behind a facade of normalcy so that the gazes come across as objective reflections of an external world rather than as something constructed and contested. Media gazes are mediacentric insofar as they are inclined to frame their particular version of reality as natural and normal (according to the dictates of a predominantly straight, white male, middle-class, and middle-aged media industry), while dismissing other versions of reality as irrelevant and inferior. Concealing the constructedness and mediacentredness produces the effect of coaxing audiences into seeing like the media as if it were no perspective at all (i.e., uncontaminated by bias).

5   *Oppositionality as gaze.* An oppositional gaze subverts a mainstream gaze. A mainstream media gaze reflects the centralized views and standardized messages aimed at a mass audience. This gaze is gendered toward male gazes, racialized toward white or Eurocentric gazes, and classed toward middle-class gazes, and so on. By contrast, Aboriginal media and ethnic media incorporate populist gazes that offer an alternative. These oppositional gazes react to negative mainstream coverage of diversities and difference by positively framing and promoting those communities and demographics unappealing to mainstream media. Online media gazes, from the Internet to social media, are no less oppositional. In some cases, this oppositionality is directed at challenging mainstream media or society at large; in other cases, it involves establishing patterns of community, conversation, and connections that circumvent the authority, elitism, and limitations of mainstream media. To be sure, there is disagreement within oppositional gazes: recurrent debates within marginalized communities pivot on whether historically disadvantaged groups should seek inclusion as equals like others, albeit as defined by society. Or alternatively, should they reject incorporation (absorption) on mainstream terms to protect their status as different yet equal?

6   *Media gazes matter.* Why do media gazes matter? The power of a media gaze resides in its resourcefulness to frame reality so that the resultant seeing (gaze) produces a hegemonic pattern of persuasion that is conceptually akin to soft propaganda. More specifically: (a) framing as media gaze involves a

process of organizing information in a way that draws attention to some versions of reality as natural and normal, desirable and acceptable, and away from other versions or aspects of reality as inferior, irrelevant, or a threat, in hopes of encouraging a preferred reading that is natural and uncontested rather than constructed and problematic; (b) hegemony as media gaze acknowledges how those in positions of power maintain power not by coercion or force but ideologically and with the implicit consent of the dominated, who are largely unaware of their complicity in the hegemonic process; (c) in equating a prevailing media gaze as a hegemonic gaze, the framing of minorities is shown to be so one-sided that this monocultural coverage is tantamount to soft propaganda – at least in behaviour and consequences if not necessarily by intent or effects (also Klaehn and Mullin 2010).

From this overview and review, the conclusion seems plausible. The concept of a media gaze provides a useful explanatory framework that accounts for representations of diversities and difference in Canadian media regardless of (1) the media sector, industry, or process under study or (2) the diversity in question, including race, gender, class, sexuality, age, or religion. Reference to the media gaze also provides insights into the *how* and *why* behind the misrepresentations of diversities and differences. In the final analysis, it has been argued, mainstream media gazes are discourses in defence of dominant ideologies by promulgating ideas and ideals that reflect, reinforce, and advance the interests of some while ignoring, distorting, or suppressing those of others (also van Dijk 1995).

The Micro-Politics of Media Proofing

Media proofing for a twenty-first-century Canada must begin by taking media seriously. It must acknowledge the necessity of taking media into account when analyzing their impact on identities, experiences, opportunities, and outcomes at both individual and group levels. Life and social reality as we know it would be unimaginable without the pervasiveness and persuasiveness of media communication. Like the air we breathe, our lives are so saturated with media messages that an obliviousness to their obviousness is understandable, but fraught with peril. Put bluntly, media are much more than a transmission technology for conveying information about reality: in many cases, media *are* reality. Media inform and infuse our perception of reality in terms of what's normal, acceptable, and desirable, with the result that the world "out there" is inconceivable outside the context of media images, symbols, and narratives. Media create the images around which reality is constructed; through repeated exposure, they then confer an aura of legitimacy on the constructed images. And although media images are constructed, hence conventional (arbitrary), these constructions create the symbolic bubble that over time envelops people's lived realities. The acquisition of "media smarts" provides a starting point for unmasking those underlying structures, internal logics, and hidden agendas that inform an increasingly mediated experience for all Canadians.

To be sure, a sense of perspective is critical. Media gazes per se are neither the source of all good nor the root of all evil. Their influence in shaping human behaviour and intergroup relations is much too complex and conditional to fall into the trap of either/or. In that mainstream media articulate and transmit powerful images and narratives regarding what is acceptable, normal, and necessary, they are influential in shaping our attitudes (why do I think like I do?), identities (why am I like I am?), and behaviour (why do I behave the way I do, and why do others behave like they do?). Minorities are no less influenced by media gazes: representations of diversities are pivotal in constructing symbolic worlds that define the parameters of their social existence. And although these constructions of a mediated world are not necessarily real in the normal sense of the term, they need not be real to produce negative consequences. Or to put a sociological spin on it, social phenomena do not have to be real to be real in their consequences, but if people act as if it were reality, the consequences are realistic. The fusing of media with reality has proven convoluted and subject to endless discussion and debate; therefore, an informed critique of the politics of seeing like the media is both timely and relevant. The alternative is nothing less than a paralysis by analysis that not only cripples public discourses but also aborts social engagement.

The Macro-Politics of Transforming the Media

Just as readers and viewers must become more critically informed about the media – to see and think like the media see and think so they can see through a media gaze – so too must the media become more aware of what they are doing, why, and how, and who they are excluding because of a business-as-usual syndrome. Mainstream media's tendency to exclude those Canadians who don't fit into the conventional mould raises several key questions: Do the media have a responsibility to advance an inclusive Canada, one that is free of prejudging and criticizing others, because of who they are? The Ontario Human Rights Commission (2008) acknowledged this when it concluded, "The media has a significant role to play in either combating societal racism [or substitute 'sexism,' 'ageism,' 'classism,' and so on for 'racism'] or refraining from communicating or reproducing it." If the media have a responsibility to inspire progressive change – and not everyone agrees with this assessment, arguing that commercial media have a responsibility only to provide coverage that makes money for shareholders – what is their role in discharging this responsibility? Should the media restrict their coverage of minorities to positive stories, if only to minimize the risk of stereotyping? Should media continue to do what they have always done, that is, "telling it like it is," regardless of whose self-esteem is crushed in the process? Or should coverage consist of a balance between positive and negative, on the grounds that such a strategy provides a more realistic insight into minority lives? The final Insight in this book tackles the issue of whether mainstream media are truly capable of inclusiveness, given their sociological status as propaganda in function rather than form.

insight

Deconstructing Media Propaganda: Hard or Soft?

Rulers and elites in democratic societies confront an age-old conundrum (Media Lens 2003): How to isolate the governed from the levers of governance without openly doing so (Fleras 2009). In democratic societies that eschew open brainwashing and an explicit police state, the uncritical acceptance of the status quo must be indirectly internalized. The mainstream media are particularly adept at advancing these vested interests by promoting a hegemonic media gaze as if it were neutral and unproblematic. In some cases, this exercise in indoctrination is blunt; in others, a hidden agenda is sustained by a sheen of impartiality and objectivity. As a result, media portrayals of diversities and difference have proven systemically (inadvertent) biasing rather than a case of systematic (deliberate) bias. That is, news media don't go out of their way to deny or demean; nevertheless, in refracting diversity and minority realities through a conventional media gaze, they end up doing exactly that. To the extent that coverage of minorities as troublesome constituents is negatively racialized, the (news) media constitute an institutionalized (soft) propaganda.

Propaganda may be defined as a process of persuasion by which the few manipulate the many. Symbols are manipulated by vested interests in an organized manner to modify attitudes or reshape behaviour. Admittedly, as Jacques Ellul (1973) recognized long ago, propaganda is not necessarily the evil opposite of truth. All communication involves the manipulation of information to persuade others of a particular point of view, resulting in the circulation of half-truths, incomplete truths, truths out of context, and misspoken truths. In that propaganda inheres in all levels of communication, there is much to commend in the following postmodernist insight: that in a mind-dependent world, there is no such thing as truth, only discourses about truth that reflect social location and power relations. Deconstructing propaganda as inherent to the media's meaning making reinforces Nancy Snow's admonition (2007) in paraphrasing Ellul: "The best way to study propaganda is to separate one's ethical judgements from the phenomenon itself. Propaganda thrives and exists for ethical and non-ethical purposes."

A distinction between institutional and institutionalized propaganda is useful. Institutional (hard or systematic) propaganda involves a purposeful distortion ("spinning") of facts or evidence to make a one-sided and uncontested point. Institutional actors act on behalf of the institutions in reshaping how people think and behave by regulating what they see or hear. In taking this perspective of coercive persuasion, institutional propaganda conjures up images of blatant brainwashing or crude displays of totalitarian censorship. But the propagation of propaganda in democratic societies is trickier: the pursuit of thought control must comply with the principles of a free society and freedom of the press. The "dirty work" of propaganda cannot afford to sink to the level of flagrant indoctrination without inciting a crisis of legitimacy. The challenge rests in assuming an air of openness, balance, and fairness to enhance credibility and effectiveness.

Opposed to institutional propaganda is the concept of institutionalized (soft or systemic) propaganda. Unlike its systematic counterpart, soft propaganda is systemic – neither reflecting personal motives nor entailing deliberate lying but whose slanted coverage is incidental. Soft propaganda as systemic bias reflects a pattern of unmarked persuasion that (1) inheres in the normal processing of information rather then a toxicity inserted by vested interests; (2) is impersonal and unconscious because of seemingly neutral rules and priorities that, when evenly and equally applied, exert an unintended yet discriminatory impact but without prejudicial intent; and (3) is so deeply embedded within institutional processes and outcomes that discriminatory effects materialize without people's awareness of the biasing at play (Fleras 2010). With a systemic (soft) propaganda, messages are wired (structured) into the system without malice or deceit; conveyed by coded language that conceal and confuse; often based on faulty assumptions, from "we know what's best" to "business as usual"; and absorbed by the public without awareness of their complicity in perpetuating these biases.

Systemic bias differs from its systematic counterparts at critical junctures – one is impersonal, the other is deliberate, with consequences prevailing over intent, routine over random, normal over deviant, and structural over attitudinal. How, then, are news media a case of systemically biasing propaganda? Put simply, news media cannot help but engage in systemic bias because of a prevailing gaze that supersedes other ways of framing reality. Just as Eurocentrism reflects an unconscious tendency to frame reality from a Western/mainstream point of view as natural or superior while assuming others are doing so as well (or would if they could), so too does a mediacentric bias reflect an institutional tendency to privilege a particular framing of reality as normal, necessary, and inevitable. Media are systemically biasing when newsworthiness reflects a media-centred bias toward the abnormal over the normal, the negative over the positive, deviance over normalcy, conflict over cooperation, the sensational over the mundane, and the episodic over the thematic. Coverage is also systemically biasing when priority is assigned to (1) blaming the victim over system blaming, (2) personalities over structure or context, (3) conflict over consensus or cooperation, (4) the "othering" of others over citizenship and justice, and (5) the status quo over social change.

Critical-Thinking Question

By distinguishing the concepts of systemic bias from systemically biasing, how does a hard (institutional) propaganda differ from soft (institutionalized) propaganda in the processing of information?

* * * * * * * * * * *

Challenging the Mediacentric Gaze

Let's put the text into perspective: diversities and difference (including women, young and old, gays and lesbians, religious persons, and racialized minorities, Aboriginal peoples, and immigrants and refugees) continue to be ignored, stereotyped, problematized, and/or depoliticized (whitewashed) by negative images that (mis)inform audiences about who they are and what they want (Weston 2003). Minorities in the broadest sense of the term do not necessarily suffer from biased news coverage – that is, coverage that is deliberately misleading, consciously slanted, or wilfully malevolent. To the contrary, they must endure coverage that is systemically biasing, namely, coverage that purports to treat everyone the same, regardless of the discriminatory consequences that flow from applying equal standards to unequal circumstances.

But it's precisely this one-size-fits-all formula – with its predilection for abnormality, conflict, and the negative as quintessentially newsworthy – that exerts a controlling/biasing effect on some and not others for reasons beyond their control. Of course, news stories that pander to the problematic are not exclusive to minority coverage. Newsworthiness in general reinforces the mediacentric notion that bad news is good news. But the framing of vulnerable minorities along these lines exerts a different impact; after all, minorities lack the institutional power to deflect, absorb, and neutralize this symbolic assault on their identities and aspirations.

Why should Canadians care about media mistreatment of diversities and minorities? To say that the media are powerful and pervasive repeats the obvious. Their potency lies in an ability to articulate who is important, what is acceptable in society, and whose voices shall be heard (Fleras 2004b). People turn to media to allay concerns, uncertainty, and confusion during times of rapid social change involving unprecedented patterns of immigration, Aboriginal peoples' politics, and ethnicity-based nationalisms (Shoemaker and Cohen 2006). They also rely on media to form attitudes about group relations or diversity politics, particularly since many lack meaningful contact with minorities except in the most superficial manner (Wilson, Gutiérrez, and Chao 2003; ter Wal, d'Haenens, and Koeman 2005). Media images define what is acceptable, important, or desirable then confer legitimacy on this *media*ted reality through selective exposure and positive reinforcement. The end result of these discursive frameworks prioritizes majority interests at minority expense (Fleras 2007b). Public discourses are generated in which certain persons or objects are normalized as acceptable and desirable, whereas others are demonized or marginalized. And although media do not necessarily set out to control, the cumulative impact of framing minorities as troublesome constituents can exert a controlling effect.

Minorities and diversities are under pressure to reclaim control of media representations. In seeking to escape those mediacentric prisms/prisons that deny or distort, minorities can and do resist and react, despite a competitive disadvantage in framing issues and setting agendas. Empowerment is conditional on their controlling the framing of issues ("counterframing," as put by Entman [2004]) to ensure the privileging of their voices on their terms (M.J. Miller 2008). In the final analysis, mastery over knowledge and its dissemination through media images is fundamental to the exercise of power in society, especially if minorities want to prevail as subjects of the world rather than as objects for manipulation, distraction, projections, or amusement (Hanamoto 1995). Such control is tantamount to empowerment by asserting a counterhegemonic alternative to those discursive frameworks that deny or exclude. But claims to ownership and control are neither simple nor straightforward (see also Corntassel and Witmer 2008). Mainstream media are so structured in dominance, as Stuart Hall (1980) once observed, that a hierarchy of discourses control the "out there" by hegemonizing the "in here."

The challenge is formidable. Initiatives for improving the quality and quantity of minority coverage will remain mired in a monocultural rut unless citizens challenge the foundational principles (news values) of the media's constitutional order (news paradigm). Proposed solutions must focus on changing those rules (foundational principles) that inform the conventions of newsworthiness instead of simply tweaking the conventions that refer to such rules. Contesting media hegemony and institutionalized power must go beyond a splash of colour or a few minority hires. Transforming the prevailing news paradigm begins with the problematizing of dominant news norms – themselves often invisibly yet powerfully normative, seemingly natural yet socially constructed, and ostensibly neutral yet ideologically infused (Jiwani 2006). In other words, modifying attitudes without corresponding institutional transformations in advancing progressive change is doable, but difficult – the metaphorical equivalent of walking up a down-escalator whose speed is controlled by seemingly invisible hands.

To the extent that media are complex and confusing enterprises, a multipronged strategy of change is critical. Any institutional transformation must begin with media workers. Content creators may be complicit in advancing mainstream media gazes that, in reflecting their privileged status in terms of race, gender, class, age, and sexuality, may unconsciously create media narratives that are raced/racialized, sexist/gendered, classed, ageist, secularist and sexualized. But no less important are structural changes. As discourses in defence of dominant ideology, there is nothing neutral or natural about media structures (from design and agendas to procedures and outputs). Rather, media structures are fundamentally raced, gendered, classed, ageist, sexualized, and secularized without much public awareness of how these deeply embedded rules and priorities can segue into a discriminatory effect. Insofar as media are structured in dominance, moves to bring about transformative change at structural levels will remain a daunting challenge. After all, changing the attitudes that refer to foundational rules is one thing; challenging the foundational rules that generate attitudes is quite another.

A sense of perspective must preside. However well intentioned a commitment to recalibrate media gazes, an agency-oriented solution may prove insufficient. To be sure, there is a place for attitudinal modification. Journalists work within a dominant culture, unconsciously absorb and espouse its values, and draw upon these beliefs for framing representations – thus constituting and reconstituting dominant ideologies and hegemonic control (Ricard and Wilkes 2007). Yet any solution must go beyond the formalities of consciousness-raising through training sessions. Insofar as news media bias is structural and systemic, proposed solutions must incorporate transformative changes that are foundational from start to finish (M. Gallagher 2005). The dislodging of those foundational principles (rules) that inform conventional media gazes may provide one possibility of giving the people what they want (justice and happiness) rather than co-opting people into what the media have to offer (consumerism and compliance).

No one said the contesting of media representations would be easy in light of formidable hurdles. At the core of this contestation is power. Control over representations will remain rooted in power inasmuch as all representations are socially constructed by those with the resources and resourcefulness to create and impose them. Of course, challenging the representational basis/bias of the media-diversity nexus may not yield a "power to the people." But a business-as-usual mindset is decidedly disempowering for the marginalized. Until the issue of power is resolved in terms of who controls what and how, and whose values will dominate in the sorting-out process, the politics of media representations will remain a paradox. On one side is the exclusionary dynamic that negatively frames coverage of diversities as discourses in defence of dominant ideology. On the other side is an inclusionary commitment to re-align diversities and difference along the lines of an inclusive Canada. The reconciling of these oppositional tensions is critical (Hodgetts et al. 2005); after all, the representational basis of media-diversity relations will improve only when prevailing media gazes move beyond an "us versus them" framework by repositioning "their" concerns as part of "our" collective interests.

References

Abel, Sue. 1997. *Shaping the News: Waitangi Day on Television*. Auckland: Auckland University Press.

Abourezk, Kevin. 2004. Native Filmmakers, Actors Depict Tribal Life – Past and Present. *Lincoln Journal Star*, 8 January.

Abrams, Brett L. 2008. *Hollywood Bohemians: Transgressive Sexuality and the Selling of the Movieland Dream*. Jefferson, NC: McFarland.

Adams, Michael. 2007. *Unlikely Utopia*. Toronto: Penguin.

Age Concern. 2007. Ageism Is the Most Common Form of Discrimination in the UK. Age Concern. http://www.ageconcern.org.uk.

Age UK. 2011. Age UK Research Shows Age-Discrimination Is Rife in Europe. European Research Group on Attitudes to Age, University of Kent. 3 March.

Ahmad, Fauzia. 2006. British Muslim Perceptions and Opinions on News Coverage of September 11. *Journal of Ethnic and Migration Studies* 32(6): 961-82.

Akdenizli, Banu. 2008. *Democracy in the Age of New Media: A Report on the Media and the Immigration Debate*. Los Angeles: Brookings Institution and Norman Lear Center, University of Southern California.

Akou, Heather Marie. 2010. Interpreting Islam through the Internet: Making Sense of *Hijab*. *Contemporary Islam* 4(3): 331-46.

Al Hidaya Association. 2008. *Debating Reasonable Accommodation: Can a Progressive Nation Overcome Racism?* Brief presented by Centre Communautaire Musulman de Montréal (Al Hidaya Association) to the Consultation Commission on Accommodation Practices Related to Cultural Differences, Montreal.

Alang, Navneet. 2009. Found in Translation. *This Magazine*. March/April, 41-42.

Aleiss, Angela. 2005. *Making the White Man's Indian: Native Indians and Hollywood Movies*. Westport, CT: Praeger.

Alia, Valerie. 1999. *Un/Covering the North: News, Media, and Aboriginal People*. Vancouver: UBC Press.

–. 2009. Outlaws and Citizens: Indigenous People and the "New Media Nation." *International Journal of Media and Cultural Politics* 5(1): 39-54.

–. 2010. *The New Media Nations: Indigenous Peoples and Global Communication.* New York: Berghahn Books.

Alia, Valerie, and Simone Bull. 2005. *Media and Ethnic Minorities.* Edinburgh: Edinburgh University Press.

Alliance for American Manufacturing. 2011. How Do Factory Workers and Blue-Collar Laborers Fare on TV? Blog entry by Scapozzola, 2 April. http://americanmanufacturing.org.

Alliance of Civilizations. 2006. *Research Base for the High Level Group Report: Analysis on Media.* New York: United Nations.

Alper, Loretta, and Pepi Leistyna. 2006. *Class Dismissed: How TV Frames the Working Class.* Northampton, MA: Media Education Foundation. Filmstrip, 62 min.

Altheide, David. 2002. *Creating Fear: News and the Construction of Crisis.* New York: Aldine de Guyter.

–. 2009. The Columbine Shootings and the Discourse of Fear. *American Behavioral Scientist* 52(10): 1354-70.

Anderson, Brooke. 2007. A Little Mosque Grows. Al Jazeera, News Americas, 3 October. http://english.aljazeera.net.

Anderson, Kim. 2009. Leading by Action: Female Chiefs and the Political Landscape. In *Restoring the Balance,* ed. Eric Guimond, Gail Guthrie Valaskakis, and Madeline Dion Stout, 99-124. Winnipeg: University of Manitoba Press.

Anderssen, Erin. 2010. Time for Breast Cancer Fundraising to Take Its Foot Off the Accelerator? *Globe and Mail,* 18 October.

Anupam, Joshi, Tim Finan, Akshay Java, Anubhav Kale, and Pranan Kolari. 2007. Web (2.0) Mining: Analyzing Social Media. Paper presented at the National Science Foundation Symposium on Next Generation Data Mining and Cyber-Enabled Discovery for Innovation, University of Maryland, Baltimore, 10 October.

Appelbe, Alison. 2003. Canada Blames Media Hype for SARS Economic Impact. CNSnews. com. http://www.cnsnews.com.

Ariely, Dan. 2009. The End of Rational Economy. *Harvard Business Review,* July/August. http://hbr.org/.

Armstrong, Jane, and John Ibbitson. 2009. Canada to Take a Hard Line With Would-Be Migrants. *Globe and Mail,* 20 October.

Armstrong, Robert. 2010. *Broadcasting Policy in Canada.* Toronto: University of Toronto Press.

Arnold, Chris. 2009. *Ethical Marketing and the New Consumer.* New York: John Wiley and Sons.

Arnold, E.L., and D.C. Plymire. 2004. Continuity within Change: The Cherokee Indians and the Internet. In *Web Studies: Rewiring Media Studies for the Digital Age,* 2nd ed., ed. D. Gauntlett and Ross Horsley. New York: Oxford University Press.

Ash, Timothy Garton. 2007. Capitalism's Contradictions. *Guardian Weekly* (Manchester), 2-8 March.

Associated Press. 1997. Fashion King Farewelled. Copy on file with author.

–. 2008. TV Showing More Gay Characters, Study Says. Msnbc.com, 23 September. http:// www.msnbc.msn.com.

Atkinson, Joe. 1994. The State, the Media, and Thin Democracy. In *Leap into the Dark: The Changing Role of the State in New Zealand since 1984,* ed. A. Sharp. Auckland: Auckland University Press.

Atkinson, Joshua D. 2010. *Alternative Media and Politics of Resistance: A Communication Perspective*. New York: Peter Lang.

Attalah, Paul, and Leslie Shade, eds. 2006. *Mediascapes*. 2nd ed. Toronto: Nelson.

Austerberry, Emerald. 2008. Disputed Lands, Failed Coverage. *Ryerson Review of Journalism*, Summer.

Australian, The. 2010. Love Her or Lobe Her: The Remaking of Julia Gillard, 27 July.

Aydin, Cemil, and Juliane Hammer. 2010. Muslims and Media: Perceptions, Participation, and Change. *Contemporary Islam* 4(1): 1-9.

Bagdikian, Ben. 2004. *The New Media Monopoly*. 7th ed. Boston: Beacon Press.

Bahdi, Reem. 2003. Racial Profiling and Canada's War against Terrorism. *Osgoode Hall Law Journal* 41(2/3): 302-16.

Bales, Susan Nall. 2003. Winning the Frame Game. *Utne Reader,* July/August, 78-80.

Baltruschat, Doris. 2004. Television and Canada's Aboriginal Communities. *Canadian Journal of Communication* 29(1): 47-59.

–. 2010. Co-Producing First Nations' Narratives: The Journals of Knud Rasmussen. In *Indigenous Screen Cultures in Canada*, ed. S.B. Hafsteinsson and M. Bredin, 127-42. Winnipeg: University of Manitoba Press.

Barker, Michael. 2005. Manufacturing Policies: The Media's Role in the Policy Making Process. Refereed paper presented at the Journalism Education Conference, Brisbane, Queensland, Australia, 29 November-2 December.

Barlow, Maude. 2004. Canada: Global Model for a Multicultural State. In *Canadian Multiculturalism: Dreams, Realities, and Expectations*, ed. M. Zachariah, A. Sheppard, and L. Barratt, 31-38. Edmonton: Canadian Multicultural Education Foundation.

Barnard, Linda. 2009. Tears of a Disney Princess. *Toronto Star,* 27 November.

Barnes, Rodney. 2010. Second Life. Traditional Media Are Scrambling to Create Online Communities. A Report on Who's Doing it Right – and Who's Doing it Wrong. *Ryerson Review of Journalism*, Spring. http://www.rrj.ca/M8437/.

Barnhurst, Kevin, ed. 2007. Visibility as Paradox. In *Media Queered: Visibility and Its Discontents*, ed. K. Barnhurst, 1-21. New York: Peter Lang.

Bashevkin, Sylvia. 2008. *Women, Power, Politics: The Hidden Story of Canada's Unfinished Democracy.* Toronto: Oxford University Press.

Bauder, Harald. 2008a. Dialectics of Humanitarian Immigration and National Identity in Canadian Public Discourse. *Refuge* 25(1): 84-94.

–. 2008b. Neoliberalism and the Economic Utility of Immigration: Media Perspectives of Germany's Immigration Law. *Antipode* 40(1): 55-78.

Baumann, Shyon, and Josée Johnston. 2007. Who Cares about Class Inequality? The Framing of a Social Non-Problem in Gourmet Food Writing. Paper presented at the annual meeting of the American Sociological Association, New York, 11 August. http://www.allacademic.com.

Beckerman, Gal. 2004. Why Don't Journalists Get Religion? A Tenuous Bridge to Believers. *Columbia Journalism Review* 43(1): 26-30.

Beckford, James A. 1999. The Mass Media and New Religious Movements. In *New Religious Movements: Challenges and Response*, ed. B. Wilson and J. Cresswell, 105-17. New York: Routledge.

Bem, Sandra L. 1994. In a Male-Centred World, Female Differences Are Transformed into Female Disadvantage. *Chronicle of Higher Education*, August 17, B1-B3.

Bendery, Jennifer. 2009. Review of *Aimee and Jaguar*. Pop Matters, 11 August. http://www.popmatters.com.

Benkler, Yoshai. 2006. *The Wealth of Networks: How Social Production Transforms Markets and Freedoms.* New Haven, CT: Yale University Press.

Benson, Rodney. 2005. American Journalism and the Politics of Diversity. *Media, Culture, and Society* 27(1): 5-20.

–. 2010. What Is News Diversity and How Do We Get It? Lessons from Comparing French and American Immigration Coverage. Paper presented at the News and Inclusion Symposium, Stanford, CA, 4 March.

Berila, Beth, and Devika Dibya Choudhuri. 2005. Metrosexuality the Middle-Class Way. *Genders* 42. http://www.genders.org.

Berkhofer, Robert. 1979. *The White Man's Indian.* New York: Vintage.

Berton, Pierre. 1975. *Hollywood's Canada: The Americanization of Our National Image.* Toronto: McClelland and Stewart.

Bharma, A.S. 2008. Media Still Make South Asians "Outsiders." *The Tyne,* 17 November.

Bibby, Reginald. 1987. *Fragmented Gods.* Toronto: Stoddart.

–. 2011. *Beyond the Gods and Back: Religion's Demise and Rise, and Why It Matters.* Toronto: Novalis.

Biernatzki, William E. 2003. Mass Media versus Religion. *Journal of the Asian Research Center for Religion and Social Communication* 1(2).

Blatchford, Christie. 2009. While Police Go in One Direction, Mother's Instinct Says Otherwise. *Globe and Mail,* 18 April.

Bledsloe, G. 1989. The Media: Minorities Still Fighting for Their Share. *Rhythm and Business Magazine,* March/April, 14-18.

Bleich, Erik. 2006. Review of *Shaping Race Policies: The United States in Comparative Perspective,* by Robert Lieberman. *Ethics and International Affairs* 20(1): 133.

Blotnicky, Karen. 2008. Creating Social Change through Advertising. In *Communication in Question,* ed. J. Greenberg and C.D. Elliott, 105-11. Toronto: Thomson Nelson.

Bordo, Susan. 1993. *Unbearable Weight: Feminism, Western Culture, and the Body.* Berkeley: University of California Press.

Bouchard, Gérard, and Charles Taylor. 2008. *Report of the Bouchard-Taylor Commission on the Reasonable Accommodation of Minorities.* Quebec City: Consultation Commission on Accommodation Practices Related to Cultural Differences.

Bouw, Brenda. 2010. Unmarried, Childless, Unelectable? *Globe and Mail,* 14 August.

Boykoff, Jules. 2006. Framing Dissent: Mass-Media Coverage of the Global Justice Movement. *New Political Science* 28(2): 201-28.

Braden, Maria. 1996. *Women Politicians and the Media.* Lexington: University of Kentucky Press.

Bradimore, Ashley, and Harald Bauder. 2011. Mystery Ships and Risky Boat People: Tamil Refugee Migration in the Newsprint Media. Working paper 11-02, Metropolis British Columbia, Vancouver.

Bramadat, Paul. 2009. Religious Diversity and International Migration: National and Global Dimensions. In *International Migration and the Governance of Religious Diversity,* ed. P. Bramadat and M. Koenig, 1-27. Montreal and Kingston: McGill-Queen's University Press.

Bramadat, Paul, and David Seljak, eds. 2008. *Christianity and Ethnicity in Canada.* Toronto: University of Toronto Press.

Bredin, Marian, and Sigurjon Baldur Hafsteinsson. 2010. Introduction. In *Indigenous Screen Cultures in Canada,* ed. S.B. Hafsteinsson and M. Bredin, 1-16. Winnipeg: University of Manitoba Press.

Breen, M., E. Devereux, and A. Haynes. 2005. *Representation of Immigration in the Irish Print Media*. Paper presented to the "Power, Trust and Ethics Conference," Dublin City University, 17 June.

Brown, Lauren. 2004. Empowerment of American Indians through Film. Paper presented at the annual meeting of the American Sociological Association, San Francisco, 14 August.

Buddenbaum, Judith. 2010. Review of *Blind Spot: When Journalists Don't Get Religion. Journal of Media and Religion* 9(1): 47-51.

Bullock, Heather E., K.F. Wyche, and W.R. Williams. 2001. Media Images of the Poor. *Journal of Social Issues* 57(2): 229-46.

Bundale, Brett. 2008. Ads Use Sex to Sell to Girls. *Montreal Gazette*, 23 June.

Bunting, Madeleine. 2007. Don't Hunker but Embrace Instead. *Guardian Weekly* (Manchester), 6 July.

Burnett, Jon. 2011. Linking Racial Violence to Media Coverage. Institute of Race Relations, April 14. http://www.irr.org.uk.

Burnside, Sharon. 2006. A Difficult News Story Well Told. *Toronto Star*, 17 June.

Buscombe, Edward. 2006. *"Injuns!" Native Americans in the Movies*. Bodmin, UK: Reaktion Books.

Butsch, Richard. 1992. *Social Class and Television*. Chicago: Museum of Broadcast Communications.

—. 2003 [1992]. Ralph, Fred, Archie, and Homer: Why Television Keeps Recreating the White Male Working-Class Buffoon. In *Gender, Race, and Class in Media: A Text-Reader*, 2nd ed., ed. G. Dines and J. Humez, 575-85. Thousand Oaks, CA: Sage.

—. 2005. Five Decades and Three Hundred Sitcoms about Class and Gender. In *Thinking Outside the Box: A Contemporary Genre Television Reader*, ed. G. Edgerton and B. Rose, 111-35. Lexington: University Press of Kentucky.

Butterwege, A. 2001. Migrants and the Mass Media. Originally appeared in *Globalization and Capitalism*, 28 August 2001. Translated from the German. http://www.mbtranslations.com.article.php?filenum=1, accessed 26 October 2008.

Callow, Simon. 2008. Foreword to *Out at the Movies: A History of Gay Cinema*, by S.P. Davies, 8-11. Harpenden Herts, UK: Kamera Books.

Campbell, Heidi. 2010. Religious Authority and the Blogosphere. *Journal of Computer Mediated Communication* 15(2): 251-76.

Campbell, Murray. 2006. Failing to Remember the Lessons of Ipperwash. *Globe and Mail*, 21 April.

Campion, M.J. 2006. Picture Perfect. *Guardian* (Manchester), 20 March.

Canadian Islamic Congress. 2001. Anti-Islam in Canadian Media Feeds Image Distortion Disorder. http://www.canadianislamiccongress.

—. 2005. Anti-Islam in the Media: Summary of the Sixth Annual Report for the Year 2003. 31 January. http://www.canadianislamiccongress.com.

Cann, Paul, and Malcolm Dean. 2009. *Unequal Ageing*. Bristol: Polity Press.

Carastathis, Anna. 2007. Gender, Race, and Religious Freedom. *The Dominion*, 28 December. http://www.dominionpaper.ca.

Cardozo, Andrew. 2005. Cultural Diversity in Canadian Broadcasting. Paper presented at the Ethnicity and Media Symposium, Toronto, 21 March.

Carroll, Hamilton. 2008. Men's Soaps: Automotive Television Programming and Contemporary Working-Class Masculinities. *Television and New Media* 9(4): 263-83.

Castells, Manuel. 2009. *Communication Power*. New York: Oxford University Press.

Cavanagh, Richard. 2004. *Reflecting Canadian: Best Practices for Cultural Diversity in Private Television.* Toronto: Connectus Consulting for Task Force for Cultural Diversity on Television.

CBC (Canadian Broadcasting Corporation). 2005. *Street Cents.* Episode 2. http://www.cbc.ca.

Centre for Immigration Policy Reform. 2010. Aims and Objectives. http://www.immigrationreform.ca.

Chan, Adrian. 2008. Reflections on Social Media's Next Phase. CenterNetworks, 10 November. http://www.centernetworks.com.

Chan, Cindy. 2009. Telecom Network Boosts Development, Support among Aboriginals. *Epoch Times,* 15-21 January.

Chan, Wendy, and Kiran Mirchandani. 2002. From Race and Crime to Racialization and Criminalization. In *Crimes of Colour: Racialization and the Criminal Justice System in Canada,* ed. W. Chan and K. Mirchandani, 9-23. Peterborough, ON: Broadview Press.

Chandler, Daniel. 2000. Notes on "The Gaze": John Berger's *Ways of Seeing.* Aberystwyth University. http://www.aber.ac.uk.

Chen, Rene, and Esther Thorson. 2007. Civic Participation by Educated Immigrant Population: Examining the Effects of Media Use, Personal Network, and Social Capital. Paper presented at the Annual Meeting of the International Communication Association, San Francisco, 23 May. http://www.allacademic.com.

Cheng, Hau Ling. 2005. *Constructing a Transnational, Multilocal Sense of Belonging: An Analysis of Ming Pao.* West Canadian ed. *Journal of Communication Inquiry* 29(2): 141-59.

Chomsky, Noam. 1997. What Makes Mainstream Media Mainstream? *Z Magazine,* October, 1-7.

Chozik, Amy. 2010. Testostero-Reality: Few Women, Brawny Men. *Globe and Mail,* 20 November.

Christchurch Press. 2006. The Good, the Bad, and the Ugly: News Reflects Life. Editorial, 27 January.

Chuang, Angie. 2010. Stories about Quran Burning Reveal Shortcomings of U.S. Media's Coverage of Islam. *PoynterOnline,* 13 September. http://www.poynter.org.

Churchill, Ward. 2000. *Fantasies of the Master Race.* San Francisco: City Lights.

–. 2002. *Perversions of Justice: Indigenous Peoples and Angloamerican Law.* San Francisco: City Lights.

Coates, Ken. 2000. *The Marshall Decision and Native Rights.* Montreal and Kingston: McGill-Queen's University Press.

Cochrane, Kira. 2007. Too Much to Bare. *Guardian* (Manchester), 6 September.

Cohen, Jeff. 1999. Racism and Mainstream Media. Fairness and Accuracy in Reporting, 1 October. http://www.fair.org.

Cohen, Nicole. 2005. All We Need Is Dove? *Toronto Star,* 23 August.

Cohen, Stanley. 1972. *Folk Devils and Moral Panic: The Creation of Mods and Rockers.* London: MacGibbon and Kee.

Columpar, Corinn. 2010. *Unsettling Sights: The Fourth World on Film.* Carbondale: Southern Illinois University Press.

Cone, L.L.C. 2007. Cause Evolution Study. Cause Marketing Forum, 26 July. http:///www.causemarketingforum.com.

–. 2008. Consumer Behavior Study Confirms Cause-Related Marketing Can Exponentially Increase Sales, 1 October. http:///www.coneinc.com.

Connell, R.W. 2005. *Masculinities.* Cambridge: Polity Press.

Connell, R.W., and J.W. Messerschmidt. 2005. Hegemonic Masculinity: Rethinking the Concept. *Gender and Society* 19(6): 829-59.

Conradi, Alexa. 2009. Uprising at Oka: A Place of Non-Identification. *Canadian Journal of Communication* 34(4): 547-66.

Corntassel, Jeff, and Richard C. Witmer. 2008. *Forced Federalism: Contemporary Challenges to Indigenous Nationhood.* Norman: University of Oklahoma Press.

Cottle, Simon. 2008. Reporting Demonstrations: The Changing Media Politics of Dissent. *Media, Culture and Society* 30(6): 853-72.

Couldry, Nick. 2003. *Media Rituals: A Critical Approach.* London: Routledge.

Courchene, Thomas J. 2005. "E-the-People": Reflections on Citizen Power in the Information Age. *Policy Options*, March/April, 43-47.

Crawford, Matthew B. 2009a. The Case for Working with Your Hands. *New York Times Magazine*, 24 May, 36-41.

–. 2009b. *Shop Class as Soulcraft: An Inquiry into the Value of Work.* New York: Penguin Press.

Critcher, Chas. 2003. *Moral Panics and the Media.* Buckingham, UK: Open University Press.

–, ed. 2006. *Critical Readings: Moral Panics and the Media.* Buckingham, UK: Open University Press.

Croteau, David, and William Hoynes. 2003. *Media/Society: Industries, Images, and Audiences.* 3rd ed. Thousand Oaks, CA: Sage.

Crowley, Brian. 2010. The Sun Sea Saga Part I: What Can We Do and Why? McDonald-Laurier Institute, 12 December.

CRTC (Canadian Radio-Television and Telecommunications Commission). 1999. Ethnic Broadcasting Policy. Public Notice CRTC 1999-117. http:///www.crtc.gc.ca.

–. 2011. Cultural Diversity on Television and Radio. http://www.crtc.gc.ca.

Crumley, Bruce. 2006. Trials and Errors. *Time Magazine World*, 25 February.

Cultural Survival Voices. 2008. On the Air. *Cultural Survival* 6(2): 2-3.

Cunningham, Brent. 2004. Across the Great Divide: Class. *Columbia Journalism Review* 43(1): 31-38.

Cushion, Stephen. 2004. Misrepresenting Youth: UK Media and Anti–Iraq War Protestors. *Bad Subjects*, January. http://bad.eserver.org.

Darian-Smith, Kate. 2004. Filming Indigenous Australia. *Otemon Journal of Australian Studies* 30: 264-70.

David, Dan. 2004. Aboriginal Media Just Whistling Dixie. *Windspeaker* 22(2): 21.

Davies, Steven Paul. 2008. *Out at the Movies: A History of Gay Cinema.* Harpenden Herts, UK: Kamera Books.

Dawson, Lorne. 2006. *Comprehending Cults: The Sociology of New Religious Movements.* Toronto: Oxford University Press.

Dawson, Lorne, and Douglas Cowan, eds. 2004. *Religion Online: Finding Faith on the Internet.* New York: Routledge.

deMause, Neil. 2009. The Recession and the "Deserving Poor." Fairness and Accuracy in Reporting, March. http://www.fair.org.

Dent, Tamsyn. 2008. Women and the Media – What Do They Want? Polis and the Gender Institute seminar, London School of Communication, March.

Desmond, Mathew. 2006. *On the Fireline: Living and Dying with Wild Land Firefighters.* Chicago: University of Chicago Press.

–. 2008. The Lie of Heroism. *Contexts* 7(1): 56-58.

–. 2009. Bottoms Up. *Contexts* 8(1): 69-71.

de Souza, Father Raymond J. 2009. A New Orthodoxy. *National Post,* 2 July.

DeSouza, Ruth, and Andy Williamson. 2006. Representing Ethnic Communities in the Media. *AEN Journal* 1(1): 20-23.

Deuze, Mark. 2006. Ethnic Media, Community Media and Participatory Media. *Journalism* 7(3): 262-80.

Devereux, Eoin. 2006. *Devils and Angels: Television, Ideology, and the Coverage of Poverty.* Luton, UK: University of Luton Press.

Diamond, Neil. 2010. *Reel Injuns.* Toronto: Mongrel Media. Filmstrip, 86 min.

Did the Microsoft Case Change the World? 2011. *New York Times* editorial, 22 May.

DiManno, Rosie. 2004. Another Unpleasant Spin on the Terror Debate. *Toronto Star,* 12 November.

DiversiPro. 2007. Research on Settlement Programming through the Media. Ontario Council of Agencies Serving Immigrants, 9 October. http://atwork.settlement.org.

Does Religious Pluralism Require Secularism? 2010. *Hedgehog Review* 12(3) (entire issue).

Dollarhide, Maya. 2002. Film on Deaths of Mexican Women Indicts Corruption. WEnews, 20 August. http://www.womensenews.org.

Donlon, Margie M., Ori Ashman, and Becca R. Levy. 2005. Re-Vision of Older Television Characters: A Stereotype-Awareness Intervention. *Journal of Social Issues* 61(2): 307-19.

Dorfman, Lori. 2000. Off Balance: Youth, Race, and Crime in the News. Berkeley Media Studies Group, California.

Douglas, Susan. 1994. *Where the Girls Are: Growing Up Female with the Mass Media.* New York: Random House.

–. 2010. *Enlightened Sexism: The Seductive Message That Feminism's Work Is Done.* New York: Times Books.

Dove. 2004. Only Two Percent of Women Describe Themselves as Beautiful: New Global Study Uncovers Desire for Broader Definition of Beauty. Dove, 29 September. http://www.dove.ca.

Dowd, Maureen. 2011. Corsets, Cleavage, Fishnets. *New York Times,* 2 May.

Downing, John. 2009. *Racism, Ethnicity, and Television.* Chicago: Museum of Broadcast Communications.

Doyle, John. 2011. How to Make a Hit TV Show: Project the Right Values. *Globe and Mail,* 26 May.

Drabinski, Emily. 2009. Teaching about Class in the Library. *Radical Teacher* 85: 15-16.

Dummitt, Christopher. 2007. *The Manly Modern: Masculinity in Postwar Canada.* Vancouver: UBC Press.

Dworkin, Shari L., and Faye Linda Wachs. 2009. *Body Panic: Gender, Health, and the Selling of Fitness.* New York: New York University Press.

Dye, Lauren. 2009. Consuming Constructions: A Critique of Dove's Campaign for Real Beauty. *Canadian Journal of Media Studies* 5(1): 114-28.

Dyer, Gwynne. 2003. West Overrates Terrorism. *Toronto Star,* 10 September.

Eagle, David E. 2011. Changing Patterns of Attendance at Religious Services in Canada, 1986-2008. *Journal for the Scientific Study of Religion* 50(1): 187-200.

Ebo, B., ed. 1998. *Cyberghetto or Cybertopia: Race, Class, and Gender on the Internet.* Westport, CT: Praeger.

Edwards, Harry. 2000. Crisis of Black Athletes on the Eve of the 21st Century. *Society* 37(3): 9-13.

Elber, Lynn. 2008. TV Still a "Whiteout": NAACP. Associated Press, reprinted in the *Toronto Star,* 19 December.

Ellul, Jacques. 1973. *Propaganda: The Formation of Men's Attitudes.* New York: Vintage.

Elmasry, Mohamed. 1999. Framing Islam. *Kitchener-Waterloo Record,* 16 December.

—. 2006. Preserving Multiculturalism through Smart Integration. *National Post,* 14 June.

Entman, Robert. 1993. Framing: Toward Clarification of a Fractured Paradigm. *Journal of Communication* 43(4): 51-58.

—. 2004. *Projections of Power: Framing News, Public Opinion, and U.S. Foreign Policy.* Chicago: University of Chicago Press.

Entman, Robert, and Andrew Rojecki. 2001. *The Black Image in the White Mind: Media and Race in America.* Chicago: University of Chicago Press.

Everitt, Joanna. 2005. Uncovering the Coverage: Gender Biases in Canadian Political Reporting. Breakfast on the Hill Seminar Series, sponsored by Social Sciences and Humanities Research Council of Canada, 17 November.

Faludi, Susan. 1991. *The Undeclared War against American Women.* New York: Anchor.

Fatah, Tarek. 2008. CBC and Jihad. *Calgary Herald,* 11 December.

Fejes, Fred, and Kevin Petrich. 1993. Invisibility, Homophobia, and Heterosexism: Lesbians, Gays, and the Media. *Critical Studies in Mass Communication* 10(4): 395-422.

Fishman, Mark. 1980. *Manufacturing News.* Austin: University of Austin Press.

Fiske, John. 1987. *Television Culture.* London: Methuen.

—. 1998. Culture, Ideology, Interpellation. In *Literary Theory: An Anthology,* ed. J. Revkin and M. Ryan, 305-11. Malden, MA: Blackwell.

Fleras, Augie. 2003. *Mass Media Communication in Canada.* Toronto: Nelson.

—. 2004a. The Conventional News Paradigm as Systemic Bias: Rethinking the Misrepresentational Basis of News Media–Minority Relations. Paper presented at the Media, Migration, Integration Conference, Siegen, Germany, June.

—. 2004b. *Social Problems in Canada.* 4th ed. Toronto: Prentice Hall.

—. 2006. The Conventional News Paradigm as Systemic Bias: Rethinking the Representational Basis of News Media–Minority Relations in Canada. In *Media and Migration: A Comparative Perspective,* ed. Rainer Geissler and Horst Pöttker, 179-222. Berlin: Transcript.

—. 2007a. Aboriginal and Ethnic Media. Paper presented at the Media, Migration, Integration Conference, Dortmund, Germany, 21-22 June.

—. 2007b. Misreading Minorities: Newscasting as Systemic Propaganda. Paper presented at the "20 Years of Propaganda" conference, Windsor, ON, 15-16 May.

—. 2009. *The Politics of Multiculturalism.* New York: Palgrave Macmillan.

—. 2010. *Unequal Relations: Race, Ethnic, and Aboriginal Relations in Canada.* 6th ed. Toronto: Prentice Hall.

—. 2011. The Politics of Multicultural Governance in a Globalizing World: A Case for Multiversalism and Multiculturalism in Canada. Paper presented to the Conference commemorating 15 Years of Canadian Studies at the University of Matanzas, Cuba, 24 February.

Fleras, Augie, and Jean Lock Kunz. 2001. *Media and Minorities: Representing Diversity in a Multicultural Canada.* Toronto: Thompson.

Foucault, Michel. 1977. *Discipline and Punish: The Birth of the Prison.* London: Allen Lane.

Francis, Daniel. 1992. *The Imaginary Indian: The Image of the Indian in Canadian Culture.* Vancouver: Arsenal Pulp Press.

Fraser Institute. 1993. Immigration, Part 1: The Human Interest Story. *On Balance* 6(3). http://oldfraser.lexi.net.

Friar, Ralph, and Natasha Friar. 1972. *The Only Good Indian ... The Hollywood Gospel.* New York: Drama Book Publishers.

Friscolanti, Michael. 2009. The Truth about Priests. *Maclean's,* 7 December.

Friscolanti, M., J. Gatehouse, and C. Gillis. 2006. Homegrown Terror: It's Not Over. *Maclean's,* 19 June, 18-25.

Frum, David. 2006. "Terrorism's Enablers." *National Post,* 19 August.

Gallagher, Margaret. 2005. *Who Makes the News?* London, UK: Global Media Monitoring Project.

Gallagher, Stephen. 2008. Canada and Mass Immigration: The Creation of a Global Suburb and Its Impact on National Unity. Immigration Watch Canada, 4 June. http://www.immigrationwatchcanada.org.

Garfield, B. 2005. Garfield's Ad Review. *Advertising Age* 76(30): 53.

Gauntlett, David. 2008. *Gender, Media, and Identity.* 2nd ed. New York: Routledge.

Geddes, John. 2009. "What Canadians Think of Sikhs, Jews, Christians, Muslims ..." *Maclean's,* 4 May, 20-24.

Geissler, Rainer, and Horst Pöttker, eds. 2005. *Media Integration of Ethnic Minorities in Germany, Canada and the USA.* Bielefeld, Germany: Transcript.

–, eds. 2006. *Mass Media-Integration: Media and Migration – A Comparative Perspective.* Berlin: Transcript.

Geist, Michael. 2008. Internet Matures as Tool for Political Advocacy. *Toronto Star,* 2 June.

Gelerenter, Lior, and Motti Regev. 2010. Internet and Globalization. In *Routledge International Handbook on Globalization Studies,* ed. Bryan Turner, 62-76. New York: Routlege.

Georgiou, Myria. 2002. *Mapping Minorities and Their Media: The National Context – The UK.* London: London School of Economics.

Gerstel, Judy. 2008. Media Bias. *Toronto Star,* 9 June.

Ginsberg, Faye. 2000. Resources of Hope: Learning from the Local in a Transnational Era. In *Indigenous Cultures in an Interconnected World,* ed. Claire Smith and Graeme K. Ward, 27-48. Vancouver: UBC Press.

Giroux, Henry A. 2001. Private Satisfactions and Public Disorders: *Fight Club,* Patriarchy, and the Politics of Masculine Violence. *JAC* 21(1): 1-31.

–. 2006. *Beyond the Spectacle of Terrorism: Global Uncertainty and the Challenge of the New Media.* Boulder, CO: Paradigm.

GLAAD (Gay and Lesbian Alliance Against Defamation). 2010. Network Responsibility Index 2009-2010. http://www.glaad.org.

Global Media Monitoring Project. 2010. Who Makes the News: Key Findings 1995-2005. London, UK: Global Media Monitoring Project.

Glynn, Kevin, and A.F. Tyson. 2007. Indigeneity, Media, and Cultural Globalisation: The Case of Mataku or the Maori X-Files. *International Journal of Cultural Studies* 10(2): 205-24.

Goldberg, Michelle. 2009. Is Sarah Palin a Narcissist? *Toronto Star,* 4 July.

Gonzales, Juan. 2001. Passion and Purpose for the Ethnic Press. *Quill* 89(3): 42-44.

Goodman, Lee-Ann. 2011. Palin, Bachmann Eye Candidacy. *Waterloo Region Record,* 28 May.

Gordinier, Jeff. 2010. The Remasculated Man. *Details,* March. http://www.details.com.

Gordon, Daphne. 2002. Disney's Girls Are Doing It for Themselves. *Toronto Star,* 17 February.

Gottschalk, Peter, and Gabriel Greenberg. 2008. *Islamophobia: Making Muslims the Enemy.* Lanham, MD: Rowman and Littlefield.

Graves, Frank. 2005. The Shifting Public Outlook on Risk and Security. The Canadian Institute, Woodrow Wilson International Center for Scholars, October.

Gray, John Maclachlan. 2006. Massive Terror Attack Averted. *Globe and Mail,* 3 June.

Gray Panthers. 1995. Help Stamp Out Ageism. *Network* 1(2): 14.

Graydon, Shari. 2001. The Portrayal of Women in the Media: The Good, the Bad, and the Beautiful. In *Communications in Canadian Society*, 5th ed., ed. C. McKie and B. Singer, 143-71. Toronto: Thompson.

Greenberg, Joshua. 2000. Opinion Discourses and Canadian Newspapers: The Case of the Chinese "Boat People." *Canadian Journal of Communication* 25(4): 517-37.

Greenspon, Edward. 2003. What Passes for the Normal in News. *Globe and Mail*, 10 May.

Gunter, Barrie. 2008. Media Violence: Is There a Case for Causality? *American Behavioral Scientist* 51(8): 1061-122.

Haas, Werner. 2006. The Portrayal of Single Moms on Television. Associated Content, 14 November. http://www.associatedcontent.com.

Hackett, Robert A., and Steve Anderson. 2010. Democratic Media Reform in Canada. Ottawa: Canadian Centre for Policy Alternatives, 1 July.

–. 2011. Research in Brief: Democratizing Communication Policy in Canada – A Social Movement Perspective. *Canadian Journal of Communication* 36(1): 161-68.

Hackett, Robert A., Richard Gruneau, Donald Gutstein, and Timothy A. Gibson. 2000. *The Missing News: Filters and Blind Spots in Canada's Press*. Aurora, ON: Canadian Centre for Policy Alternatives/Garamond Press.

Hackett, Robert A., and Yuezhi Zhao. 1998. *Sustaining Democracy: Journalism and the Politics of Objectivity*. Toronto: Garamond Press.

Hafsteinsson, Sigurjon Balder. 2010. Aboriginal Journalism Practices as Deep Democracy: APTN National News. In *Indigenous Screen Cultures in Canada*, ed. B. Hafsteinsson and M. Bredin, 53-68. Winnipeg: University of Manitoba Press.

Hafsteinsson, Sigurjon Balder, and Marian Bredin, eds. 2010. *Indigenous Screen Cultures in Canada*. Winnipeg: University of Manitoba Press.

Hall, Stuart. 1978. *Policing the Crisis*. London: Palgrave Macmillan.

–. 1980. Encoding/Decoding. In *Culture, Media, Language*, ed. S. Hall, C. Critcher, T. Jefferson, J.N. Clarke, and B. Roberts, 117-27. London: Hutchinson.

Haller, Beth, and Sue Ralph. 2001. Profitability, Diversity, and Disability Images in Advertising in the United States and Great Britain. *Disabilities Studies Quarterly* 21(2).

Halperin, Mark. 2010. It's Her Party Now. *Time*, 12 April, 32.

Hanamoto, Darrell. 1995. *Monitored Peril: Asian Americans and the Politics of Representation*. St. Paul: University of Minnesota Press.

Haniff, Ghulam M. 2009. Muslims Need to Make Their Own Images. *New America Media*, 26 January. http://www.newamericamedia.org.

Hanke, Robert. 1998. Theorizing Masculinity with/in the Media. *Communication Theory* 8(2): 183-201.

Harding, Robert. 2005. The Media, Aboriginal People, and Common Sense. *Canadian Journal of Native Studies* 25(1): 311-25.

–. 2006. Historical Representations of Aboriginal People in the Canadian News Media. *Discourse and Society* 17(2): 205-35.

–. 2010. The Demonization of Aboriginal Child Welfare Authorities in the News. *Canadian Journal of Communication* 35(1): 85-108.

Harper, Tim. 2008. Michelle Obama Softens Her Public Image. *Toronto Star*, 21 June.

Hart, K.-P.R. 2000. Representing Gay Men on American Television. *Journal of Men's Studies* 9(1): 59-79.

Hartley, J. 1999. *Use of Television*. London: Routledge.

Harvard Project on American Indian Economic Development. 2008. *The State of the Native Nations Conditions under U.S. Policies of Self-Determination*. New York: Oxford University Press.

Harvey, Frank. 2006. Terrified of Terrorism. *National Post,* June 26.

Haskell, David. 2009. *Through a Lens Darkly: How the News Media Perceive and Portray Evangelical Christians.* Toronto: Clements Publishing.

Haythornthwaite, Caroline, and Lori Kendall. 2010. Internet and Community. *American Behavioral Scientist* 53(8): 1083-94.

Heider, Don, ed. 2004. *Class and News.* Lanham, MD: Rowman and Littlefield.

Henry, Frances, and Carol Tator. 2002. *Discourses of Domination: Racial Bias in the Canadian English-Language Press.* Toronto: University of Toronto Press.

–. 2005. Racial Profiling in Toronto: Discourses of Domination, Mediation, and Opposition. Final draft submitted to the Canadian Race Relations Foundation, September, Toronto.

–. 2006. *The Colour of Democracy.* 3rd ed. Toronto: Nelson/Thompson.

Herman, Edward. 2003a. Propaganda in the Free Press. Interview by David Ross. *ZNet,* http://www.zmag.org.

–. 2003b. The Propaganda Model: A Retrospective. *Against All Reason* 1: 1-14.

Herman, Edward, and Noam Chomsky. 2002 [1988]. *Manufacturing Consent.* New York: Pantheon Books.

Herzberg, Bob. 2008. *Indians in Motion Pictures.* Jefferson, NC: McFarland.

Hesse, Monica. 2011. Wikipedia's Just Getting Started, Founder Says. *Washington Post,* 14 January.

Hier, Sean. 2008. Representing Race: Are Canadian News Media Racist? No. In *Communication in Question,* ed. J. Greenberg and C.D. Elliot, 131-38. Toronto: Thomson Nelson.

–. 2010. More Than a Vernacular Commentary: A Response to Minelle Mahtani. *Canadian Journal of Communication* 35(2): 173-78.

Hier, Sean, and Joshua Greenberg. 2002. News Discourses and the Problematization of Chinese Migration to Canada. In *Discourses of Domination,* ed. F. Henry and C. Tator, 138-62. Toronto: University of Toronto Press.

Higginbotham, Anastasia. 1996. Teen Mags: How to Get a Guy, Drop 20 Pounds, and Lose Your Self-Esteem. *MS,* March/April, 84-87.

Higgins, Michael. 2011. Of Gods and Men and the Purity of Faith. *Globe and Mail,* 22 April.

Hirst, Martin, and Roger Patching. 2005. *Journalism Ethics.* Victoria, Australia: Oxford University Press.

Hitchens, Christopher. 2007. *God Is Not Great: How Religion Poisons Everybody.* New York: Twelve.

Hodgetts, Darrin, Alison Barnett, Andrew Duirs, Jolene Henry, and Anne Schwanen. 2005. Maori Media Production, Civic Journalism and the Foreshore and Seabed Controversy in Aotearoa. *Pacific Journalism Review* 11(2): 191-208.

hooks, bell. 1992. *Black Looks: Race and Representation.* New York: South End Press.

Houpt, Simon. 2009. Back on the Soap Box. *Globe and Mail,* 28 August.

–. 2010. Blowing the Whistle on Men's Marketing. *Globe and Mail,* 12 February.

Howard, Philip N. 2010. *The Digital Origins of Dictatorship and Democracy.* New York: Oxford University Press.

Howard, Philip N., Laura Busch, and Penelope Sheets. 2010. Comparing Digital Divides: Internet Access and Social Inequality in Canada and the United States. *Canadian Journal of Communication* 35(1): 109-28.

Howley, Kevin, ed. 2010. *Understanding Community Media.* Thousand Oaks, CA: Sage.

Hsu, Hua. 2002. Ethnic Media Grow Up. *ColorLines,* Fall, http://colorlines.com.

Hubert, Susan J. 1999. What's Wrong with This Picture? The Politics of Ellen's Coming Out Party. *Journal of Popular Culture* 33(2): 31-36.

Huijser, Henk. 2007. Representing Indigenous Stories in the Cinema: Between Collaboration and Appropriation. *International Journal of Diversity in Organisations, Communities and Nations* 7(3): 1-10.

Husband, Charles. 2005. Minority Ethnic Media as Communities of Practice: Professionalism and Identity Politics in Interaction. *Journal of Ethnic and Migration Studies* 31(3): 461-79.

Huysmans, Jef. 2006. *The Politics of Insecurity: Fear, Migration, and Asylum in the EU.* London: Routledge.

Ibbitson, John. 2005. *The Polite Revolution: Perfecting the Canadian Dream.* Toronto: McClelland and Stewart.

Ibrahim, Dina. 2010. The Framing of Islam on Network News Following the September 11th Attacks. *International Communication Gazette* 72: 111-25.

Ibrahim, Yasmin. 2009. New Visibilities: Mobile Technology and Media Event. *Re-Public.* http://www.re-public.gr.

International Longevity Center. 2006. *Ageism in America.* New York: Anti-Ageism Task Force, sponsored by the Open Society Institute.

International Women's Media Foundation. 2011. A Global Report on Women in the News Media. 23 March.

Jackson, John D., Greg M. Nielsen, and Yon Hsu. 2011. *Mediated Society: A Critical Sociology of Media.* Toronto: Oxford University Press.

Jenicek, A., A.D. Wong, and E.O.J. Lee. 2009. Dangerous Shortcuts: Representations of Sexual Minority Refugees in the Post–9-11 Canadian Press. *Canadian Journal of Communication* 34(4): 635-58.

Jhally, Sut. 2007. Dreamworlds 3: Desire, Sex, and Power in Music Video. Media Education Foundation.

Jhally, Sut, and Justin Lewis. 1992. *Enlightened Racism: The Cosby Show, Audiences, and the Myth of the American Dream.* Boulder, CO: Westview Press.

Jhaveri, Hemal. 2008. NAACP Slams the TV Industry. *TV Squad,* 21 December. http://www. tvsquad.com.

Jiwani, Yasmin. 2001. Intersecting Inequalities: Immigrant Women of Colour, Violence, and Health Care. July. http://www.harbour.sfu.ca/ freda/articles/hlth.htm.

–. 2006. *Discourses of Denial: Mediations on Race, Gender, and Violence.* Vancouver: UBC Press.

–. 2009. Helpless Maidens and Chivalrous Knights: Afghan Women in the Canadian Press. *University of Toronto Quarterly* 78(2): 728-44.

–. 2010. Race(ing) the Nation: Media and Minorities. In *Mediascapes,* 3rd ed., ed. L.R. Shade, 271-86. Toronto: Nelson.

Jiwani, Yasmin, and Mary Lynn Young. 2006. Missing and Murdered Women: Reproducing Marginality in News Discourse. *Canadian Journal of Communication* 31(4): 895-917.

Johnson, Brian D. 2010. Hollywood's Shocking Reel Indians. *Maclean's,* 23 February.

–. 2011. Feeling the Pain of Rich Alpha Males. *Maclean's,* 21 January, 57.

Johnson, Matthew. 2010. Social Networks: How Facebook Changed the Internet. Media Awareness Network, 30 September. http://www.media-awareness.ca/blog.

Jonas, George. 2011. Innocent Till Proven Guilty – Unless You're Rich. *National Post,* 21 May.

Juergens, Brian. 2008. Review of Gus Van Sant's *Milk. After Elton,* 25 November. http://www. afterelton.com.

Kalant, Amelia. 2004. *National Identity and the Conflict at Oka.* New York: Routledge.

Kamalipour, Y.R., and T. Carilli, eds. 1998. *Cultural Diversity and the U.S. Media.* New York: State University of New York Press.

Kanellakis, Abigail. 2007. Women through the Eyes of Mainstream Media. *Associated Content,* 7 September. http://www.associatedcontent.com.

Karan, Kavita, and Michelle Khoo. 2007. The Power of the Gaze in the Media: Visual Representations. *For Him Magazine* (FHM). Singapore. Paper presented at the Visual Studies Division of the annual conference of the International Communication Association, San Francisco, June.

Karim, Karim. 2002. *Islamic Peril: Media and Global Violence.* Montreal: Black Rose Books.

–. 2003. *The Media of Diaspora.* New York: Routledge.

–. 2006a. American Media's Coverage of Muslims: The Historical Roots of Contemporary Portrayals. In *Muslims and the News Media,* ed. E. Poole and J.E. Richardson, 116-27. New York: I.B. Taurus.

–. 2006b. The Media and Muslims. *Research Works,* March.

–. 2010. The National-Global Nexus of Ethnic and Diasporic Media. In *Mediascapes,* 3rd ed., ed. L.R. Shade, 256-70. Toronto: Nelson.

Katz, Jackson. 1999. *Tough Guise: Violence, Media and the Crisis in Masculinity.* Northampton, MA: Media Education Foundation. Filmstrip, 82 min.

Kay, Jonathan. 2006. Islam as Goth. *National Post,* 13 June.

Kellner, Douglas. 1995. *Media Culture.* New York: Routledge.

Kelly, Deirdre M. 2006. Frame Work: Helping Youth Counter Their Misrepresentations in Media. *Canadian Journal of Education* 29(1): 27-48.

Kelly, Jennifer. 1998. *Under the Gaze: Learning to Be Black in White Society.* Halifax: Fernwood Publishing.

Kendall, Diana. 2005. *Framing Class: Media Representations of Wealth and Poverty in the United States.* Lanham, MD: Rowman and Littlefield.

Keung, Nicholas. 2006. Mainstream Media Advertising Misses Some Ethnic Segments. *Toronto Star,* 17 March.

Kilbourne, Jean. 2000. *Can't Buy My Love: How Advertising Changes the Way We Think and Feel.* New York: Simon and Schuster.

Kilbourne, Jean, and Diane Levin. 2008. *So Sexy So Soon: The New Sexualized Childhood and What Parents Can Do to Protect Their Kids.* New York: Random House.

Killingbeck, Donna. 2001. The Role of Television News in the Construction of School Violence as a "Moral Panic." *Journal of Criminal Justice and Popular Culture* 8(3): 186-202.

Kimmel, Michael S. 2008. *The Gendered Society.* 3rd ed. New York: Oxford University Press.

–. 2010. *Misframing Men: The Politics of Contemporary Masculinities.* Piscataway, NJ: Rutgers University Press.

King, Samantha. 2006. *Pink Ribbons Inc.: Breast Cancer and the Politics of Philanthropy.* Minneapolis: University of Minnesota Press.

Klaehn, Jeffery. 2002. A Critical Review and Assessment of Herman and Chomsky's Propaganda Model. *European Journal of Communication* 17(2): 147-82.

Klaehn, Jeffery, and Andrew Mullin. 2010. The Propaganda Model and Sociology: Understanding the Media and Society. *Synaesthesia* 1(1): 10-23.

Knopf, Kerstin. 2010. Aboriginal Media on the Move: An Outsider Perspective on APTN. In *Indigenous Screen Cultures in Canada,* ed. S.B. Hafsteinsson and M. Bredin, 69-86. Winnipeg: University of Manitoba Press.

Kollmeyer, Christopher J. 2004. Corporate Interests: How the News Media Portray the Economy. *Social Problems* 51(3): 432-52.

Kozlowski, Kim. 2007. Think Pink Marketing Takes Off. *Detroit News,* 12 October.

Krahn, H.J., G.S. Lowe, and K.D. Hughes. 2007. *Work, Industry and Canadian Society.* 5th ed. Scarborough: Thomson Nelson.

Krashinsky, Susan. 2009. Why Men in Ads Are Dumb, Goofy, or Completely Inept. *Globe and Mail,* 7 August.

Kular, Kulvinder. 2006. Making the Case for More Third-Language Television. *Toronto Star,* 22 July.

Kumar, Sangeet. 2010. Google Earth and the Nation State: Sovereignty in the Age of New Media. *Global Media and Communication* 6(2): 154-76.

Kunkel, D., S. Smith, P. Suding, and E. Biely. 2002. Coverage in Context: How Thoroughly the News Media Report Five Key Children's Issues. Commissioned by Casey Journalism Centre on Children and Families. University of Maryland: College Park.

Kunz, Jean. 2009. *Religious Diversity in a Multicultural Canada: Quo Vadis?* Ottawa: Policy Research Initiative.

Kunz, Jean, and Augie Fleras. 1998. Women of Colour in Mainstream Advertising: Distorted Mirror or Looking Glass? *Atlantis* 22(2): 27-38.

Kupu Taea. 2007. *Media and Te Tiriti O Waitangi.* Wellington: Media and Te Tiriti Project. Treaty Resource Centre. http://www.trc.org.nz.

Kurien, Prema A. 2006. Multiculturalism and American Religion: The Case of Hindu Indian Americans. *Social Forces* 85(2): 723-41.

Kusz, Kyle. 2008. Remasculinizing White Guys in/through New Millennium American Sports Films. In *Sport in Films,* ed. E. Poulton and M. Roderick, 93-110. New York: Routledge.

Kuypers, Jim A. 2002. *Press Bias and Politics: How the Media Frame Controversial Issues.* Westport, CT: Praeger.

Kymlicka, Will. 2008. The Current State of Multiculturalism in Canada. Prepared for the Multiculturalism and Human Rights Branch, Goverment of Canada.

Lakoff, George, and Sam Ferguson. 2006. *The Framing of Immigration.* Posted on Cognitive Policy Works, http://www.cognitivepolicyworks.com/resource-center/rethinking -immigration/.

Lam, Lawrence. 1996. The Role of Ethnic Media for Immigrants: A Case Study for Chinese Immigrants and Their Media in Toronto. In *The Mass Media and Canadian Diversity,* ed. S. Nancoo and R. Nancoo, 233-58. Toronto: Canadian Education Services.

Lambertus, Sandra. 2004. *Wartime Images, Peacetime Wounds: The Media and Gustafsen Lake Standoff.* Toronto: University of Toronto Press.

Landzelius, Kyra, 2006. Introduction: Native on the Net. In *Native on the Net,* ed. K. Landzelius, 1-42. New York: Routledge.

Lasica, J.D. 1996. Net Gain: Journalists in an Interactive Age. *American Journalism Review* 18(9): 20-33.

Ledger, Brent. 2008. Penn Plays It Straight and Gets It Right. *Toronto Star,* 6 December.

Lee, Monica M., Brian Carpenter, and Lawrence S. Meyers. 2006. Representations of Older Adults in Television Advertisements. *Journal of Aging Studies* 21(1): 23-30.

Lee, Timothy B. 2010. Seeing Like a Movie Mogul. Reaction essay for the Cato Institute, 14 September. http://www.cato-unbound.org.

Leistyna, Pepi. 2009. Exposing the Ruling Class in the United States Using Television and Documentary Film. *Radical Teacher* 85: 12-15.

Leistyna, Pepi, and Debra Mollen. 2008. Teaching Social Class through Alternative Media and by Dialoging across Disciplines and Boundaries. *Radical Teacher* 81: 20-27.

Leong, Melissa. 2008. If She Had Just Worn a Pantsuit. *National Post,* 28 May.

Leroy, Christophe J. 2005. Threat Perceptions in the United States and Canada: One Issue, Two Voices. Canadian Institute, Woodrow Wilson International Center for Scholars, October.

Lewis, Charles. 2009. Newfoundland Anglican Priest Facing Charges of Child Porn. *National Post,* 10 December.

Lewis, Justin, Paul Mason, and Kerry Moore. 2009. "Islamic Terrorism" and the Repression of the Political. In *Media, Religion, and Conflict,* ed. L. Marsden and H. Savigny, 17-38. Burlington, VT: Ashgate.

Li, Charlene, and Josh Bernoff. 2008. *Groundswell: Winning in a World Transformed by Social Technologies.* Boston: Harvard Business Press.

Li, Peter S. 2003. *Destination Canada: Immigration Debates and Issues.* Toronto: Oxford University Press.

Lieberman, David. 2006. Media Tune into Ethnic Audiences. *USA Today,* 6 June.

Lin, Wan-Ying, and Hayeon Song. 2006. Geo-Ethnic Storytelling. *Journalism* 7(3): 362-88.

Lincoln, Clifford, Roger Tasse, and Anthony Cianciotta. 2005. *Integration and Cultural Diversity: Report of the Panel on Access to Third-Language Public Television Services.* Ottawa: Department of Canadian Heritage.

Lindsey, Linda L. 1997. *Gender Roles: A Sociological Perspective.* Upper Saddle River, NJ: Prentice Hall.

Lockett, Christopher. 2010. Masculinity and Authenticity: Reality TV's Real Men. Memorial University, 15 October, http://flowtv.org/.

Lofton, Kathryn. 2011. *Oprah: The Gospel of an Icon.* Berkeley: University of California Press.

Lumme-Sandt, Kirsi. 2011. Images of Ageing in a 50+ Magazine. *Journal of Aging Studies* 25(1): 45-51.

Lunt, Andrea. 2011. Media: It's Still a Man's World, Especially at the Top. *Global Geopolitics and Political Economy,* 24 March. http://globalgeopolitics.net.

Maaka, Roger, and Augie Fleras. 2005. *The Politics of Indigeneity: Perspectives from Canada and New Zealand.* Dunedin, New Zealand: Otago University Press.

–. 2008. Contesting Indigenous Peoples Governance: The Politics of State-Determination vs. Indigenous Self-Determining Autonomy in Canada and New Zealand. In *Aboriginal Self-Government in Canada: Current Trends and Issues,* 3rd ed., ed. Y. Belanger, 176-211. Saskatoon: Purich Publishing.

MacCharles, Tonda. 2008. Ad Blitz Touts Reforms of Immigration System. *Toronto Star,* 21 April.

Mace, Eric. 2005. Race Representations in French TV Programmes: Realistic Discriminations of a National Social Imaginary. Paper presented at the Centre for Research in Ethnic Relations, Warwick, UK, 1 November.

Maclean's. 2009. Divided by Religion: What Canadians Think of Sikhs, Jews, Christians and Muslims. 4 May.

–. 2010. Outraged Moms, Trashy Daughters. 16 August.

MacNeill, Margaret. 2009. Opening Up the Gendered Gaze: Sports Media Representations of Women, National Identity, and Racialised Gaze in Canada. In *Olympic Women and the Media,* ed. P. Markula, 50-69. New York: Palgrave Macmillan.

Macpherson, Cluny, and Paul Spoonley. 2004. Mediated Ethnicity: Media and the Management of Ethnic Images in Aotearoa. In *Tangata Tangata: The Changing Ethnic Contours of New Zealand,* ed. P. Spoonley, D. Pearson, and C. Macpherson, 221-46. Southbank, Victoria, New Zealand: Dunmore Thomson.

Mahtani, Minelle. 2001. Representing Minorities: Canadian Media and Minority Identities. *Canadian Ethnic Studies* 33(3): 99-131.

–. 2008a. How Are Immigrants Seen – And What Do They Want to See? Contemporary Research on the Representation of Immigrants in the Canadian English-Language Media. In *Immigration and Integration in Canada in the Twenty-First Century,* ed.

John Biles, Meyer Burstein, and James Frideres, 231-52. Montreal and Kingston: McGill-Queen's University Press.

—. 2008b. Racializing the Audience: Immigrant Perceptions of Mainstream Canadian English Language TV News. *Canadian Journal of Communication* 33(4): 639-60.

—. 2009. Critiquing the Critiques on Media and Minority Research in Canada. *Canadian Journal of Communication* 34(4): 715-19.

Mahtani, Minelle, Frances Henry, and Carol Tator. 2008. Discourse, Ideology, and Constructions of Racial Inequality. In *Communication in Question*, ed. J. Greenberg and C.D. Elliott, 120-30. Toronto: Thomson Nelson.

Males, Mike A. 1999. *Framing Youth: Ten Myths about the Next Generation.* Monroe, ME: Common Courage Press.

Malin, Brenton J. 2010. Viral Manhood: Niche Marketing, Hard-Boiled Detectives, and the Economics of Masculinity. *Media, Culture, and Society* 32(3): 373-89.

Mallia, Karen L. 2009. From the Sacred to the Profane: A Critical Analysis of the Changing Nature of Religious Imagery in Advertising. *Journal of Media and Religion* 8(3): 172-90.

Mantsios, Gregory. 2001. Media Magic: Making Class Invisible. In *Race, Class, and Gender in the US*, 5th ed., ed. P. Rothenberg. New York: St. Martin's Press.

Manzoor, Sarfraz. 2008. The Forgotten People. *Guardian* (Manchester), 3 March. http://www.guardian.co.uk.

Maracle, Brian. 1996. One More Whining Indian Tilting at the Windmills. In *Clash of Identities*, ed. J. Littleton, 15-20. Toronto: Prentice Hall.

Marche, Stephen. 2008. The Sexiest Woman (Barely) Alive. *Toronto Star*, 3 May.

Markula, Pirkko. 2009. Introduction. In *Olympic Women and the Media*, ed. P. Markula, 1-29. New York: Palgrave Macmillan.

Marsden, Lee, and Heather Savigny, eds. 2009. *Media, Religion, and Conflict.* Burlington, VT: Ashgate.

Marshall, P., L. Gilbert, and R.G. Ahmanson, eds. 2009. *Blind Spot: When Journalists Don't Get Religion.* New York: Oxford University Press.

Marubbio, M. Elise. 2006. *Killing the Indian Maiden: Images of Native American Women in Film.* Lexington: University Press of Kentucky.

Masood, Ehsan. 2008. Muslims and Multiculturalism: Lesson from Canada. Open Democracy. http://www.opendemocracy.net.

Mazzarella, Sharon R. 2008. Men, Media, and Machines: Fabricating Masculinities in *American Chopper. Popular Communication* 6(2): 68-84.

McAndrew, Marie. 1992. Combatting Racism and Ethnocentrism in Educational Materials: Problems and Actions Taken in Quebec. In *Racism and Education: Different Perspectives and Experiences*, 49-60. Ottawa: Ontario Teachers Federation.

McChesney, R.W. 1999. *Rich Media, Poor Democracy: Communication Politics in Dubious Times.* Urbana: University of Illinois Press.

McCreanor, Tim. 2006. Sticks and Stones May Break My Bones: Talking Pakeha Identities. In *New Zealand Identities*, ed. J.H. Liu, T. MacIntosh, T. McCreanor, and T. Teaiwa, 52-68. Wellington: Victoria University Press.

McDonald, Alyssa. 2009. If You Got Elected to Westminster, What Would Your Husband Do for Sex during the Week? *New Statesman*, 6 July.

McGowan, William. 2001. *Coloring the News: How Political Correctness Has Corrupted American Journalism.* New York: Encounter Books.

McGuire, Brian C. 2008. Ageism: Media Influences and Older Americans. Socyberty, 16 January. http://www.socyberty.com.

McKinney, M.S., L.A. Rill, and R.G. Watson. 2011. Who Framed Sarah Palin? Viewer Reactions to the 2008 Vice-Presidential Debate. *American Behavioral Scientist* 55(3): 212-31.

McKnight Foundation. 2008. Youth in the Media: Overview. http://www.mcknight.org.

McLeod, Judi. 2006. Terrorism Comes to Canada. *Canadian Free Press*, 3 June.

McMullin, Julie. 2010. *Understanding Social Inequality in Canada: Intersections of Class, Age, Gender, Ethnicity, and Race.* 2nd ed. Toronto: Oxford University Press.

McRobbie, Angela, and Sarah L. Thornton. 1995. Rethinking "Moral Panic" for Multimediated Social Worlds. *British Journal of Sociology* 46(4): 559-74.

Meadows, M., and H. Molnar. 2001. *Songlines to Satellites.* Sydney: Pluto Press.

"Media and Youth." Media@Youth. http://peer-educator.tripod.com.

Media Awareness Network. 2009. Dove's Campaign for Real Beauty. http://www.media -awareness.ca.

Media Lens. 2003. Thought Control, the Chains of Seduction. http://www.medialens.org.

Media Monitor. 2000. *What's the Matter with Kids Today? Images of Teenagers on Local and National TV News.* Washington, DC: Center for Media and Public Affairs.

Mediam'Rad. 2009. Ethnic Media in Europe: Media, Diversity and Pluralism. Mira Media. http://www.miramedia.nl.

Meer, Malik. 2007. Range of Responses to *Little Mosque on the Prairie.* Guardian TV and Radio (blog), 15 January. http://www.guardian.co.uk/culture/tvandradioblog/2007/jan/ 15/post7.

Meltzer, Kimberly. 2010. A Different Sort of Reality TV Hero: Extreme Fishermen, Loggers, and Truckers on the Edge. In *Reel Politics: Reality Television as a Platform for Political Discourse,* ed. L. Baruh and J.H. Park, 249-64. Newcastle Upon Tyne, UK: Cambridge Scholars Publishing.

Messner, Michael A., and Cheryl Cooky. 2010. *Gender in Televised Sports: News and Highlight Shows, 1989 to 2009.* Los Angeles: Center for Feminist Research, University of Southern California.

Metropolis Presents. 2004. Conference Notes on Media, Immigration and Diversity: Informing Public Discourse or Fanning the Flames of Intolerance? Ottawa, 30 March.

Miel, Persephone, and Robert Faris. 2008. *News and Information as Digital Media Come of Age.* Harvard, MA: Berkman Center for Internet and Society.

Miller, David, ed. 2004. *Tell Me No Lies: Propaganda and Media Distortion in the Attack on Iraq.* London: Pluto Press.

Miller, John. 2005. Ipperwash and the Media: A Critical Analysis of How the Story Was Covered. Paper prepared for the Aboriginal Legal Foundation, Toronto.

–. 2006. Media Coverage of Ipperwash Affair Biased, Untrue. *News and Events.* Ryerson University, 31 January. http://www.ryerson.ca/news/media.

Miller, Mary Jane. 2008. *Outside Looking In: Viewing First Nations Peoples in Canadian Dramatic Television.* Montreal and Kingston: McGill-Queen's University Press.

Moeller, Susan. 2006. Regarding the Pain of Others: Media, Bias, and the Coverage of International Disasters. *Journal of International Affairs* 59(2): 173-95.

Mohammed, Noha. 2007. *Little Mosque on the Prairie*: A Canadian Sitcom Takes a Biting Look at the Life of Muslims in the West. *Egypt Today,* July. http://www.egypttoday.com.

Moller, Stephanie. 2008. Review of *Framing Class,* by Diana Kendall. *Social Forces* 86(3): 1347-49.

Morgenson, Donald. 2010. Being Aged in the Land of the Young. *The Cord* (Wilfrid Laurier University), 22 September.

Morozov, Evgeny. 2011. *The Net Delusion: The Dark Side of Internet Freedom*. New York: Public Affairs Books.

Morris, Andrew. 2006. In Good Faith: Portrayals of Islam in the Media. 11 November. http://blogcritics.org.

Morrow, Martin. 2009. The Longest Winter. CBC News, 26 March. http://www.cbc.ca.

MRTW (Media Report to Women). 1996. New York AFRA Panel Hits Continuing Stereotyping on TV. *Media Report to Women*, Winter 24(1): 6-7.

–. 2000. U.S. Women Surging Online, Closing Gender Gap, Reshaping Social Landscape, Study Says. *Media Report to Women* 28(2): 1-2.

Mulvey, Laura. 1975. Visual Pleasure and Narrative Cinema. *Screen* 16(3): 6-18.

Mumby, Dennis K. 1998. Organizing Men: Power, Discourse, and the Social Construction of Masculinity(s) in the Workplace. *Communication Theory* 8(2): 164-83.

Murray, Catherine. 2002. *Silent on the Set: Cultural Diversity and Race in Canadian TV Drama*. Burnaby, BC: School of Communication, Simon Fraser University.

–. 2008a. Lost in Translation? *Media*, Spring/Summer, 18-19.

–. 2008b. Media Infrastructure for Multicultural Diversity. *Policy Options*, April, 63-68.

–. 2009a. Designing Monitoring to Promote Cultural Diversification in TV. *Canadian Journal of Communication* 34(4): 675-99.

–. 2009b. Not Another Solitude: Third Language Media Matter. Address to the Panel on Heritage Languages, Integration, and Globalization, Ottawa, 22 October.

Murray, Catherine, S. Yu, and D. Ahadi. 2007. *Cultural Diversity and Ethnic Media in BC*. Report to the Canadian Heritage Western Regional Office, no. 45193670, October.

Murray, John P. 2008. Media Violence: The Effects Are Both Real and Strong. *American Behavioral Science* 51: 1212-24.

NAACP. 2008. Out of Focus, Out of Sync: Take 4. Published by the Hollywood Bureau of the NAACP, California.

Nagourney, Adam. 2008. An Election That Changed Everything. *New York Times*, global ed., 5 November.

Nation Talk. 2009. *About APTN: APTN Launches a New Season and a New Look*. 20 June. http://www.nationtalk.ca.

Nelson, Adie. 2006. *Gender in Canada*. 3rd ed. Toronto: Pearson.

–. 2010. *Gender in Canada*. 4th ed. Toronto: Pearson.

Nelson, Joyce. 1976. Review of *Hollywood's Canada: Jump Cut. Review of Contemporary Media* 2(13): 69.

Nesbitt-Larking, Paul. 2001. *Politics, Society, and the Media: Canadian Perspectives*. Peterborough, ON: Broadview Press.

Newspapers Canada. 2010. Ownership: Daily Papers. http://www.newspaperscanada.

Nicholson, Judith A. 2010. Mobiles and Mobilities. In *Mediascapes*, 3rd ed., ed. L.R. Shade, 371-90. Toronto: Nelson.

Nicolo, Alessandro. 2007. TV review, *Little Mosque on the Prairie*. *Blogcritics*. http://blogcritics.org.

Niezen, Ronald. 2005. Digital Identity: The Construction of Virtual Selfhood in the Indigenous Peoples' Movement. *Comparative Study of Society and History* 45(2): 532-51.

Niles, Robert. 2008. Ethnic Media Publishers Are the Original Niche Media Pioneers. *Online Journalism Review*, 31 January. http://www.ojr.org.

Nixon, Darren. 2009. "I Can't Put a Smiley Face On": Working-Class Masculinity, Emotional Labour, and Service Work in the "New Economy." *Gender, Work, and Organization* 16(3): 300-21.

Nordyke, Kimberly. 2008. NAACP: Industry "Out of Sync." *Hollywood Reporter,* 17 December.

O'Doherty, Kieran, and Martha Augoustinos. 2008. Protecting the Nation: Nationalist Rhetoric on Asylum Seekers and the Tampa. *Journal of Community and Applied Social Psychology* 18(6): 576-92.

Ohmann, Richard, and Frinde Maher. 2008. Introduction: Teaching about the Upper Class. *Radical Teacher* 81: 1.

Ojo, Tokunbo. 2006. Ethnic Print Media in the Multicultural Nation of Canada: A Case Study of the Black Newspaper in Montreal. *Journalism* 7(3): 343-61.

Olsson, Eva Karin. 2009. Rule Regimes in News Organization Decision Making. *Journalism* 10(6): 758-76.

Onstad, Katrina. 2010. Thin Is Inviolate. *Globe and Mail,* 20 November.

Ontario Human Rights Commission. 2008. *Commission Statement Concerning Issues Raised by Complaints against* Maclean's *Magazine.* Toronto: Queen's Printer for Ontario.

Orenstein, Peggy. 2011. *Cinderella Ate My Daughter.* New York: HarperCollins.

Palfrey, John, and Urs Gasser. 2008. *Born Digital: Understanding the First Generation of Digital Natives.* New York: Basic Books.

Pare, Daniel J. 2010. Internet Governance: What a Long and Not So Strange Trip It's Been. In *Mediascapes: New Patterns in Canadian Communications,* 3rd ed., ed. L.R. Shade, 326-40. Toronto: Nelson.

Parry-Giles, Shawn. 2000. Mediating Hillary Rodham Clinton. *Critical Studies in Media Communication* 17(2): 205-26.

Patterson, Mike. 2010. Wearing the White Man's Shoes: Two Worlds in Cyberspace. In *Indigenous Screen Cultures in Canada,* ed. S.B. Hafsteinsson and M. Bredin, 143-62. Winnipeg: University of Manitoba Press.

Perigoe, Ross. 2006. Muslims and Media. Paper presented at the Congress of Social Sciences, York University, Toronto, 29-31 May.

Perlmutter, David D. 2000. *Policing the Media: Street Cops and Public Perception of Law Enforcement.* Thousand Oaks, CA: Sage.

Pew Research Center. 2009. Women Outnumber Men on Social Networking Sites. Pew Internet and American Life Project. http://www.pewinternet.org.

–. 2010. Many Say Coverage of the Poor and Minorities Is Too Negative. Pew Research Center for the People and the Press, 19 August, http://people-press.org.

Pew Research Center Project for Excellence in Journalism. 2006. Ethnic Media, Content Analysis. 13 March. http://www.journalism.org.

–. 2008. The State of the News Media: Ethnic Media. http://www.journalism.org.

–. 2010a. Media, Race, and Obama's First Year: A Study of African Americans in US News Coverage. 26 July. http://www.journalism.org.

–. 2010b. New Media, Old Media: How Blogs and Social Media Agendas Relate and Differ from the Traditional Press. 23 May. http://www.journalism.org.

–. 2011. Religion in the News: Islam Was No. 1 Topic in 2010. 24 February. http://www.journalism.org.

Pietikäinen, Sari. 2003. Indigenous Identity in Print: Representations of the Sami in News Discourse. *Discourse and Society* 14(5): 581-609.

Policy Research Initiative. 2009. *Understanding Canada's "3M" Reality in the 21st Century.* Ottawa: Government of Canada.

Potter, James. 2005. *Media Literacy.* 3rd ed. Thousand Oaks, CA: Sage.

Power, Nicole Gerarda. 2008. Occupational Risks, Safety and Masculinity: Newfoundland Fish Harvesters' Experiences and Understandings of Fishery Risks. *Health, Risk, and Society* 10(6): 565-83.

Pozner, Jennifer. 2005. Dove's "Real Beauty" Backlash. *Bitch: Feminist Response to Pop Culture* 30.

—. 2010. *Reality Bites Back: The Troubling Truth about Guilty Pleasure TV.* Berkeley, CA: Seal Books.

Prashad, Sharda. 2006. "CRTC Pushes Diversity Strategies." *Toronto Star,* 22 March.

Prensky, Marc. 2001. Digital Natives, Digital Immigrants. *On the Horizon* 9(5): 1-4.

Purdum, Todd. 2009. It Came from Wasilla. *Vanity Fair,* August.

Putnam, Robert D. 2001. *Bowling Alone: The Collapse and Revival of American Community.* New York: Simon and Schuster.

—. 2007. E Pluribus Unum: Diversity and Community in the Twenty-First Century. *Scandinavian Political Studies* 30(2): 137-74.

Quill, Greg. 2011. The Girls Who Kicked Butt. *Toronto Star,* 21 April.

Raboy, Marc. 1988. Canada's Broadcasting Policy Debate. *Canadian Issues* 10(6): 41-54.

Rahoi-Gilchrist, Rita L. 2010. Examining the Successes and Struggles of New Zealand's Maori TV. In *Understanding Community Media,* ed. K. Howley, 161-67. Thousand Oaks, CA: Sage.

Rakauskas, Robert. 2006. Ned Romero: The Definitive Native American Actor. *Wildest Westerns* 6. http://www.wildestwesterns.com/no_6/ned_romero.htm.

Ramirez, Eddy. 2002. Ageism in the Media Is Seen as Harmful to the Health of the Elderly. *LA Times,* 5 September.

Ramji, Rubina. 2009. Representations of Islam in American News and Film: Becoming the "Other." In *Mediating Religion: Conversations in Media, Religion, and Culture,* ed. J. Mitchell and S. Marriage. New York: T. and T. Clark.

Ramsay, Christine. 2010. Regina's *Moccasin Flats:* A Landmark in the Mapping of Urban Aboriginal Culture and Identity. In *Indigenous Screen Cultures in Canada,* ed. S.B. Hafsteinsson and M. Bredin, 105-26. Winnipeg: University of Manitoba Press.

Raymond, Diane. 2003. Popular Culture and Queer Representation: A Critical Perspective. In *Gender, Race, and Class in Media,* 2nd ed., ed. G. Dines and J. Humez, 98-110. Thousand Oaks, CA: Sage.

Raza, Raheel. 2003. Talk given at the Jihad in the Newsroom session, Innoversity Creative Summit Conference, Toronto, 22 May.

Razack, Sherene. 2002. *Race, Space, and the Law: Unmapping a White Settler Society.* Toronto: Between the Lines.

RCAP (Royal Commission on Aboriginal Peoples). 1996. *Looking Forward, Looking Backward.* Vol. 3. Ottawa: Royal Commission on Aboriginal Peoples.

Reitz, Jeffrey, Rupa Bannerjee, Mai Phan, and Jordan Thompson. 2009. Race, Religion, and the Social Integration of New Immigrant Minorities in Canada. *International Migration Review* 43(4): 695-726.

Rendall, Steve, and Isabel Macdonald. 2008. Making Islamophobia Mainstream. Fairness and Accuracy in Reporting, November/December, http://www.fair.org.

Rendleman, Todd. 2008. "I Know Y'all Think I'm Pretty Square, but tuh, I Believe What I Believe": Images of Evangelicals in American Film. *Journal of Media and Religion* 7(4): 271-91.

Rennie, Ellie. 2006. *Community Media: A Global Introduction.* Toronto: Rowman and Littlefield.

Ricard, Danielle, and Rima Wilkes. 2007. Newspaper Framing of Protest by Indigenous Peoples and the Construction of National Identity. Paper presented at the annual meeting of the American Sociological Association, New York, NY, 11 August. Available at http://www.allacademic.com.

Richardson, Chris. 2007. "Canada's Toughest Neighbourhood": Surveillance, Myth, and Orientalism in Jane-Finch. MA Thesis, Brock University.

Riggins, Stephen, ed. 1992. *Ethnic Minority Media: An International Perspective.* Newbury Park, CA: Sage.

Roberts, David J., and Minelle Mahtani. 2010. Neoliberalizing Race, Racing Neoliberalism: Placing "Race" in Neoliberal Discourses. *Antipode* 42(2): 248-57.

Robinson, T., M. Callister, D. Magoffin, and J. Moore. 2007. The Portrayal of Older Characters in Disney Animated Films. *Journal of Aging Studies* 21(3): 203-13.

Rockler-Gladen, Naomi. 2008. Minority Media Representations: Common Representations of Gays, African Americans, and Other Minorities. Media Literacy, 29 April. http://medialiteracy.suite101.com.

Rollins, Peter C., and John E. O'Connor, eds. 2003. *Hollywood's Indians: The Portrayal of the Native American in Film.* Lexington: University Press of Kentucky.

Rook, Katie. 2008. Too Close for Comfort. *National Post,* 14 October.

Rosas-Moreno, Tanya Cantrell. 2010. Media Representations of Race: Cue the State of Media Opening in Brazil. *International Journal of Communication* 261: 261-82.

Rose, Mike. 2009. Blue Collar Brilliance: Questioning Assumptions about Intelligence, Work, and Social Class. *Utne Reader,* November/December, 58-61. Originally published in *American Scholar* 78(3): 43-49.

Rosenstiel, Tom. 2011. Five Myths about the Future of Journalism. *Washington Post,* 7 April.

Roszak, Theodore. 2010. *The Making of an Elder Culture: Reflections on the Future of America's Most Audacious Generation.* Gabriola Island, BC: New Society.

Roth, Lorna. 2005. *Something in the Air: The Story of First Peoples Television Broadcasting in Canada.* Montreal and Kingston: McGill-Queen's University Press.

–. 2006. *First Peoples Television Broadcasting in Canada.* Chicago: Museum of Broadcast Communications. http://www.museum.tv.

–. 2010a. Canadian First Peoples' Landscapes: A Snapshot with Three Corners. In *Mediascapes,* 3rd ed., ed. L.R. Shade, 237-55. Toronto: Nelson.

–. 2010b. First Peoples' Television in Canada: Origins of Aboriginal Peoples Television Network. In *Indigenous Screen Cultures in Canada,* ed. S.B. Hafsteinsson and M. Bredin, 17-34. Winnipeg: University of Manitoba Press.

Rozanova, Julia. 2006. The Master of Disguise: Hidden Faces of Media Ageism. *International Journal of Ageing and Later Life* 1(2): 111-21.

Rupp, Shannon. 2008. What's So Great about Beauty? *The Tyee,* 9 June. http://thetyee.ca/mediacheck.

Ryan, John, and William M. Wentworth. 1999. *Media and Society: The Production of Culture in the Mass Media.* Toronto: Allyn and Bacon.

Ryan, Phil. 2010. *Multicultiphobia.* Toronto: University of Toronto Press.

Salon.com. 2005. "Real Beauty" – or Really Smart Marketing? 22 July. http://www.dir.salon.com.

Saloojee, Raid. 2003. Talk given at the Jihad in the Newsroom session, Innoversity Creative Summit Conference, Toronto, 22 May.

Saunders, Eileen. 2006. Good Kids/Bad Kids: What's a Culture to Do? In *Mediascapes,* 2nd ed., ed. P. Attalah and L.R. Shade, 77-94. Toronto: Nelson.

–. 2008. Real Curves: Democratizing Beauty or Selling Soap? In *Communication in Question,* ed. J. Greenberg and C.D. Elliott, 112-19. Toronto: Thomson Nelson.

Sauvageau, Florian, David Schneiderman, and David Taras. 2006. *The Last Word: Media Coverage of the Supreme Court of Canada.* Vancouver: UBC Press.

Sax, Leonard. 2010. *Girls on the Edge.* New York: Basic Books.

Schneller, Johanna. 2009. Three Things That Defined the Year in Film. *Globe and Mail,* 29 December.

Schuck, Andreas, and Claes H. de Vreese. 2006. Between Risk and Opportunity: News

Framing and Its Effects on Public Support for EU Enlargement. *European Journal of Communication* 21(1): 5-32.

Scott, Marion. 2009. Refugees to Canada in Catch 22 Situation. *Montreal Gazette,* 26 November.

Seelye, Katharine, and Julie Bosman. 2008. Networks Challenge Sexism Charges. Reprinted in *Toronto Star,* 18 June. Originally published in *New York Times.*

Seljak, David. 2009. *Dialogue among the Religions in Canada.* Ottawa: Policy Research Initiative.

Shade, Leslie Regan, ed. 2010. *Mediascapes: New Patterns in Canadian Communications.* 3rd ed. Toronto: Nelson.

Shah, Shamir. 2008. Foreword to *A Tale of Two Englands: "Race" and Violent Crime in the Press,* by K.P. Sveinsson. London: Runnymede Trust.

Shaheen, Jack. 2001. *Reel Bad Arabs: How Hollywood Vilifies a People.* New York: Olive Branch Press.

–. 2009. *Guilty: Hollywood's Vilification of Arabs after 9-11.* New York: Olive Branch Press.

She, Kay. 2007. Women in Advertising. *Gauntlet News* (University of Calgary), 8 November.

Sheffield, Tricia. 2002. Towards a Theory of Divine Female Embodiment. *Journal of Religion and Society* 4: 1-12.

Sheikh, Aisha, and Mueen Farooq. 2007. Square Peg, Round Hole. *Silhouette,* 16 February.

Shoemaker, Pamela J., and Akiba A. Cohen. 2006. *News Around the World.* New York: Routledge.

Shugart, Helene. 2003. Reinventing Privilege: The New (Gay) Man in Contemporary Popular Media. *Critical Studies in Media Communication* 20(1): 67-91.

Siebert, Monika. 2006. Atanarjuat and the Ideological Work of Contemporary Indigenous Filmmaking. *Public Culture* 18(3): 531-50.

Silk, Mark. 2009. Islam and American News Media Post September 11. In *Mediating Religion: Conversations in Media, Religion, and Culture,* ed. J. Mitchell and S. Marriage. New York: T. and T. Clark.

Simmons, Alan. 2010. *Immigration and Canada: Global and Transnational Perspectives.* Toronto: Canadian Scholars' Press.

Skinner, David. 2006. Alternative Media. In *Mediascapes,* 2nd ed., ed. P. Attallah and L.R. Shade, 213-30. Toronto: Nelson.

–. 2010. Minding the Growing Gaps: Alternative Media in Canada. In *Mediascapes,* 3rd ed., ed. L.R. Shade, 221-36. Toronto: Nelson.

Smith, Jo, and Sue Abel. 2008. Ka Whawhai Tonu Matou: Indigenous Television in Aotearoa/ New Zealand. *NZJMS* 11(1): 1-15.

Smolash, Wendy Naava. 2009. Mark of Cain(ada): Racialized Security Discourse in Canada's National Papers. *University of Toronto Quarterly* 78(2): 1-15.

Snider, Clifton. 2008. Queer Persona and the Gay Gaze in *Brokeback Mountain*: Story and Film. *Psychological Perspectives* 51(1): 54-69.

Snow, Nancy. 2007. 10 Things That Everyone Should Know about Propaganda. http://www.nancysnow.com/snow-tracks.

Solis, Brian. 2010a. *Engaged: The Complete Guide for Brands and Businesses to Build, Cultivate, and Measure Success in the New Web.* New York: John Wiley and Sons.

–. 2010b. The Future of Broadcast Media Is Social. *Social Media Today* post, 19 March. http://socialmediatoday.com/SMC/182824.

Solutions Research Group. 2006. Study Explores Media Use among Growing Ethnic Groups. Solutions Research Group, 16 March. http://www.srgnet.com.

Somerville, Will, J. Durana, and A.M. Terrazas. 2008. *Hometown Associations: Untapped Resource for Immigration Integration?* Washington, DC: Migration Policy Institute.

Sommers, S.R., E.P. Apfelbaum, K.N. Dukes, N. Toosi, and E.J. Wang. 2006. Race and Media Coverage of Hurricane Katrina: Analysis, Implications, and Future Research Questions. *Analysis of Social Issues and Public Policy* 6(1): 1-17.

Soroka, Stuart, and Antonia Maioni. 2006. Little Signs of Bias in News Coverage. *Toronto Star,* 1 February.

Spoonley, Paul. 2005. Print Media Representations of Immigration and Immigrants, 1993-2003. In *New Zealand and International Migration: A Digest and Bibliography,* no. 4., ed. A. Trlin, P. Spoonley, and N. Watts, 86-106. Palmerston North, New Zealand: Massey University.

Spoonley, Paul, and Andrew Butcher. 2009. Reporting Superdiversity: The Mass Media and Immigration in New Zealand. *Journal of Intercultural Studies* 30(4): 355-72.

Spoonley, Paul, and Andrew Trlin. 2004. *Immigration, Immigrants, and the Media: Making Sense of Multicultural New Zealand.* Palmerston North, New Zealand: New Settlers Programme, Massey University.

SSRC (Social Science Research Council). 2010. The New Landscape of the Religion Blogosphere. 2 March. http://blogs.ssrc.org.

Starck, Kenneth. 2007. Perpetuating Prejudice or Merely Telling a Story? Media Portrayal of Arabs in the United States. Paper presented at the "Media, Migration, Integration" conference, Dortmund, Germany, 21-22 June.

Steimel, Sarah J. 2010. Refugees as People: The Portrayal of Refugees in American Human Interest Stories. *Journal of Refugee Studies* 23(2): 219-37.

Stein, Janice. 2007. Religion versus the Charter. *University of Toronto Magazine,* Winter.

Stern, Jessica. 2003. *Terror in the Name of God: Why Religious Militants Kill.* New York: HarperCollins.

Stevenson, Seth. 2005. When Tush Comes to Dove. *Slate,* 1 August. http://www.slate.com.

Stone, Sharon D. 2001. Lesbians, Gays, and the Press: Covering Lesbian and Gay Pride Day in Kelowna 1996. *Studies in Political Economy* 64 (Spring): 59-72.

Stout, Daniel A., and Judith Buddenbaum. 2008. Approaches to the Study of Media and Religion. *Religion* 38: 226-32.

Strauss, Marina. 2010. There's a "Menaissance" in the Ad World. *Globe and Mail,* 9 August.

Surette, Ray. 2004. *Media, Crime, and Criminal Justice: Images and Realities.* Toronto: Wadsworth.

−. 2007. *Media, Crime, and Criminal Justice: Images and Realities.* 2nd ed. Toronto: Wadsworth.

Suro, Roberto. 2008. *The Triumph of No: How the Media Influence the Immigration Debate.* Washington, DC: Governance Studies at the Brookings Institution.

−. 2009. *Promoting Misconceptions: News Media Coverage of Immigration.* Los Angeles: Center for the Study of Immigrant Integration, University of Southern California.

Sveinsson, Kjartan Pall. 2008. *A Tale of Two Englands: "Race" and Violent Crime in the Press.* London: Runnymede Trust.

Swain, Harry. 2010. *Oka: A Political Crisis and Its Legacy.* Vancouver: Douglas and McIntyre.

Tahmahkera, Dustin. 2008. Custer's Last Sitcom. *American Indian Quarterly* 32(3): 309-33.

Takeuchi, Craig. 2006. Updating Aboriginals in Films. *Straight.com,* 26 January. http://www.straight.com.

Tapscott, Don. 2008. *Growing Up Digital: The Rise of the Net Generation.* New York: McGraw-Hill.

−. 2011. Why Did We Ignore Obama's Social Media Lesson? *Globe and Mail,* 2 May.

Tapscott, Don, and Anthony D. Williams. 2007. *Wikinomics: How Mass Collaboration Changes Everything.* Expanded ed. New York: Portfolio.

Taras, David. 2001. *Power and Betrayal in the Canadian Media*. Peterborough, ON: Broadview Press.

Tatchell, Peter. 2001. Beyond Equality. *New Humanist* 116(1).

–. 2009. Bruno Will Both Incite Homophobia or Make Bigots Squirm. *Independent* (London), 2 July.

Taylor, Kate. 2007. TV Loves Wealth, but Not the Wealthy. *Globe and Mail*, 29 December.

ter Wal, Jessika. 2004. European Day of Media Monitoring: Quantitative Analysis of Daily Press and TV Content in the 15 EU Member States. Pilot study in the framework of the Online/More Colour in the Media. http://www.multicultural.net/edmm/index.htm.

ter Wal, Jessika, Leen d'Haenens, and Joyce Koeman. 2005. (Re)presentation of Ethnicity in EU and Dutch Domestic Views: A Quantitative Analysis. *Media, Culture, and Society* 27(6): 937-50.

Thompson, Cressida. 2005. Migration and the Media. Issue paper prepared for the European Migration Dialogue, October.

Thorburn, David, and Herb Jenkins. 2003. Introduction: Toward an Aesthetic of Transition. In *Rethinking Media Change: An Aesthetics of Transition*, ed. D. Thorburn and H. Jenkins, 1-18. Cambridge, MA: MIT Press.

Thussu, Daya Kishan. 2008. *Media on the Move: Global Flow and Counter Flow*. New York: Routledge.

Toughill, Kelly. 2000. Burnt Church Natives Reject Lobster Deal. *Toronto Star*, 10 August.

Transatlantic Trends. 2010. Immigration 2010: Key Findings. German Marshall Fund of the United States.

Trudeau, Alexandre. 2006. We Have to Defeat Fear. *Maclean's*, 11 September, 40-41.

Turner, Graeme. 2010. *Ordinary People and the Media: The Demotic Turn*. New York: Oxford University Press.

Turner, James. 2010. The Workplace (as Seen on TV). *Christian Science Monitor* 102(13): 3.

Tweedy, Ann, and Elizabeth Perry. 2006. Toward a Native Voice in Filming History. *Cultural Survival Quarterly*, Summer, 43-46.

Tyyskä, Vappu. 2009. *Youth and Society: The Long and Winding Road*. 2nd ed. Toronto: Canadian Scholars' Press.

Vallis, Mary. 2009. Why Ads Paint Dads as Buffoons. *National Post*, 20 June.

Valpy, Michael. 2010. The Future of Religion in Canada. *Globe and Mail*, 13 December.

van der Zon, Marian. 2000. "Aliens Go Home": A Critical Media Analysis of Chinese Migrants. Vancouver Island Public Interest Research Group. http://www.vipirg.ca.

van Dijk, Teun A. 1991. *Racism and the Press*. New York: Routledge.

–. 1995. The Mass Media Today: Discourse of Domination or Diversity. *Javnost/The Public* 2(2): 28-42.

–. 2000. New(s) Racism: A Discourse Analytical Approach. In *Ethnic Minorities and the Media*, ed. S. Cottle, 33-49. Philadelphia: Open University Press.

–. 2006. Racism and the European Press. Paper presented to the European Commission against Racism and Intolerance, Strasbourg, 16 December.

Viccari, Ben. 2007. Daily News. *Mediacaster Magazine*. http://www.mediacastermagazine.com.

Vieira, Paul. 2011. Canada's Demographic Time Bomb. *Financial Post*, 2 April.

Vincent, Norma. 2008. *Self-Made Man*. London: Atlantic Books.

Vitales, Christopher. 2010. A New Queered Gaze? Reading "Spartacus: Blood and Sand" as Symptom of a Shift in the Male Gaze. Blog entry, Networkologies, 22 March, http://networkologies.wordpress.com.

Vukov, Tamara. 2003. Imagining Communities through Immigration Policies. *International Journal of Cultural Studies* 6(3): 335-53.

Vultee, Fred, Stephanie Craft, and Matthew Velker. 2010. Faith and Values: Journalism and the Critique of Religion Coverage of the 1990s. *Journal of Media and Religion* 9(3): 150-64.

WACC (World Association of Christian Communication). 2009. World Association of Christian Communication Statement on International Women's Day. http://www.whomakesthenews.org.

Wacker, Watts. 2003. The Future of Media. *MediaPost*, 1 April. http://www.mediapost.com.

Wakeman, Jessica. 2008. *Huffington Post* Mutes Women's Voices. Fairness and Accuracy in Reporting, *Extra!*, November/December. http://www.fair.org.

Walker, Susan. 2007. *The 2007 Hollywood Writers Report: Whose Stories Are We Telling?* Writers Guild of America, West.

Walkom, Thomas. 2006. The Problem with Losing Perspective. *Toronto Star*, 12 June.

Wallis, Jim. 2005. *God's Politics: Why the American Right Gets It Wrong and the Left Doesn't Get It.* New York: HarperCollins.

Watkins, Craig. 2009. *The Young and the Digital.* Boston: Beacon Press.

Weber-Menges, Sonia. 2005. The Development of Ethnic Media in Germany. Paper presented at the ICI conference, New York, May.

Weinman, Jaime. 2008. The Curse of *Sex and the City. Maclean's*, 28 April, 59.

Wente, Margaret. 2009. We Are Witnessing the Passing of Working-Class Masculinity. *Globe and Mail*, 23 May.

West, Cornell. 2001. *Race Matters.* New York: Vintage Books.

Weston, Mary Ann. 2003. Journalists and Indians: The Clash of Cultures. Keynote speech at the American Indian Issues in the California Press Symposium, Los Angeles, CA, 21 February. http://www.bluecorncomics.com/weston.htm.

Whittington, Les. 2010. Investigations Will Proceed. *Toronto Star*, 14 August.

Whyte, John D., Lynn Wells, Rick Salutin, Joyce Green, and Gennadiy Chernov. 2007. Media and Politics. Saskatchewan Institute of Public Policy, Briefing note no. 20 (May). http://www.uregina.ca/sipp.

Whyte, Murray. 2006. Forgotten in Media's Culture Gap. *Toronto Star*, 24 June.

Wilkes, Rima, Catherine Corrigall-Brown, and Daniel J. Myers. 2010. Packaging Protest: Media Coverage of Indigenous People's Collective Action. *Canadian Review of Sociology* 47(4): 327-57.

Will, Gudrun. 2005. Ethnic Media. *Vancouver Review* 5.

Wilson, Clint C. II, Félix Gutiérrez, and Lena M. Chao. 2003. *Racism, Sexism, and the Media: The Rise of Class Communication in Multicultural America.* 3rd ed. Thousand Oaks, CA: Sage.

Wilson, Pamela, and Michele Stewart, eds. 2008. *Global Indigenous Media: Cultures, Poetics, and Politics.* Durham, NC: Duke University Press.

Winograd, Morley. 2008. *Millennial Makeover: MySpace, YouTube and the Future of American Politics.* Piscataway, NJ: Rutgers University Press.

Winseck, Dwayne. 2008. Media Merger Mania. *Canadian Dimension* 42(1): 30-32.

Winseck, Dwayne, and Robert Pike. 2008. Communication and Empire: Media, Markets, and Globalization, 1860-1910. *Global Media and Communication* 4(1): 7-37.

Winter, James. 2001. *Media Think.* Montreal: Black Rose Books.

Winter, N.J.G. 2008. *Dangerous Frames: How Ideas about Race and Gender Shape Public Opinion.* Chicago: University of Chicago Press.

Wise, Tim. 2008. *Between Barrack and a Hard Place: Racism and White Denial in the Age of Obama.* San Francisco: City Lights Books/Open Media Series.

Wiwchar, David. 2006. When Will We Learn to Cover Native Peoples Properly? *Media,* Winter, 26-27.

Wolf, Naomi. 1993. *Fire with Fire: The New Female Power and How It Will Challenge the 21st Century.* New York: Random House.

Women in Film and Television. *Frame Work: Employment in Screen-Based Media – A National Profile.* Toronto, 2005.

Wood, Huston. 2008. *Native Features: Indigenous Films from Around the World.* New York: Continuum International.

Working-Class Perspectives. 2008. Stereotyping the Working Class. Center for Working Class Studies, 8 September. http://workingclassstudies.wordpress.com.

Wortley, Scot. 2003. Misrepresentations or Reality? The Depiction of Race and Crime in the Canadian Print Media. In *Critical Criminology,* ed. B. Schissel and C. Brooks, 87-111. Halifax: Fernwood Publishing.

Wu, Esther. 2005. Study Details Rising Tide of Ethnic Media. *Dallas Morning News,* 15 June.

Wyatt, David A. 2008. Gay/Lesbian/Bisexual Television Characters. http://home.cc.umanitoba.ca.

Xing, Jun. 2009. Cinematic Asian Representation in Hollywood. In *Performing Difference,* ed. J.C. Friedman, 113-35. New York: University Press of America.

York, Geoffrey. 1991. *People of the Pines: The Warriors and the Legacy of Oka.* Toronto: Little Brown.

YouthNet. 2008. Young People Urged to Seize the News Media. http:// www.youthnet.org.

Zerbisias, Antonia. 2010. A Girl Crisis? *Toronto Star,* 25 April.

Zimmerman, Larry J., Karen Zimmerman, and Leonard Bruguier. 2000. Cyberspace Smoke Signals: New Technologies and Native American Ethnicity. In *Indigenous Cultures in an Interconnected World,* ed. C. Smith and G. Ward, 69-88. Vancouver: UBC Press.

Zook, K.B. 1999. *The Fox Network and the Revolution in Black Television.* New York: Oxford University Press.

Index

Printed and bound in Canada by Friesens

Set in Futura Condensed, Warnock, and Meta by
Artegraphica Design Co. Ltd.

Copy editor: Judy Phillips

Proofreader: Lesley Erickson